Constitutionalism Justified

Constitutionalism Justified

Rainer Forst in Discourse

Edited by
ESTER HERLIN-KARNELL
AND MATTHIAS KLATT

HÉCTOR MORALES
Assistant Editor

OXFORD
UNIVERSITY PRESS

OXFORD
UNIVERSITY PRESS

Oxford University Press is a department of the University of Oxford. It furthers the University's objective of excellence in research, scholarship, and education by publishing worldwide. Oxford is a registered trademark of Oxford University Press in the UK and certain other countries.

Published in the United States of America by Oxford University Press
198 Madison Avenue, New York, NY 10016, United States of America.

Library of Congress Cataloging-in-Publication Data

Names: Herlin-Karnell, Ester, editor | Klatt, Matthias, editor. | Morales Zúñiga, Héctor A., editor.
Title: Constitutionalism justified : Rainer Forst in discourse / edited by Ester Herlin-Karnell and Matthias Klatt ; Héctor Morales, Assistant Editor.
Description: New York : Oxford University Press, 2019. | Includes bibliographical references and index.
Identifiers: LCCN 2019031615 (print) | LCCN 2019031616 (ebook) | ISBN 9780190889050 (hardback) | ISBN 9780190889074 (epub) | ISBN 9780190889067 | ISBN 9780190889081
Subjects: LCSH: Constitutional law—Philosophy. | Forst, Rainer, 1964- —Influence. | Justification (Ethics) | Critical theory.
Classification: LCC K3165 .C6265 2019 (print) | LCC K3165 (ebook) | DDC 342/.001—dc23
LC record available at https://lccn.loc.gov/2019031615
LC ebook record available at https://lccn.loc.gov/2019031616

---

1 3 5 7 9 8 6 4 2

Printed by Integrated Books International, United States of America

Note to Readers

This publication is designed to provide accurate and authoritative information in regard to the subject matter covered. It is based upon sources believed to be accurate and reliable and is intended to be current as of the time it was written. It is sold with the understanding that the publisher is not engaged in rendering legal, accounting, or other professional services. If legal advice or other expert assistance is required, the services of a competent professional person should be sought. Also, to confirm that the information has not been affected or changed by recent developments, traditional legal research techniques should be used, including checking primary sources where appropriate.

(Based on the Declaration of Principles jointly adopted by a Committee of the American Bar Association and a Committee of Publishers and Associations.)

Contents

Contributors

Sameer Bajaj
Assistant Professor of Philosophy, University of Warwick

Claudio Corradetti
Associate Professor of Political Philosophy, University of Rome Tor Vergata

Eoin Daly
Lecturer in Law, National University of Ireland, Galway

Rainer Forst
Professor of Political Theory and Philosophy, Goethe University Frankfurt, and Research Professor of Political Theory, WZB Berlin Social Science Centre

Alon Harel
Phillip and Estelle Mizock Chair in Administrative and Criminal Law, Hebrew University of Jerusalem

Ester Herlin-Karnell
Visiting Research Fellow, Uppsala University

Christian Hiebaum
Associate Professor of Legal and Social Philosophy and Sociology of Law, University of Graz

Matthias Klatt
Chair of Jurisprudence, University of Graz

Lois McNay
Professor of the Theory of Politics and Fellow of Somerville College, Oxford University

Arthur Ripstein
Professor of Law and Philosophy and University Professor, University of Toronto

Enzo Rossi
Associate Professor in the Department of Political Science, University of Amsterdam

Christian F. Rostbøll
Professor in the Department of Political Science, University of Copenhagen

Andrea Sangiovanni
Professor of Social and Political Theory, European University Institute, and Professor of Philosophy, King's College London

Bernhard Schlink
Professor emeritus of Public Law and Legal Philosophy, Humboldt University Berlin

Introduction

Ester Herlin-Karnell and Matthias Klatt

I. Discursive Constitutionalism and the Right to Justification

This book explores Rainer Forst's work on the basic right to justification from three different perspectives: a philosophical, a legal-philosophical, and a constitution-theoretical one. Although this is already the third collected volume to date devoted to discussing Forst's work,[1] this book is unique in combining insights from philosophy, Kantian theory, constitutionalism, legal theory, and law.

The chapters in the first part address issues relating to the philosophical argument laying fundament to the basic right to justification. The contributions in the second part gradually move away from the philosophical fundaments towards issues that are embedded in the constitutional and legal frameworks. They thus represent attempts to explore in detail the implications Forst's right to justification has for conceptualizing constitutional democracy and its foundations, and how the moral right to justification may translate into particular practices of justification which are constrained by a specific legal framework.

The heart of a legal framework is represented in its constitution. Constitutionalism is a theoretical concept that highlights certain characteristics of legal systems which acknowledge a special normative role of constitutional law, in contrast to all other law. The special normative role of constitutional law norms stems from both their subject matter and their status. As regards their subject matter, constitutional norms not only regulate the creation and the exercise of political power, by means of principles like the rule of law, the separation of powers, and democracy, together with institutions and procedures safeguarding and implementing these principles. Constitutions also contain substantive principles

[1] Rainer Forst, *Justice, Democracy and the Right to Justification: Rainer Forst in Dialogue* (Bloomsbury Academic 2014). See also his dialogue with Wendy Brown and Rainer Forst, *The Power of Tolerance: A Debate* (Luca Di Blasi and Christoph FE Holzhey eds, Columbia University Press 2014) and the special issues of *Philosophy & Social Criticism* (2015, Vol. 41, 3), *Netherlands Journal of Legal Philosophy* (2016, Vol. 45, 3), and *Journal of Political Power* (2018, Vol. 11, 2). See also several contributions in the special issue "Dimension of Justice and Justification in EU and Transnational Context" (2017, Vol. 8, 1), *Transnational Legal Theory*, discussing Forst's work.

of political morality that comprise the legitimating basis of a legal system.[2] The core of these substantive principles are fundamental rights *qua* legal rights which link the constitution directly to human rights *qua* moral rights.

As regards their status, constitutional norms take precedence over all other legal norms. They enjoy a higher rank and thereby influence the content and the validity of lower-ranked norms. Thus, constitutional law 'occupies a middle ground between the routine administration of ordinary law . . . and moral theorizing from first principles of justice'.[3] The ultimate aim of constitutional law is regulating the justification of the legitimate authority of law. Constitutional norms create and allocate burdens of justification.[4] Under the principle of justification, law can claim legitimate authority according to reasons that 'those over whom laws claim authority might reasonably accept as free and equals . . . or cannot reasonably reject as free and equals'.[5] Since these questions are to be answered under conditions of reasonable disagreement about what justice requires, constitutionalism necessarily attains a discursive character.

Constitutions institutionalize specific forms of justificatory arrangements. The particular notion of discursive constitutionalism acknowledges that we need to justify what the dignity of persons and their relations of freedom and equality mean in the legal and the political spheres. Constitutions contain fundamental rights, and thus constitutionalism requires discourses about what rights we have, and how they can be realized. It is vital, therefore, to understand what justification means and how it ought to be used in rights discourse. Precisely that is the project of discursive constitutionalism, and the right to justification bears significant impact upon it. The present volume takes its starting point in the claim that Forst's account of the right to justification is a powerful theory that helps spelling out in more detail the notion of 'reflexive constitutionalism'.[6]

Several common issues addressed by a number of authors keep recurring in this volume. They include, inter alia, the influence of Kantian thought upon the right to justification;[7] the deontological versus teleological fundament of justification;[8] the tension between moral pluralism or particularism versus

[2] Ronald Dworkin, *Freedom's Law: The Moral Reading of the American Constitution* (Harvard University Press 1996) 1–38.

[3] TRS Allan, 'The Deliberative Constitution at Common Law' in Ron Levy and others (eds), *The Cambridge Handbook of Deliberative Constitutionalism* (Cambridge University Press 2018) 141.

[4] Thomas Kleinlein, *Konstitutionalisierung im Völkerrecht: Konstruktion und Elemente einer idealistischen Völkerrechtslehre* (Springer 2012) 687.

[5] Mattias Kumm, 'Global Constitutionalism and the Rule of Law' in Anthony F Lang and Antje Wiener (eds), *Handbook on Global Constitutionalism* (Edward Elgar Publishing 2017) 202.

[6] On reflexive constitutionalism, see eg Martin Loughlin, *Foundations of Public Law* (Oxford University Press 2010) 311.

[7] See contributions in this volume by Corradetti, Herlin-Karnell, Ripstein, and Rostbøll.

[8] See contributions in this volume by Ripstein and Sangiovanni.

universalism;[9] the relation of the right to justification to social and distributive justice;[10] the value of constitutional law in general[11] and, in particular, the value of democracy and its instrumental or non-instrumental justification;[12] the relation between the formal structure of democracy and substantive justice;[13] the problem of whether and how constitutionalism stretches beyond the national state and is capable of becoming 'global' or 'cosmopolitan'.[14] This entails the intricate and highly relevant problem of the inclusion of outsiders in the constitutional setting.[15] Human rights are the substantial core of constitutionalism, and the contributions in this volume address the relations of Forst's principle of justification to the justification of human rights in general.[16] In particular, the authors discuss whether an intrinsic right to a hearing exists,[17] as well as the links between power and justification.[18] Human rights law is largely global in nature and often connected to a proportionality test. Hence several chapters discuss to what extent and how precisely proportionality analysis can be reconstructed as a particular form of justification in constitutional rights adjudication.[19] How is the proportionality test as a universal element of constitutionalism linked to the right to justification? Finally, our authors also engage with the related problem of the legitimacy of judicial review as a justificatory practice vis-à-vis deliberative democracy.[20]

II. Rainer Forst

A Leibniz Price Awardee (German Research Foundation, 2012), Rainer Forst is the leading figure of the fourth generation of the Frankfurt School.[21] Drawing upon Kant's critical philosophy and Habermas's discourse theory—among other

[9] See contributions in this volume by Corradetti, Sangiovanni, and Schlink.
[10] See contributions in this volume by Hiebaum and Schlink.
[11] See contributions in this volume by Herlin-Karnell and Rostbøll.
[12] See contributions in this volume by Harel, Herlin-Karnell, Ripstein, and Rostbøll.
[13] See contributions in this volume by Hiebaum, Klatt, and Schlink.
[14] See contributions in this volume by Harel, Herlin-Karnell, Ripstein, and Sangiovanni. cf Jürgen Habermas, 'Does the Constitutionalization of International Law Still Have a Chance?' in Jürgen Habermas, *The Divided West* (Ciaran Cronin tr, Polity 2006); Mattias Kumm, 'The Cosmopolitan Turn in Constitutionalism: On the Relationship between Constitutionalism in and beyond the State' in Jeffrey L Dunoff and Joel P Trachtman (eds), *Ruling the World?: Constitutionalism, International Law, and Global Governance* (Cambridge University Press 2009).
[15] See contributions in this volume by Bajaj & Rossi, Herlin-Karnell, and McNay.
[16] See contributions in this volume by Klatt and Sangiovanni.
[17] See contributions in this volume by Harel and Schlink.
[18] See contributions in this volume by Bajaj & Rossi, Herlin-Karnell, Hiebaum, and McNay.
[19] See contributions in this volume by Daly, Harel, Herlin-Karnell, Klatt, and Schlink.
[20] See contributions in this volume by Daly, Harel, Herlin-Karnell, and Klatt.
[21] Forst himself, though, is sceptical about picturing the Frankfurt School as composing a family with generations of descendants: Rainer Forst, 'The Right to Justification: Towards a Critical Theory of Justice and Democracy. An Interview with Rainer Forst' in Gary Browning, Raia Prokhovnik, and Maria Dimova-Cookson (eds), *Dialogues with Contemporary Political Theorists* (Palgrave MacMillan 2012) 107.

sources—Forst has introduced new perspectives on core topics of the Frankfurt School, such as the concept of reason, the relation between modernity and emancipation, the structure of democracy, and the idea of social justice, to name but a few. His works have stimulated pervasive interest by scholars from many disciplines.

Forst has been professor of philosophy and political theory since 2004 and, since 2007, co-director of the Cluster of Excellence *Normative Orders* at Goethe-University Frankfurt. He has published three collections of essays to date. The first of these collections stand in the centre of the current volume, *The Right to Justification: Elements of a Constructivist Theory of Justice* (German 2007, English 2011).[22] This book was followed by *Justification and Critique: Towards a Critical Theory of Politics* (German 2011, English 2013)[23] and by *Normativity and Power: Analyzing Social Orders of Justification* (German 2015, English 2017).[24] These books, together with other papers published in journals[25] and edited volumes,[26] shape a systematic and stimulating body of work as well as an original approach to Frankfurt critical theory.

Forst studied philosophy, political science, and American studies in Frankfurt, Binghamton, and Harvard in the mid-80s. He then commenced doctoral studies under the auspices of Jürgen Habermas, joining the latter's Leibniz research group on legal theory.[27] This group was the laboratory incubating Habermas's masterpiece *Between Facts and Norms*. Forst also studied with John Rawls at

[22] Rainer Forst, *Das Recht auf Rechtfertigung: Elemente einer konstruktivistischen Theorie der Gerechtigkeit* (Suhrkamp 2007); Rainer Forst, *The Right to Justification: Elements of a Constructivist Theory of Justice* (Jeffrey Flynn tr, Columbia University Press 2011).

[23] Rainer Forst, *Kritik der Rechtfertigungsverhältnisse: Perspektiven einer kritischen Theorie der Politik* (Suhrkamp 2011); Rainer Forst, *Justification and Critique: Towards a Critical Theory of Politics* (Ciaran Cronin tr, Polity Press 2013).

[24] Rainer Forst, *Normativität und Macht: Zur Analyse sozialer Rechtfertigungsordnungen* (Suhrkamp 2015); Rainer Forst, *Normativity and Power: Analyzing Social Orders of Justification* (Ciaran Cronin tr, Oxford University Press 2017).

[25] Particularly relevant, Rainer Forst, 'The Justification of Basic Rights: A Discourse-Theoretical Approach' (2016) 45(3) Netherlands Journal of Legal Philosophy 7; Rainer Forst, 'Political Liberalism: A Kantian View' (2017) 128 Ethics 123; Rainer Forst, 'Noumenal Power Revisited: Reply to Critics' (2018) 11 Journal of Political Power 294.

[26] Particularly relevant, Rainer Forst, 'Two Stories About Toleration' in Lorenzo Zucca and Camil Ungureanu (eds), *Law, State and Religion in the New Europe: Debates and Dilemmas* (Cambridge University Press 2012); Rainer Forst, 'The Point and Ground of Human Rights: A Kantian Constructivist View' in David Held and Pietro Maffettone (eds), *Global Political Theory* (Polity Press 2016); Rainer Forst, 'What's Critical About a Critical Theory of Justice' in Banu Bargu and Chiara Bottici (eds), *Feminism, Capitalism, and Critique: Essays in Honor of Nancy Fraser* (Palgrave 2017); Rainer Forst, 'A Critical Theory of Human Rights—Some Groundwork' in Penelope Deutscher and Cristina Lafont (eds), *Critical Theory in Critical Times: Transforming the Global Political and Economic Order* (Columbia University Press 2017).

[27] Jürgen Habermas, *Between Facts and Norms: Contributions to a Discourse Theory of Law and Democracy* (William Rehg tr, MIT Press 1996) xliii; Forst, 'The Right to Justification: Towards a Critical Theory of Justice and Democracy. An Interview with Rainer Forst' (n 21) 107f. See also Stefan Müller-Doohm, *Habermas: A Biography* (Polity Press 2016) 244f.

Harvard University. He performed a mediating role between Habermas and the American professor, who at that time had already finished his manuscript of *Political Liberalism*.[28]

In his doctoral dissertation (German 1994, English 2002),[29] Forst engages in the vivid dispute between liberalism and communitarianism. Asked for a list of the most important philosophical books published since 1950, Habermas mentioned Forst's doctoral dissertation.[30] Forst was assistant professor at Free University in Berlin and at the Department of Philosophy at Goethe-University Frankfurt, as well as visiting professor at the New School for Social Research in New York. He received his habilitation for his erudite monograph *Toleration in Conflict* (German 2003, English 2013).[31]

III. Summaries

Arthur Ripstein discusses two different versions of the idea that everyone who is suitably affected by actions of others has a right to have these actions justified to them. Both versions turn to Kant's *Doctrine of Right*, which according to Ripstein provides a powerful conception of the right to justification. The first model, which Ripstein labels the co-deliberation model, is based upon a system of giving and asking for reasons. Significantly, the notion of a reason in this model is unconstrained and open-ended. The sole criterion to decide upon the acceptability of reasons is the scrutiny of the justificatory process itself. The ultimate relevance of a reason thus becomes a matter of degree, and any reason may be outweighed by colliding reasons. Co-deliberation may turn out to justify multiple and differentiated moral and legal rules, thus allowing for pluralism. The process of co-deliberation itself, however, is universal.

In contrast, the second model roots in a narrow Kantian understanding of the right to justification. This model assumes an antecedent right to be the ultimate foundation of a right to justification, namely Kant's innate right of humanity in one's own person. The innate right of humanity is normatively and conceptually prior to the right to justification. It therefore delimits and structures the right to

[28] Forst, 'The Right to Justification: Towards a Critical Theory of Justice and Democracy. An Interview with Rainer Forst' (n 21) 108.

[29] Rainer Forst, *Kontexte der Gerechtigkeit: Politische Philosophie jenseits von Liberalismus und Kommunitarismus* (Suhrkamp 1994); Rainer Forst, *Contexts of Justice: Political Philosophy Beyond Liberalism and Communitarianism* (John MM Farrell tr, University of California Press 2002).

[30] cf Brian Leiter's blog, <https://leiterreports.typepad.com/blog/2009/05/the-most-important-philosophical-books-since-1950.html> accessed 24 February 2019.

[31] Rainer Forst, *Toleranz im Konflikt: Geschichte, Gehalt und Gegenwart eines umstrittenen Begriffs* (Suhrkamp 2003); Rainer Forst, *Toleration in Conflict: Past and Present* (Ciaran Cronin tr, Cambridge University Press 2013).

justification by means of providing a background set of normative entitlements. Furthermore, the innate right of humanity represents a starting point for any processes of justification that is non-comparative and does not admit of degrees.

Ripstein explores the two models and provides a number of questions of political philosophy that allow demonstrating their differences. He acknowledges that most times Forst seems to adopt the co-deliberation model, while his theory was also compatible with the narrow Kantian model. Since Ripstein finds the narrow Kantian model to provide a more powerful conception of the right to justification, he invites Forst to explicitly adopt the narrow Kantian model.

Rainer Forst admits, in his reply to Ripstein, with whom he agrees on the deontological framework, to be 'somewhat torn' between these two models—for good reasons, though, since he wanted to construct a third model *qua* middle way. Forst explains why he finds the co-deliberation model too wide and Ripstein's narrow model too narrow. He demonstrates how his third model could, on the one hand, allow for a special realm of narrower justifications for basic rights while, on the other hand, still insisting that it is justificatory practices that bring this realm about, rather than some deduction from the innate right. That way, Forst stresses the dynamic and the relational character of his constructivist justification of human rights.

Claudio Corradetti takes issue with two specific aspects of Forst's theory. First, he challenges the compatibility of the right to justification with a Kantian ethics of duty. While Forst sees both a right and a corresponding duty as the two sides of his principle of justification, Corradetti finds the analogy between the unconditional Kantian moral imperative and an unconditional duty of justification unconvincing. After all, Kant did not couple the universal duty of the categorical imperative with a universal subjective right. To ground a moral duty in someone else's right would not be consistent with individual autonomy. It followed that the right to justification could not be complemented with the categorical imperative. In consequence, Corradetti urges Forst either to substitute the right to justification with a duty to justification or to drop the Kantian fundament to his theory. It would be more promising, Corradetti claims, to base the right to justification in Kant's universal principle of right. This line of argument, however, would demand to spell out the shift from a moral principle to a legal one as well as the relation between the two. This first challenge ultimately leads to doubts about whether the right to justification really is the fundament of a justificatory theory of justice, as Forst claims.

Second, Corradetti raises the problem of identifying the subjects of justification properly. He claims that Forst's theory did not explain sufficiently what it takes an individual to become an equal actor of justification in a legal system. He problematizes the potential calamity of rightless people that stand outside the legal system. Referring to Forst's criterion that a person has to be 'affected' in order to raise a claim for justification, Corradetti challenges that this status could be interpreted as being of a pre-defined legal, rather than of a morally inclusive quality. In result, he criticizes the right of justification for not having sufficient resources to vindicate the rights of the excluded.

Rainer Forst, in his reply to Corradetti, stresses that the principle of justification is relevant in both moral and legal-political contexts. He maintains that, in the moral context, the categorical duty of justification did indeed imply a general moral right. Forst urges Corradetti to make a distinction between moral rights and coercive rights regulating external freedom. Furthermore, Kant himself justified his Doctrine of Right on the categorical imperative. As for pluralism of reasonable views on morality, Forst stresses that he does not depend on dubious metaphysics. Rather, the reasonableness is presupposed by the discursive conception of practical reason in processes of justification. Forst also underlines that his theory did not restrict the membership of a normative order, and that his concept of normative order was a particularly broad and inclusive one, thus grounding possibly critique and development of specific legal status.

Andrea Sangiovanni focuses on the justification of human rights by identifying three different approaches, which he labels the orthodox view, the political view, and the legal view. Each of these approaches displayed certain advantages as well as shortcomings, and Sangiovanni diagnoses a stalemate between them. None of the three approaches is capable of providing sustainable solutions to all of the three most important challenges in human rights theory, which Sangiovanni locates in the contingency problem, the specificity problem, and the direction problem. Either human rights are made dependent upon contingent political arrangements; or they do not provide the appropriate specific guidance along the spectrum between the highly abstract and the very concrete; or lastly, they are incapable of establishing a binding practical-normative relationship between individuals, rather than merely justifying monopolar duties or directed duties of collectives or aggregated individual interests.

Sangiovanni then embarks upon offering a distinct reconstruction of Forst's theory. According to him, Forst's account offers a series of promising avenues for responding to all three challenges, thus dissolving the stalemate in current human rights theory. In the course of his discussion, Sangiovanni places distinct emphasis on the impossibility to justify an abstract universal list of human rights. He underlines the significant role of specific institutions in grounding human rights, and he finds Forst's theory wanting in that respect. The answer that Sangiovanni gives to the problem of spelling out the details of the role of institutions, in his 'revised Forst account', is that human rights were best justified as systems in which institutions and individuals are bound together under the dominion of the right to justification. It follows that institutions matter not only for the application of human rights, but for specifying their content, grounds, and scope in the first place. A consequence from this view is that a wide variation of human rights lists and interpretations, for different legal orders and institutional contexts, gets centre stage. It is precisely the task of philosophical conceptions of human rights to address these specific questions, Sangiovanni argues, rather than engaging in a purely abstract discourse and leaving the details for further implementation.

Rainer Forst, in his reply to Sangiovanni, emphasizes that his integration between the three approaches to human rights required a deontological grounding, while Sangiovanni favoured a teleological basis. Forst insists that an abstract core conception of basic rights is necessary. As for the role institutions play, he distinguishes between processes of rights justification and rights application and highlights important differences between his account and Sangiovanni's. That way, Forst underlines the necessity to refrain from privatizing the justification of rights regimes and, in contrast, insists on the democratic and public character of rights justification. Referring to an earlier exchange with Sangiovanni, Forst also takes occasion to argue against the European Court of Human Rights' margin of appreciation practice which gave rise to relativism and power politics.

Christian Hiebaum discusses the right to justification in the wider context of politico-philosophical debates on equality. He addresses in some detail two major paradigms of egalitarianism, distributive and social egalitarianism, analyzing their strengths and weaknesses. Hiebaum criticizes distributive egalitarianism for not providing a more encompassing conception of social justice. Social egalitarianism, in turn, can incorporate other values into the egalitarian framework. It hence better accounts, Hiebaum argues, for the political urgency of inequality concerns. This paradigm, furthermore, allowed for addressing specifically the justifications of distributions as well as the decision-making processes, by way of connecting democratic politics with social equality. This, then, leads naturally to Forst's discursive theory of social justice. Hiebaum is sceptical, however, of Forst's claim that the right to justification was the core and centre of justice as such. He raises two objections: First, while many instances of injustice were indeed arbitrary exercises of power, failing to provide adequate justification, this was not always the case. Second, and more importantly, it was unclear who the addressee of a right to justification was, specifically in scenarios that lack clear structures, institutions, and procedures of justification. It was impossible, Hiebaum argues, to identify a single democratically established authority in today's global society. The difficulties of identifying persons or institutions who bear concrete responsibility for injustice, then, unjustly clears the privileged from any justificatory obligations. Hiebaum also distinguishes, following Caney, between political legitimacy, to which practices of justification contributed, and philosophical legitimacy, which was neither guaranteed nor constituted by justificatory practices. Today's struggles for justice occurred mainly in the transnational sphere, and hence outside of democratic justificatory practices. Furthermore, Hiebaum is not convinced that political decision-making ought to be responsive to public discourse at all, given that in populist contexts such responsivity will bring about an even greater risk of maldistribution. Hiebaum then develops his own account of an egalitarian theory of social justice. He bases this account on a closer link between distributive egalitarianism and relational equality, a link that the notion of rights provided.

Rainer Forst, in his answer to Hiebaum, agrees that social contexts of arbitrary rule and domination are standard cases of injustice, calling for the establishment of structures of justification in the first place. The right of justification entailed a right of dominated people to participate in the establishment of these structures. Huge as this political task may be, it did not count against a normative approach. Forst also rejects Hiebaum's (and Caney's) separation between democratic legitimacy and substantive justice by insisting on their internal connection. Commenting on Hiebaum's own proposal, Forst diagnoses a tension between distributional and relational elements. He traces this tension back to Hiebaum's teleological view, to which he juxtaposes his own (and Ripstein's) deontological account.

Bernhard Schlink juxtaposes Forst's paradigm of justice as justifiability with a paradigm of distributive justice. Contradicting Adorno's famous dictum that there could be no right life within the false one, Schlink follows an ethos of practice, which consists in acting in accordance with the demands of justice notwithstanding unjust contexts around us. He then defends the distributive paradigm against criticism, noting that justice also distributes the burden of argumentation in a particular way, as well as the close relation between equality and freedom. Linking equality reasoning to both justificatory practices in general and proportionality analysis in particular, Schlink underlines that the reasons put forward to substantiate unequal treatment will represent the standards of a specific time and place. Furthermore, and in contrast to a notion of justification *ex post*, he claims that any decision should be preceded by an institutionalized debate in which the people affected must have a say—an argument that closely resembles with Harel's right to a hearing. Schlink then takes issue with the relationship between the two paradigms of justice specifically. He argues that the paradigm of justification presupposes an established knowledge of what is just. Any justificatory practices must operate, he claims, in existing contexts of experiences and standards lending some certainty to those practices from their very beginning. Justice, Schlink claims, exists already prior to democratic discursive-constructive processes, and the former is the guiding notion for the latter. We can and must raise the question of justice independently of instances of justificatory exercises. Justificatory power is, Schlink argues, neither a sufficient nor even a necessary condition for justice.

A second consequence Schlink derives from these considerations is that in the light of the huge diversity of contexts and constellations of justice in our highly differentiated world, the importance and relevance of the highly abstract notion of justice as justifiability is diminished. Instead, problems of distributive justice should be answered on a situation-by-situation basis. Starting from an assumption of equality, any deviation from equality needs to be supported by reasons. Schlink concludes by underlining the critical potential of justice as an explosive, transformative force directed against instances of injustice—rather than lending justice a constructive power to create a just order of state and society. To achieve the latter, we had better take resort to the virtues of compassion and solidarity.

Rainer Forst, in his answer to Schlink, addresses Schlink's claim that the procedural discursive justification of justice was always secondary to a substantive justification of justice. Forst acknowledges that his account of justice of justification does imply substantive notions and pre-judgments. His theory included a substantive form of proceduralism. Otherwise social discursive practices would be in danger of merely reproducing the unjustifiable. Yet Forst disagrees with Schlink's conclusion that substantive notions of justice existed always prior to justification. The justificatory reconstruction of justice was neither lacking a guiding notion of justice nor operating *ex nihilo*, rather it was an exercise combining substance and procedure. Against Schlink's appeal to the virtues of compassion and solidarity, Forst underlines the capacity of justice as justification to provide sufficient guidance in, eg refugee and migration issues. He is also concerned that his account was not misinterpreted as some utopian framework too detected from practical struggles for concrete justice.

Sameer Bajaj and *Enzo Rossi* address the connection between the right to justification and power. They reconstruct Forst's noumenal understanding of power by analyzing his argumentative steps from the recognition of reasons by subjects of power to the thesis that this recognition required justification and, ultimately, to the result that power required justification. The authors then challenge this account in different aspects, relating to a conceptual and a normative link between power and justification, respectively. As far as the conceptual link is concerned, they critically explore Forst's various premises (as reconstructed by the authors) in order to rebut his conclusion that power required justification. This critical exploration entails raising doubts upon Forst's starting point that to be a subject of power was to be moved by reasons. Power, they claim, does not have to be an object of normative enquiry. Against this dominant view of normative political theory, which was oblivious to the importance of factual power-relations, the authors put their own more 'realist' account that primarily constructs power as a contingent instrument. Another point of criticism regards Forst's premise that recognition of reasons required justification. Bajaj and Rossi claim that justification was merely a sufficient, rather than a necessary condition of the recognition of reasons. Reasons could also be recognized in a non-justificatory sense. From that it followed that power qua recognition of reasons did not sufficiently ground a right to justification. The authors claim that subjects of power are justificatory beings. Their argument is based upon a distinction between reason-giving and reason-recognizing, combined with the claim that only the former required justification. In contrast to Forst, the authors defend a functional, compliance-inducing normative order whose recognition did not depend on its justification. They defend the possibility to evaluate the appropriateness of a response of a human agent to a reason without any justification of the power in question.

Second, Bajaj and Rossi explore the possibility of defending a normative link between power and justification by means of the right to justification. They deny this possibility, because rational disagreement existed on whether a structure of justification was required in the first place. The authors claim that Forst's theory fails by its own standard, because imposing a justificatory standard on human agents amounted to projecting specific reasons onto those who reject the principles of justification. Thus, Forst arbitrarily privileged the right to justification to 'competing narratives of justification'. A possible response to that objection could be to claim that such privileging was not arbitrary, but justified—but this response, the authors claim, would represent a petitio principii. They also deny that agents need to have a practical insight into a moral right to justification in order to engage in rational moral discourse; the latter was possible without the former.

Rainer Forst, in his answer to Bajaj and Rossi, underlines that his theory of power, while bearing relevance to his normative conception of justice, was not in itself normative, but rather a conceptual and descriptive theory. Hence, Bajaj and Rossi offered too strong a normative reading. In the context of power and motivating reasons, Forst points out, he employs a rather broad, non-normative notion of reason-giving. His descriptive theory of power aimed at explaining all types of power exercises, and not only justified ones. Regarding his Kantian transcendental argument, Forst objects to the social relativism in Bajaj and Rossi's alternative account. For them, the term 'reasonable' would lose its critical bite. In contrast, Forst maintains that the mere fact of disagreement did not imply that the disagreement was reasonable. Social relativism, in turn, reduced reason to mere positivist descriptivism, and could not account for the necessary validity claim inherent in labelling a disagreement as reasonable. Addressing the further objection that his theory was amounting to an ideal theory, Forst underlines that the right to justification did not appeal to a teleological ideal prior to justificatory practices. His practical transcendentalism did not entail any metaphysical or ontological element. Lastly, denying that justificatory agents must have moral insight, as Bajaj and Rossi do, fails to meet, Forst argues, the participant's perspective.

Lois McNay focuses her critical discussion on the limits of Forst's right to justification. Her main objection is that Forst did not succeed to integrate the transcendental and the critical dimension of justification by establishing an immanent connection. Rather, as she argues, he oscillated inconsequently between these dimensions in a methodologically indecisive manner. For her, Forst shielded the right to justification, qua universal principle, in a self-contradictory way from systematic and self-reflective criticism, thereby hiding the presumptions, blind spots, and potential exclusions of his own theory. The main reason for these failures, according to McNay, lies in Forst's concept of noumenal power. This concept was incapable of advancing beyond on empty formalism, thus preventing an adequate analysis of indirect perpetuations of inequality and oppression. McNay juxtaposes Forst's 'hyper-rationalist' concept of power with a more material concept of embodied power and non-cognitive dynamics, drawing on the theories of Foucault, Bourdieu, and Butler.

Moreover, according to McNay, Forst's rather limited concept of justification resulted in numerous negative consequences as it was incapable of explaining the dynamics in which major structural inequalities were reproduced. Forst disregarded the latent power dynamics prevailing in actual, rather than ideal, debates on justice. He did not consider adequately entrenched asymmetries of power in real contexts. His theory did not ensure that equality will be realized in actual practice, rather than in the idealized space of reasons. Ultimately, the purportedly universal practice of justification was merely a contingent socio-cultural practice, amounting to hegemonic imposition of Western ideals. McNay claims that the idea of reasonable justification was tacitly exclusionary and reflected the limited sensibility and habitus of Western elites. She acknowledges that Forst had addressed this objection by raising a counter-charge of ethnocentrism to this criticism, but she does not see how Forst's theory could overcome its considerable barriers to the inclusion of marginal and oppressed voices in actual practice. Smoothing this problem down by referring to a distinction between ideal and real justificatory discourses does not help, according to McNay, since this amounted to pre-determining the outcomes of justificatory processes in a circular way. Ultimately, McNay suggests a theory of justification she claims to be quite divers from Forst's, which would be grounded in personal experience and the willingness of render oneself vulnerable to others, thus ending epistemic blindness and insensitivity to injustice and oppression. This new theory of justification, the author hopes, would combat the 'inherited cognitive and discursive habits' she finds of so limited capacity.

Rainer Forst, in his answer to McNay, agrees that critical theory should be sociologically informed and emancipatory. He maintains, however, that self-reflexivity and normatively grounded critique were impossible without the principle of justification. The principle of justification was at the same time situated in social contexts and still generated transcending power. Reason, Forst claims, had a distancing power, and thus his dialectical approach was both immanent and transcendental. The main point of critical theory was to reconstruct the counterfactual principles of rationality amidst factual irrationality. In contrast, McNay's non-dialectical suggestion of a purely immanentist approach necessarily lost the emancipatory critical power and exhibited historicist relativism. Without a conception of discursive justification and reflective reason, there could be none of the critical processes McNay considered as so important. Forst further insists on the categorical distinction between real practices of justification and counterfactual principles of critical reason. McNay, Forst claims, mistook the latter for the former.

Matthias Klatt aims at providing a deep normative justification for proportionality analysis. He defends proportionality as a universally valid form of argument in rights reasoning by identifying the moral right to justification as its normative basis. He explores Forst's idea of humans as justificatory beings and matches it with Brandom's normative pragmatics, discussing whether this anthropologic-existentialist basis of Forst's theory makes it vulnerable to the is-ought-fallacy. The author demonstrates how Forstian normativity depends on sociality and existentialist decision, bringing about a relative necessity of practical normativity. Klatt then explores in detail how proportionality analysis translates the moral right to justification into constitutional practice. He stresses that these practices are necessarily connected to an overarching claim to correctness. In particular, the three elements of the claim to correctness fulfil Forst's criteria of generality and reciprocity. Even though the more specific criteria for correctness may vary according to contexts and legal systems, the elements guiding the correctness in the first place are universally valid.

Klatt further reconstructs how proportionality analysis is capable of integrating the form and the substance of justificatory practices in rights reasoning. In contrast to Forst, he claims that the two formal criteria of reciprocity and generality are necessary, but not sufficient conditions for the correctness of legal propositions. Human rights, to which the right to justification is not analytically prior, have to be added to Forst's account in order to allow for substantive correctness. Klatt defends that proportionality is one of the rules that institutionalize the space of reasons in constitutional law. He stresses that the open-endedness of the space of reasons lends the right to justification a diachronic dimension. It follows that proportionality analysis gets the character of a chain novel, operated by a default-and-challenge-structure in the sense of Brandomian commitments and entitlements. Klatt uses the distinction between internal and external justification to develop his proportionality as integrity model. Based on the same distinction, he demonstrates how proportionality combines universal validity with cultural sensitivity. This leads, ultimately, to a concept of discursive global constitutionalism, which institutionalizes the moral right to justification in a specific form of deliberative democracy. In this arena, the right to justification not only applies to substantial questions of material justice but also to the institutional questions of competence and legal authority.

Rainer Forst, in his comment to Klatt, disagrees with Klatt's claim that the normativity of the right to justification rested ultimately on existentialist decision. From a first-person perspective, moral normativity was valid apart from those decisions, lest the categorically binding moral normativity would turn into ethical normativity, binding only for individuals. Moral principles did not depend on moral agents deciding in favour of them. In consequence, Forst also denies Klatt's social relativity thesis, which may be factually true but not from a normative perspective. Furthermore, Forst comments on Klatt's thesis that the claim to correctness, in the legal realm, was more fundamental than the right to justification. Forst highlights that the very notion of correctness was already determined by the general normative perspective, including the right to justification. Forst also denies Klatt's thesis that human rights were analytically prior to the right to justification. Forst is concerned here that the attempt to account for a normative plurality and heterogeneity of rights regimes would be incompatible with his deontological view. The question Forst raises is to what extent proportionality analysis could accommodate deontological views. As for constitutional review, Forst is sceptical of Klatt's thesis that such review should be allocated to a court, rather than a legislative body. He is eager to stress that no institutional form whatsoever could exhaust the principle of justification.

Eoin Daly defends a republican concept of constitutional rights and contrasts it with a liberal understanding. He reconstructs the standard picture of republican political thought according to which the very concept of judicially enforceable rights are in tension with republican values like procedural democracy, social solidarity, and the common good. In the context of severe disagreement about rights, liberal rights claims are highly contextual, contingent, and utterly political. The liberal concept of constitutional adjudication, then, is at odds with the intrinsically political character of rights. In contrast, republicans maintain that conflicting rights claims are best reconciled in political processes of democratic procedures. It seems to follow that the proportionality test, used in constitutional review, is not compatible with republican concepts of rights.

It is precisely this point that Daly wants to disprove. He sets out to demonstrate how proportionality analysis allows for accommodating the instability and contestability of rights in constitutional adjudication. Rather than assisting a notion of rights as areas of non-interference, proportionality required public authorities to act non-arbitrarily. Daly further claims that Forst's right to justification supported precisely this understanding of proportionality. Freedom, according to Daly, is not a guarantee of non-interference, but rather of non-domination, and citizens themselves realize it through participation in politics. Hence, we must shift our focus of attention away from the individual rights-holder's isolated guarantees of non-interference towards more complete political processes of determining contents and scopes of rights.

Daly then outlines a republicanized conception of constitutional rights adjudication. In contrast to a widely shared assumption, Daly claims that the institution and practice of constitutional adjudication does not necessarily depend on a liberal conception of rights. On the contrary, constitutional review could well account for the contingent and indeterminate, intrinsically political character, of rights. This was possible by conceptualizing rights as bulwarks against arbitrary exercises of state power. Constitutional adjudication then controls special kinds of justification for certain state actions, and Daly finds support for this in Forst's theory.

Constitutional law is seen by Daly as being concerned with the predicates of government action, rather than with the moral rights of individuals. Accordingly, the focus of constitutional review moves from individual liberties towards patterns and purposes of government action. The aim of constitutional review was not to protect individual spheres of non-interference, but rather to control arbitrariness in the exercise of state power. This was reflected in proportionality analysis whose more technical-rational parts could properly control arbitrariness, based on a republican understanding of rights as non-domination.

Rainer Forst, in his comment to Daly, agrees that basic rights raise the threshold for justification of interferences. He again stresses, however, the deontological grounding of basic rights. While the concrete form and content of rights only get constructed in particular political communities, their core was not at the disposal of majorities. Unlike many constitutional theorists, Forst derives this point from the principle of democracy itself, interpreted as an institution of non-domination. Furthermore, Forst joins Daly's notion of rights as bulwarks, but unlike Daly he is critical of the notion of balancing rights as inherent in proportionality analysis.

Alon Harel juxtaposes two versions of constitutionalism, an instrumentalist and a robust version. He criticizes the former and defends the latter. Aquinas, Kelsen, and Dworkin, all are representatives of instrumentalist constitutionalism, according to Harel. They employ result-driven accounts, placing the legitimacy of constitutionalism on extrinsic ends. Harel finds these instrumentalist accounts wanting for two reasons. First, they rested on empirical claims as to the factual consequences of constitutions and their institutions. These claims were too general and context-dependent, and we could not validate them properly. Second, Harel maintains that instrumental constitutionalism was inauthentic. The real attitudes and sentiments of its proponents remained hidden.

They refer, Harel claims, to the symbolic significance of entrenched and explicit rights norms.

In contrast to instrumental accounts, Harel values constitutionalism as such and irrespective of its outcomes. Against communitarian thought, he stresses the 'individualistic sentiments' of constitutionalism. Two distinct features characterize Harel's robust constitutionalism: it imposes duties on the legislature, and it institutionalizes judicial review. Binding the legislature by mandatory directives, Harel argues, had a value quite independent of any effect on rights protection because it underlined that the protection of rights was a mandatory task for the legislature. The protection of rights was not the free choice of the legislature. Furthermore, we could also use a structurally similar argument beyond the state, in order to defend the global notion of constitutionalism.

Judicial review, in particular, granted individuals a right to a hearing. The right to a hearing, Harel claims, is essentially a robust version of Forst's right to justification, to which it was inextricably connected. Judicial review, then, is not valuable for instrumentalist reasons, in the sense that it helped protecting individual rights. Rather, judicial review functions as an irreducible fundament of any protection of rights. It is itself a (deliberative) right, requiring a distinct mode of justification that addresses the particular grievance raised by a claimant. Harel refers to Forst's account of deliberative democracy in this context, which also opposes instrumentalist views. Harel, however, draws attention to the limits of public deliberation. He demands more stringent forms of justification, which submit legislative decisions to adjudicative scrutiny. In result, only the right to a hearing, interpreted as a special right to justification and institutionalized in judicial review, could ground the overall legitimacy of the constitutional state.

Rainer Forst, in his comment to Harel, agrees with the emphasis on dignity and non-domination. However, he reminds us of the dynamic, self-reflective quality of constitutions as learning structures of justification. No concrete form of constitutionalism, including Harel's right to a hearing, Forst claims, could have intrinsic value since the founding right to justification transcended all particular constitutional structures. Forst also underlines that democracy and basic rights are not separate values.

Christian F. Rostbøll addresses the problem of the justification of democracy. He distinguishes between instrumentalist and non-instrumentalist justifications. The former bases the justification of democracy upon its desired outcomes, while the latter interprets democracy as a good in itself. Rostbøll lists six different requirements for a sound justification of democracy and uses them to reject instrumentalist theories, eg the natural law theory of Aquinas or the legal positivist theories of Bentham or Kelsen. Instrumentalist theories, according to Rostbøll, lack robustness because the justification they provide was dependent upon both contingent empirical factors and specific but contested views on social justice.

Furthermore, they would be compatible with inegalitarian institutions and could not differentiate properly between democratic and undemocratic institutions. Lastly, by focusing on long-term consequences, instrumentalist justifications of democracy were unable to account for the bindingness of particular decisions.

Rostbøll then develops his own account of a non-instrumentalist justification of democracy by addressing two different interpretations of the idea that democracy is good in itself, namely Aristotelian and justice-first non-instrumentalism, respectively. From both interpretations, he takes some aspects while rejecting others. That way, he develops his own understanding as a third way of a non-instrumentalist justification. Rostbøll agrees, on the one hand, with Aristotelian non-instrumentalism, as developed by Mill, Arendt, and Anderson, on the constitutive value of democracy. He rejects, however, its focus on a specific notion of a fulfilling human life for reasons of sectarianism and its inability to account for the equality of citizen's political influence. From justice-first non-instrumentalism, on the other hand, Rostbøll adopts the notion of egalitarian relationships. Discussing Forst's and Christiano's non-instrumentalist theories of democracy, Rostbøll rejects the idea of a separate, democracy-independent idea of justice, as represented, eg by the right to justification. Forst, Rostbøll argues, neglected the special norm created by constitutional democracy specifically. The two-step structure of justice-first theories failed to provide a truly constitutive justification of democracy. In result, the non-instrumentalist justification Rostbøll favours bases democracy upon relationships of equal freedom, which are however constituted by, and not prior to, democracy itself. In this respect, Rostbøll also criticizes Harel's claim to provide a non-instrumentalist justification for ultimately holding to an instrumentalist account.

The argument Rostbøll provides for his third, Kantian non-instrumentalist theory, draws upon Kant's idea of freedom as autonomy as realized by public and reciprocal coercion possible only in the constitutional state. Democracy, under this account, is interpreted as a specific organization of the political community, combining individual freedom with binding positive laws by providing equal participatory standings for its citizens. Constitutional democracy, then, is the morally obligated form of political system.

Rainer Forst, in his comment to Rostbøll, disagrees with the idea that his own account was belonging to the category of justice-first justifications of democracy. Forst reconstructs democracy as the political form of justice as justification which rests on a deontological Kantian justification. Democracy, therefore, was not capable of trumping the value of human beings as ends in themselves. It rather expressed the correct form of respect for equal normative authorship in the political world. Pointing towards differences between their Kantian accounts, Forst goes on to suggest a reading of Rostbøll's account that allows to interpret democracy as realizing the moral norm of equal standing in a form of collective political co-authorship.

Ester Herlin-Karnell explores how the republican concept of freedom as non-domination can help to understand the European Union's security regulation. The latter comprises, in particular, the establishment of an Area of Freedom, Security and Justice, which seeks to reconcile free movement, migration, and asylum policy with criminal laws and anti-terrorist strategy. Herlin-Karnell addresses the notion of freedom as non-domination as a status a person enjoys in relation to other people, and contrasts the republican writings with Forst's right to justification. The chapter underlines that the idea of non-domination is the most important means to determine the level of freedom in a society. The concept of domination is then juxtaposed with the concept of coercion, as used, eg by Dworkin and Ripstein. This leads Herlin-Karnell to the problem of the legitimacy of domination, which was interwoven with the problem of justification. As an exemplary issue for these considerations, Herlin-Karnell discusses the legitimacy of judicial review, exercised by means of proportionality test. She defends the use of proportionality analysis as a more intelligible notion than the abstract right to justification. Moving to the EU level specifically, Herlin-Karnell identifies instances of coercion in the use of arbitrary powers, stemming from poorly drafted legislation and deficient reasoning in the EU Court of Justice. This is then exemplified with an eye on the Area of Freedom, Security and Justice specifically. Another question addressed is how this could supply justifications of EU legislation not only to the Member States but also to the citizens as well as to outsiders, along the Kantian idea of a cosmopolitan right. Finally, Herlin-Karnell discusses if and how the proportionality test can be used to strike a balancing between the EU's security needs and human rights.

Rainer Forst, in his answer to Herlin-Karnell, welcomes the consideration of the right to justification in the EU context. At the same time, he issues warning against downplaying the critical and democratic implications of his theory. In particular, he adds that rights systems beyond the state as addressed by Herlin-Karnell must be democratic, rather than merely an inter-state contractual system. Forst agrees with Herlin-Karnell in her analysis that focusing on state power often tends to overlook supranational forms of potential domination. He takes the opportunity to underline that the logic of justification did not stop at the borders of national normative systems.

IV. Acknowledgements

The origins of this volume lie in a workshop held in Amsterdam in January 2016. Ester Herlin-Karnell wants to acknowledge support by the *Dutch Scientific*

Research Council (NWO) and by *Access Europe Amsterdam* for kindly sponsoring the workshop. Both editors wish to express their sincere gratitude to Héctor A. Morales Zúñiga for his truly committed and astute assistance.

All contributions to this volume are original, with one exception: The contribution by Lois McNay is reprinted with permission from McNay L, 'The Limits of Justification: Critique, Disclosure and Reflexivity' (2016) European Journal of Political Theory, doi: 10.1177/1474885116670294 (10 October 2016).

References

Forst R, *Contexts of Justice: Political Philosophy Beyond Liberalism and Communitarianism* (John MM Farrell tr, University of California Press 2002).

Forst R, *The Right to Justification: Elements of a Constructivist Theory of Justice* (Jeffrey Flynn tr, Columbia University Press 2011).

Forst R, 'The Right to Justification: Towards a Critical Theory of Justice and Democracy. An Interview with Rainer Forst' in Gary Browning, Raia Prokhovnik and Maria Dimova-Cookson (eds), *Dialogues with Contemporary Political Theorists* (Palgrave MacMillan 2012).

Forst R, 'Two Stories About Toleration' in Lorenzo Zucca and Camil Ungureanu (eds), *Law, State and Religion in the New Europe: Debates and Dilemmas* (Cambridge University Press 2012).

Forst R, *Justification and Critique: Towards a Critical Theory of Politics* (Ciaran Cronin tr, Polity Press 2013).

Forst R, *Toleration in Conflict: Past and Present* (Ciaran Cronin tr, Cambridge University Press 2013).

Forst R, 'The Point and Ground of Human Rights: A Kantian Constructivist View' in David Held and Pietro Maffettone (eds), *Global Political Theory* (Polity Press 2016).

Forst R, 'A Critical Theory of Human Rights – Some Groundwork' in Penelope Deutscher and Cristina Lafont (eds), *Critical Theory in Critical Times: Transforming the Global Political and Economic Order* (Columbia University Press 2017).

Forst R, *Normativity and Power: Analyzing Social Orders of Justification* (Ciaran Cronin tr, Oxford University Press 2017).

Forst R, 'What's Critical About a Critical Theory of Justice' in Banu Bargu and Chiara Bottici (eds), *Feminism, Capitalism, and Critique: Essays in Honor of Nancy Fraser* (Palgrave 2017).

Habermas J, *Between Facts and Norms: Contributions to a Discourse Theory of Law and Democracy* (William Rehg tr, MIT Press 1996).

Habermas J, 'Does the Constitutionalization of International Law Still Have a Chance?' in Jürgen Habermas, *The Divided West* (Ciaran Cronin tr, Polity 2006).

Kleinlein T, *Konstitutionalisierung im Völkerrecht: Konstruktion und Elemente einer idealistischen Völkerrechtslehre* (Springer 2012).

Kumm M, 'The Cosmopolitan Turn in Constitutionalism: On the Relationship between Constitutionalism in and Beyond the State' in Jeffrey L Dunoff and Joel P Trachtman (eds), *Ruling the World? Constitutionalism, International Law, and Global Governance* (Cambridge University Press 2009).

Kumm M, 'Global Constitutionalism and the Rule of Law' in Anthony F Lang and Antje Wiener (eds), *Handbook on Global Constitutionalism* (Edward Elgar Publishing 2017).

PART I
THE RIGHT TO JUSTIFICATION

1

The Innate Right of Humanity and the Right to Justification

*Arthur Ripstein**

I. Introduction

At the centre of Rainer Forst's systematic approach to political philosophy is the 'right to justification' which, he contends, underlies and provides the basis for all other rights that people have against each other. Drawing on Kant, Rawls, and Habermas, Forst seeks to characterize this right through an examination of the claims that human beings, as free and equal and as rational and social, have against those whose acts affect them. In this chapter, I will consider two versions of the idea that everyone who is suitably affected has a right to have the actions (including the effects of those actions) of others justified to them.

On one interpretation, the right to justification is situated within an idea of the system of norms that is generated through the giving and assessing of reasons, the aim of which is to create a system of which every citizen can regard himself or herself as author of as well as subject to those norms. On this first interpretation, the acceptability of a reason depends upon whether it survives critical scrutiny through mutual justification; there is no antecedent constraint on acceptable reasons. Many of Forst's explicit formulations emphasize this first interpretation, and treat its specification as itself part of the process of giving justifications. On this first account, the subjects of justification are seen as co-legislators of the general will, but, crucially, each citizen owes each of the other co-legislators a justification for any rule that might affect them. I will call this the 'co-deliberation' model of the right to justification.

I will suggest that the alternative account, found not in Kant's *Groundwork* or the writing of Rawls or Habermas, but rather in Kant's *Doctrine of Right*, provides a more powerful conception of the right to justification. On this alternative account, persons have different claims against others depending on different kinds of questions, including first-order questions about how one person may affect

* I am grateful to Rainer Forst, Ester Herlin-Karnell, Matthias Klatt, and Malcolm Thorburn for comments on an earlier draft of this chapter, and to George Pavlakos for discussion.

Arthur Ripstein, *The Innate Right of Humanity and the Right to Justification* In: *Constitutionalism Justified: Rainer Forst in Discourse.* Edited by: Ester Herlin-Karnell and Matthias Klatt, Oxford University Press (2020),

DOI: 10.1093/oso/9780190889050.003.0001

another, secondary questions about the enforcement of rights, and tertiary questions about the acts of public officials. On the second interpretation, some antecedent idea of a right to stand in a certain type of normative relation, not exhausted by claims to justification, is essential. For the second interpretation, the right to justification follows from each person's innate right of humanity in his or her own person, and crucially, the resources available for justification are to be found in each person's status as *sui iuris*. I will call this second interpretation 'the narrow Kantian interpretation'.

II. Some Similarities

In this chapter, I want to engage with Forst's idea of the right to justification, drawing attention to these two different ways in which it might be read. Before turning to the differences between them, it is worth noting some similarities between them. First, both accounts are broadly republican, seeking to articulate principles of social life in which domination is the paradigmatic problem. The co-deliberation model does this through an idea of arbitrariness; the narrow Kantian model through the idea that each person is *sui iuris*. Second, both are resolutely antifoundationalist, in a way that might strike a critic as circular. Both seek to develop interdefined accounts of justification, dignity, freedom, and reciprocity, never fully breaking out of these interrelated concepts. The co-deliberation model seeks no deeper vindication than its own ability to survive the very process of giving and asking for reasons in a non-dominating context that it characterizes. The narrow Kantian model begins with a norm of reciprocal independence and, perhaps unsurprisingly, generates a republican account of non-domination in public law. I mention these similarities between the two conceptions of the right to justification because they already reveal that the significant differences between them are not primarily a matter of their first order moral recommendations or of broader epistemological debates about the concept of justification more generally. Instead, they are specifically about the context within which justifications may be demanded and the kinds of factors that qualify as adequate responses to those demands.

With that in mind, I turn to the two conceptions.

III. Some Contrasts

The first interpretation of the right to justification, which I believe to be most prominent in Forst's formulations, understands it as a general kind of moral status, an entitlement to have others give you reasons for whatever they do that has an effect on you. On this understanding, the idea of reciprocity figures centrally, because one of the standard ways in which others can justify something to you, some effect that their action has on you or your interests, is to point out that to prohibit that kind of action would burden them too greatly. This first reading understands everyone as equal in the sense that everyone has the same kind of claim to the moral attention of others. This conception of equality and the idea of reciprocity fit together: everyone is equal because everyone is alike in being entitled to demand from everyone else the same justification of the effects that rules proposed by others have on them. Further, no one is entitled to any kind of exemption from, or special status within, a general system of rules that can be justified to all, in keeping with what Forst describes as the 'veto' that each of us has.

On this first interpretation, the right to justification is the structuring principle of what Scanlon, in a related context, calls 'a system of co-deliberation'[1] in which moral peers construct a system of rules for regulating their common affairs. Crucially, this system of co-deliberation may lead to a morality marked by multiple differentiations and distinctions—the morality of making and keeping promises is different from the morality of friendship, which is different again from the morality of mutual aid, and all of these are different from the negative morality of refraining from interfering with other people's bodies or property. But on the co-deliberation approach, any such differentiations are the product of the process of co-deliberation and justification, a process which is itself undifferentiated. The reason that unauthorized touching of another person's body is prohibited, that contracts are binding on the parties who enter into them (absent defeating circumstances such as deception, duress, or unconscionability), that discrimination is prohibited, and taxes must be paid are all to be analyzed in terms of the justifications that citizens could give to each other.

A second, superficially similar, but ultimately fundamentally different approach, understands the right to justification in terms of an irreducible idea of *standing*. On this view, central to Kant's *Doctrine of Right*, any right to place demands on others, for justification or for anything else, is structured by a right that is normatively and conceptually prior to it, the innate right of humanity in one's own person. In 'The Normative Order of Justice and Peace', Forst describes the innate right as the 'claim to a kind of liberty that is justifiable between us reciprocally.'[2] In a more recent piece he puts it this way: 'In my Kantian view, the right to justification operates between the moral and the legal-political level.

[1] Thomas M Scanlon, *What We Owe to Each Other* (The Belknap Press of Harvard University Press 1998) 268. He first introduces this term in Thomas M Scanlon, 'The Significance of Choice' in Sterling M McMurrin (ed), *The Tanner Lectures on Human Values* (University of Utah Press 1988) 166.

[2] Rainer Forst, 'The Normative Order of Justice and Peace' in Rainer Forst, *Justification and Critique: Towards a Critical Theory of Politics* (Ciaran Cronin tr, Polity Press 2013) 74.

Thus it performs a similar function as Kant's "innate" or "original" right of persons.'[3] On this more narrowly Kantian formulation, the innate right is a right to equality, *not* in the sense that everyone is alike in some morally significant respect, or that all rules must be general or acceptable to all, but rather in the sense that nobody is the superior (and thus nobody is the subordinate) of any other. This contrastive conception of equality figures in basic moral relations between private persons, but, perhaps more significantly, in what Kant characterizes as 'the right to be beyond reproach', that is, the right to be presumed to have done no wrong. This right to be beyond reproach is a familiar fixture of legal systems, figuring in such things as the right to a fair trial, structured by the presumption of innocence, the burden of proof and burden of coming forward with the evidence in legal proceedings and, most significantly, the right against defamation, that is, the juridical standing to compel anyone who accuses you of having done wrong either to prove their claim in court or to withdraw it.

One way of understanding the difference between these two approaches is to notice that the co-deliberation model is *open* with respect to what counts as a reason in the relevant sense. That doesn't necessarily mean that anything goes as far as a reason, but rather that reasons themselves—as opposed to the specific political rights and principles issuing from exercises of the right to justification—are not themselves reasons of right, but rather *inputs* to rights. That does not mean that they are somehow aggregated to generate those rights, or that the rights are reducible to interests, only that on the co-deliberation model they are assessed (and perhaps reworked) under the ideas of reciprocity and generality. Different formulations of the co-deliberation model may have different conceptions of the relevant types of reasons that might be brought forward, ranging from Rawls's interest in doing justice in setting and pursuing a conception of the good (which generates a catalogue of primary goods, that is, preconditions of exercising these moral powers) through the broader range of factors that Habermas and Scanlon are prepared to include. Crucially, on the co-deliberation model, as preliminary inputs, the relevant reasons need not make explicit reference to other persons; other persons come in at the stage of co-deliberation about relevant principles governing their interactions, establishing that the rules that are imposed meet the tests of reciprocity and generality, rather than as the first-order reasons put forward to generate those principles. Further, on the co-deliberation model, the reasons to be exchanged in co-deliberation need not be essentially general. To use a Kantian distinction, they are material rather than formal. Forst writes that the reasons must be 'shareable', so that they can apply to more than one person, and in that sense, they must be general. But the idea of the reason being shareable

[3] Rainer Forst, 'The Justification of Basic Rights: A Discourse-Theoretical Approach' (2016) 45(3) Netherlands Journal of Legal Philosophy 7, 12.

requires only that it be something that could count as a reason for someone other than some specific individual. The requirement that reasons be shareable rules out subjective or idiosyncratic claims, but not, for example, that it would be burdensome for me to have a certain legal rule or requirement. This reflects another feature of the co-deliberation model: many of the shareable reasons or questions of degree, that something would be too difficult, or too burdensome. Which rights persons have on the co-deliberation model will depend on these matters of degree: shareable reasons would need to be processed through co-deliberation to determine whether they are outweighed by competing reasons.

Instead, on this view, the generality of moral and legal rules is the *product* of the reciprocal exercise of the right to justification by citizens concerned to be able to justify their institutions to each other. That is, moral and legal rules are general because they must include everyone, be acceptable to everyone, and be the same for everyone. Scanlon is especially perspicuous on this point: it provides the rationale for going through the contractualist procedure, rather than simply moving directly from the reasons to conclusions about what to do. Morality demands that first order reasons, which are primitive in his account, be brought together in the right way; co-deliberation is the specific subject matter of moral reasoning for beings already conversant with reasons, both acting for and offering them. That is the sense in which any generality is the product of the right to justification on the co-deliberation view.

By contrast, on the narrow Kantian account, the starting point cannot be expressed in terms of anything other than a perfectly general rule. Each person's right to independence as against each of the others is already general, not merely in the sense that it holds in every case, but rather in that it restricts the form of thought appropriate to justification. On the narrow Kantian view, the basic form of a demand for justification objects to some way of treating another person, or some public law rule, on the grounds that it is inconsistent with someone's innate right; the basic form of a justification is the demonstration of consistency. Because of that right, certain things do not need to be justified, and certain other things cannot be justified. The distinctive form of relational generality that animates the narrow Kantian account is reflected in the fact that the starting point for any analysis of rights is non-comparative, that is, does not admit of any questions of degree.

By focusing on each person's innate right as the precondition of a structuring principle for any further right to justification, this second approach distinguishes itself from the first in two fundamental respects. First, on this second reading of the right to justification, the right to demand that somebody justify their action to you only arises against the background of a set of already differentiated entitlements to formal independence. It might be thought that these entitlements must also undergo a process of justification, but on this second conception, each person's innate right of humanity is the presupposition of any morally coherent right to justification. So rather than seeing rules as the output of a process of justification, the second, Kantian, approach sees one rule—that each person is *sui iuris*, and has no juridical master—as the presupposition of the demand for justification. Rather than focusing on benefits and burdens or the preconditions of moral agency, the second approach instead restricts the operation of the demand for justification to occasions in conformity with each person's innate right. Rather than treating domination as a particularly significant pathology against which the right to justification must protect, the narrow Kantian view makes the wrongfulness of domination—the violation each person's standing as *sui iuris*—its presupposition.

These contrasts manifest themselves most significantly with respect to the relevance of benefits and burdens. On the open conception of the relevant reasons, the fact that it would be particularly difficult for me to moderate my conduct counts against finding me to have an obligation to do so; conversely, the fact that it would be particularly difficult for me to lead an autonomous life if a rule did not provide me with what I need also counts as relevant. The narrower Kantian view can allow such factors in, but only at a later stage. As I shall explain, this will have the consequence that on the co-deliberation account, there is an important sense in which justification is unstructured, and any procedures giving effect to the right to justification are merely implementations of it, while on the narrower Kantian account, justification is fundamentally sequenced.

Second, the narrow Kantian approach leads to a differentiated conception of justification itself: interpersonal justification differs from the justification of public policies and practices. These differences manifest themselves in several ways, perhaps the most significant of which is that interpersonal justification focuses only on how things stand as between two individual human beings; the justification of public policies and practices goes to the entitlement of institutions purporting to act on behalf of everyone to put restrictions on the operation of individual rights, and typically proceeds not by looking at how things stand comparatively between this person and that one, not asking the question 'how bad would it be for others if they were not permitted to do this?' but instead looking to some idea of a properly public purpose, a purpose that belongs not to any at specific individual, nor to the intersection between the multiple private purposes of each of the members of a multitude of individual persons, but rather to the citizens considered as a collective body. This public order of justification focuses on the exercise of distinctively public powers, determining whether a policy, rule, or practice can be justified by a distinctive idea of the public.

I mentioned that many of Forst's most prominent formulations suggest a commitment to the first, co-deliberation interpretation. I do not, however, think that anything that he says rules out the second, narrow Kantian one. And so, by way of friendly amendment, I propose to develop the second, and to invite him to make its role explicit. One of the animating thoughts behind all of Forst's work is that basic rights are not in dispute; the task for philosophers is to properly and perspicuously characterize their normative basis and structure. Although, as an empirical matter, I fear that some recent political events have revealed that basic rights to freedom and against domination are more controversial than Forst allows, at least there is no dispute between the two of us about those rights. Whether there is a dispute about the perspicuous characterization of their nature and source is less clear. That is what I propose to examine here.

IV. Forst's Characterizations of the Right to Justification

Consider several of Forst's general characterizations of the right to justification:

> Reciprocity means that no one may make a normative claim (such as a rights claim) he or she denies to others (call that reciprocity of content) and that no one may simply project one's own perspective, values, interests, or needs onto others such that one claims to speak in their 'true' interests or in the name of some truth beyond mutual justification.[4]
>
> That is a political notion of dignity as a relational concept, referring to the social and political standing of human beings as agents of justification who are equal to one another.[5]
>
> This means that moral actions or norms have to be justifiable with moral reasons in moral discourse (free from coercion or delusion) and that political or social structures or laws have to be based on or (at least) to be compatible with moral norms applicable to them and must be justifiable within appropriate legal and political structures (and practices) of justification.[6]
>
> Rather, dignity means that a person is to be respected as someone who is worthy of being given adequate reasons for actions or norms that affect him or her in a relevant way. And this kind of respect requires us to regard others as autonomous sources of normative claims within a justificatory practice. Each person is an 'authority' in the space of reasons, so to speak.[7]
>
> In the first place, the Kantian character of Rawls's theory implies that the autonomy of free and equal persons, which is at the normative heart of the approach, is not the autonomy of individuals who are primarily conceived as

[4] Rainer Forst, 'The Justification of Human Rights and the Basic Right to Justification: A Reflexive Approach' (2010) 120 Ethics 711, 719.

[5] ibid 721.

[6] ibid 734.

[7] ibid.

> recipients of goods which they would need in order to lead a 'good life'. It is rather the constructive autonomy of free and equal subjects of justification which manifests itself in the fact that the persons are able to regard the principles of justice as morally self-given; hence, the citizens view the social basic structure which is grounded in this way as the social expression of their self-determination. The essential conception of autonomy is the autonomy to actively determine the basic structure, not the autonomy to enjoy its goods (even though this is also important).[8]
>
> [W]e may want to ask whether the justifications given for certain relations are good justifications (and we need a standard for that), and we ask whether the existing practices of justification, including those that are institutionalized, are adequate for the purpose of generating generally binding and acceptable justifications.[9]
>
> It is a game that humans cannot opt out of without violating a basic moral demand, namely that of treating others as autonomous 'ends in themselves', that is, as beings with a right to justification with respect to how one treats them. The insight relevant here is an insight of reason and morality at the same time: you see the other as like and as unlike you; like you, he or she can use and in any case deserves reasons in moral contexts of action; unlike you, he or she might have justifiable claims and reasons you did not recognize and at first may not understand. So my moral 'outlook' is not 'humanist' in the sense that I project one form of recognition onto all others; what I mean is that morality is a particular practice of respect, and it involves not essentializing or idealizing others, but seeing them as reason-giving and reason-deserving autonomous and yet vulnerable beings.[10]

Finally,

> a normative basis that the principle of justification provides—as a principle immanent to and at the same time transcending social practice.[11]

Each of these claims seems to me to allow for either of the interpretations I identified above. On the one hand, they all speak in the vocabulary of standing, justification, and authority. As Forst formulates them, each of these concepts appears as irreducible. To say that each of us has authority in the space of reasons is, as

[8] Rainer Forst, 'Two Pictures of Justice' in Rainer Forst, *Justification and Critique: Towards a Critical Theory of Politics* (Ciaran Cronin tr, Polity Press 2013) 18.

[9] Rainer Forst, 'Justifying Justification: A Reply to My Critics' in Rainer Forst, *Justice, Democracy and the Right to Justification: Rainer Forst in Dialogue* (Bloomsbury Academic 2014) 190.

[10] Forst, 'Two Pictures of Justice' (n 8) 30.

[11] Forst, 'Justifying Justification: A Reply to My Critics' (n 9) 199.

I understand it, to reject the thought that the concept of authority must itself be analyzed in some further away, focused on the service it provides or the way in which it tracks reasons that are already determinable and significant in the absence of that type of authority. So, too, to speak of the standing that each of us has is to treat standing as a primitive, rather than something that is conferred on us in the service of some other set of moral ideas.

Again, the notion that dignity must in some way be the starting point for analysis, that norms of what can be asserted in the process of justification preclude direct appeals to the correctness of a moral principle, or true (but unasserted) interests, or even the unvarnished assertion of mere perspectives and interests suggests that each person's standing enters as an irreducible premise of the entire analysis. Does dignity function as a restriction on means that can be used, or is it instead a property of a human life, so that each person is entitled to demand to be provided with the conditions of a dignified life?

At the same time, other formulations appear to treat this standing as undifferentiated, as in the reference to 'adequate reasons for actions or norms that affect him or her in a relevant way.' The word 'relevant' in the phrase, 'affect him or her in the relevant way', could take either 'way' or 'affect' as its object. On the first 'way' reading, the relevant way of affecting someone can only be characterized in terms of a system of rights that is already differentiated. To affect you in the relevant way in this sense would just be to violate some genuine claim of yours, for example, violating your right to bodily integrity or to your own good name, each of which is understood as a (wrongful) way of affecting you. In public law, it might be affecting you by restricting the operation of some right that you have, for example, restricting the scope of your freedom of expression in light of the equality rights of others, in the context of hate speech laws, or restricting commercial speech in light of the obligation of the state to protect children. On this narrow Kantian structure, what needs to be justified is any apparent departure from the organizing thought that no person is in charge of any other. How easy or difficult it is to meet this burden in a particular context will vary. Certain limitations on fundamental rights, like those mentioned in the last few examples, may be comparatively easy to justify; other, historically familiar examples may be much harder to justify.

Alternatively, if 'relevant' modifies 'affect', then another person bringing about a result (or a rule permitting that person to bring about that results) is a thing to which you are entitled to object. On the second reading, then, your complaint is grounded in some interest of yours, such as your interest in having an adequate range of options, leading an autonomous life, continuing your current project, continuing your general life trajectory, or even continuing your life at all. On the first, narrower interpretation, with its focus on the way, that is, the means through which, I affect you, the right to justification treats as presumptively unjustified a number of things that I might do to you; on the second, broader, one it contains things that I might cause to (or perhaps fail to prevent from) happening to you. These differences manifest themselves in the range of things that require justification. If only actions specified in terms of relations between persons need to be justified, then your right to justification does not go to any questions of my failure to organize my activities in ways that will better accommodate your preferred way of organizing your life. By contrast, if the production of effects (or failure to produce them) is what needs to be justified, then I owe you a justification for a much wider variety of things.

The same space of possibilities governs the idea that human beings are ends in themselves. This idea admits of a formal interpretation, on which each human being's standing as a person restricts the means that human beings can use in relation to each other. But it also admits of a material interpretation, on which as an end in to himself or herself, a human being's interests are to be promoted. On the material reading, Ronald Dworkin's familiar claim that a normative order must treat people with 'equal concern and respect' is an interpretation of human beings as ends in themselves.

Forst distinguishes between injustice and misfortune,[12] noting that the conceptual home of the right to justification is in dealing with domination and injustice, rather than with unfortunate facts of nature. At the same time, the question of what a normative order makes of natural facts—the institutional resources available to those who find that their skills are not in demand or their seaside homes destroyed by mudslides (to mention two very different classes of persons)—is always within the space of justification. So, although I do not dominate you if I fail to assist you, perhaps the legal order creates or reinforces domination does if it permits me to stand by or concern myself with other matters in your moment of need.

All of these contrasts mark the difference between a narrow Kantian understanding of the right to justification in purely relational terms, focused exclusively on the standing of individual human beings as against each other (plurality) and as against the citizens considered as a collective body (totality), and the twentieth-century co-deliberation understanding of it, according to which each person's right to justification is rooted in that person's fundamental interest in leading an autonomous life on terms commonly acceptable to a plurality of persons. The co-deliberation approach is monadic in that the moral significance of an autonomous (or dignified) life can be characterized (at the most general level) apart from questions about the relations in which one person stands to others. That is the sense in which its conception of the reasons it considers is open.

[12] Forst, 'Two Pictures of Justice' (n 8).

Relations with others may be among the most important *material* conditions of the autonomous or dignified life, but they are not constitutive of it in the way in which they are on the relational conception. On the monadic interpretation, the role of citizens as co-legislators enters as yet another factor in assessing the acceptability of proposed rules. On both the relational and monadic conceptions, the actual operation of the right to justification is partially contextual, turning as it does on social, cultural, and technological aspects of the context in which questions of justification arise. But although both approaches can be understood in this contextual way, they differ fundamentally in their starting point.

Forst's remark that 'A discourse theory of justice has a variety of substantial normative presuppositions and implications, none of which can be validated nondiscursively, for each one must be justifiable in correctly structured discourses',[13] might be thought to resolve these differences in favour of the co-deliberation model. But the idea of a correctly structured discourse seems to me to admit of the same pair of interpretations. Although I believe that starting with the innate right of humanity can also be justified recursively, in the way in which, on any Kantian approach, the vindication of reason may help itself to reason's own standards,[14] without it being the case that the form of reasoning appropriate to innate right depends upon any conception of discursive vindication that does not itself already presuppose that each person is *sui iuris*. Although it could past a test based on a suitable interpretation of reciprocity and generality, the suitability of any such test would presuppose rather than explain the sense in which each person is *sui iuris*.

In the next two sections I will fill out these contrasts more fully.

V. Co-Deliberation

As I noted, many of Forst's formulations appear to work with an undifferentiated conception of the reasons available to co-deliberation, and to generate the generality of moral and especially legal rules as the product of the exchange of reasons, where those reasons being exchanged themselves need not be general. In this section I want to briefly sketch some features of this approach, as it figures prominently in the work of twentieth-century philosophers whose influence Forst

[13] Rainer Forst, 'Introduction: The Foundation of Justice' in Rainer Forst, *The Right to Justification: Elements of a Constructivist Theory of Justice* (Jeffrey Flynn tr, Columbia University Press 2011) 7.

[14] See Kant's discussion in the 'Canon of Pure Reason' in Immanuel Kant, *Critique of Pure Reason* (Paul Guyer and Allen W Wood eds and trs, Cambridge University Press 1998) 672ff; and Onora O'Neill, 'Vindication of Reason' in Paul Guyer (ed), *The Cambridge Companion to Kant* (Cambridge University Press 2009).

acknowledges, Habermas, Rawls, and Scanlon. These three thinkers differ on many fundamental points, but share an acknowledged Kantian orientation combined with a desire to formulate positions that, as Rawls put it, are free of Kant's 'dualisms'[15] or, in Scanlon's words, to formulate a Kantianism 'on the cheap'.[16] For Habermas, 'Kant's irreconcilable worlds, the objective world of appearances and the moral world of autonomous action, shed their transcendental-ontological dignity, and return in everyday communicative practice.'[17] Each of the three seeks to replace Kant's framework with a system in which moral rules emerge through the process of ordinary people giving reasons to each other. At the same time, each of them hopes to keep Kant's focus on human beings as active rather than passive, that is, as co-legislators as well as recipients of the law. In Scanlon's work this focus manifests itself in contractualism, through which proposed moral principles are assessed on the basis of whether they could be 'reasonably rejected' by people concerned to justify their conduct to each other, in Rawls in his use of the original position as a 'device of representation', and in Habermas in the 'ideal speech situation'. I trust that the broad outlines of each of these approaches will be familiar, and that any attempt on my part to delineate the significant differences among them will be controversial and, worse yet, distracting.

I do, however, want to draw attention to the way in which each of Habermas, Rawls, and Scanlon proposes a structure of justification within which the concept of a reason is open-ended. Habermas emphasizes 'the procedural aspects of the public use of reason', and its readiness to derive 'the system of rights from the idea of its legal institutionalization'.[18] Scanlon proposes constructivism about morality but not about reasons.[19] Rawls represents the choice of principles of political morality as structured by the interest that representative persons, unaware of their particular identities, abilities, and conception of the good, would choose from behind a veil of ignorance. Rawls's use of these ideas is considerably narrower than those of Scanlon or Habermas, and indeed both contrast their position with his in a number of places. Still, even when restricted, Rawls focuses on a broad conception of reasons that are related to the interests of the parties, and ultimately to how their lives go. Although Rawls's characterization of the way in which the parties reason shifted over the decades, a fundamental idea running

[15] John Rawls, 'Kantian Constructivism in Moral Theory' (1980) 77 The Journal of Philosophy 515, 516.

[16] Alex Voorhoeve, 'Kant on the Cheap: Thomas Scanlon Interviewed' (2001) The Philosophers' Magazine 29, 29f.

[17] Jürgen Habermas, 'The Unity of Reason in the Diversity of Its Voices' in Jürgen Habermas, *Postmetaphysical Thinking: Philosophical Essays* (William Mark Hohengarten tr, MIT Press 1992) 142.

[18] Jürgen Habermas, 'Reconciliation Through the Public Use of Reason: Remarks on John Rawls's *Political Liberalism*' (1995) 92 The Journal of Philosophy 109, 131.

[19] Thomas M Scanlon, 'The Appeal and Limits of Constructivism' in James Lenman and Yonatan Shemmer (eds), *Constructivism in Practical Philosophy* (Oxford University Press 2012).

throughout was the 'strains of commitment', that is, the thought that a person could not agree to terms that it would be too difficult to fulfil. Indeed, Rawls uses this argument to show that slavery could never be acceptable in the original position, even in economic circumstances in which it would raise standards of living.[20] As I will explain in more detail later, the reasons with which this analysis begins are non-relational—it starts with each individual's interest in getting on with his or her life—and is worked up into a reciprocal and general concept of not asking too much of others. Readers will all be familiar with the enormous secondary literature that uses Rawlsian apparatus to figure out appropriate rules for all manner of situations.[21]

These ideas of citizens as active rather than passive in so far as they must be seen to participate in the making of the laws that bind them, combined with an open conception of reasons that might be relevant to satisfying their demands for justification, has produced much of the most influential political philosophy of the past half-century. But, I now want to suggest, this non-dualistic, post metaphysical, bargain-priced Kantianism is not the only viable Kantian alternative. In advocating a more Kantian Kantianism, I will not make a plea for extravagant metaphysics or untenable dualisms. Instead, I will focus on the formal, structural features of Kant's own formulation of the innate right of humanity, arguing that it provides an alternative understanding of what a right to justification could be. The innate right explains the standing to demand justifications from others, without itself being the product of any process of co-deliberation that can be characterized in terms of anything more basic than each human being's entitlement to be independent of the determining choice of others.

VI. Innate Right

In the *Introduction to the Doctrine of Right*,[22] Kant characterizes the 'Universal Principle of Right':

> Any action is *right* if it can coexist with everyone's freedom in accordance with a universal law, or if on its maxim the freedom of choice can coexist with everyone's freedom in accordance with the universal law. (6:230)

[20] John Rawls, *A Theory of Justice* (Harvard University Press 1971) 176ff.

[21] As Ronald Dworkin remarked at a memorial for Rawls: 'the other day I saw him cited twice in the British press, once in an argument calling for more far-reaching thought about Iraq, and once, in what you might think the opposite level of importance, in a sports-page argument about the realignment of teams in the British Rugby League.' Ronald Dworkin, 'Remembrance: John Rawls' (2003) XI The Harvard Review of Philosophy 7.

[22] Immanuel Kant, 'The Metaphysics of Morals' in Immanuel Kant, *Practical Philosophy* (Mary J Gregor ed and tr, Cambridge University Press 1996) 386ff.

After explaining the structure of this principle and its relation to coercion, he goes on to say that 'there is only one innate right'. He characterizes this right as:

> *Freedom* (independence from being constrained by another's choice), insofar as it can coexist with the freedom of every other in accordance with a universal law, is the only right belonging to every human being by virtue of his humanity. This principle of innate freedom already involves the following authorizations which are not really distinct from it . . . Innate *equality*, that is independence from being bound by others to more than one can in turn bind them; hence a human being's quality of being *his own master* (*sui iuris*), as well as being a human being *beyond reproach (iusti)* since before he performs any act affecting rights he has done no wrong to anyone; and finally, his being authorized to do to others anything that does not in itself diminish what is theirs, so long as they do not want to accept it . . . (6:237)

The structure of innate right sets up the basic entitlements for free beings to interact with each other. Kant continues:

> The aim in introducing such a division within the system of natural right (in so far as it is concerned with innate right) is that when a dispute arises about an acquired right and the question comes up, on whom does the burden of proof (*onus probandi*) fall, either about a controversial fact or, if this is settled about a controversial right, someone who refuses to accept this obligation can appeal methodically to his innate right to freedom (which is now specified in its various relations), as if he were appealing to various bases for rights. (6:238)

Your innate right is thus your fundamental status as a human being in relation to other human beings. Although there is an innocent way of understanding the claim that you enjoy this status *because of* your dignity, or your humanity, or your moral personality, each of these is highly misleading. Your innate right of humanity in your own person is your entitlement to stand in certain types of relations to other human beings. It is not in the service of anything that can be usefully described as a basis apart from the relation. Although it is true that there are certain ways that others may not treat you because you are a human being, and so that they must always treat you as an end and never merely as a means, the force of the word 'because' in this formulation does not flow from the idea that humanity has value *apart* from your innate right to be treated in certain ways. Instead, your dignity consists in your entitlement to be treated in certain ways by others, to stand in certain relations to them. The distinction between a person and a mere thing is just the distinction between beings that may not be subordinated to the purposes of other (purpose having) beings and those that may be so subordinated. That is, the thought that you are a person rather than a thing, entitled to set your own purposes rather than having others set purposes for you, is a thought for two.[23] Its content is exhausted by the prohibition on others choosing the purposes you must serve.

Confusion about this point is easy, because only beings capable of setting purposes can stand (or fail to stand) in this relation: only a chooser can subordinate the choice of another, or be subordinated to the choice of another. As a result, the distinctive wrong of a violation of innate right can only be committed by persons against other persons. This is just the distinction between injustice and misfortune. But the restriction of the scope of wrongdoing to interpersonal wrongs does not reflect any assumption about the non-relational (monadic) value of choice or autonomy. It is not that there is some respect, which can be characterized *without* reference to innate right, in which you and every other human being are equal. Or rather, if there is such a respect, it has no bearing on your right of humanity in your own person. Nor is it something that comes in degrees, in which you participate in the same degree or, in Rawls's formulation, in the same 'range' of degree. Instead, your right to equality reflects the fact that none is subject to another. Human beings all have that property, but the relation they stand in is the basis of the property, rather than vice versa.

The Kantian refusal to ground innate right in anything non-relational, not even autonomy, might strike some as an evasion, a premature abandonment of the question of justification. This apparent weakness of the Kantian account actually reveals its strength, because it shows that the demand for justification is itself irreducibly relational. Different people might disagree about what grounds the value of humanity in each of us, but those disagreements don't need to be resolved in order for each of us to demand justifications from each other; the right to do so is grounded in nothing more than our independence of each other, and the correlative thought that none of us has the standing to impose our views unilaterally upon anyone else.

To paraphrase Kant, using Forst's vocabulary, the innate right of humanity structures the right to justification. In cases of dispute—not only in the context of a trial, but no less when one person contests a second person's entitlement to do something to the first, or an individual citizen contests the state's lawmaking power—the structure of interpersonal justification is determined by the fact that each has an innate right to freedom. That is, a free person can never be compelled to refrain from doing anything to another that does not diminish that person's rights. The burden of establishing that another has acted without justification lies with the person who alleges it. More generally, anyone asserting a right against

[23] I owe this lovely formulation to Ariel Zylberman, 'Why Human Rights? Because of *You*' (2016) 24 Journal of Political Philosophy 321.

another must explicate it in a way that is consistent with that other person's innate right of humanity.

Kant says that the aspects of innate right that he catalogs are not several rights but only one right, because each of what might seem to be 'incidents' of innate right just is part of what it is for a human being to be independent of the choice of other human beings. You get to determine the ends that you will pursue; others do not. Instead, both you and I (and all others) must accept limitations on the means that we use in pursuing our ends, but nobody is entitled to require that you pursue an end that you have not chosen. The innate right of humanity is thus structured by a sharp distinction between wronging someone by doing something to that person and merely failing to benefit that person. Indeed, ideas of benefit and burden, which figure centrally in Rawls's and Scanlon's formulations of co-deliberation, have no part in the Kantian conception. Its formality entails that the fact that something would be difficult for you and easy for someone else cannot be relevant to how things stand as between you, because there is no conceptual space for any consideration of ease or difficulty. Ease or difficulty is simply a function of the adequacy of a person's means to some end that is treated as given. From the Kantian standpoint, no ends count as given in the relevant sense.

On Kant's view, then, a normative structure is always already in place, prior to any specific demand for justification. Moreover, occasions on which the demand for justification are most pressing are just those in which some right is at issue. Kant sets up the problem of the *Doctrine of Right* by asking how positive, that is, institutionally given, law could be binding. That question gets its force from every human being's innate right of humanity in his or her own person, that is, it gets its start from the thought that no person is in charge of another. Positive law is always in some way chosen law—it must be enacted through appropriate procedures, and it purports to bind those who are subject to those procedures. That is, positive law has authority, inasmuch as it binds based on its sources rather than exclusively on its merits. This familiar, indeed unremarkable, feature of the institutional world calls out for explanation because it presents itself in such stark opposition to each person's innate right of humanity, each person's right to be *sui iuris*, that is, to have no master. If people had masters in the way that slaves or serfs were once thought to, the question of authority would not be philosophically demanding. The doctrine of right contends that the category of beings who have duties of obedience but no rights is empty, 'for these would be human beings without personality (serfs, slaves).' Instead, the only non-empty possibility is 'the relation in terms of rights of human beings towards beings that have right as well as duties' which is 'a relation of human beings to human beings.'[24] The question of how positive law can be binding thus emerges

[24] 6:241.

against the background assumption that it binds beings that have rights as well as duties. Anarchists imagine that the act of an institution could never be binding; Kantians seek to articulate the conditions under which positive law could be binding by showing how one would need to establish that it was consistent with innate right, that is, showing that the authoritative institution has a mandate that is consistent with every person's innate right, and that it is acting within the scope of that mandate.

Many of the other central questions of political philosophy come out of innate right when it is understood in this way. For example, questions about democracy get their moral interest not from questions about what will produce the best outcome, but from the morally antecedent question of the relevant ground for assessing legal and political decisions. A benevolent despot might make high-quality decisions. I rather doubt this, but mention it because the Kantian argument in favour of institutions that represent the citizens does not turn on any purported epistemic virtues of such institutions, or of any anticipation of things that might go wrong if powerful rulers lack popular oversight. Instead, democratic institutions are required so that the citizens are able to rule themselves through the institutions that exercise power over them. At the same time, the putative tension between popular rule and entrenched constitutional rights is revealed to be an illusion, because the powers of legislative bodies are *in subsidium* of their role in creating an institutional culture consistent with every human being's innate right.[25] As such, they have no untrammeled discretion to pursue private purposes. Instead, a legislative body is charged exclusively with providing a rightful condition for its citizens, and all of the particular powers that it has are incidents of that mandate.

I do not purport to have given an account of the significance of innate right for all of these other topics in political philosophy; I mention them here only because they illustrate the significance of innate right in all of the contexts in which the right to justification seems most compelling because the demand for justification seems so appropriate.

The answer that Kant gives to his own question presupposes innate right at two different levels. First, positive law can be legitimate in so far as it eliminates dependence of one person's choice on the private choice of another, that is, if it solves the problem of unilateral action in a state of nature. This is the answer provided by the Postulate of Public Right. Individual human beings give up their 'wild lawless freedom' as against each other, and in return acquire their freedom as against each other under law. Second, positive law can be fully rightful only against the Idea of a condition in which the elimination of private choice as

[25] See Jacob Weinrib, *Dimensions of Dignity: The Theory and Practice of Modern Constitutional Law* (Cambridge University Press 2016).

between individual human beings does not lead to its replacement with private choice of the ruler over his subjects. This is the answer provided by the Idea of the Original Contract, according to which everyone enjoys his or her freedom under laws that can be understood as collectively and severally self-imposed. The idea that law is self-imposed is, once again, relational and contrastive: the citizens rule themselves when they are not ruled by the private will of another, but instead by public laws. Positive, that is, chosen law, is only fully rightful, then, if the making of laws is itself subject to law. Natural law mandates positive, chosen law, demanding that it be consistent with independence, both horizontally, as guaranteed by the Postulate of Public Right, and vertically, as demanded by the Idea of the Original Contract. Despotism can satisfy the Postulate of Public Right, as it can solve the horizontal problems as between individual human beings in a state of nature, and so eliminate private dependence between private persons; it is still defective from the standpoint of the Idea of the Original Contract because human beings remain dependent on the private choice of the ruler. The ruler thus remains problematically private, and so the relation between ruler and ruled is defective.

Forst appears to endorse something similar when he writes:

> This right implies that all those who are subjected to a normative order should be its co-authors as equal participants and normative authorities in adequate justificatory practices that critically reflect on and constitute that order.[26]

But, I shall now argue, the relevant idea of co-authorship can be understood in a broad or in a narrow way, corresponding to what I earlier called the co-deliberation model and the narrow Kantian model. Understood broadly, the co-authors jointly create a system of rules in light of the reasons that secure conviction when offered back and forth. Understood narrowly, the citizens must be co-authors of the law because they lack the moral standing to bind each other in ways inconsistent with innate right, and, so, too, they lack the standing to 'throw away' their freedom.

VII. Deciding between the Accounts

A number of things might be said in favour of each of the Kantian model and the co-deliberation model. The fact that the Kantian model is Kantian seems to me to count in its favour, but I will not lean heavily on that; you, gentle reader, might

[26] Rainer Forst, 'Noumenal Power' (2015) 23 Journal of Political Philosophy 111, 117.

stand on your right to justification and tell me I haven't discharged my correlative duty by an appeal to authority. You would be correct of course, but your rejection of my appeal to authority brings the actual advantages of the Kantian approach into focus. As it turns out, all of the questions of political philosophy come out of the fact that no person is in charge of another.

1. Why Justify at All?

The central strength of the narrow Kantian account is that it captures something fundamental about the nature and importance of justification and of the distinctive relationship we stand in as juridical equals, where neither is the superior nor the subordinate of the other. That is, the narrow Kantian view understands us as free in a fundamental normative and transcendental (but not transcendent or metaphysical) sense: our respective freedom consists in the fact that neither of us is master of or subject to the other. That idea is sufficient to discharge any burdens of further justification. It isn't that in some process of co-deliberation, antecedent to any talk of the right each of us has to our own person or our own good name, we would agree that this was more important than other things. Any such imagined exercise in justification would seem to presuppose an account of why we have the standing to demand this of each other, and so to need to reintroduce our non-derivative status, each entitled to be independent of the other, neither superior nor subordinate. The idea of standing, however, is not merely a spatial metaphor. Like spatial concepts more generally, it is irreducibly relational.[27] The fact that the interests of some, or all, or the equal interests of all would be served or equally served by granting standing to individual human beings to demand justifications of each other does not, without some relational characterization of that standing, generate any explanation of why the demand for justification must be given weight. Although one could try to trace this to some still deeper, or (as Rawls sometimes puts it) 'higher order' interests in doing justice and setting and pursuing a conception of the good,[28] these ideas are either unmotivated and in

[27] As Kant already established in the Transcendental Aesthetic, the first part of the *Critique of Pure Reason*, relational ideas cannot be reduced to, or derived from, monadic ones. Kant makes this point in noting that the concept of spatial location could not be abstracted by comparing particular instances of it, because parts of space are not each spatial to some degree in the way in which, for example, different shades of the colour blue might differ in their saturation or hue. Instead, spatial location is already relational rather than comparative. See Kant, *Critique of Pure Reason* (n 14) 157 (A23, B38). See also Daniel Warren, 'Kant and the Apriority of Space' (1998) 107 The Philosophical Review 179.

[28] 'The parties in the original position have no direct interests except an interest in the person each of them represents and they assess principles of justice in terms of primary goods. In addition, they are concerned with securing for the person they represent the higher-order interests we have in developing and exercising our . . . moral powers and in securing the conditions under which we

need of some account of why bearers of these interests are entitled to demand the assistance or even non-obstruction by others, that is, to demand justification with respect to them. Alternatively, these higher-order interests might be taken to simply be implications of the innate right of humanity.[29] Empirically, we may be interested in justifying ourselves to others—in an early article, the late G.A. Cohen suggested that as a matter of human psychology, the basis of all ideology is to be found in human sociability, in particular, the eagerness of human beings to appear justified, if not always to others, then at least to their peers, and if not always even to their peers at least in their own eyes.[30] But this psychological conception of justification has no bearing on any kind of right. Your entitlement to demand of me that I justify what I am doing is not part of a joint exercise of mutual reassurance; it arises instead against the background of a form of interaction in which justificatory resources are available, antecedent to any particular ends or interests either of us might have. The most basic of these justificatory resources is the thought that I am not in charge of you. Put slightly differently, the right to justification is not an interest in participating in a process, or even in living with others on terms all can accept. It is a right, a constraint on the conduct of others, that they must treat you on terms consistent with the fact that no other person is your master. Put in yet another way, living with others on terms all can accept matters because each of us is *sui iuris*.

2. Sequenced Justification

A second difference between the two models comes out in the contrast between the structure of justification for individuals and the structure for a public authority.

Kant's description of the way in which innate right figures, 'when a dispute arises about an acquired right and the question comes up on whom does the burden of proof fall', might be taken to have its natural home in disputes between private persons. Innate right does, indeed, structure the resolution of private disputes and, further, provides the form (although not always the matter) of private litigation. The person who disputes another's title to property, demands

can further our determinate conceptions of the good, whatever it is.' John Rawls, *Political Liberalism* (Columbia University Press 1996) 105f.

[29] Corresponding, as they do, to the first and third of the Ulpian precepts that Kant identifies before articulating innate right, *honeste vive* and *sum cuique tribue*. *Honeste vive* is explicitly tied to the right of humanity in our own person, and *sum cuique tribue* is said to be subsumed under it (6:236).

[30] GA Cohen, 'The Workers and the Word: Why Marx Had the Right to Think He Was Right' (1968) 3–4 Praxis (Zagreb) 376.

performance of a contract, or seeks a remedy for injury to body or property faces the burden of coming forward with the evidence and establishing the wrong. The person who alleges that another has done wrong, more generally, can be called upon to prove it in court or be liable for defamation. In all of these private, 'horizontal' transactions, Kantian right does not engage in an open-ended give-and-take form of justification. Instead, it is always structured by the right to be beyond reproach, and each person's claim to be secure in what they have as against all other private persons. Significantly, when no right is at issue, one person does not need to justify the failure to look to the effects of his or her action on others.

The horizontal exercise of the Kantian right to justification turns on rejecting a fundamental feature of the co-deliberation model. On the latter model, the subject matter of justification is not a particular act that is brought under a rule that is structured by each person's innate right; instead, the subject matter of justification is the general rule itself, which must, as we saw previously, be treated as the product of the process of giving and asking for reasons. On the co-deliberation model, no sharp distinction can be drawn between cases in which no right is at issue, and no conclusions drawn or even presumptions made about each person's entitlement to be beyond reproach. Instead, all of the reasons that might be brought forward are material rather than formal, and their relative significance in favour of a rule must be somehow measured against reasons opposing the adoption of that rule. As a result, the Kantian (and more generally juridical) idea that private persons are entitled to pursue their own purposes, and do not need to use their possessions or abilities in the way that best suits the choices of their neighbours cannot be characterized as a direct implication of each person's innate right of humanity. Instead, on the co-deliberation view, it must be understood as at best a provisional rule, one that might be fine-tuned depending on how much was at stake for each of the parties. A sharp division between misfeasance (interfering with another's right) and nonfeasance (failing to provide others with assistance, either directly or by providing them with a favourable context for their preferred purposes) does not appear as a structuring principle, or indeed anything at all, on the co-deliberation account.

Unsurprisingly, the narrow Kantian conception also generates a further distinction in kind between the right to justification in private contexts and in the context of Public Law, while the co-deliberation model neither draws nor even permits any such distinction. Instead, because the co-deliberation model treats rules as outputs but not inputs, the only way there can be a question about what one private person can be required to do for another private person is by asking about the balance of reasons for this kind of case, precisely the same exercise that governs rules of public law, including constitutional law.

On the distinctively public ('vertical') relation between the state and its citizens, the two models might appear more similar, with the narrow Kantian model assessing rules by asking whether free beings could give such laws to themselves, where lawgiving is thought of both individually and collectively. In discussing such examples as hereditary offices and established religions, Kant asks whether citizens could agree to a law, and also speaks of citizens individually and collectively being unable, as a matter of right, to 'throw away' their freedom. The organizing thought is in some ways similar to the co-deliberation model: it looks as though Kant is suggesting that as potential subjects of the law, citizens considered also as authors of that law could not choose to impose it upon themselves.

Even here, however, the differences are significant, because the reasons that are available, and the possibility of assessing their respective significance, are constrained on the narrow Kantian model. Most significantly, the only material considerations relevant to the justification of public law come from the state's mandate of providing a rightful condition for all of its citizens. It cannot act to advance the private purposes of particular citizens, not even the particular purposes that are shared by all private persons; it can only act to provide a rightful condition. Further, the restrictions on the means that it can use are structured by every citizen's status as a co-legislator of the laws and every individual human being's innate right of humanity in his or her own person.

The restricted resources available for justification generate a sequenced model of justification, different from the univocal or flat model characteristic of the co-deliberation account. As George Fletcher pointed out some decades ago,[31] a flat system of justification brings all of the relevant factors into consideration at once, generating a decision (or in this case a rule) based on the full assessment of all of the merits. A structured, or sequenced, system of justification, by contrast, regards certain factors as relevant at one stage in the justification, and others as potentially relevant at another, later stage. The difference is important, because on a sequenced understanding, the sense in which fundamental rights, especially constitutional rights such as freedom of expression, are subject to limitation comes into focus. So, too, is the difference between rights that implicate in a right and rights that are fundamentally rights of full citizenship.

The significance of a structured approach can be brought out through several examples: the right to be beyond reproach structures the tort of defamation, for which there is an exemption for defamatory statements made in the context of a public proceeding such as an accusation in court by a plaintiff or prosecutor, or in parliament. Even outside of these explicitly juridical contexts, many jurisdictions include a privilege for responsible journalism. In these cases, a private person can be defamed without having the legal power to demand retraction. As a matter of how things stand between the person who falsely accuses another of a wrong and

[31] George P Fletcher, 'The Right and the Reasonable' (1985) 98 Harvard Law Review 949.

the person who has been defamed, there is no (private) justification; the defamer acted inconsistently with the innate right of the person defamed. A sequenced approach to justification can explain how this can, in restricted contexts, be wrongful but not actionable. Although there is a rights violation at the first (private, horizontal) stage, justification for failing to give effect to the private right in question arises at a second (public, vertical) stage. The broad structure of justification for limiting the operation of a private right comes from the fact that a robust but responsible press is a precondition of the operation of political institutions in which the citizens can rule themselves through the law and their representatives. This is not a matter of some all things considered judgment about how things will go from the perspective of the non-relational interests of individual human beings, whether biological or (in Rawls's idiom) 'representative'; instead, it turns on the relation of the acceptable limitations on horizontal rights that are imposed by the possibility of lawmaking institutions that are themselves consistent with innate right.

I am not suggesting that it is a simple matter to determine the appropriate limitations on freedom of expression and the right to be beyond reproach within an integrated normative scheme. The point of the example instead is to draw attention to the structure of the task of justification. At no point in the analysis is some balance to be struck between how well democracy will function on the one hand and how bad (painful, harmful, burdensome, costly) it is to have other people believe false things about you on the other. The analysis is sequenced because *any* protection of speech that is false and defamatory is an infringement of each person's right to be beyond reproach. The question then becomes whether such an infringement can be justified, and the only possible justification must be framed in terms of a compelling public purpose, that cannot be achieved in any other way, and minimal and proportionate restriction of the right.

The co-deliberation model also has resources to ask whether it works to the advantage of all to give certain advantages to certain officials. That is, both approaches recognize the distinctive character of public authority, and both also begin with standpoint from which general rules must be justified that is not itself already constituted by those very same general rules. But here the differences begin to emerge. For what I have been calling the narrow Kantian view, the equivalent of what Forst calls the 'veto right',[32] is not the interest in the morally justifiable claims to freedom of movement, security, participation, or access to social institutions, but rather just the manifestation of each person's innate right of humanity in relation to public institutions. Those institutions need to protect rights in a way that is consistent with everyone's innate right to freedom. That

[32] Rainer Forst, 'The Justification of Justice: Rawls's Political Liberalism and Habermas's Discourse Theory in Dialogue' in Rainer Forst, *The Right to Justification: Elements of a Constructivist Theory of Justice* (Jeffrey Flynn tr, Columbia University Press 2011) 112.

in turn generates a new set of claims, which hold as against those institutions, rather than against individual human beings. The right to participate in political life is such a right, as is the political right to freedom of expression. But so, too, does it include the right to such things as the preconditions of economic independence, a right that does not hold against other private persons.

Rather than showing that the adoption of this rule works, on balance, to everyone's advantage—something that could only be shown to hold generally, based on some assessment of the frequency with which various kinds of situations came up—how likely you are to misidentify a wrongdoer, how likely you are to be misidentified, how likely you are to be the victim of a crime, how likely you are to be wrongfully convicted, and so on, things that, not only would we not be in a very good position to know in advance, but, more significantly, that might turn out to justify some quite extreme measures.

These abstract philosophical contrasts have significant implications for the practice of justification in constitutional democracies. In a passage in *A Theory of Justice* that might be regarded either as telling,[33] or merely unfortunate, (depending on how representative is taken to be) Rawls considers the possibility of a regime of strict criminal liability for possession of a firearm in one's dwelling in a time of civil unrest. Such a regime would hold someone accountable even if the tenant or homeowner was unaware of its presence. Rawls remarks that such a statute 'trespasses upon the precept ought implies can', but that 'it might be accepted by the Representative Citizen as a lesser loss of liberty, at least if the penalties imposed are not too severe. . . . citizens may affirm the law is the lesser of two evils, resigning themselves to the fact that while they may be held guilty for things they have not done, the risks to their liberty on any other course would be worse.'[34] This Rawlsian proposal regards each citizen as interested in maximizing his or her own liberty and, although Rawls seeks to seal off liberty from other considerations, writing 'the conclusion once again is that arguments for restricting liberty proceed from the principle of liberty itself. To some degree anyway, the priority of liberty carries over to partial compliance theory. Thus in the situation discussed the greater good of some has not been balanced against the lesser good of others. Nor has a lesser liberty been accepted for the sake of greater economic and social benefits.'[35]

From the perspective of the co-deliberation account, any such trade-offs would have to be regarded as unremarkable. From the perspective of the Kantian

[33] Pogge argues that Rawls's theory is entirely patient-centred, and advocates focusing on the greater seriousness of harm done by the state. But this difference seems only to be one of degree; an agent-centred theory would face the same problem if the stakes were higher: Thomas W Pogge, 'The Incoherence between Rawls's Theories of Justice' (2004) 72 Fordham Law Review 1739, 1742.

[34] Rawls, *A Theory of Justice* (n 20) 242.

[35] ibid 243f.

account, by contrast, they are ruled out *ab initio*, because inconsistent with each person's innate right of humanity, because they violate the presumption of innocence. For Rawls, the presumption of innocence is just an expression of the priority of liberty, that is, of H.L.A. Hart's idea that ordinarily people should be given the opportunity to organize their behaviour so as to avoid legal sanction.[36] For Kant, by contrast, the right to be beyond reproach is *not* a general rule assigned in order to see to it that individual human beings have as broad a range of options as possible, including the option of breaking the law and accepting the penalty. Your right to be beyond reproach is not in the service of anything non-relational, and certainly not in the service of broadening your range of options (including the option of lawbreaking). Instead, each person's right to be beyond reproach is the precondition of the existence of any rightful options for anyone.

I described this Rawlsian example as unfortunate, and it might be thought to not fully reflect the aspirations of the Rawlsian account. Rawls's later focus on 'higher order' interests in exercising 'the two moral powers', that is, the capacity to give justice and the capacity to set, pursue, and revise a conception of the good, makes his position look more like the narrow Kantian position. Nonetheless, the example illustrates the fundamental difference in thinking about rules such as the presumption of innocence as an element of an already rule-governed idea of innate right, and thinking of it instead as the product of a process of justification the currency of which concerns benefits and burdens, even if an idea of autonomy figures prominently (or even exclusively) among the benefits, and even if an idea of co-deliberation is included. If the right to justification operates on interests that can be characterized *apart* from the juridical relations in which human beings stand, then the type of balancing exercise that Rawls contemplates in the quoted passage is not merely unavoidable, but is itself the very essence of the exercise of public reason and the right to justification. Moreover, narrowing its scope, so as, for example, to prohibit all forms of aggregation (as Scanlon seeks to do in developing his contractualist method) addresses an instance of the difficulty without engaging with the underlying problem. The problem is not that one person's right to be beyond reproach is sacrificed for the sake of another person's security; the exact same problem can be generated if, as Rawls himself suggests, we think of 'representative citizens', and even, in the limiting case, if we imagine running the argument from the original position with only one person, assessing how things would go from the standpoint only that individual's higher order moral interests.[37] The root of the difficulty, then, is not the particular balance struck, but rather the thought that the right to be beyond reproach is in the service of making lives go better from any perspective whatsoever, including the

[36] ibid.

[37] ibid 139.

perspective of higher order moral interests. The right to be beyond reproach is relational, and is not in the service of anything monadic.

Just as prohibiting aggregation does not address the underlying difficulty, so, too, focusing on the role of citizens as both authors and subjects of the law cannot solve it except by presupposing the Kantian idea of innate right, or some formal analog of it. Innate right functions as a basis for other rights, but, at the same time, it also generates a disability on lawgiving power: free beings cannot 'throw away their freedom', by giving themselves laws that are inconsistent with innate right. The claim that a people could not assent to something cannot be understood empirically; at most that could establish that it is very unlikely that anyone would so assent. Instead, the claim must be understood normatively: the citizens considered as a collective body lack the power to make such a decision for itself, just as an individual human being lacks the moral power to throw away his or her freedom. The claim that an individual human being cannot throw away his or her freedom is not, plainly, an empirical claim. Human beings throughout history have done so. Instead, the claim is about the basis of moral powers; you cannot act in a way that is inconsistent with your rightful honour. The same point applies to the citizens considered as a collective body, acting through their representatives. Those representatives are not delegates, but they nonetheless must act on behalf of the citizens. Nobody acting on your behalf can act in a way that is inconsistent with your rightful honour. Once more, the claim is not that it is factually impossible to, but rather that anyone who does so exceeds the moral basis of his lawmaking power.

By contrast, if co-legislation is understood in terms of lawgivers needing to be able to live with the rules that they have made for themselves—the strains of commitment idea that figures prominently in Rawls—then the only constraint imposed by the idea of co-legislation is material; it is simply the structure through which particular material concerns are taken up, and so it cannot avoid questions of the form 'how much?' 'how many?' or 'how often?' That is, the strongest modality available to the idea of the strains of commitment is what people *would* do is the specified choice situation; the Kantian approach goes with the stronger and more significant question of what people (rightfully) *could* do.

The idea of the strains of commitment is not an idea of aggregation of interests across persons, but rather one of a (certain type of) reciprocity and generality of rules governing their interactions, an idea that nobody should be compelled to do anything, or be understood to have undertaken a commitment to do anything, that, in practice, would be so demanding that they would be unable to follow through. Material factors—how difficult it would be—are reprocessed through these ideas of reciprocity and generality, rather than simply being added up. For all that, however, they remain material, and the question of whether something would be too much to ask of a person, even when rendered reciprocal so that too much is not asked of others either, ultimately remains material.

Forst does not discuss strict criminal liability or the presumption of innocence; his concern instead is with what he characterizes as 'basic rights'. Nonetheless, the Rawlsian example brings out the difference between two fundamentally distinct ways of thinking about the right to justification, whether in terms of higher order interests or whether instead in terms of innate right understood relationally.

3. Borders and Cosmopolitan Right

These contrasts are especially important to an issue of pressing global concern: the questions clustered around what Kant called *cosmopolitan* right, the right that individual human beings have against political societies of which they are not members. Kant famously (or notoriously, depending on how you look at it) limited cosmopolitan right to the 'right to visit' rather than the right to settle. In Kant's day, its urgency followed the claims of European colonial powers to settle and then rule distant lands in Africa, Asia, the Americas, and Australia. Today the same questions arise in relation to the claim of (typically, but not always) wealthy states to control their borders and exclude (classes of) migrants.

If the right to justification is a matter of co-deliberation, such questions can only be engaged by asking about the weight or importance of the relative claims of insiders and outsiders: can the exclusion, or the rule conferring the power to exclude, be justified to (some of) those who are excluded? More generally, what reasons can be given by those unwilling to share their more fortunate circumstances? Conversely, can a demand for entry be justified to those who are already members of the affluent state? More generally, can people demand that others share their resources and advantages? If, as the co-deliberation model proposes, these are matters of asking for reasons framed in terms of the material interests on both sides, the relevant question is whether people could agree to a world in which governments could deny them access to their territory and resources, a question that would finally have to be answered in terms of the strains of commitment, that is, just how unbearable it would be for those most disadvantaged by the relevant rules. By contrast, if the right to justification is identified with the innate right of humanity, those on both sides of the border have a much narrower range of reasons to assert against each other: Material comfort is not available as a reason to exclude, but comparative material disadvantage is not, without more, available as a reason to demand entry. Instead, cosmopolitan right limits the right to exclude where exclusion violates the excluded person's innate right to humanity. As Peter Niesen has demonstrated in an insightful recent essay,[38] the idea of innate right, and its development in cosmopolitan right, does not tell us *what* to think about the enforcement of borders or the claims of refugees and other migrants; it only tells us *how* to think about the challenges that they raise.

VIII. Conclusion

I noted in the earlier part of this chapter that Forst's formulations can be understood as consistent with both ways of thinking about the right to justification. My aim has not been to criticize him for adopting the wrong approach, but rather to urge him to explicitly adopt the right one.

References

Cohen GA, 'The Workers and the Word: Why Marx Had the Right to Think He Was Right' (1968) 3–4 Praxis (Zagreb) 376.

Dworkin R, 'Remembrance: John Rawls' (2003) XI The Harvard Review of Philosophy 7.

Fletcher GP, 'The Right and the Reasonable' (1985) 98 Harvard Law Review 949.

Forst R, 'The Justification of Human Rights and the Basic Right to Justification: A Reflexive Approach' (2010) 120 Ethics 711.

Forst R, 'Introduction: The Foundation of Justice' in Rainer Forst, *The Right to Justification: Elements of a Constructivist Theory of Justice* (Jeffrey Flynn tr, Columbia University Press 2011).

Forst R, 'The Justification of Justice: Rawls's Political Liberalism and Habermas's Discourse Theory in Dialogue' in Rainer Forst, *The Right to Justification: Elements of a Constructivist Theory of Justice* (Jeffrey Flynn tr, Columbia University Press 2011).

Forst R, 'The Normative Order of Justice and Peace' in Rainer Forst, *Justification and Critique: Towards a Critical Theory of Politics* (Ciaran Cronin tr, Polity Press 2013).

Forst R, 'Two Pictures of Justice' in Rainer Forst, *Justification and Critique: Towards a Critical Theory of Politics* (Ciaran Cronin tr, Polity Press 2013).

Forst R, 'Justifying Justification: A Reply to My Critics' in Rainer Forst, *Justice, Democracy and the Right to Justification: Rainer Forst in Dialogue* (Bloomsbury Academic 2014).

Forst R, 'Noumenal Power' (2015) 23 Journal of Political Philosophy 111.

Forst R, 'The Justification of Basic Rights: A Discourse-Theoretical Approach' (2016) 45(3) Netherlands Journal of Legal Philosophy 7.

Habermas J, 'The Unity of Reason in the Diversity of Its Voices' in Jürgen Habermas, *Postmetaphysical Thinking: Philosophical Essays* (William Mark Hohengarten tr, MIT Press 1992).

[38] Peter Niesen, 'What Kant Would Have Said in the Refugee Crisis' (2017) 50 Danish Yearbook of Philosophy 83.

Habermas J, 'Reconciliation Through the Public Use of Reason: Remarks on John Rawls's *Political Liberalism*' (1995) 92 The Journal of Philosophy 109.
Kant I, 'The Metaphysics of Morals' in Immanuel Kant, *Practical Philosophy* (Mary J Gregor ed and tr, Cambridge University Press 1996).
Kant I, *Critique of Pure Reason* (Paul Guyer and Allen W Wood eds and trs, Cambridge University Press 1998).
Niesen P, 'What Kant Would Have Said in the Refugee Crisis' (2017) 50 Danish Yearbook of Philosophy 83.
O'Neill O, 'Vindication of Reason' in Paul Guyer (ed), *The Cambridge Companion to Kant* (Cambridge University Press 2009).
Pogge TW, 'The Incoherence between Rawls's Theories of Justice' (2004) 72 Fordham Law Review 1739.
Rawls J, *A Theory of Justice* (Harvard University Press 1971).
Rawls J, 'Kantian Constructivism in Moral Theory' (1980) 77 The Journal of Philosophy 515.
Rawls J, *Political Liberalism* (Columbia University Press 1996).
Scanlon TM, 'The Significance of Choice' in Sterling M McMurrin (ed), *The Tanner Lectures on Human Values* (University of Utah Press 1988).
Scanlon TM, *What We Owe to Each Other* (The Belknap Press of Harvard University Press 1998).
Scanlon TM, 'The Appeal and Limits of Constructivism' in James Lenman and Yonatan Shemmer (eds), *Constructivism in Practical Philosophy* (Oxford University Press 2012).
Voorhoeve A, 'Kant on the Cheap: Thomas Scanlon Interviewed' (2001) The Philosophers' Magazine 29.
Warren D, 'Kant and the Apriority of Space' (1998) 107 The Philosophical Review 179.
Weinrib J, *Dimensions of Dignity: The Theory and Practice of Modern Constitutional Law* (Cambridge University Press 2016).
Zylberman A, 'Why Human Rights? Because of *You*' (2016) 24 Journal of Political Philosophy 321.

2

Engaging with Forst's *Right to Justification*

Kantian Analogies and the Problem of Subjectivity

Claudio Corradetti

I. Introduction

Rainer Forst's theory of a right to justification is a powerful attempt to renovate the liberal tradition from an analytical critical theory perspective. Forst develops his views on right and justice along a number of different articles collected essentially around two books: *The Right to Justification* and *Justification and Critique*.[1] Forst's project wants also to provide further insight into advancing the Rawls-Habermas debate on public deliberation and justice. Distinctively, Forst believes that to be a legitimate subject to 'a normative order: [is] to have standing as equal normative authorities within such an order'.[2] This element is what he calls 'the first demand of justice'.[3] This view presupposes a number of deep commitments. To begin with, for Forst, practical reason is reason for justification.[4] Together, practical reason and justification define fundamental justice as 'a basic structure of justification'.[5] Here moral and political autonomy converge into a 'basic right to justification', a springboard for the further definition of a system of human rights.[6]

The moral right to justification is thus the core aspect of Forst's theory of justice. It aims to ground the reflexive procedure of practical reason for the justification of norms among free and equal persons. This aims to present itself also as a constructivist process whereby all human rights are discursively justified—not 'derived'—[7] from the adoption of a fundamental right to justification. From such

[1] Rainer Forst, *The Right to Justification: Elements of a Constructivist Theory of Justice* (Jeffrey Flynn tr, Columbia University Press 2011) and Rainer Forst, *Justification and Critique: Towards a Critical Theory of Politics* (Ciaran Cronin tr, Polity Press 2013).
[2] Rainer Forst, 'Noumenal Power' (2015) 23 Journal of Political Philosophy 111, 118.
[3] ibid.
[4] Rainer Forst, 'Practical Reason and Justifying Reasons: On the Foundation of Morality' in Rainer Forst, *The Right to Justification: Elements of a Constructivist Theory of Justice* (Jeffrey Flynn tr, Columbia University Press 2011) 13–42.
[5] Forst, 'Noumenal Power' (n 2) 127 and Rainer Forst, 'The Justification of Human Rights and the Basic Right to Justification: A Reflexive Approach' (2010) 120 Ethics 711, 736.
[6] Forst, 'The Justification of Human Rights and the Basic Right to Justification' (n 5) 712.
[7] ibid 735.

Claudio Corradetti, *Engaging with Forst's* Right to Justification: *Kantian Analogies and the Problem of Subjectivity*
In: *Constitutionalism Justified: Rainer Forst in Discourse*. Edited by: Ester Herlin-Karnell and Matthias Klatt,
Oxford University Press (2020), © Ester Herlin-Karnell and Matthias Klatt.
DOI: 10.1093/oso/9780190889050.003.0002

principle there departs two strands of constructivism, one moral and the other political. Together, they define what appears to be 'the twofold nature of human rights as general moral rights and as concrete legal rights'.[8] Such double-sided constructivist process aims to vindicate the respect for the autonomy of human beings as both moral and political agents. Duplicity affects human rights also in another sense. Within Forst's theory of justice, human rights ground not only justificatory claims of justice but they empower also people to restore defective social structures, by justifying claims to basic income, goods, freedom and so forth.[9]

Forst distinguishes, between a *transcendental-foundational* function of human rights (as the role that the basic right to justification plays in establishing a normative precondition for community affiliations), and a *critical-emancipatory* function of human rights (as that which allows individuals to enact social transformations).[10] It is due to this kind of duplicity that Forst then claims that 'the principle of justification must be situated within moral and political contexts such that these contexts are partially (not completely) congruent'.[11]

All in all, Forst's right to justification mobilizes several layers of enquiry: a *historical dimension*, where emancipatory claims of justification activate dynamics of social struggle; a *reconstructive-pragmatic* dimension, which clarifies the conditions for the justification of validity claims; and, finally, a *reflexively-moral transcendental* dimension answering, respectively, the question of what it means to be a subject of justification and to treat others as ends in themselves.[12]

In the following sections, I engage with Forst's treatment of justification and how this relates to a fundamental 'duty' to justification. I raise doubts on the equation that he establishes between the unconditionality of a Kantian moral imperative and the pretense of unconditionality of the duty to justification.[13] As a result, I contest that the right to justification stands as a *fundamentum inconcussum*[14] of a justificatory theory of justice and suggest, alternatively, that the Kantian account takes the justification of morality and law as elements of a

[8] ibid.

[9] ibid 733.

[10] Rainer Forst, 'The Basic Right to Justification: Toward a Constructivist Conception of Human Rights' in Rainer Forst, *The Right to Justification: Elements of a Constructivist Theory of Justice* (Jeffrey Flynn tr, Columbia University Press 2011) 205.

[11] Rainer Forst, 'The Justification of Justice: Rawls's Political Liberalism and Habermas's Discourse Theory in Dialogue' in Rainer Forst, *The Right to Justification: Elements of a Constructivist Theory of Justice* (Jeffrey Flynn tr, Columbia University Press 2011) 111.

[12] Rainer Forst, 'The Right to Justification: Moral and Political, Transcendental and Historical. Reply to Seyla Benhabib, Jeffrey Flynn and Matthias Fritsch' (2015) 43 Political Theory 822, 835.

[13] Forst, 'Practical Reason and Justifying Reasons' (n 4) 35ff.

[14] Rainer Forst, 'Introduction: The Foundation of Justice' in Rainer Forst, *The Right to Justification: Elements of a Constructivist Theory of Justice* (Jeffrey Flynn tr, Columbia University Press 2011) 5.

cooperative scheme of justice. A corollary to this point is the problem of pluralism and the dialogical nature of reason as a capacity to take the standpoint perspective of the other. I will argue that at times, Forst's moral grounding of justice might raise concerns with a truly post-metaphysical doctrine of justice. Attached to this point and to the charge of selectivity is the problem of legal subjectivization that arises for those 'affected subjects' in a Forstian sense, that might nevertheless never enter into a process of justification of justice.

Therefore, secondly, and connected to the first point, I hold that Forst's justificatory theory of justice needs a more robust theory of subjectivity, one that is capable of accounting why and how individuals become moral subjects in a full concrete way, that is, as subjects of *these societies*. Indeed, it is the case that either the demands of justification could be brought in by individuals who are excluded and prevented from becoming subjects of a polity and therefore could seek inclusion into a system of justification (demands of recognition); or, that demands of justification could be deliberately disattended by those same members of a system of justice that distribute unevenly the power of justification from which social struggles arise (struggles of recognition). I refer here to individuals of societies as we know them, that is, as egoist and greedy beings who are selfishly oriented. This point contributes to closing the gap between the normativity of the moral standpoint and the transformation of preferences by self-interested people. The shift is required for individuals also in order to acquire the moral standpoint. It is the case, indeed, that the endorsement of a standard of justification is possible only if individuals acquire a moral property as subjects of a cooperative system of mutual justification—which Forst links to 'political autonomy' as being 'authors of the law'.[15]

Can one hold that this notion of autonomy is satisfactory? Habermas certainly thought it was not, and this is why he thought that 'autonomy must be conceived more abstractly' and accordingly, as identifiable with 'a discourse principle that is initially indifferent vis-à-vis morality and law'.[16]

As it appears, the lack of this fundamental distinction affects deeply Forst's purchase of his right to justification. Indeed those cases where misrecognitions affect equal distributory patterns of justification, I fear that the principle of justification remains impotent to ground 'a norm to be equally justifiable to *all* affected'[17] absent a process of inclusion of the subjects as right-members of a system of justice.

[15] Forst, 'The Justification of Justice' (n 11) 102.

[16] Jürgen Habermas, *Between Facts and Norms: Contributions to a Discourse Theory of Law and Democracy* (William Rehg tr, MIT Press 1996) 121.

[17] Rainer Forst, 'Ethics and Morality' in Rainer Forst, *The Right to Justification: Elements of a Constructivist Theory of Justice* (Jeffrey Flynn tr, Columbia University Press 2011) 65.

Struggles of subjectivity are struggles of misrecognition, but these require recognition as subjects of law. These dynamics hint to a social scenario where actors strive for a re-equalization of power-imbalances and injustices within law. Since the political terrain appears to be crossed by a radically irreconcilable dichotomy between the social processes of subject formation and the formulation of justificatory claims of justice, Forst's preordained conception of individuality faces the risk of becoming a non-starter for a socially embedded justification of justice that is incapable of including the rightless other as a subject of law.

II. Is the Principle of Justification Compatible with a Kantian Ethics of Duty?

In several parts of his works Forst refers to justification alternatively as 'a principle', or as 'a duty', or, finally, as 'a right'.[18] With Forst's words: 'According to the principle of reciprocal and general justification, moral persons have a fundamental *right* to justification and a corresponding unconditional *duty* to justify morally relevant actions'.[19]

Forst makes explicit the relation between the principle of justification and its articulation in a right-duty language when he says: 'The principle of justification would be left hanging in the air, so to speak, if the recursive insight into this principle were not part of the second-order practical insight into the duty to justify and the right to justification'.[20] To begin with, Forst's right-duty structuring of the principle of justification aims at clarifying in what consists a secondary level of investigation for the justification of moral reasoning in so far as a moral dimension of autonomy is concerned. The relation between the principle of justification and its corresponding duty discloses an unconditional dimension, namely, 'the unconditional duty of justification'.[21] This duty claims that moral contexts require that reasons of justification are *owed* to others.[22] For Forst, such unconditionality of the duty to justification corresponds to Kant's idea of the unconditionality of

[18] Variations include Forst's mentioning at times of either the 'principle of justification' or the 'principle of reciprocal and universal justification': Forst, 'Practical Reason and Justifying Reasons' (n 4), respectively, 18 and 20.

[19] ibid 21.

[20] In a footnote, ibid n 108, Forst specifies that 'The concept of second-order practical insight fills the theoretical gap (located at the third level), which arises through Habermas's separation of "a 'must' of a weak transcendental necessity" of "unavoidable" presuppositions of argumentation and the "prescriptive 'must' of a rule of action", that is between the principle of argumentation (U) and that of discourse (D).'

[21] See ibid 35: '*Second-order practical insight*, a fundamental insight not only into the . . . principle of justification but into the *unconditional* duty of justification to which it corresponds.'

[22] As Forst puts this: 'in moral contexts one *owes* others (reciprocally and generally) justifying reasons'. Ibid 35.

the moral law as a 'fact of reason'.[23] Furthermore, when considering the right to justification, Forst claims that it is from the consideration of the autonomy of the moral person 'as an "end in itself" ',[24] that one can derive such right and endorse the 'moral point of view' according to the respect of standards of reciprocity and generality.

I find that the analogy Forst draws between a duty of justification and the way in which Kant conceives the unconditionality of moral command is not so persuasive. One reason being that the universal duty of compliance with the categorical imperative (in any of its formulations),[25] is not accompanied in Kant by a universal subjective right. On the contrary, Forst makes to correspond his right to justification by someone else's duty to justify. Moreover, Kant's categorical imperative is a duty-based principle of ethics. There, the content of the moral law is independent from the objects of volition.[26] On its side, instead, Forst's right to justification pretends to be a constructivist principle of justice conceived along the lines of a right-duty correspondence. In the latter case, the subjective right-claim to have a justified political order is grounded in a universal duty, on third parties, to comply with such right. Each view defines, each in its own domain, an autonomous route to ethics and to normative justice. For Forst we are subjects of justice primarily in so far as we participate to a process of justification both as right-holders as well as duty-bearers. For Kant, instead, we are moral entities primarily because we are bound to a moral imperative and this is what imposes itself as a 'fact of reason'.[27] Accordingly, it seems that the Kantian unconditionality of the moral imperative cannot be equated to the transcendental level of unconditionality that Forst assigns to justification as a right.

Indeed, the unconditionality of Kant's ethical duty is such precisely because nobody else can advance a right-claim *against* the moral duty. For Kant, the will is heteronomous every time that it 'does not give itself the law; [and] instead the

[23] ibid.

[24] ibid 37.

[25] See Immanuel Kant, 'Groundwork of the Metaphysics of Morals' in Immanuel Kant, *Practical Philosophy* (Mary J Gregor ed and tr, Cambridge University Press 1996).

[26] As Wood puts this point: 'The moral law, that is, must get its content independently of all "properties of its objects of volition." Here the phrase "properties of the objects of volition" might bear two distinct meanings: It might mean "the properties of all ends to be produced that are set by volition" but also "the properties of those things in the world toward which volition might be directed, including the properties of the things the will might use as means to its ends". If the moral law's commands depended on the properties of objects in the first sense, then their rational bindingness would be conditional on those objects' having those (desirable) properties. If they depended on the properties of objects in the second sense, then they would be conditional on facts about the way those objects might serve as means. In either case, the moral law would be a hypothetical rather than a categorical imperative'. Allen W Wood, *Kantian Ethics* (Cambridge University Press 2007) 114.

[27] Immanuel Kant, 'Critique of Practical Reason' in Immanuel Kant, *Practical Philosophy* (Mary J Gregor ed and tr, Cambridge University Press 1996) 164, also Immanuel Kant, 'The Metaphysics of Morals' in Immanuel Kant, *Practical Philosophy* (Mary J Gregor ed and tr, Cambridge University Press 1996) 407.

object, by means of its relation to the will, gives the law to it'.[28] If one were to follow Forst's reasoning and consider that moral duty is grounded into someone else's right, as a protected interest, then one would cease to be autonomous and become *heteronomous*. The unconditionality of the moral duty would become thus *conditioned* by the fulfilment of someone's else claim. This certainly does not mean that acting in compliance to duty excludes categorically the co-occurrence of a duty-compatible interest (as for instance a protected right). But even though Kant discusses only those cases where inclinations are contrary to a moral duty, ie lying, the bulk of his argument is that one should never conflate *material* motivations with the *formal requirement* of the moral command. This means that respect of someone else's right is *compatible* with respect of the moral law as long as this does not represent its motivational grounding.

This distinction is relevant in Kantian terms since it explains the reason a distinction is drawn between a system of morality and a system of rights, each endowed, in its own terms, with relatively autonomous principles. Whereas the system of moral legislation constrains the dimension of internal freedom, a system of coercive rights constraints the system of external freedoms. Accordingly, I find hard to accept Forst's reference to the Kantian categorical imperative when he says: 'In Kantian terms, this *right to justification*—or the duty of justification that is its reverse side—is a Categorical Imperative.'[29]

Since, as I have noticed, Kant never drew a correlation between the unconditionality of the categorical imperative and the unconditionality of a moral right, similarly I think, Forst should not attempt to make such a move. The moral law indeed imposes itself on the will as a 'fact of reason', assuring its self-legislating character without relying on an external, right-dependent dimension owed to any other. In *Groundwork*, Kant is even more explicit by saying that '[c]onsciousness of this fundamental law [moral law] may be called a fact of reason because one cannot reason it out from antecedent data of reason, for example, from consciousness of freedom (since this is not antecedently given to us)'.[30] From which it can be concluded that for Kant there holds no correlation between the categorical duty of morality and the innate right to freedom.[31] If one were to construct the moral law on a duty-right correlation, then, the unconditionality of the law would immediately cease to self-impose as a 'fact' and appear

[28] Kant, 'Groundwork of the Metaphysics of Morals' (n 25) 89 (4:441).

[29] Rainer Forst, 'The Normative Order of Justice and Peace' in Rainer Forst, *Justification and Critique: Towards a Critical Theory of Politics* (Ciaran Cronin tr, Polity Press 2013) 83.

[30] Kant, 'Groundwork of the Metaphysics of Morals' (n 25) 164 (5:31).

[31] Kant seems rather to express the connection in the following terms: '. . . categorical imperatives are possible by this: that the idea of freedom makes me a member of an intelligible world and consequently, if I were only this, all my actions *would* always be in conformity with the autonomy of the will; but since at the same time I intuit myself as a member of the world of sense, they *ought* to be in conformity with it'. Ibid 100 (4:454).

to consciousness without any mediation of yet another principle as it would be instead with its dependence on a right as a source of its justification.[32]

What we can understand—the consciousness we have of the moral law—is instead one where the unconditionality of the moral law is conceived as coming only from the respect of a duty upon which it is established: 'The objective necessity of an action from obligation'.[33] From this, I believe, it follows also that an interpretation coherent with a Kantian idea of morality and moral autonomy would refuse the idea that the unconditionality of the moral duty is one based on an external 'claim that he [the other] makes on me and to which I must respond'.[34] Since the type of argument that Kant submits for the unconditionality of the moral imperative is so central in characterizing his views on practical rationality, I fear that no compromise would be possible here without losing entirely—not just in the letter but also in the spirit—the overall significance of Kant's moral doctrine.[35]

Forst might reply by rebutting the claim that the right to justification is ultimately connected to the protection of sensible interests, ie objects of private possession, since its conceptual grounding is made to derive from the notion of 'humanity as an end in itself'.[36] But here my answer to Forst is that the notion of humanity as an end in itself for Kant is not itself a right, even if it is right-generating. Indeed to think of humanity as an end allows one to conceive the moral duty in accordance to its form and not to its matter—as would be the case if a member of humanity was used as a means for an end. Were this the case, though, the duty to *respect humanity* as a whole would be infringed since subordinated to the right of an individual. Instead, humanity as an end in itself remains for Kant a formal constraint for thinking the unity and the unconditionality of the moral duty without being also its conceptual grounding. Let me clarify this point further. For Kant, duties are either '*duties of right* (*officia iuris*)' or '*duties*

[32] As Kant says: 'it cannot make comprehensible as regards its absolute necessity an unconditional practical law (such as the categorical imperative must be); for, that it is unwilling to do this through a condition—namely, by means of some interest laid down as a basis—cannot be held against it, since then it would not be the moral law, that is, the supreme law of freedom', and this is also the reason Kant concludes the *Groundwork* with 'we indeed do not comprehend the practical unconditioned necessity of the moral imperative, but we do comprehend its *incomprehensibility*...'. Ibid 108 (4:463).

[33] ibid 16 (4:439).

[34] Rainer Forst, 'Moral Autonomy and the Autonomy of Morality: Toward a Theory of Normativity after Kant' in Rainer Forst, *The Right to Justification: Elements of a Constructivist Theory of Justice* (Jeffrey Flynn tr, Columbia University Press 2011) 59.

[35] As Wood remarks: 'The moral law has no author because it is a natural law, so its content is determined by no will at all. Instead of having an author, it is "practically necessary"—it commands regarding what is "[good or] bad in itself." The content of the moral law is no more dependent on anyone's will (yours, mine, or God's) than the fact that a triangle has three angles. The content of the moral law is laid down by no will but rather "lies in the nature of things . . . in the essence of things." Once again we see clearly that Kant is a *metaethical realist*'. Wood (n 26) 113.

[36] Kant, 'Groundwork of the Metaphysics of Morals' (n 25) 81 (4:430–4:431).

of virtue (*officia virtutis s. ethica*), for which external lawgiving is not possible'.[37] Duties of virtue 'have to do with an end which . . . is also a duty'.[38]

In *The Metaphysical First Principles of the Doctrine of Virtue* of the *Metaphysics of Morals*, Kant specifies that '[a]n *end* is an object of the choice . . . Now, I can indeed be constrained by others to perform *actions* that are directed as means to an end, but I can never be constrained by others *to have an end*', meaning implicitly that my end is not determined by someone else's right to an end, for instance. And, Kant adds, in practical reasoning to have an end that countervails 'the end arising from sensible impulses', this would be an '*an end that is in itself a duty*'.[39] Therefore, within the ethical discourse, humanity as an end in itself is for Kant a mere duty that one gives to oneself, and it cannot be equated to a right that someone else imposes on me. The principle of virtue, differently from the principle of right that is analytic, is rather synthetic: 'the principle of the doctrine of virtue goes beyond the concept of outer freedom and connects with it, in accordance with universal laws, an *end* that it makes a *duty*. This principle is therefore synthetic'.[40] Not so much different is the case of treatment of external freedom in this respect, particularly when Kant connects 'the right of humanity [*Rechte der Menschheit*]' to the duty of *Rightful Honor*, that is, when self-consideration as 'an end' is said to be an 'obligation [*Pflicht*]' derived 'from the right of humanity in our own person (*Lex iusti*)'.[41] What it appears from this passage is that even when the notion of humanity is considered as a 'right', in the context of coerciveness, the duty that is attached to this is a duty to oneself which obligates one to not enter an agreement as a means.

Finally, this same point can be made and reinforced also from another perspective. When Kant discusses the possibility of a conflict of ethical duties, he never mentions that this is a result of a clash of rights. For Kant, duties of ethics differ from duties of right: the first ones are wide duties that might require the help of casuistry for their determination; the others instead are strict and make use of judgment in a more precise way.[42] Moreover, Kant argues that a conflict of ethical duties can never really arise because 'duty and obligation are concepts that express the objective practical *necessity* of certain actions and two rules opposed to each other cannot be necessary at the same time . . . a *collision of duties* and obligations is inconceivable (*obligationes non colliduntur*)'.[43]

[37] Kant, 'The Metaphysics of Morals' (n 27) 394 (6:239).
[38] ibid 395 (6:239).
[39] ibid 513 (6:381).
[40] ibid 526 (6:396).
[41] ibid 392 (6:236).
[42] See citation of Kant: '. . . unlike duties of right, ethical duties cannot be determined with precision, but are wide duties . . . ethics will add a casuistry that sharpens the understanding in its judgment of duties. (*Vorarbeiten*, XXIII 419.5–10)', in Jens Timmermann, 'Kantian Dilemmas? Moral Conflict in Kant's Ethical Theory' (2013) 95 Archiv für Geschichte der Philosophie 36, 54.
[43] Kant, 'The Metaphysics of Morals' (n 27) 378f (6:224).

Since it is not the case, according to Kant, that a moral obligation to action arises out of the pursuance of certain ends—which may vary if attached to a plurality of rights—a conflict of duty cannot be even conceived from the perspective of an a priori view on morality. Instead, for Kant, the obligating force of ethical duties stands on the normative force of the reason that grounds them—the obligating reasons.[44] Whenever two mutually contradicting obligations arise, only one prevails due to the supreme obligating force of the reasons that make one duty superior to the other.[45]

To conclude, for Kant there cannot hold a right-duty relation in the justification of the categorical imperative. Kant's duties of ethics arise out of a categorical imperative which is a principle of practical reason and not a right. Duties arising out of rights are of a different type; they might be either duties connected to natural rights or to positive rights established by a legislator. Since Forst establishes a parallel between his theory of a principle of justification and Kant's moral theory, my argument is that this analogy does not hold. On the contrary, Kant explicitly defines his doctrine of morals as a doctrine of duties and not of rights, as when he says: 'But why is the doctrine of morals usually called (especially by Cicero) a doctrine of *duties* and not also a doctrine of *rights, even though rights have reference to duties?*—The reason is that we know our own freedom (from which all moral laws, and so all rights as well as duties proceed) only through the *moral imperative*, which is a proposition commanding duty, from which the capacity of putting others under obligation, that is, the concept of a right, can afterwards be explicated'.[46]

I think that Kant's theory of ethics is clear enough on this point. Accordingly, I solicit Forst to either switch to a notion of 'duty of justification', if he dares to remain an orthodox Kantian, or to drop Kantianism if he wants to maintain a right-duty correlation as a way of articulating internally a grammar of the principle of justification.

A corollary to this point concerns, according to the Habermasian conception, the 'monological'[47] character of the categorical imperative as a principle for moral deliberation and the necessity of transforming this into a dialogical

44 Timmermann (n 42) 48.

45 As Kant says: 'two *grounds* of obligation (*rationes obligandi*), one or the other of which is not sufficient to put him under obligation (*rationes obligandi non obligantes*), so that one of them is not a duty. When two such grounds conflict with each other, practical philosophy says, not that the stronger obligation takes precedence (*fortiori obligation vincit*) but that the stronger *ground of obligation* prevails (*fortiori obligandi ratio vincit*)'. Kant, 'The Metaphysics of Morals' (n 27) 379 (6:224).

46 ibid 395 (6:239).

47 As J. Habermas explicitly considers: 'discourse ethics rejects the monological approach of Kant, who assumes that the individual tests his maxims of action *foro interno* or, as Husserl put it, in the loneliness of his soul'. Jürgen Habermas, 'Morality and Ethical Life: Does Hegel's Critique of Kant Apply to Discourse Ethics?' in Jürgen Habermas, *Moral Consciousness and Communicative Action* (Christian Lenhardt and Shierry Weber Nicholsen trs, Polity Press 1990) 203.

process for practical reasoning as with the endorsement of the point of view of the other—a problem that is raised by Habermas both at the value level, as with the inherent plurality of the visions of the self and the good, as well as at the level of reasonable (but also unreasonable) comprehensive views.

The outcome of such argument is that the Kantian categorical imperative is an inadequate resource if taken as a procedure for the justification of justice. Indeed, Kantian uniformity in the subjective visions of the good life could not account for what also Rawls considered to be the turning point, conceptually and historically of modernity, namely, the 'fact of reasonable pluralism'.[48] It is for these reasons that the Habermasian construction of a principle of universalization 'U' sets an explicit preclusion to 'a monological application of the principle'.[49]

If one were to construct a justification of justice through the procedure displayed by Kant's categorical imperative, it would be difficult to address the irreducible radical pluralism of moral perspectives that characterizes modern societies. That Forst, despite his general intent, at times tends to think of the political in reductivist moral terms is apparent from remarks like the following, as when he says: '*moral justification* is—*in a normative-formal sense—the core of political justification*'.[50] If respect for standards of generality and reciprocity means that reasons of justification 'have to be shareable by all affected persons, given their (reciprocally) legitimate interests and claims',[51] so 'that no one may make a normative claim (such as a rights claim) he or she denies to others (call that reciprocity of content)' or 'project one's own perspective, values, interests, or needs onto others such that one claims to speak in their "true" interests',[52] then, we would need to separate the morally reasonable comprehensive level from the public deliberative level of the political. It is indeed only when reasonable comprehensive pluralism finds expression in a political model of justification incorporating standards of public reason that a justification of justice could be said to truly satisfy the interests of 'all affected persons'.[53] If Forst's views on standards of generality and reciprocity fly in the face of a plurality of reasonably comprehensive views,[54] then, the principle of justification back-steps from the political justification of justice hiding again in the heights of metaphysics.[55]

48 John Rawls, *Political Liberalism* (2nd edn, Columbia University Press 1996) XVII.

49 Jürgen Habermas, 'Discourse Ethics: Notes on a Program of Philosophical Justification' in Jürgen Habermas, *Moral Consciousness and Communicative Action* (Christian Lenhardt and Shierry Weber Nicholsen trs, Polity Press 1990) 66.

50 Forst, 'The Basic Right to Justification' (n 10) 218.

51 Forst, 'The Justification of Human Rights and the Basic Right to Justification' (n 5) 720.

52 ibid 719.

53 ibid 720.

54 Forst, 'The Basic Right to Justification' (n 10) 219.

55 See John Rawls, 'Justice as Fairness: Political Not Metaphysical' (1985) 14 Philosophy and Public Affairs 223, 223–51.

All in all, therefore, it seems that Forst's suggestion of an analogy between his right to justification and Kant's Categorical Imperative is open to encounter difficulties as with regards to its extension to the political terrain and the pluralism of reasonable doctrines that comes with it in liberal democracies. Forst could draw a more promising analogy, I think, with Kant's Universal Principle of Right, in so far as this plays a significant role in generating standards of rights. For Kant, such principle of right postulates that 'Any act is *right* if it can coexist with everyone's freedom in accordance with a universal law, or if on its maxim the freedom of choice of each can coexist with everyone's freedom in accordance with a universal law'.[56] Kant believes that freedom of choice, as an instance of external freedom, can be legitimately coerced only under the compliance to a universal principle. Whenever my freedom is hindered by someone else's freedom, it follows that there is a presumption of legitimate coercion. This explains why Kant concludes that 'coercion that is opposed to this [hindrance of freedom]', that is, 'a *hindering of a hindrance to freedom* . . . it is right'.[57]

But if Forst were to accept this suggestion, then he would have to abandon the monistic view of his right to justification and supplement the moral principle of justification with a principle of right in whatever form he wants to conceive this. The result is that we would be back hypothetically to a differentiation of the principle of justification into a moral and a juridical sense; or, alternatively to a dualistic grounding of practical reasoning in a sphere of morality and a sphere of law. If Forst's right to justification is to be supplemented by Kant's Universal Principle of Right, then the authority of justifications has to incorporate some notions on the authority of the law and only through this passage, next, a notion of legitimate coercion can become justified (the authority of power). Absent a Universal Principle of Right, Forst deprives himself from the possibility to give coercive power a legitimacy character.

Contrariwise, as it seems, for Kant this strand of argumentative strategy is apparent from the notion that acquisition assume with regard to the notion of an 'omnilateral'[58] will, that is, as the power to coerce individuals to enter into a space of justifications organized according to right. When Kant speaks of the shift from a unilateral to an omnilateral will, as that which his discussion into the categories of roman private law hints of, he establishes the conditions for the emerge of a reason of authority that appeals to an authority of reasons, namely, to reasons that we all would agree on once we strive to exiting a lawless condition as it is that

[56] Kant, 'The Metaphysics of Morals' (n 27) 387.
[57] ibid 388.
[58] As Kant says: 'For the acquisition of a public rightful condition by the union of the will of all for giving universal law would be an acquisition such that none could precede it, yet it would be derived from the particular wills of each and would be *omnilateral*, whereas original acquisition can proceed only from a unilateral will'. Ibid 412 (6:259).

of the state of nature. To conclude this corollary point: I think that it would be beneficial to Forst's overall argument if supplementary clarification was provided with regard to the interlink that can be established between the normative status of a right to justification and its relation to a legal conception of rights. But perhaps, a lack of explanation on this might be a hint to a deeper difficulty.

I believe that Forst is correct in thinking that the fundamental issue concerning justice 'is not *what you have* but *how you are treated*'.[59] As he says, justice issues arise out of a 'moral-political imperative' that countervails relations of domination.[60] Subjugation to a rule lacking justification is indeed arbitrary because it violates the freedom and equality of persons and therefore the possibility of their free assent in *actual* processes of justification.[61] But then one might wonder whether the requirement of justice as 'a fundamental *right to justification* . . .',[62] in so far as it offers 'appropriate reasons for the norms of justice that are supposed to hold generally',[63] is in fact bound to a specific legal discourse from within which—only—one can coerce others to a public justification of their actions.

Indeed, if it is the case, as Forst considers that 'whatever norms and institutions persons are subject to, they always have the fundamental right to ask for reasons for those norms and institutions—and to question these reasons',[64] it is also true that for Forst norms are ultimately proffered by powers that 'serve their function if they are seen as reason-giving'.[65] I think here comes one of the major difficulties of shifting away too easily from a moral normative principle of discourse to a juridical one. The conclusion, I think, is that Forst needs to explain which principle of law, or *Rechtsprinzip* in Kantian terms, he can establish in relation to his starting moral principle of justification and in what terms he conceives of the relation, if any, between the two.[66]

[59] Rainer Forst, 'Two Pictures of Justice' in Rainer Forst, *Justice, Democracy and the Right to Justification: Rainer Forst in Dialogue* (Bloomsbury Academic 2014) 20.

[60] 'I have defined justice as the human virtue and moral-political imperative to oppose relations of arbitrary rule or domination'. Ibid 33.

[61] ibid 34.

[62] ibid.

[63] ibid.

[64] Forst, 'The Normative Order of Justice and Peace' (n 29) 83.

[65] Rainer Forst, 'Justifying Justification: A Reply to My Critics' in Rainer Forst, *Justice, Democracy and the Right to Justification: Rainer Forst in Dialogue* (Bloomsbury Academic 2014) 180f.

[66] To this purpose J. Habermas dedicates entire sections of his *Between Facts and Norms*. For a detailed investigation of this point, see Habermas, *Between Facts and Norms* (n 16) 82ff. Evidence that Forst is aware of this line of development of the theory is a recent symposium on his work together with a reply, Rainer Forst, 'The Justification of Basic Rights: A Discourse-Theoretical Approach' (2016) 45(3) Netherlands Journal of Legal Philosophy 7; and Rainer Forst, 'What Does It Mean to Justify Basic Rights? Reply to Düwell, Newey, Rummens and Valentini' (2016) 45(3) Netherlands Journal of Legal Philosophy 76.

III. What does it mean to Become a Subject in a System of Justification?

On these premises one can move to the consideration of a second point, namely, the problem of subjectivity and the process of becoming an equal subject of law.

Forst argues that the notion of legitimate power implies that forms of coercion are justified only if they are conceived as in accordance with demands of reason that imply in turn, a procedure of mutual justification.[67] The authority of power deprived of reason, on the contrary, is neither legitimate nor justified. It constitutes, instead, an unbound form of domination. Since power is justified if it establishes the imposition of coercive measures based on non-rejectable reasons, the possibility for a power-entity to set a normatively justified order depends on its pre-commitment to respect human beings in terms of 'autonomous agents who have the right not to be subjected to certain actions or institutional norms that cannot be adequately justified to them'.[68]

For Forst this prerogative is reflexively upheld by 'one basic moral right, the *right to justification*', one which reinstates from within the perspective of a political system—in an embedded form—the idea that 'no one should be subjected to a set of rights and duties—to a political-legal rights regime—the determination of which he or she cannot participate in as an autonomous agent of justification'.[69] It is because we are primarily autonomous agents in a Kantian moral sense, that any form of coercion becomes legitimate if it can be un-coercively accepted by 'all affected persons'.[70]

The requirements of a justification of justice and the idea of justice as justification, respectively, mobilize different kinds of reasons for what should count as relevant in shareable standards among participants of a community of equals. Here I maintain that the cognitive force of justification (the power of justification) does not appear to capture either the mandatory character or the justice element of reasons. Indeed, justification vindicates a mandatory requirement but not, by that same token, also a requirement of justice. This is, instead, independently posed in terms of a self-standing value. It follows that whereas (cognitive) justice and justification *might* coincide, they *do not necessarily* do so. I suggest, therefore, to separate the question of what it means to justify power, from the concern of what is justice as justification and conclude that justification of power

[67] Allegedly, parallel to this, is the question of what confers legitimate authority to a certain power-entity. This aspect, unfortunately, does not fuel Forst's normative account of power and therefore difficulties arise with regard to a lack of consideration of what are the mutual implications of justification between authority and power.

[68] Forst, 'The Justification of Human Rights and the Basic Right to Justification' (n 5) 712.

[69] ibid.

[70] ibid 720.

and the power of justification trigger reasons of a different kind even if aligned on one overall account.

Forst reveals what appears to be an enabling and emancipatory aspect of his theory, one which he refers to someone 'who offers and demands justifications' as a subject of justice.[71] A 'victim of injustice', in this respect, is not someone who is deprived of goods, but rather one who does 'not "count" when it comes to deciding about the process of producing and allocating of goods'.[72] So, if justice implies justification, the latter requires political inclusion with regard to the submission of one's views to public scrutiny. But can the grammar of justice be exhausted by reference to the moral idea of justification as something in the absence of universal legal rights?

Human rights, yet only as moral constraints, play certainly a crucial role in Forst's theory of justice. They are, in one sense, 'basic claims for justificatory standing as a full member, and, in another sense, they can also be means to address particular shortcomings of a social structure'.[73] For this reason, human rights for Forst do not address any particular goods. They define, rather, 'persons as "norm-givers"'.[74] To be a norm-giver, though, means to have become already a member of a cooperative system of justice. Normativity, in the 'corrective' role that Forst assigns to human rights within a social structure, requires preliminary subjectivity, that is, the attainment of a cooperative system of justice by compliance with publicly agreed standards.

The question, next, turns on how Forst's right to justification operates in actual legal contexts where priority goes to the remedying striving of 'particular shortcomings'.[75] I consider that this fundamental condition mobilizes a dimension requiring subject-formation and transformation. That is, one needs to formulate the type of principle that explains the legal subjectivization of the individuals in their becoming equal actors of a system of law and thus co-authors of a principle of justification. I propose to refer to this process with the expression: *Rechtsubjektsfähigkeit*—something indicating the 'capacity of becoming a subject of law'. Indeed it appears that it is from the status of an individual that becomes a subject to a system of law—to a community of rights—that it follows Forst's subjective claim of justice as justification. But then one could go on and notice that to have a capacity of becoming a subject of law triggers an intersubjective process of recognition whereby mutual subjectivity is accounted for.

[71] Rainer Forst, 'Two Pictures of Justice' in Rainer Forst, *Justification and Critique: Towards a Critical Theory of Politics* (Ciaran Cronin tr, Polity Press 2013) 22.
[72] ibid.
[73] Forst, 'The Justification of Human Rights and the Basic Right to Justification' (n 5) 733.
[74] ibid.
[75] ibid.

Let me address this point by considering what Arendt aimed to point out when she referred to 'the calamity of the rightless' as 'not that they are deprived of life, liberty, and the pursuit of happiness, or of equality before the law . . .', but rather that 'they no longer belong to any community whatsoever'.[76] Here rightless is not simply a temporary condition of legal deprivation that *anticipates* the creation of a system of rights. It is rather a permanent, irreversible, status-condition from which subjectivity is *prevented* from arising precisely because it never individualizes within a system of *legally protected liberties*. Such absence of consideration of individuals as subjects of rights transforms lives into 'perfectly "superfluous"' entities.[77] So, Arendt concludes, 'deprivation of human rights' is 'deprivation of a place in the world which makes opinions significant and actions effective'.[78]

On a similar note, Agamben conceptualizes philosophically and actualizes with regard to victims of the Holocaust as well as refugees, the Roman legal notion of the *homo sacer* (the sacred man)—one who can be killed without being sacrificed.[79] The interesting perspective disclosed by Agamben and which integrated Arendt's concerns for the refugees, those who incarnate *par excellence* the subjects in need of human rights protection, is that of the 'sacred man' who from the inside shakes the pillars of the legal system of the state.[80]

The paradox of an unqualified human rights discourse in both cases is that it is precisely when men lose all of their qualities except that of 'humanity' that human rights enter into a crisis.[81] It follows that modern international charters of human rights and strikingly the '89 French Declaration, in drawing a separation between the rights of man and the rights of citizens, have contributed unwittingly to the legitimization of biopolitical powers in ways that are certainly paradoxical. Agamben's concept of the *nuda vita* (the bare life),[82] understood in terms of 'birth' by Arendt and as biological life by Foucault, represents an ultimate and unattainable condition of human rights which remains always as an implicit presupposition for qualified prerogatives of state citizens.[83] As a limit concept (*concetto limite*),[84] the bare life reveals the paradoxical status of state sovereignty, one where attempts to protect individuals through the language

[76] Hanna Arendt, *The Origins of Totalitarianism* (Harvest Book/Harcourt Brace & Company 1973) 295ff.
[77] ibid 295.
[78] ibid 296.
[79] Similarly is the condition of the homo sacer in Agamben as a man who can be killed but not sacrificed: 'Protagonista di questo libro è la nuda vita, cioè la vita *uccidibile e insacrificabile* dell'*homo sacer* . . .'. Giorgio Agamben, *Homo Sacer: Il Potere Sovrano e la Nuda Vita* (Einaudi 2005) 11.
[80] ibid 139.
[81] ibid.
[82] Agamben (n 79).
[83] Agamben (n 79) 142.
[84] ibid 148.

of human rights ends, unexpectedly, in separating the rights of humans from those of the citizens, leaving the first uncoercible. It is in such sense that I read Agamben's insight into apparently protected areas, which instead de-subjectivize individuals, as in concentration or refugee camps.

Also nowadays the language of human rights, articulated in both national constitutions and international conventions, has not solved this internal tension. By taking seriously the ever increasing prominence of refugees in today's politics, it becomes clear how the legal objectification which accompanies the bare life—the process of what can be termed, by playing with words, with another neologism: *Rechtsobjektsfähigkeit* ('becoming an object of law'). With such expression, one can come to refer, ultimately, to a polemical process, in a Schmittian sense, of a juridical order that by objectifying its addressees of rights it ends, paradoxically, in determining their same social expulsion. In either of these cases, state powers and international human rights organizations, unwittingly, end up becoming those same biopolitical powers that they themselves aimed to contrast.[85]

So my puzzle here with Forst's principle of justification concerns the fact that, a principle of law mediating between individual preferences and universal principle of right, is a necessary tool to transform tendencies of objectification of individual claims to inclusion in to a system of justice. I fear that the property of 'all-affectedness' or 'all affected people' that the right to justification mobilizes is pre-defined by a juridical status quo that remains unchallenged by Forst's principle of morality, in so far as it never becomes, or, it is never accompanied by a principle of right.

It is from the consequence of the distancing of the moral standpoint from the juridical one, the 'humanitarian' from the 'legal-political' one, that it should be seen one of the causes of the fading away of the Enlightenment project of social emancipation through human rights in their Janus-face connotation of abstract universality as the rights of man and their concrete enforceability as rights of the citizens. I fear that it is precisely in view of these historical and conceptual challenges that Forst's right to justification risks remaining an unattainable resource for the vindication of the rights of those who are excluded.

IV. Conclusion

Forst's theory of justice as justification is certainly a praiseworthy project that throws light on what are the determinants of justice from which only a renewed paradigm of critical theory can rehabilitate. In this respect I find myself

[85] ibid 147ff.

sympathetic with Forst's overall vision, one inspired by an intellectual project of renovation of classical Enlightenment. Forst places, indeed, a lot weight on the role that the principle of justification assumes in equalizing justificatory powers and in critically redeeming social injustices through a grammar of rights. Yet, as I have attempted to show, there seem to be difficulties with regard to the possibility of arguing for a right to justification from within the perspective of a duty-based Kantian ethics. All Forst can derive from Kant, I believe, is an unconditional 'duty to justification'. What might appear, at first sight, as a possibly mere academic diatribe on Kantian exegesis, I think could instead have a more profound repercussion within Forst's normative system—if left unsolved. Indeed, lack of redemption of a right-based justice leads to uncritical acceptance, due to a lack of resources for inclusion of those subjects that cannot attain as equals to a system of justice.

All this contributes to raise a concern on whether Forst's right to justification has enough inclusive capacity as a principle of justice. The right to justification, as a principle of morality, succeeds at most to show only that *if* we are already subjects of a legal system of interaction, *then* we have a right to demand a justification for those norms that are adopted therewith. The principle, though, does not suffice to establish that because we are equal moral subjects of justification *we have a right to be part* of a coercive legal system as subjects of rights.

I consider therefore that the development of a legal dimension would help Forst's argument in stabilizing mutual relations of recognition and in allowing for the possibility of activating dynamics of legal subjectivization. This process would also integrate, on the empirical level, Forst's and Habermas's consideration for which 'valid norms must *deserve* recognition by *all* concerned', thus bringing into a concrete dimension of coercibility a value-based expectation of justice.[86] Following such reasoning, then, Forst's pledge for equal standing as the 'first demand of justice',[87] signifies primarily that the recognition for individual inclusion in a system of justice has to integrate the recognition of individual moral worthiness together with their legal subjectivity. In this respect, the subjectivization of an individual, both as a legal and as a moral member of a system of justice, *anticipates* her possibility to stand as an equal member along a process of justification.

With this double-tracking process, of both moral/legal normativity and of subjectivity, one comes to define in a more precise way what it means for a subject to be included into a social community as an equal member 'for whom certain norms of justice are supposed to be binding'.[88] Certainly, the remarks here

[86] In Jürgen Habermas, 'Discourse Ethics: Notes on a Program Philosophical Justification' in Seyla Benhabib and Fred R Dallmayr (eds), *The Communicative Ethics Controversy* (MIT Press 1990) 70.

[87] Forst, 'Noumenal Power' (n 2) 118.

[88] Forst, 'Two Pictures of Justice' (n 71) 35.

presented start from the general conviction of the praiseworthiness of Forst's neo-Enlightenment project, as I might call it. It is certainly true that more fully fledged reflection is needed, as Forst notices, on how 'to indicate the sense in which a practically reasoning person has an insight not only into the "how" but also into the "that" of justification'.[89] But if a 'critically sympathetic' contribution can be offered to Forst from my side in view of stimulating future developments of his theory, then, I believe that it would go in the direction of urging a more fundamental understanding of the interconnection between the 'just' and the 'right', what Kant saw in one single word: *Recht*.

References

Agamben G, *Homo Sacer: Il Potere Sovrano e la Nuda Vita* (Einaudi 2005).

Arendt H, *The Origins of Totalitarianism* (Harvest Book/Harcourt Brace & Company 1973).

Forst R, 'The Justification of Human Rights and the Basic Right to Justification: A Reflexive Approach' (2010) 120 Ethics 711.

Forst R, 'Ethics and Morality' in Rainer Forst, *The Right to Justification: Elements of a Constructivist Theory of Justice* (Jeffrey Flynn tr, Columbia University Press 2011).

Forst R, 'Introduction: The Foundation of Justice' in Rainer Forst, *The Right to Justification: Elements of a Constructivist Theory of Justice* (Jeffrey Flynn tr, Columbia University Press 2011).

Forst R, 'Moral Autonomy and the Autonomy of Morality: Toward a Theory of Normativity after Kant' in Rainer Forst, *The Right to Justification: Elements of a Constructivist Theory of Justice* (Jeffrey Flynn tr, Columbia University Press 2011).

Forst R, 'Practical Reason and Justifying Reasons: On the Foundation of Morality' in Rainer Forst, *The Right to Justification: Elements of a Constructivist Theory of Justice* (Jeffrey Flynn tr, Columbia University Press 2011).

Forst R, 'The Basic Right to Justification: Toward a Constructivist Conception of Human Rights' in Rainer Forst, *The Right to Justification: Elements of a Constructivist Theory of Justice* (Jeffrey Flynn tr, Columbia University Press 2011).

Forst R, 'The Justification of Justice: Rawls's Political Liberalism and Habermas's Discourse Theory in Dialogue' in Rainer Forst, *The Right to Justification: Elements of a Constructivist Theory of Justice* (Jeffrey Flynn tr, Columbia University Press 2011).

Forst R, *The Right to Justification: Elements of a Constructivist Theory of Justice* (Jeffrey Flynn tr, Columbia University Press 2011).

Forst R, *Justification and Critique: Towards a Critical Theory of Politics* (Ciaran Cronin tr, Polity Press 2013).

Forst R, 'The Normative Order of Justice and Peace' in Rainer Forst, *Justification and Critique: Towards a Critical Theory of Politics* (Ciaran Cronin tr, Polity Press 2013).

Forst R, 'Two Pictures of Justice' in Rainer Forst, *Justification and Critique: Towards a Critical Theory of Politics* (Ciaran Cronin tr, Polity Press 2013).

[89] Forst, 'Practical Reason and Justifying Reasons' (n 4) 32.

Forst R, 'Justifying Justification: A Reply to My Critics' in Rainer Forst, *Justice, Democracy and the Right to Justification: Rainer Forst in Dialogue* (Bloomsbury Academic 2014).

Forst R, 'Two Pictures of Justice' in Rainer Forst, *Justice, Democracy and the Right to Justification: Rainer Forst in Dialogue* (Bloomsbury Academic 2014).

Forst R, 'Noumenal Power' (2015) 23 Journal of Political Philosophy 111.

Forst R, 'The Right to Justification: Moral and Political, Transcendental and Historical. Reply to Seyla Benhabib, Jeffrey Flynn and Matthias Fritsch' (2015) 43 Political Theory 822.

Forst R, 'The Justification of Basic Rights: A Discourse-Theoretical Approach' (2016) 45(3) Netherlands Journal of Legal Philosophy 7.

Forst R, 'What Does It Mean to Justify Basic Rights? Reply to Düwell, Newey, Rummens and Valentini' (2016) 45(3) Netherlands Journal of Legal Philosophy 76.

Habermas J, 'Discourse Ethics: Notes on a Program of Philosophical Justification' in Jürgen Habermas, *Moral Consciousness and Communicative Action* (Christian Lenhardt and Shierry Weber Nicholsen trs, Polity Press 1990).

Habermas J, 'Discourse Ethics: Notes on a Program Philosophical Justification' in Seyla Benhabib and Fred R Dallmayr (eds), *The Communicative Ethics Controversy* (MIT Press 1990).

Habermas J, 'Morality and Ethical Life: Does Hegel's Critique of Kant Apply to Discourse Ethics?' in Jürgen Habermas, *Moral Consciousness and Communicative Action* (Christian Lenhardt and Shierry Weber Nicholsen trs, Polity Press 1990).

Habermas J, *Between Facts and Norms: Contributions to a Discourse Theory of Law and Democracy* (William Rehg tr, MIT Press 1996).

Kant I, 'Critique of Practical Reason' in Immanuel Kant, *Practical Philosophy* (Mary J Gregor ed and tr, Cambridge University Press 1996).

Kant I, 'Groundwork of the Metaphysics of Morals' in Immanuel Kant, *Practical Philosophy* (Mary J Gregor ed and tr, Cambridge University Press 1996).

Kant I, 'The Metaphysics of Morals' in Immanuel Kant, *Practical Philosophy* (Mary J Gregor ed and tr, Cambridge University Press 1996).

Rawls J, 'Justice as Fairness: Political Not Metaphysical' (1985) 14 Philosophy and Public Affairs 223.

Rawls J, *Political Liberalism* (2nd edn, Columbia University Press 1996).

Timmermann J, 'Kantian Dilemmas? Moral Conflict in Kant's Ethical Theory' (2013) 95 Archiv für Geschichte der Philosophie 36.

Wood AW, *Kantian Ethics* (Cambridge University Press 2007).

3

Human Rights, Interests, and Variation

Andrea Sangiovanni

I. Introduction

The debate on human rights is currently divided between three camps, namely, the Orthodox View—associated with, for example, James Griffin and John Tasioulas—the Political View—associated with, for example, John Rawls, Charles Beitz, and Joseph Raz—and the Legal View—associated with Allen Buchanan. The debate is reaching somewhat of a stalemate, with all three sides backed into defensive and unattractive positions. Rainer Forst gives us a distinctive, and distinctively appealing, way to play a different game. In this chapter, I will reconstruct what makes the Forstian game distinctive (though in a different way than Forst himself), highlight a tension in Forst's view that threatens to make it indistinguishable from the Orthodox View, and show how to resolve it. The resolution will suggest a novel way of conceiving of human rights that allows for much greater institutional variation in conceptions of human rights than we are accustomed to.

II. The Three Camps, and Why We Need to Look Elsewhere

According to the Political View, human rights are moral rights whose violation makes various forms of international interference permissible that would have otherwise been impermissible. According to the Legal View, human rights should neither be conceived of as moral rights nor justified solely in terms of moral rights; they are rather best understood as naming an international system of *legal* rights whose justification need not make any reference to underlying individual moral rights. According to the Orthodox View, human rights are moral rights that we have merely in virtue of our humanity. These characterizations are rough, but they give us enough to recount the main problems that each view faces, and how Forst offers us an alternative.

The Legal View seem excessively narrow. While of course international legal human rights are an essential aspect of human rights practice, they do not exhaust that practice. Indeed, the Legal View seem to mischaracterize a crucial

Andrea Sangiovanni, *Human Rights, Interests, and Variation* In: *Constitutionalism Justified: Rainer Forst in Discourse.* Edited by: Ester Herlin-Karnell and Matthias Klatt, Oxford University Press (2020), © Ester Herlin-Karnell and Matthias Klatt.
DOI: 10.1093/oso/9780190889050.003.0003

aspect of the way the language of human rights is used in the main legal treaties and conventions. The authors and signatories of those treaties and conventions do not conceive of themselves as *creating* a new class of individual rights, actionable in international contexts, and then giving them a name, 'human rights'. Rather, they conceive of themselves as *declaring* or *recognizing*, in law, a series of moral rights that we possess independently of that law. It is those pre-existing moral rights that are properly called human rights, and that shape the character and function of the law of human rights. While of course the legal remedies, duties, and rights that define how human rights matter in international and domestic politics cannot be fully justified simply by referring to the underlying moral rights—they must include, for example, reference to a whole range of further moral, practical, and prudential considerations—it is essential to human rights practice that the legal instruments be understood as giving legal weight and significance to what are, at root, ultimately moral rights.[1]

The Political View might seem to do better. Because they focus on human rights as ultimately *moral* rights with a special function in international politics, they can remain true to both the declaratory aspect of legal human rights instruments and to the fact that human rights discourse is so often dominated by reference to legal texts, treaties, and judgments. The Political View, however, face what we might call the *argument from contingency*. If human rights are moral rights whose possession *qua* human rights depends on whether it is permissible to interfere internationally (in whatever way stipulated by the advocate of such a view), then the human rights we have will seem to depend in the wrong way on the shifting dynamics of international politics. For example, Charles Beitz, a prominent supporter of the Political View, claims that many of the concerns defended in the Convention on the Elimination of All Forms of Discrimination against Women cannot be bona fide human rights because it would be infeasible to pursue international action to change them:

> The inference is that a government's failure to comply with those elements of women's human rights doctrine that require efforts to bring about substantial cultural change does not supply a reason for action by outside agents because there is no plausibly effective strategy of action for which it could be a reason. But if this is correct, then these elements do not satisfy one of our schematic conditions for justifying human rights: they are not appropriately matters of international concern . . . But human rights are supposed to be matters of

[1] For a fuller account of this objection, see Andrea Sangiovanni, *Humanity without Dignity: Moral Equality, Respect, and Human Rights* (Harvard University Press 2017) ch 4. For a response, see Allen Buchanan, 'Human Rights: A Plea for Taking the Law and Institutions Seriously' (2016) 30 Ethics & International Affairs 501.

> international concern, and if there are no feasible means of expressing this concern in political action, then perhaps to this extent women's human rights doctrine overreaches.[2]

Whether women have human rights turns out to vary according to how feasible international efforts at social change in fact would be. This seems to make the possession of human rights too contingent, too yielding with respect to the way power and self-interest shapes the limits of political possibility.[3]

In light of the problems faced by the Legal and the Political View, the Orthodox View might seem best placed to provide a philosophical grounding to human rights. Moral rights that we have *merely in virtue of our humanity*, after all, are rights that do not vary with the shifting sands of political circumstance or legal judgment. They are rights that we have independently of politics, independently of legal institutions, and hence independently of power. In this light, they are moral rights that can serve as bulwarks against *all* forms of authority in *any* context. Given common reference to rights possessed 'in our virtue of humanity' in human rights discourse, the Orthodox View also seem to be more faithful with the way practitioners conceive of their own practice. But the Orthodox View face two problems (both of which will be crucial to our discussion of Forst later). The first I will refer to as the *argument from specificity*; the second, the *challenge from direction*.

The *argument from specificity* departs from the premise that, to be plausible, the Orthodox View must be able to specify, as bona fide human rights, a subclass of the class of moral rights *simpliciter* that is neither too narrow nor too wide. For example, if the Orthodox View say that human rights are those moral rights that we would possess in a state of nature, then the subclass seems too narrow. Rights to education, health, fair trial, and political participation, for example, cannot plausibly be construed as moral rights that we possess in any meaningful sense in a state of nature. Accepting that such rights are *not* bona fide human rights would bound the subclass by a mere fiat—a fiat, moreover, that has little connection to human rights discourse.[4] On the other hand, if the Orthodox View say that human rights are those moral rights that we possess (as, for example, John Tasioulas claims) in 'modernity', then the class seems too broad and normatively *ad hoc*. By 'modernity', Tasioulas refers to an era in which the following are accessible:

> significant levels of scientific and technological expertise and capacity; heavy reliance on industrialized modes of production; the existence of a market-based

[2] Charles R Beitz, *The Idea of Human Rights* (Oxford University Press 2009) 195.

[3] I develop this critique in more depth in Sangiovanni (n 1) ch 4. Forst makes the same point in Rainer Forst, 'Moral Autonomy and the Autonomy of Morality: Toward a Theory of Normativity after Kant' in Rainer Forst, *The Right to Justification: Elements of a Constructivist Theory of Justice* (Jeffrey Flynn tr, Columbia University Press 2011).

[4] For this critique, see Beitz (n 2).

> economy of global reach; a developed legal system that is both efficacious and broad-ranging; the pervasive influence of individualism and secularism in shaping forms of life, and so on.[5]

On this view, promissory rights and rights not to be insulted must surely count as moral rights that we possess in 'modernity' since the duties correlated to them do not seem impossible to satisfy in current conditions. And they are also rights possessed 'in virtue of our humanity' since their force does not depend on who we are, what we have done, or where we come from. So, on Tasioulas's view, they must be human rights. This looks implausible. Furthermore, even if we grant that human rights are those moral rights we possess in conditions of modernity, what normative reason do we have to accept this restriction? What special importance do such rights have to merit the attention that human rights usually get in inter-, trans-, and national politics?

The *challenge from direction* is addressed to the two most prominent Orthodox theorists, namely, Griffin and Tasioulas, both of whom rest their theories of human rights on an interest-based account of their justification. On such accounts, human rights share three essential features.[6] First, they are grounded in *individual* human interests taken, as it were, one by one, rather than in the value of aggregate welfare or in interests held by collectives. Second, such individual interests must be significant enough to impose *directed* moral duties on others. The emphasis on directed duties is important: human rights do not simply articulate goals for the promotion of individual human well-being, or broader non-directed moral duties to promote their good. Rather, they establish moral duties whose violation does not just do wrong in general but wrong *to* the individual right-holder. Third, as rights, human rights must have *categorical* and *exclusionary* force: they must provide reasons that do not depend on duty-holders' motivations and that *exclude* rather than *outweigh* a range of other, first-order reasons (such as reasons to increase aggregate welfare or to pursue narrowly self-interested concerns).

The challenge faced by such accounts is to explain how to 'get from' a fundamental concern with generic human interests and hence welfare to (1) individualistically grounded, (2) directed, (3) categorical, and (4) exclusionary duties, or,

[5] John Tasioulas, 'On the Nature of Human Rights' in Ernst Gerhard and Jan-Christoph Heilinger (eds), *The Philosophy of Human Rights: Contemporary Controversies* (Walter de Gruyter 2011) 36.

[6] These three features are emphasized by Tasioulas (but not by Griffin) but are required to make James Griffin's account plausible. Tasioulas explains why Griffin should have done more to emphasize them in John Tasioulas, 'Taking Rights Out of Human Rights' (2010) 120 Ethics 647. I agree with him, which is why I put Griffin and Tasioulas together.

in short, *bipolar* duties, as I will refer to them.[7] Suppose, for example, that I am ill with a common form of malignant cancer. I have a weighty individual interest in extending my life by a year, but the treatment required to do so would cost over €10,000,000. Why would my weighty individual interest fail to impose a bipolar duty on others to provide for my treatment in this case but would if the cost were much lower? Notice that to respond here that the idea of a 'right' explains why only shifts the problem one step further back: How and when do the interests grounding the rights generate the quadruple, bipolar character of the duties in some cases but not others? How do we decide where the threshold lies? Tasioulas and Griffin leave the answer to intuition, but this leaves us wondering whether there might be a better answer.

The challenge can be sharpened by considering the other crucial feature of bipolar duties, namely, their directed character. There are, as I have said, two kinds of deontic obligations. I might have a duty, for example, to change my halogen bulbs to LED, but this is not a duty I owe *to* anyone in particular. It is non-directed, or monopolar. Unless I have made a promise or other commitment, I do not say: 'I have a duty *to Jane* to change my halogen bulbs'. So what changes when I, say, make a promise to Jane to change my lightbulbs? It is not just that Jane can hold me to account; anyone can hold me to account for failing to change my lightbulbs even in the previous case. It is also not simply that Jane has the power to relieve me of my obligation to her; there are many bipolar duties where those to whom the duty is owed—ie the right-holder—do not have the power to loose; duties not to enslave provide an example. The key feature of a bipolar duty—hence the name—is that it is *essentially*, or *noncomparatively, relational*;[8] it binds together two individuals in a distinctive, pairwise practical nexus that cannot be understood without the presence of the other 'pole'.[9]

The relation 'to the left of' is noncomparatively relational in this sense. There is no way to define what the relation consists in by referring solely to facts about the nonrelational properties of the relata. The relation 'taller than', on the other hand, is only *comparatively* relational: the relation 'taller than' consists in one thing having a nonrelational property, namely, height, to a greater degree than another thing. There is no comparable degree of 'leftness' that a thing possesses independently of its relation to other things. The bipolar relations at the heart of directed duties are analogous: there is no way to identify why or what someone owes without referring to the one to whom it is owed. Contrast the duty to change

[7] The term 'bipolar' duty is from Michael Thompson, 'What Is It to Wrong Someone? A Puzzle about Justice' in RJ Wallace and others (eds), *Reason and Value: Themes from the Moral Philosophy of Joseph Raz* (Oxford University Press 2004).

[8] cf Arthur Ripstein, 'Civil Recourse and Separation of Wrongs and Remedies' (2011) 39 Florida State University Law Review 163.

[9] I draw the idea of a 'practical nexus' from Thompson (n 7).

one's lightbulbs: while the duty places all those who must change their lightbulbs in a relation both to a collective good and to each other, it does so only because each one is under the same duty, rather than because the duty's content and justification requires essential reference to the one to whom it is owed.

The challenge the Orthodox View face is then the following. The Orthodox View identify generic human interests as the grounds for rights, but how and why do the interests justify bipolar rather than merely monopolar duties? How does the fact that something is in someone's interest, above some 'threshold', not only impose *a* duty on others to promote, protect, respect, etc., the interests but establish a *directed* duty? Put another way: How does the mere idea of something's being good for someone bind that individual in a practical nexus with the particular others on whom the duties fall? And why, especially in view of the Orthodox Views' emphasis on well-being, must the interests that ground the duties be *individual* rather than *collective* or *aggregated* interests? It might be true that human rights discourse assumes the bipolarity of duties and rights and their individualistic character, but we want to know not merely how the practices in which human rights figure operate—as if we were anthropologists—but why, and whether, such practices are justified. Human rights theories are normative and evaluative rather than merely descriptive. So the challenge cannot be dodged.[10]

III. The Forstian Alternative

So far we have presented three problems that the predominant views of human right face: the *argument from contingency*, the *argument from specificity*, and the *challenge from direction*. In this section, I will show how Forst's conception of human rights provides a series of promising avenues for responding to all three. In the next section, I will, however, also argue that a full answer to all three requires some modifications to the underlying theory—modifications that will orient the account in a different direction.

The foundation stone of Forst's conception of human rights is the *right to justification*. We find ourselves necessarily implicated as human beings in practices of discursive justification, some of which require one to justify one's actions in specifically moral terms. Put another way: if someone asks us—'With what right do you act in such and such a way?'—we must answer. And, once we do, we become enmeshed in practices of moral justification. Moral discourses of justification, in turn, have a certain normative structure, which can be reconstructed by

[10] Could a conception of human dignity fill the gap? For an argument showing that the idea of dignity *qua* unconditional worth gives us at most a monopolar conception of duty, see Ariel Zylberman, 'Why Human Rights? Because of *You*' (2016) 24 Journal of Political Philosophy 321.

considering what is (necessarily) presupposed in 'redeeming' a claim to rightness. This is what makes them practices of *justification* rather than, say, forms of command, advice, warning, exhortation, or questioning. If we do not respect the standards internal to justification as a practice, we must therefore fail in justifying ourselves to others, and hence fail in something we must do. As Forst writes in the first passages from *The Right to Justification*: 'Human beings' are 'justificatory beings . . . If we want to understand human practices, we *must* conceive of them as practices bound up with justifications; *no matter what we think or do*, we place upon ourselves (and others) the demand for reasons, whether they are made explicit or remain implicit'.[11] In recognizing that (inescapable) practical deliberation requires that we justify ourselves to others, we recognize at the same time others' claim-rights to demand justification of us. This is the basis, Forst argues, for our equal moral status *qua* dignity.

Forst then claims that such practices, given their structure, necessarily presuppose that the reasons we offer others must meet criteria of generality and reciprocity. Forst writes:

> [C]riteria of reciprocity and generality are essential: the former means that nobody claims special privileges and everyone grants others all the claims one raises for oneself, without projecting one's own interests, values, or needs onto others and thereby unilaterally determining what counts as a good reason; the latter means that no affected person's objections may be excluded to achieve general agreeability. Only by adhering to these criteria can it be claimed that nobody has good reasons for challenging the validity of a norm and particular, corresponding ways of acting.[12]

These criteria are intended to tell us which reasons—including reasons deriving from individuals' interests—are valid reasons and hence that could be used to reject principles or norms for the general regulation of action.[13]

We now have enough to see how Forst can answer the *challenge from direction*. Recall that the Orthodox View do not offer resources to explain how, when, and why an individual's interests can give rise to specifically bipolar duties. When, why, and how, that is, does the fact that an action promotes someone's welfare put others under a special relationship to that person such that a failure to act in

[11] Rainer Forst, 'Introduction: The Foundation of Justice' in Rainer Forst, *The Right to Justification: Elements of a Constructivist Theory of Justice* (Jeffrey Flynn tr, Columbia University Press 2011) 1 (emphasis added).

[12] Rainer Forst, 'Ethics and Morality' in Rainer Forst, *The Right to Justification: Elements of a Constructivist Theory of Justice* (Jeffrey Flynn tr, Columbia University Press 2011) 66.

[13] I question whether Forst's criteria of reciprocity and generality are sufficient to filter valid from invalid reasons, and hence can be used to support Forst's argument for human dignity, in Sangiovanni (n 1) ch 1. Here I simply assume that the argument goes through.

the relevant way counts as *wronging that individual* rather than merely *violating a general duty to promote the good*? As Forst writes, 'There are many . . . interests—think of the interest in being loved; but how do we single out those that qualify for grounding human rights? Furthermore, how does a claim of subjective importance translate into a binding general claim to rights? What is the mediating factor which generates that kind of normativity?'[14] For Forst, the mediating factor is the right to justification. But how does the right of justification put two individuals in the relevant practical nexus, that is, in a practical nexus binding the two in the bipolar relation of claimant and claimee? Justification, understood in its most basic sense as a practice of reason-giving, is an inherently pairwise affair between two individuals: we do not justify ourselves to no one in particular or to aggregates. Justification is always justification *to* someone in particular. And, if Forst is right that justification is inescapable once we address others with claims and demands, then justification necessarily yokes individuals together into the relevant kind of practical nexus between a claimant and a claimee. So, if a particular claim or demand—say, to seek special protection of an interest—cannot reasonably be rejected according to the constitutive norms of justification (reciprocity and generality), then the interest is transformed from something merely 'subjective' to the basis for an agent-relative duty to act so as to protect the interest. This duty is directed because its normative force arises from the constitutive demands of justification to another, which, as we have seen, are essentially relational. By violating the duty, we thereby also violate another person's right to justification and therefore don't just do wrong in general but wrong them in particular.

We can now turn to the *argument from specificity*. It is essential that human rights are not derived directly from the *ur*-right to justification as Athena was from Zeus's head.[15] There is no unmediated route from the right to justification to human rights. In a common refrain, Forst writes: 'Human rights can only be grounded on a fundamental notion of a right to have all those rights that free and equal normative authorities cannot reciprocally and generally deny each other *if they want to secure and operationalize that status . . . in the legal, political and social world*'.[16] He also writes, 'the essential political message of human rights [is] the claim to be not just a fully integrated member of society, but to be a social and political subject who is, negatively speaking, free from arbitrary social

[14] Rainer Forst, 'The Justification of Human Rights and the Basic Right to Justification: A Reflexive Approach' in Rainer Forst, *Justification and Critique: Towards a Critical Theory of Politics* (Ciaran Cronin tr, Polity Press 2013) 40.

[15] For this point, see eg Rainer Forst, 'The Basic Right to Justification: Toward a Constructivist Conception of Human Rights' in Rainer Forst, *The Right to Justification: Elements of a Constructivist Theory of Justice* (Jeffrey Flynn tr, Columbia University Press 2011) 212.

[16] Rainer Forst, 'The Point and Ground of Human Rights: A Kantian Constructivist View' in David Held and Pietro Maffettone (eds), *Global Political Theory* (Polity Press 2016) 33 (emphasis added).

or political domination'.[17] The way I read him in these passages is that human rights would not exist in a Rousseauvean state of nature (in which individuals do not share in any significant social, political, or legal practices). Rather, human rights are those moral rights we must grant one another once (but only once) we interact via shared social, political, and legal practices. They must be, therefore, identified and justified not *in abstracto*—for example, as logical derivations from the right to justification—but in terms of the specific scope, functions, and content the practices they are meant to regulate.[18] More precisely, they are those civil, political, social, and cultural rights that we must grant one another if we are to justify the institutional orders we share with others. I leave the idea of an 'institutional order' vague at this point. It obviously includes coercive legal orders such as the state. But it is essential to the account that it is not limited to the state. In principle (a point to which we will return later), sharing *any* institutional order gives rise to a demand to justify that order to those who are both subject to it and, if not subjects, then affected by it, and hence a demand to regulate that order by human rights standards. We might think here not only of international organizations, such as the World Bank but also non-state organizations, such as corporations and non-governmental organizations. As Forst writes, 'I disagree with an institutional view which not merely argues that the state is the central institution for securing human rights but also contends that it is only violations perpetrated by official actors that count as human rights violations'.[19]

This aspect of the account is crucial in meeting the *argument from specificity*. Because human rights are rights that apply when (and only when) we share institutional orders (even if we are not 'official actors'),[20] they form a subclass of all the moral rights we possess. The account, for example, makes it easy to explain why promissory rights and rights not to be insulted—as long as they remain merely interpersonal violations—are not human rights. We might wonder whether, however, it is specific enough: If human rights are simply the moral rights we must grant one another once we share an institutional order, how are

[17] Forst, 'The Justification of Human Rights and the Basic Right to Justification' (n 14) 44.

[18] The strategy here is similar, but not the same, as the one pursued by Habermas where the discourse principle 'D'—here functionally equivalent to the right to justification—'interpenetrates' with the idea of a legal order—functionally equivalent to Forst's 'legal, political, and social world'—to deliver an abstract system of (human) rights: Jürgen Habermas, *Between Facts and Norms: Contributions to a Discourse Theory of Law and Democracy* (William Rehg tr, MIT Press 1996). For Forst's own account of his differences from Habermas, including his understanding of 'legal form', see Rainer Forst, 'The Justification of Justice: Rawls's Political Liberalism and Habermas's Discourse Theory in Dialogue' in Rainer Forst, *The Right to Justification: Elements of a Constructivist Theory of Justice* (Jeffrey Flynn tr, Columbia University Press 2011) 101–16. This strategy is, of course, also a central part of Kant's *Doctrine of Right*.

[19] Forst, 'Ethics and Morality' (n 12) 68.

[20] Though it must be said that if Forst intends human rights to apply to persons whether or not they interact via an institutional order, then his account would collapse into an Orthodox View. More on this later.

human rights any different from standards of justice (especially once we allow, as Forst does, for social rights, including social rights to a fair distribution of the benefits and burdens of social production)?

Here Forst draws a distinction between a 'basic structure of justification' and a 'fully justified basic structure'.[21] I interpret Forst to mean that human rights specify the 'basic' (but not 'minimal') requirements that an order must meet to earn the respect of its subjects and those affected by it, by which are included duties of compliance where one is a subject, and duties of non-interference where one is not. This respect is due to the order, then, even when it does wrong, as long as the wrong it does was produced as a result of deliberative procedures in which everyone had a say as an equal and free agent. Human rights, that is, set criteria for what is often called 'internal' legitimacy understood in this thin sense, where by internal legitimacy we mean standards for the assessment of an order from subjects and those affected rather than standards for the assessment of external interference. Criteria for a fully justified basic structure, on the other hand, require much more: they require that the order not only merit our *respect* but also merit our *endorsement* as fully just. Using this distinction, Forst can say that human rights standards form a subclass of the class of moral rights *simpliciter* but also a subclass of standards of justice.

This move also allows Forst to answer the *argument from contingency*. Because human rights are indexed to *institutional orders* rather than to *types of international, legitimate, and feasible remedial action*, they do not fall prey to political circumstances or remain hostage to shifting balances of power. While of course whether a particular institutional order exists depends, indeed relies, on the existence of power, human rights standards apply to it whether or not violations of such rights would justify (even *pro tanto*) external interference or action of any kind.

IV. The Role of Institutions

So far we have seen that the key to overcoming the *argument from specificity* is to make human rights a function of institutional orders that include, but are not limited to, the state. But this looks too easy. For we might then wonder: If human rights are not rights that we possess *merely* in virtue of our humanity, as the Orthodox View argue, but rights that we possess only within institutional orders, then what role do institutions play in fixing the human rights we have (without falling afoul of a slightly reworked *argument from contingency*)? Forst does not

[21] Forst, 'The Justification of Justice' (n 18) 119f.

offer an answer to this question—leaving it to be worked out by a further application of his theory—but it is, in fact, central. To see why, note why it is not available to Forst to respond that our question simply asks us how we might *apply* a conception of human rights worked out *a priori*, and therefore can be left either to deliberative publics or to a further downstream stage of the theory. The reason is that, if the conception of human rights—which includes both a 'list' of rights and an account of their justification—was available *prior* to any institution, then, in fact, the theory would be no different from the Orthodox View, and so fail in just the same ways. Sometimes Forst himself is ambiguous on just this point. For example, he writes:

> Starting from the claims people have raised and do raise in social conflicts, a constructivist theory arrives at a list of human rights that cannot reasonably (i.e., with reasons) be withheld from a person, in any social context whatsoever, without violating his or her right to justification.[22]

If human rights were in fact prior in this theoretical sense, then Forst's view would be no different in its essential characteristics from Tasioulas's. In distinguishing his account from Legal and the Political View, Tasioulas, for example, writes:

> Orthodoxy better enables us to accommodate [the possibility of human rights that do not depend on the existence of states] by giving us a purer, moral concept of human rights, free of any such specific institutional entanglements. Insofar as an (additional) institutional dimension potentially enters into human rights discourse, it does so in a non-conceptual, flexible and context-dependent ways, for example: as part of the specification of the socio-historical conditions over which particular human rights claims are supposed to hold, and in deliberation concerning the concrete specification and practical implementation of human rights.[23]

In the rest of this section, I will provide a reconstruction of Forst's view that can explain how institutions matter at a more fundamental level without falling afoul of a revamped contingency objection or collapsing into the Orthodox View. I will also suggest, however, how this revised Forstian account points in a slightly different direction, especially when we consider how much variation a theory of human rights must allow between the systems of human rights that ought to govern different institutions.

22 Forst, 'The Basic Right to Justification' (n 15) 217.
23 Tasioulas, 'On the Nature of Human Rights' (n 5) 48.

Forst's account can best be interpreted as having a three-stage structure of justification.[24] At the first stage, we ground the right to justification in the general structure of reason-giving. At the second stage, we identify a particular institutional context that the right to justification is meant to organize. For example, the right to justification could organize interaction via a state, an international organization, or a private association. In this capacity, the *ur*-right can serve both enabling functions—as when the right to justification mandates a particular participatory structure whose point and purpose is defined by the *ur*-right itself—and limiting functions—as when the right to justification specifies particular standards that must be met by an institutional order whose point and purpose is identified independently. At the third stage, we identify the particular institutions, rules, and policies that might actually realize the standards and structures fixed at the second stage.

The second stage, rather than the first or the third, is where human rights first make their appearance. They are, as we have said, the civil, political, social, cultural rights that participants (taking into account affected third parties) must grant one another to justify (in a basic sense) the institutional order in question. But *which* rights (and corresponding duties)? To fill in this part of the justificatory sequence, I want to suggest that we need more information about the kind of institution involved. Is it coercive? What public goods does it provide? What agents are principally involved in this production?

To make this more concrete, let us take up a specific example. Suppose we are wondering what human rights, if any, ought to govern corporations. We resist the temptation, as the Orthodox View might suggest, to imagine a list of human rights as given *a priori*, and then ask which ones *apply* to corporations. This is because we reject the idea that there is any such list knowable *a priori*. As we have seen, mere reflection on our humanity leaves us with only those rights we might have in a state of nature—which would leave us with a narrow list indeed—or those rights we have in a vaguely characterized 'modernity'—which would leave us with a list that is far too broad and normatively inert. Instead, we ask: What rights must corporations recognize in order to be justifiable (in a basic sense) both to participants (eg employees and shareholders) and to affected third parties (eg a community downstream of a projected dam)? What particular rights, in other words, does the right to justification require corporations to promote, respect, and fulfil in order to be legitimate? I have used the UN-inspired triad 'promote, respect, and fulfill' to put emphasis not just on the rights *in abstracto* but also the *directed, noncomparatively relational* duties associated with the rights. This is essential to see why an abstract list is insufficient. Imagine, for example,

[24] In this connection, one might compare Forst's view to Rawls's four-stage sequence. See John Rawls, *A Theory of Justice* (revised edn, Oxford University Press 1999) 171–76.

that we said that corporations must promote, respect, and fulfil the *full* list of human rights listed in the Universal Declaration of Human Rights (UDHR). This seems reasonable only if we assume that 'realizing' human rights only requires meeting a list of correlated *negative* duties to refrain from a proscribed action—say, torture or discrimination—rather than *positive, noncomparatively relational* duties to establish conditions for securing the object of a right—say, setting up and maintaining a health-care or educational system, or a system of adjudication to monitor, remedy, and prosecute abuses. However, this assumption, as Henry Shue famously argued, is misguided: promoting, respecting, and fulfilling human rights—even human rights against torture—requires much more (of states) than refraining from torture; it also requires establishing and maintaining a system of police to enforce anti-torture standards, a norm-making body to set up general guidelines, and adjudicatory bodies to settle cases that fall under the guidelines. Seen in this light, our question about human rights then becomes: Must corporations have responsibilities to do all of those things? If so, why? When and under what circumstances? Must chess clubs also do the same? International organizations such as the International Organization for Standardization? Or do those duties only fall upon states, and other associations, organizations, or institutions derivatively? (But then in what sense must corporations promote, respect, and fulfil the full list of rights listed in the UDHR directly?)

Once we go beyond the notion of an abstract list (with associated, but merely negative, duties), and once we remember the noncomparatively relational character of human rights, it becomes obvious that the particular nature and character of the institution in question matters. In our example, we need to evaluate the point and purpose of the corporation, its relations to its participants and those affected by its decision, as well as its place in a wider system of institutions. Corporations are legally recognized entities organized to pursue a particular purpose. A business corporation, for example, is organized to pursue, primarily, profit. A not-for-profit can have many ends, including charitable ones. Corporations are thus voluntary organizations with legal personality that, unlike the state, are not designed to provide a comprehensive set of public goods, or to legislate and enforce their norms coercively over a territory. Corporations are, furthermore, usually subject to the legislative authority of a state that determines their legal rights and regulates their creation and dissolution. For corporations operating in well-functioning states,[25] it therefore does not seem plausible to claim that their legitimacy—their entitlement to the respect of those subject to

[25] Special duties will apply to states operating in conflict zones, for example, as Ruggie himself argues in John G Ruggie, *Just Business: Multinational Corporations and Human Rights* (W.W. Norton & Company 2013). But even there, they should not mirror those of states.

them and affected by their decisions—rests on their willingness to provide (or even directly subsidize) the creation of an educational or health-care system, or a system of courts designed to provide a fair trial to all citizens in a territory. This is not only because we assume that the state in which the corporation operates is already doing so but also, more importantly, because corporations have a very different function from states (and indeed rely on state authority to exist *qua* legal entities). If we imagined, for example, a non-legalized corporation designed to promote the playing of chess in a Rousseauvean state of nature, it would seem absurd to say that, simply in virtue of being incorporated to pursue *some* goal, it ought to pursue *all* the goals typical of states. As John Ruggie writes, 'While corporations may be considered "organs of society". they are specialized economic organs, not democratic public interest institutions. As such, their responsibilities cannot and should not simply mirror the duties of States'.[26]

This doesn't mean, of course, that corporations are not bound by human rights norms, or indeed norms that go beyond a narrow concern with profit (or in the case of non-profits, a narrow concern with their specific objectives).[27] But it does mean that those norms will take a very different form, precisely in virtue of the character and function of corporations, their distinctive operating environment, and the fact that human rights require one to identify *both sides* of the practical nexus associated with any right. A focus on the directed, bipolar duties associated with rights should therefore push us to see that the shape, nature, and justification of human rights will differ greatly when considering different kinds of institutions. Given such variation, it is misleading to claim that underlying the duties are the 'same' rights. While the interests involved in the justification of the rights—given their fundamental nature—will most often be the same (as will the right to justification that underlies all rights), human rights are *not* merely interests that others have a duty to promote. If we miss the essentially relational, directed character that makes human rights *rights*, we miss the fact that rights are claims against particular others in bipolar contexts, rather than merely non-directed goals, interests, or duties owed by and to no one in particular. By focusing on the essentially bipolar character of rights, then, we must also recognize that institutions matter in specifying the content, grounds, and scope of human rights *themselves*—as my reconstruction of Forst's second stage suggests—rather than merely in adjusting how they are applied or implemented.

To illustrate, let us return to corporations. What does a corporation need to do to be legitimate—to merit the respect and compliance of its participants

[26] John G Ruggie, 'Report of the Special Representative of the Secretary-General on the Issue of Human Rights and Transnational Corporations and Other Business Enterprises' (2008) para 53. See also Ruggie, *Just Business* (n 25) ch 2.

[27] cf the wider category of what goes under the name of 'Corporate Social Responsibility'.

(even when they disagree with its particular policies, strategies, and organization), and at the very least the non-interference of those affected by it? The best method in answering this question begins by considering the standard ways in which corporations threaten the most important claims of participants and third parties. In *Just Business*, John Ruggie has drawn up an impressive list of the incredibly diverse ways in which corporations significantly threaten to impinge (or have consistently impinged) on the most important interests and claims (for example, to fair treatment) underlying the human rights listed in the UDHR. This list includes claims and interests to fair working conditions, freedom of association, health, equal treatment under the law, freedom of movement, participation in cultural life, and even education.[28] But when does a corporation set back these interests and infringe these claims in a way that violates a human right, or, in Forst's terms, when does a corporation ultimately violate the right to justification that gives these interests and claims their normative weight? To answer this further question, we need to point to the directed, bipolar duties correlated with the right, and so with the special relations that bind together corporations and their employees, managers, shareholders, and affected third parties. At the same time, as we have seen, we should resist the conclusion that these are the same duties as apply to states. To distinguish what duties are held by states as opposed to corporations, it is misleading to suppose that there is a single 'list' of human rights that everyone, everywhere should 'promote, respect, and fulfill'. Rather, we should query when and whether the very same actions as performed by a corporation as opposed to state—say a failure to set up a system of schools—counts as a violation of a human right (and so of a correlated duty) or not. If there is a divergence between the duties of states and corporations in cases like these—cases, that is, in which the interests and claims underlying the rights are set back to the same degree—then we should not say that corporations can violate human rights in ways that states can't. Rather, we should say that different conceptions of human rights apply to the actors. And if we do that, then we would be, I am suggesting, adopting my institutionalist reconstruction of Forst's account and therefore rejecting the Orthodox View.

So far, I've claimed that adopting an institutionalist account allows Forst to counter the *argument from specificity*. I have also argued that, once we do so, we must accept that different conceptions of human rights will apply in different contexts, especially once we shift from seeing rights only in terms of the interests they protect to seeing rights in terms of the quadruple, bipolar duties correlated with them. Of course, where the duties are the same no matter who the actors are, the underlying rights will be the same—the purely negative aspect of

[28] Ruggie, *Just Business* (n 25) ch 2.

rights against torture provide an example. But, once we have in view the positive, noncomparatively relational, and bipolar aspects of rights, we should also accept that human rights are best justified as *systems* binding together institutions and individuals under the dominion of the right to justification.[29] This is why I have spoken of different *conceptions* of human rights for different contexts. To return to our running example, even if some of the rights will have the same *objects* and protect the same *interests/claims*, the overall *system* of human rights that ought to govern corporations will be different from the one that ought to govern states. This will be most evident, as we have seen, when we speak of rights to health, or education, or participation, but it will also be the case when we speak of rights to freedom of expression, association, and a fair trial. In the latter cases, the positive, bipolar duties associated with the rights, including how they interact with other rights-correlated positive duties, will be distinct given the different relations, operating environment, and functions of corporations. In some cases, it will not make sense to speak of a right to education, and in others the rights to 'association', 'participation', 'family life' will take very different forms. For example, rights to association, expression, and participation will have a special meaning and basis given the particular conditions of workers in firms and their relations to employers—especially in relation to labor rights such as the right to bargain collectively and participation rights in relation to the governance of the firm. And they will be different again when we consider different kinds of international organizations, such as the World Bank, the International Organization for Standardization, or the World Trade Organization. Finally, it is worthwhile to note that a full theory of human rights, of course, would also have to take into account how different systems of human rights *interact*, especially how they interact with the system with which we are most familiar, that governs the most important institutions in the international order, and that is the main agent and subject in the international system of *legal* human rights (the UN system), namely, the state.

Accepting such variation in conceptions of human rights on the basis of facts about institutional orders may seem to bring back the *argument from contingency*: Does affirming such institutionalism mean that the human rights we possess depend on arbitrary balances of power? Because institutionalism yokes variation to the kinds of institutional order rather than to judgments of feasibility or appropriate, contextually sensitive responses to violation, the variation in institutional order is not a problem. While of course participants in an institutional order could disband the order by collective action, and thus free themselves of the human rights obligations that apply to it, the moment they set up a new one

[29] For a discussion of how to understand interdependence among human rights, especially in light of UN doctrine regarding indivisibility, see Sangiovanni (n 1) ch 6.

a new set of human rights standards will apply. Given this fact, it seems far out to worry that participants would return to a state of nature in order simply to avoid human rights obligations. Similarly, the function of an institution is not determined by stipulation (or, narrowly, by simply taking a survey of practitioner's beliefs); it is determined by interpretation of what the institution actually does and how it does it.

Accepting this variation, in turn, means that we must also reject the idea that there is a 'master list' of human rights—say, the rights listed in the UDHR—that are simply applied differently in different contexts. Rather, there are different systems, and hence conceptions, of human rights that must be constructed for each institutional context. It therefore makes no sense to imagine that we can give a philosophical defence of an abstract list of human rights for *any* context (as Forst often claims to do).[30] To do so would be to revert to the Orthodox View. To be sure, along with the right to justification, many of the interests/claims protected by human rights will be the same, given their fundamental nature, and so the justification for each of these systems will resemble each other in important ways. But the crucial point that I have stressed in this chapter is that to associate human *rights* with the *interests/claims* they protect leads us to overlook their essentially relational, bipolar character—the way such rights claims bind together individuals *and* institutions, rather than simply 'express' something essential about individuals *per se*.

This has implications, too, for the way we understand, from a philosophical point of view, different practices or discourses of human rights as deployed by different human rights practitioners. When we consider what conception of human rights should, for example, both *apply to*[31] and *govern* Amnesty International's aims and methods, on our best understanding of what Amnesty's aims are, it is not a foregone conclusion that it will be the same as the conception of human rights that ought to apply to and govern the framers or judges of the European Convention on Human Rights, or the World Bank. Because the institutional contexts in which they operate are so different—one a legal context designed to oversee and monitor states, the other a non-legal context designed to bring international attention to the way institutional agents of all kinds subvert the most important fundamental interests/claims of individuals, and the last designed to provide development assistance and loans—it should not be surprising if the

[30] See, especially, his critique of my own account of human rights, which is very similar to the reconstruction of Forst's view that I have given in this chapter, with the important difference that I understand the grounds for both basic and equal moral status, and hence the demand for justification, very differently from Forst. For my critique of Forst's arguments for the right to justification, my account of basic and equal moral status and its application to human rights, see ibid 57–64.

[31] Indeed: What conception of human rights ought to govern the conduct and projects of Amnesty's personnel *itself* in, say, conflict zones?

conceptions, understood as systems including abstract statements of rights *and* their correlated bipolar duties, will be different as well. While there will be much overlap, for example, when Amnesty pursues state violations of human rights that have also been recognized by international treaty bodies and courts, like the European Court of Human Rights (ECtHR), there is no guarantee that this will always be the case. There are many cases where, for example, we might agree that some violation by a state ought *rightly* to count as a human rights violation by the standards appropriate for Amnesty but not for the standards appropriate to the ECtHR (consider, for example, how the 'margin of appreciation' is often used by the ECtHR in ways it would make no sense for Amnesty to use), or where standards appropriate for the World Bank's projects are different from the ones that apply (internally) to Amnesty's. This will not be because we ought to accept some sort of moral relativism,[32] but because the aims and purposes of both organizations, including the institutional-legal-political-social contexts in which they operate, mean that the systems of rights and correlated bipolar duties they ought to be concerned with will be very different as well. The only way we might miss this is if we focus too much on the abstract interests/claims underlying the rights, rather than on the rights themselves (which, as I have argued, requires us to consider the role of institutions as well).

Would admitting this variation into our working account of human rights mean that we could no longer understand practitioners as engaged in a single project?[33] In brief, no, but we would need to understand the idea of a single project differently than most practitioners probably do. Adopting the institutionalist framework I have suggested previously requires us to abandon the idea that there is a single list of human rights that everyone, everywhere must respect, protect, and fulfil (such as the list in the UDHR, which is specifically designed for states and has in view future legal institutionalization in international law). But it doesn't require us to abandon the idea that human rights—in whatever form they appear in different contexts and different institutions—aim to protect the same underlying, fundamental interests/claims that are most threatened by political, legal, social, economic, and cultural orders of all types. Those interests/claims, when systematically set back by an institutional order in such a way as to violate

[32] This is, I think, misunderstood by Forst: Rainer Forst, 'Human Rights in Context: A Comment on Sangiovanni' in Adam Etinson (ed), *Human Rights: Moral or Political?* (Oxford University Press 2018).

[33] I answer the same objection in Sangiovanni (n 1) ch 4. Whereas in that book I emphasized the idea that human rights are standards whose violation ought to trigger universal moral, legal, and political concern (where the type of concern varies by context), here I emphasize the idea that human rights are standards that protect the fundamental interests/claims associated with participants in varying institutional orders. Despite these differences in emphasis, the two accounts—my own one and the Forstian one reconstructed in this chapter—are functionally equivalent. The divergence between Forst and me, therefore, does not occur at this structural level, but in our very distinct understanding of basic and equal moral status.

the correlated bipolar duties associated with that order, undermine the legitimacy of that order. That is all that is needed to make sense of 'human rights' as a single project; once we make this shift, there is no need any more to speak of a 'master list'. There will be different lists for different orders and institutional contexts—all of which are justified by the single aim of protecting fundamental interests/claims, including general claims, as Forst often writes, to being recognized as an equal author and addressee of the institutional orders to which we are subject, and including the claim to have whatever order we are subjected to justified to us.

This leads me to a last point. A common objection to human rights practice is that the rights it champions, such as those listed in the UDHR or the two Covenants (International Covenant on Civil and Political Rights and International Covenant on Economic, Social and Cultural Rights), are much too abstract and vague to be truly action-guiding. In response, it is often said that this abstraction—especially given legal, cultural, and political disagreement—is an advantage, precisely because it leaves so much to local interpretation and variation. Nothing I have said here needs to be in tension with this response. One might then wonder whether a *philosophical* account of human rights ought to be similarly abstract and noncommittal. In this chapter, I have argued that it should not. I have argued that philosophical conceptions of human rights should be able to build in and explain the nature of institutional variation, rather than leave it to further discussion or implementation. Indeed, once we have fully in view the way quadruple, bipolar duties are correlated with rights, we will see that philosophical specifications of human rights themselves should be allowed to vary much more with context than we might otherwise expect. We should not confuse, that is, what is politically and legally expedient—namely, a declaration, treaty, or constitution's abstraction and lack of specificity—with a philosophically illuminating account of the rights underlying those instruments. Philosophical conceptions of human rights should propose ways of thinking *beyond* abstract declarations; they should allow us to illuminate what the grounds, content, scope, and role of the moral rights that support the major declarations, treaties, and constitutions *really* are. And to do this, I have argued, we have to spend much more time thinking about the quadruple, bipolar duties that bind institutions and individuals together rather than merely focus our gaze solely on the abstract interests/claims that rights protect.

References

Beitz CR, *The Idea of Human Rights* (Oxford University Press 2009).

Buchanan A, 'Human Rights: A Plea for Taking the Law and Institutions Seriously' (2016) 30 Ethics & International Affairs 501.

Forst R, 'Ethics and Morality' in Rainer Forst, *The Right to Justification: Elements of a Constructivist Theory of Justice* (Jeffrey Flynn tr, Columbia University Press 2011).

Forst R, 'Introduction: The Foundation of Justice' in Rainer Forst, *The Right to Justification: Elements of a Constructivist Theory of Justice* (Jeffrey Flynn tr, Columbia University Press 2011).

Forst R, 'Moral Autonomy and the Autonomy of Morality: Toward a Theory of Normativity after Kant' in Rainer Forst, *The Right to Justification: Elements of a Constructivist Theory of Justice* (Jeffrey Flynn tr, Columbia University Press 2011).

Forst R, 'The Basic Right to Justification: Toward a Constructivist Conception of Human Rights' in Rainer Forst, *The Right to Justification: Elements of a Constructivist Theory of Justice* (Jeffrey Flynn tr, Columbia University Press 2011).

Forst R, 'The Justification of Justice: Rawls's Political Liberalism and Habermas's Discourse Theory in Dialogue' in Rainer Forst, *The Right to Justification: Elements of a Constructivist Theory of Justice* (Jeffrey Flynn tr, Columbia University Press 2011).

Forst R, 'The Justification of Human Rights and the Basic Right to Justification: A Reflexive Approach' in Rainer Forst, *Justification and Critique: Towards a Critical Theory of Politics* (Ciaran Cronin tr, Polity Press 2013).

Forst R, 'The Point and Ground of Human Rights: A Kantian Constructivist View' in David Held and Pietro Maffettone (eds), *Global Political Theory* (Polity Press 2016).

Forst R, 'Human Rights in Context: A Comment on Sangiovanni' in Adam Etinson (ed), *Human Rights: Moral or Political?* (Oxford University Press 2018).

Habermas J, *Between Facts and Norms: Contributions to a Discourse Theory of Law and Democracy* (William Rehg tr, MIT Press 1996).

Rawls J, *A Theory of Justice* (revised edn, Oxford University Press 1999).

Ripstein A, 'Civil Recourse and Separation of Wrongs and Remedies' (2011) 39 Florida State University Law Review 163.

Ruggie JG, 'Report of the Special Representative of the Secretary-General on the Issue of Human Rights and Transnational Corporations and Other Business Enterprises' (2008).

Ruggie JG, *Just Business: Multinational Corporations and Human Rights* (W.W. Norton & Company 2013).

Sangiovanni A, *Humanity without Dignity: Moral Equality, Respect, and Human Rights* (Harvard University Press 2017).

Tasioulas J, 'Taking Rights Out of Human Rights' (2010) 120 Ethics 647.

Tasioulas J, 'On the Nature of Human Rights' in Ernst Gerhard and Jan-Christoph Heilinger (eds), *The Philosophy of Human Rights: Contemporary Controversies* (Walter de Gruyter 2011).

Thompson M, 'What Is It to Wrong Someone? A Puzzle about Justice' in RJ Wallace and others (eds), *Reason and Value: Themes from the Moral Philosophy of Joseph Raz* (OUP 2004).

Zylberman A, 'Why Human Rights? Because of *You*' (2016) 24 Journal of Political Philosophy 321.

4

Distributions, Relations, and Justifications

Mixing Flavours of Egalitarianism

Christian Hiebaum[*]

I. Introduction

Equality is a notoriously contested value. There is no agreement on what equality consists in and whether inequality is bad in itself or unjust or, if bad at all, only because of its bad consequences, such as poverty, higher crime rates, political corruption, decline of mutual trust, and other phenomena of social disintegration. Whatever they disagree about, genuine egalitarians believe in equality *not just* for instrumental reasons.[1] Some egalitarians assume 'equality' to be conceptually akin to 'community', 'mutual respect', and 'esteem' or even 'love'; others prefer to keep these notions more distinct or even strictly separated. But they all consider equality either intrinsically worthwhile or a requirement of justice. Yet they know as well as their opponents that there are also morally unattractive states of equality or equal treatment. Society is a system of differences and differentiation, and no egalitarian resents this abstract fact. Egalitarianism is not mysticism. However, what egalitarians do strongly believe is that many political, economic, and other social disparities between people in the actually existing capitalist society are not compatible with equality and regardless of their further effects not just undesirable, but even intolerable. Beyond that, their views diverge. Thus egalitarians spend considerable effort arguing with each other about the proper understanding of equality. This debate is part of a broader conversation about the nature of justice and the distinction between justice and the

* For useful comments on an earlier version of this chapter I'm most grateful to Stefan Arnold, Peter Koller, and Héctor A. Morales Zúñiga.

[1] Egalitarians can certainly accept instrumental reasons for quality. As a matter of fact, outside of academic debates and ideological purity contests, they tend to not care much about the distinction between genuine and mere instrumental egalitarianism, and they are happy to form alliances with anyone pressing for a reduction of objectionable inequality. For an account of the diversity of good reasons to care about equality and inequality, not all of them genuinely egalitarian, see Thomas Scanlon, *The Difficulty of Tolerance: Essays in Political Philosophy* (Cambridge University Press 2003) ch 11; Martin O'Neill, 'What Should Egalitarians Believe?' (2008), 36 Philosophy & Public Affairs 119; and Martin O'Neill, 'Constructing a Contractualist Egalitarianism: Equality after Scanlon' (2013), 10 Journal of Moral Philosophy 429.

Christian Hiebaum, *Distributions, Relations, and Justifications: Mixing Flavours of Egalitarianism* In: *Constitutionalism Justified: Rainer Forst in Discourse.* Edited by: Ester Herlin-Karnell and Matthias Klatt, Oxford University Press (2020), © Ester Herlin-Karnell and Matthias Klatt.
DOI: 10.1093/oso/9780190889050.003.0004

good, but I believe it is also relevant to the *legal* analysis of basic rights and to debates in jurisprudence about the principle of proportionality, its content and its grounding.

In political theory, it has become common to distinguish two paradigms of egalitarianism: distributive and social egalitarianism. Section II provides a rough reconstruction of those two paradigms and their respective strengths and weaknesses. Recently, social egalitarianism has got explicit support from discourse ethics, notably from Rainer Forst, who claims that 'the first question of justice [is] the question of the justifiability of social relations and, correspondingly, how much "justification power" individuals or groups have in a political context.'[2] In Section III of this chapter, I offer some doubts as to whether there is such a thing as the first question of justice, or, rather, whether justice *in its essence* consists of nothing else than 'the prevention of social domination' within 'political relations of rule' or 'social relations of cooperation in the production and distribution of goods—or, as is often the case, . . . relations of "negative cooperation"'.[3]

My main aim, however, is constructive and 'ecumenical'. In Section IV, I shall draw an egalitarian picture of justice with the notion of rights at its centre that blends the focuses on distributions, relations, and justifications.[4] Actually, rather than a picture, it's an *approach to drawing a picture of egalitarian relations consisting in, not merely resulting from, distributions of goods and burdens*. Such an approach, I think, not only allows for more intellectual exchange between political theory and jurisprudence, but should also throw some slightly brighter light on the relationship between equality and freedom (often, especially by non-egalitarians, viewed as antagonists, sometimes with freedom conceived of as a value in need of balancing even against social justice as such).[5]

[2] Rainer Forst, 'Two Pictures of Justice' in Rainer Forst, *Justice, Democracy and the Right to Justification: Rainer Forst in Dialogue* (Bloomsbury Academic 2014) 6.

[3] ibid 10f.

[4] It is a version of what Martin O'Neill refers to as non-intrinsic genuine egalitarianism (as opposed to mere instrumental egalitarianism and to egalitarianism that treats equality as a value independent of justice: Martin O'Neill, 'What Should Egalitarians Believe?' (n 1)).

[5] Though freedom and equality are often supposed to be fundamentally at odds, most people committed to democracy, or modernity in general, agree that every reasonable conception of social justice must include both values. To put it more precisely: in order to be reasonable, they say, every conception of social justice has to present itself as a *balance* of freedom and equality (and some other values such as solidarity). This is not implausible. Obviously, demands for economic liberty based on the value of social freedom often conflict with demands for more equality of outcome. Yet sometimes freedom is not even located within the realm of justice. It is rather treated as a side-constraint on, or as a value beside, justice. It is not only libertarians who think of freedom (implemented through legal rights) as something outside of social justice, in particular of distributive justice. Some egalitarians seem to hold a similar view.

II. Two Pictures of Equality

According to distributive egalitarianism, equality is essentially a property of distributions, or of distributional patterns. Distributive justice requires an equal distribution of something. Accordingly, the first and most important task of an egalitarian theory of distributive justice is to identify the goods that are to be distributed equally. Or rather, given that some differences and disparities between people are unavoidable or obviously not objectionable, not even on the grounds of distributive justice, we have to determine a common metric. So what is to be equalized? Several *equilisanda* have been proposed: (access to) welfare, opportunities, (access to) advantages, capabilities, resources, or something else.[6] Still, even such abstract good may be distributed unequally provided that such unequal distribution can 'be vindicated by some choice or fault or desert on the part of (some of) the relevant affected agents'.[7] That is, at least some kinds of luck are to be neutralized. This is the view now known as 'luck egalitarianism', and it is the epitome of distributive egalitarianism.

I cannot go into details here; after all we are just dealing with a *picture* of equality and egalitarian thought. But notice that luck egalitarianism relies heavily on a distinction between choice and (unchosen natural as well as social) circumstances. Thereby, despite having become quite an arcane and often boringly sophisticated academic exercise without much political force, it retains some connection to widespread intuitions about why, for example, racist and sexist discrimination is wrong. For being discriminated is commonly conceived of as being disadvantaged (by authorities, norms, and institutions) just because of an unchosen property. Luck egalitarianism also appears compatible with the belief that humans are free and responsible agents, and that individual efforts and achievements should make a difference to the distribution of goods, especially of material wealth.

Inequality resulting from mere luck may also be allowed by values different from distributive justice, values such as peace or aggregate welfare. That is,

[6] See GA Cohen, *On the Currency of Egalitarian Justice, and Other Essays in Political Philosophy* (Princeton University Press 2011) chapters 1 and 2; Richard Arneson, 'Luck Egalitarianism—A Primer' in Carl Knight and Zofia Stemplowska (eds), *Responsibility and Distributive Justice* (Oxford University Press 2011) 24; Richard Arneson, 'Justice Is Not Equality' (2008) 21 Ratio 371; John E Roemer, *Equality of Opportunity* (Harvard University Press 1998); Ronald Dworkin, *Sovereign Virtue: The Theory and Practice of Equality* (Harvard University Press 2000) chapters 1 and 2; Amartya Sen, *Inequality Reexamined* (Harvard University Press 2002) 12–30; Daniel M Hausman and Michael S McPherson, *Economic Analysis, Moral Philosophy, and Public Policy* (Cambridge University Press 2002) 135–59.

[7] GA Cohen, *Rescuing Justice and Equality* (Harvard University Press 2008) 7.

distributive egalitarians do not exclusively care about distributive equality. Most of them concede that it may well be all things considered best to accept inequality or simply impossible to achieve equality *hic et nunc*, but they insist that any amount of inequality means a loss of distributive justice, however well justified a trade-off with competing values may be. That is, in the words of Gerald Cohen, 'an unequal distribution whose inequality cannot be vindicated by some choice or fault or desert on the part of (some of) the relevant affected agents is unfair, and therefore, *pro tanto*, unjust, and nothing can remove that particular injustice'.[8] Hence such theories do not constitute all-encompassing conceptions of social justice, let alone political programs. They are best understood as explorations of 'the very nature of distributive justice, not [of] the different question as to what principles, to be influenced by distributive justice *but also by other things*, a society should adopt as its basic ones.'[9] Interestingly, we do not find much in luck-egalitarian writings about what raises the question of distributive justice and equality in the first place.[10] Luck-egalitarian theories more or less simply start with the assumption that, for whatever reason, something is to be distributed among potential recipients.

In that respect, distributive egalitarianism differs from theories of social justice, such as Rawls's,[11] that are, according to the prevailing interpretation, primarily (and explicitly) distributive as well as equality-oriented without, however, assuming the equal distribution of a single good to *define* equality. Indeed, Rawls does not draw a distributive picture of equality itself. He conceives of equality as the result of the distribution of a plurality of (primary) goods satisfying certain criteria or fulfilling certain principles, thus aiming at a distribution that persons who mutually recognize each other as free and equal within a system of cooperation can agree to. To distributive egalitarians, Rawls's theory, despite its insistence on equal liberty rights (including their fair value to the members of society) and fair equality of opportunities, does not qualify as a proper egalitarian theory at all, but should rather be viewed as an instance of

[8] ibid.

[9] ibid 301. For example, Cohen was not just an egalitarian; he identified himself as a *socialist* characterizing (his) socialism as being based upon two, as he thought, often competing principles: (distributive) equality and community: GA Cohen, *Why Not Socialism?* (Princeton University Press 2009).

[10] What we do find, however, are thought experiments such as the case of a divided world where two populations exist entirely independent of each other at different levels of welfare. This is supposed to elucidate the distinction between 'telic egalitarianism' and 'deontic egalitarianism' within the distributive paradigm. For in contrast to 'deontic egalitarians', who believe we should aim for equality for reasons of justice and fairness, 'telic egalitarians' are characterized as assuming that 'it is in itself bad if there are or have been, even in unrelated communities, and in different centuries, people who are not equally well off.' Derek Parfit, 'Equality or Priority?' in Matthew Clayton and Andrew Williams (eds), *The Ideal of Equality* (Palgrave MacMillan 2002) 88.

[11] John Rawls, *A Theory of Justice* (Harvard University Press 1971).

'prioritarianism'. For the difference principle that applies particularly to the distribution of income and wealth and requires, roughly, the maximum for the least advantaged 'is concerned with how people fare, but *not* with how they fare relative to each other'.[12]

In contrast to distributive egalitarianism, social egalitarianism is primarily concerned with equality as freedom from oppression and dominance, as equal standing and status. It takes aim at 'different types of social hierarchy, including slavery, serfdom, debt patronage, feudalism . . . oligarchy, caste and class inequality, racism, patriarchy, colonialism, and stigmatization based on sexuality, disability, and bodily appearance'.[13] Among the most important questions guiding social-egalitarian research and reflection are the following: What exactly constitutes egalitarian relationships not only on the personal but also on the societal level? What precisely is the role of social equality in evaluating institutions and actions and in designing decision-making procedures? Which set of principles of distribution, retribution, restitution, and other treatments of human beings are compatible with, or conducive to, social equality? Which principles are egalitarian *as such*, that is, just in virtue of their content, however, is not an issue social egalitarians are much interested in. Whether a principle is an egalitarian principle, they maintain, cannot be determined by analyzing the principle as an isolated ideational entity, but only by linking the principle to particular goods and distributional social contexts (one of them being the basic structure of society as a whole). And in order to justify deviations from distributive equality, social egalitarians often refer to values luck egalitarians believe to be different from equality. As I said, so do luck egalitarians themselves, but social egalitarians do not think of such reasoning as compromising. That is, to some extent, they incorporate other values than distributive equality into their egalitarian framework, eg by saying that equal social standing *requires* liberties, a certain amount of solidarity, and the protection of legitimate expectations. They take equality to be a 'complex ideal whose distinctively egalitarian aspects cannot be identified,

[12] Larry S Temkin, *Inequality* (Oxford University Press 1993) 246. Notice that 'relative' here refers to a comparison of how people fare, and not exactly to a social relationship between people.

[13] Elizabeth S Anderson, 'Equality' in David M Estlund (ed), *The Oxford Handbook of Political Philosophy* (Oxford University Press 2012) 40. See also Elizabeth S Anderson, 'What Is the Point of Equality?' (1999), 109 Ethics 287; Carina Fourie, Fabian Schuppert, and Ivo Wallimann-Helmer (eds), *Social Equality: On What It Means to Be Equals* (Oxford University Press 2015); Timothy Hinton, 'Must Egalitarians Choose between Fairness and Respect?' (2001), 30 Philosophy & Public Affairs 72; Samuel Scheffler, 'What Is Egalitarianism?' (2003), 31 Philosophy & Public Affairs 5; Michael Walzer, *Spheres of Justice: A Defense of Pluralism and Equality* (Basic Books 1983); Jonathan Wolff, 'Fairness, Respect, and the Egalitarian Ethos' (1998), 27 Philosophy & Public Affairs 97; Jonathan Wolff, 'Fairness, Respect and the Egalitarian Ethos Revisited' (2010), 14 The Journal of Ethics 335; Iris M Young, *Justice and the Politics of Difference* (Princeton University Press 1990).

nor their appeal appreciated, independently of their connections with other values, such as reciprocity and respect, that also help to define the ideal'.[14] By linking equality to such values and principles, social egalitarians, I believe, give us a clearer sense of the political urgency of concerns about inequality.

However, this asset of social egalitarianism comes with a price. While distributive egalitarians mainly disagree about the *equilisandum* and how to draw the exact line between choice and circumstances, the scope of disagreement among social egalitarians seems broader. Not only is there philosophical disagreement of a more conceptual type, there is another level at which views may diverge. Questions such as those mentioned above can hardly be tackled without an account of (modern) society and its hierarchies, and such accounts are notoriously as controversial as anything can be. For example, many theorists of justice, with quite a few social egalitarians among them, think that Rawls's view of society as a system of cooperation and of cooperation as the primary trigger of concerns for justice, though far from completely wrong or useless, is insufficient. It does not properly account for other types of community, such as communities of mere possession and of solidarity, which, however, would demand for slightly different or further principles of distribution.[15] Or take as another example, closer to current political controversies, the debate about multiculturalism. It is now a commonplace that leftist social thought all too long ignored the fact that there are dimensions of social life that cannot be treated as mere epiphenomena of the division of classes. One such dimension is often supposed to be culture. Though most political thinkers and social scientists agree that, in modern society, no social sphere is in principle more basic than all the others, there is still some debate about whether culture constitutes such a sphere, whether 'culture' is an analytically useful concept, what 'cultural equality' means, how cultural identity relates to other aspects of individual identity, and, finally, whether or under what conditions collective rights to cultural difference should rank high on the egalitarian agenda.[16]

As a framework for reasoning about justice, social egalitarianism is more comprehensive than distributive egalitarianism in that it is not just concerned with distributive justice but also with transactional justice, political justice,

[14] Samuel Scheffler, 'The Practice of Equality' in Carina Fourie, Fabian Schuppert and Ivo Wallimann-Helmer (eds), *Social Equality: On What It Means to Be Equals* (Oxford University Press 2015) 41.

[15] Peter Koller, 'Economic Distributive Justice' in Sonja Puntscher Riekmann, Alexander Somek, and Doris Wydra (eds), *Is There a European Common Good?* (Nomos 2013) 70–72; Charles Taylor, 'The Nature and Scope of Distributive Justice' in Charles Taylor, *Philosophical Papers*, vol 2 (Cambridge University Press 1985).

[16] Brian Barry, *Culture and Equality: An Egalitarian Critique of Multiculturalism* (Polity Press 2001); Will Kymlicka, *Multicultural Citizenship: A Liberal Theory of Minority Rights* (Clarendon Press 1995).

and corrective justice. But with regard to distributive justice, one should avoid exaggerating the difference between distributive and social egalitarianism. It's not that social egalitarians care much less about distribution than distributive egalitarians. They may even accept that in some contexts justice has a lot to do with neutralizing luck in distribution, but they do not aim at determining a cardinal good whose equal, or 'ambition-sensitive'/'endowment-insensitive',[17] distribution defines equality. And egalitarians of both varieties face the popular levelling down objection, which says that merely bringing someone from a higher to a lower level of welfare or endowment with resources cannot improve a situation in terms of justice.[18] This objection is a corollary of the trickle-down idea, and it's usually raised against distributive egalitarianism, but it also applies to the social egalitarianism.[19] Yet, social egalitarians can often avoid the challenge by pointing out that their account of equality is sufficiently complex to not only allow but even demand for economic inequality that distributive egalitarians could not tolerate without resorting to values different from equality. In any case, egalitarians of both types should stick to the claim (and come up with some arguments for it) that levelling down may well improve a situation in terms of justice precisely by reducing inequality. They should not treat the objection as always being based on a misunderstanding of egalitarianism. If they give up that claim they sacrifice too much of what is distinctive of genuine, ie non-instrumental, egalitarianism of whatever variety.[20]

In contrast to distributive egalitarians, social egalitarians see the significance of distributions as deriving from the broader and more basic ideal of equal social standing and status. Sometimes this ideal is even construed as transcending justice;[21] more often, however, it is located right at the centre of social justice, as its core. Most importantly, social egalitarians hold that, as far as social equality is appropriately described as a matter of distribution, it is *a variety of social goods* the distribution of which amounts to relations of equality or inequality.

What is more, much depends not only on distributions themselves but also on the *justifications of distributions*. In this vein Scheffler speaks of an 'egalitarian deliberative constraint', meaning 'that each of our equally important interests constrains our joint decisions to the same extent . . . It is a distinctively egalitarian element in the complex ideal of an egalitarian relationship.'[22] Whatever

[17] Dworkin (n 6) 89f.

[18] Temkin (n 12) ch 9.

[19] As a matter of fact, even sufficientarians may face it if they consider not just absolute but also relative poverty to be a problem of justice.

[20] To be sure, in a political world more susceptible to empirical facts egalitarians would seldom need to defend their policies against the levelling down objection in philosophical terms. For most of the time fears of levelling down, just like trickle-down hopes, are empirically groundless.

[21] David Miller, 'Equality and Justice' (1997), 10 Ratio 222.

[22] Scheffler, 'The Practice of Equality' (n 14) 25.

follows from such constraint for cases where we lack knowledge of each other's needs and preferences, as it is usually the case in non-personal, largely anonymous relationships at the societal level, it certainly means something for the design of decision-making processes and the provision of what people need for meaningful participation in politics. Thus it is assumed that there is a connection between substantially democratic politics and social equality that goes deeper than the striking relation of mutual reinforcement between de-democratization and increasing economic inequality.[23] Rainer Forst goes even further than most social egalitarians and claims that justification, or rather *the right to justification* constitutes the *foundation* of justice, not just one important element among others.

III. Justice and the Right to Justification

Though largely in agreement with social egalitarians like Anderson, Scheffler, or O'Neill, Forst is not content with analyzing justice and equality as complex ideals owing their content and appeal to a plurality of interrelated values. As he ironically confesses at the beginning of his reply to Simon Caney's criticisms, he's more a Harvard- than an Oxford-style thinker:

> I am reminded of [Caney's] teacher Jerry Cohen's remark about the difference between 'Harvard people' and 'Oxford people': according to Cohen, the former seek to unify the plurality of values and principles by way of spurious constructivist methods, while the latter have more tolerance for moral pluralism and possible tensions . . . I am not sure about this characterization and shall not comment upon it, except for saying that seen in this light . . . a 'Frankfurt man' like me shares enough Kantian constructivism to find himself on the Harvard side.[24]

Accordingly, Forst aims for a single source of justice and believes to have found it in the right to justification.[25] What was once developed as the core of a discourse-ethical conception of tolerance as a political virtue,[26] is now assumed to ground *justice*—actually, not only justice but morality as a whole. As everybody

[23] See also Anderson, 'What Is the Point of Equality?' (n 13); O'Neill, 'Constructing a Contractualist Egalitarianism' (n 1). For empirical data, see Martin Gilens, *Affluence and Influence: Economic Inequality and Political Power in America* (Princeton University Press 2012).

[24] Forst, 'Two Pictures of Justice' (n 2) 205f.

[25] Rainer Forst, *The Right to Justification: Elements of a Constructivist Theory of Justice* (Jeffrey Flynn tr, Columbia University Press 2011); Forst, 'Two Pictures of Justice' (n 2).

[26] Rainer Forst, *Toleration in Conflict: Past and Present* (Ciaran Cronin tr, Cambridge University Press 2013).

familiar with Forst's writings and the intellectual tradition out of which he comes can imagine, it's quite a challenge to give a fully adequate account of this theory within a few pages. It's certainly too much of a challenge for me. So I won't even try but restrict myself to the central claims and arguments, and to problems that, as far as I can see, are rarely brought up.

Though somewhat critical of Forst's positive account of social justice, I largely subscribe to his criticism of the narrow distributive paradigm of justice.[27] In fact, I share more of Forst's objections than Caney.[28] I think, for example, that Forst's complaint about the much too strong focus of distributive egalitarians on *recipients* of goods (as opposed to *producers*) is not actually based on an unfair caricature of luck egalitarianism. Such strong focus does exist. It is reflected, among other things, by the centrality in luck-egalitarian reasoning of the notion of compensation (for disadvantages caused by bad luck). However, as will become clear in this section and in the following, I remain sceptical of Forst's claim that 'justified claims . . . can be arrived at only through discourse in the context of corresponding procedures of justification in which . . . all can in principle participate as free and equal individuals'.[29]

But now let's take a look at Forst's discourse theory of social justice. This is it in a nutshell:

> The fundamental impulse that runs counter to injustice is not primarily that of wanting to have or have more of something, but that of wanting to no longer be oppressed, harassed, or have one's claims and *basic right to justification* ignored. This right expresses the demand that there be no political or social relations of governance that cannot be adequately justified to those affected by them. In whatever specific or 'thick,' situated language this indignation—this protest—is also expressed, at its core it always goes back to the right not to be subjected to laws, structures, or institutions that are 'groundless,' that is, that are regarded as an expression of power or rule without sufficient legitimation. The demand for justice is an emancipatory demand, which is described with terms like fairness, reciprocity, symmetry, equality, or balance; putting it reflexively, its basis is the claim to be respected as an agent of justification, that is, in one's dignity as a being who can ask for and give justifications.[30]

[27] Forst, 'Two Pictures of Justice' (n 2) 4f.

[28] Simon Caney, 'Justice and the Basic Right to Justification' in Rainer Forst, *Justice, Democracy and the Right to Justification: Rainer Forst in Dialogue* (Bloomsbury Academic 2014).

[29] Forst, 'Two Pictures of Justice' (n 2) 5.

[30] Rainer Forst, 'Introduction: The Foundation of Justice' in Rainer Forst, *The Right to Justification: Elements of a Constructivist Theory of Justice* (Jeffrey Flynn tr, Columbia University Press 2011) 2.

As to the form of justificatory reasons:

> This basic right to justification is based on the *recursive* general principle that every norm that is to legitimize the use of force (or, more broadly speaking, a morally relevant interference with other's actions) claims to be reciprocally and generally valid and therefore needs to be justifiable by reciprocally and generally non-rejectable reasons. *Reciprocity* here means that neither party makes any claim to certain rights or resources that are denied to others (reciprocity of content) and that neither party projects its own reasons (values, interests, needs) onto others in arguing for its claims (reciprocity of reasons). One must be willing to argue for basic norms that are to be reciprocally and generally valid and binding with reasons that are not based on contested 'higher' truths or conceptions of the good that can reasonably be questioned and rejected. *Generality*, then, means that the reasons for such norms need to be shareable among all persons affected, not just the dominant parties.[31]

These are interesting claims. Instead of going into all the details here, I shall pick out two points that seem most relevant to me.

There are certainly many cases of injustice that may be described as arbitrary exercise of power. And often the arbitrary exercise of power is nothing else than a failure to provide adequate reasons that can be accepted or not reasonably rejected by those affected. Often, though apparently not always—for among the affected may be human beings who are simply not capable of asking for and giving justifications. But I'll skip this problem (which Forst may well be able to handle somehow) as well as the issue of who exactly the bearers of a basic right to justification are when they are supposed to be those 'affected by actions and norms in morally relevant ways',[32] that are 'concretely affected'[33] or 'possibly affected',[34] that are finding themselves in 'a context of force and domination'[35] or are 'subjected to laws, structures, or institutions'.[36] Instead, I want to raise

[31] Rainer Forst, '"To Tolerate Means to Insult": Toleration, Recognition, and Emancipation' in Rainer Forst, *Justification and Critique: Towards a Critical Theory of Politics* (Ciaran Cronin tr, Polity Press 2013) 140.

[32] Rainer Forst, 'The Basic Right to Justification: Toward a Constructivist Conception of Human Rights' in Rainer Forst, *The Right to Justification: Elements of a Constructivist Theory of Justice* (Jeffrey Flynn tr, Columbia University Press 2011) 214.

[33] Rainer Forst, 'Practical Reason and Justifying Reasons: On the Foundation of Morality' in Rainer Forst, *The Right to Justification: Elements of a Constructivist Theory of Justice* (Jeffrey Flynn tr, Columbia University Press 2011) 19.

[34] ibid 20.

[35] Rainer Forst, 'Constructions of Transnational Justice: Comparing John Rawls's *The Law of Peoples* and Otfried Höffe's *Democracy in the Age of Globalisation*' in Rainer Forst, *The Right to Justification: Elements of a Constructivist Theory of Justice* (Jeffrey Flynn tr, Columbia University Press 2011) 234.

[36] Forst, 'Introduction: The Foundation of Justice' (n 30) 2.

another question. Who is supposed to be the *addressee* of such a right when no structure, institution, or procedure of justification exists, or, rather, when it is precisely the existing social structure that prevents powerful actors from giving the justifications we are looking for, ie reasons that *justify the structure as such*? Notice that the 'right to justification is not just the right to political participation and representation but more fundamentally a right to be a justificatory equal in all relevant "spheres" of justice'.[37] It is 'a *veto right* against basic norms, arrangements, or structures that cannot be justified reciprocally and generally to him or her',[38] thus arguably more than just another name for strong moral reasons to object to inegalitarian institutional arrangements and to fight for reform. The assumption of a basic right to justification seems to go beyond the well-known and widely shared idea that a just social order is an order in which the members of society can live as free and equal. At least, we should understand Forst's proposal as a very special interpretation or specification of that idea. Otherwise it would be far less interesting.

Now, imagine a social state, not so different from today's global society, in which there is just a complex set of partly overlapping, partly competing authorities that provides for some sort of market system, thereby serving some and disadvantaging others. In short, there is simply no single established democratic authority capable of making things significantly better in terms of justice; and due to serious collective action problems it's unlikely that the powerful and advantaged develop shared agency and become a unified actor who may offer justifications. Add to this the fact that many disadvantaged themselves support different authorities and things look even murkier.[39]

[37] Rainer Forst, 'Justifying Justification: A Reply to My Critics' in Rainer Forst, *Justice, Democracy and the Right to Justification: Rainer Forst in Dialogue* (Bloomsbury Academic 2014) 210.

[38] Rainer Forst, 'Introduction: On the Idea of a Critique of Relations of Justification' in Rainer Forst, *Justification and Critique: Towards a Critical Theory of Politics* (Ciaran Cronin tr, Polity Press 2013) 6.

[39] Notice that various anti-cosmopolitans in the theory of justice such as Thomas Nagel, 'The Problem of Global Justice' (2005), 33 Philosophy & Public Affairs 113; or David Heyd, 'Justice and Solidarity: The Contractarian Case against Global Justice' (2007), 38 Journal of Social Philosophy 112, who conclude from the fact that we lack appropriate political institutions on the global level that principles of social justice cannot apply to the sphere beyond the nation state, rely on assumptions that come pretty close to Forst's idea of a basic right to justification as the foundation of justice. But unlike Forst, they believe that as long as there are no institutions which bind people together within a polity, providing for adequate decision-making and making reasonably reliable and impartial law-enforcement possible, there is strictly nothing to implement that would reach beyond international justice, that is, justice between states. That is, they attribute to the global political structure, to the system of sovereign states, the status of a strong *normative* constraint defining the proper object of any discourse on social justice. Cosmopolitans such as Forst, in contrast, take the lack of proper political institutions just as something which, together with self-interest, tribal passions, and empirical misapprehension, plausibly *explains* the widespread reluctance to seriously engage in reflection about, and politics of, global justice. But it does little to *justify* the lack of concern. They hold that the lack of such institutions is more a *problem* than proof that standards of justice (beyond the most

To be sure, it is not an implausible thought that there is a legitimate and weighty *interest* in the establishment of democratic political institutions conducive to inclusive deliberation and reasonable justification. Moreover, political struggles typically involve claims to justification against whoever acts as an opponent in a particular context of justice. But can such claims amount to a genuine individual right to a democratic structure of justification? I doubt it, at least, if the basic right to justification as a veto right against norms and structures is to be, as Forst maintains, different from a right 'to participation in a practice of establishing proper procedures and institutions of justification.'[40] It's easy to imagine addressees and violations of such a moral right to participation. It is also much easier to determine those who are responsible for fulfilling certain human rights presumably slightly less basic than the right to justification, such as the right to freedom from poverty—even if some questions about the precise allocation and ranking as well as the content of responsibilities corresponding to this right remain open and controversial.[41]

From the view that injustice essentially amounts to a violation of a right to justification it follows that the identification of an injustice implies an attribution of responsibility: 'A judgment of injustice . . . also locates the responsibilities for that situation. A context of justice is then a concrete context of justification.'[42] This claim, I believe, lets too many of the unjustly advantaged off the hook, namely, those who benefit from injustice without being individually responsible for it in any meaningful sense. Locating concrete responsibilities for injustices is often more difficult than identifying injustices. Hence the requirement of such an attribution may even do harm to our sense that there is an injustice in the first place, an injustice to be removed by political action

obvious rules of justice between states) do not apply. To them it seems that in such a case justice actually *requires* a reform of political institutions and structures of authority; see also Forst, 'Justifying Justification: A Reply to My Critics' (n 37) 201. And I think they are right, though I suspect that, given the conditions for the functioning of democracy, some trade-offs between justice and democracy will prove inevitable.

[40] Forst, 'Justifying Justification: A Reply to My Critics' (n 37) 205.

[41] See Thomas W Pogge (ed), *Freedom from Poverty as a Human Right: Who Owes What to the Very Poor?* (Oxford University Press 2007).

[42] Rainer Forst, 'Toward a Critical Theory of Transnational Justice' in Rainer Forst, *The Right to Justification: Elements of a Constructivist Theory of Justice* (Jeffrey Flynn tr, Columbia University Press 2011) 257. In the German version, it reads 'konkrete Verantwortlichkeiten' ('concrete responsibilities'): Rainer Forst, 'Zu einer kritischen Theorie transnationaler Gerechtigkeit' in Rainer Forst, *Das Recht auf Rechtfertigung: Elemente einer konstruktivistischen Theorie der Gerechtigkeit* (Suhrkamp 2007) 367.

one of whose aims may well be to establish appropriate procedures of collective decision-making.[43]

One might object that concerns such as these rest on a misunderstanding of the special nature of the right to justification as the most basic right people have. After all, the right to justification is not 'a specific, intersubjectively established and recognized human right, but rather the basis of a justification of concrete rights itself'.[44] It is the right we need to assume in order to make sense of all the other, less basic, rights of justificatory beings:

> The moral basis for human rights . . . is the respect for the human person as an autonomous agent who possesses a right to justification, that is, a right to be recognized as an agent who can demand acceptable reasons for any action that claims to be morally justified and for any social or political structure or law that claims to be binding upon him or her. Human rights secure the equal standing of persons in the political and social world, based on a fundamental moral demand of respect.[45]

Now, it seems plausible that a right to justification is implied by human rights. It also makes sense that the right to justification is the 'right to be recognized as an agent who can demand acceptable reasons for any action that claims to be morally justified.' I'm less sure about the claim that it provides the sole or most fundamental basis for human rights (if that's the claim). And I have serious trouble with the idea of a right to 'demand acceptable reasons . . . for any social and political structure or law that claims to be binding'.[46] Again, demand from whom? Actually, it is the trope of a *structure* (not: persons, authorities, or decision-makers) *making claims* that lies at the heart of what I perceive as a theoretical problem. Normally, this way of talking does not create any problems. But here it suggests a right to a just social order one possesses against the actually existing order as such, thus perhaps against no one in particular. This claim is not totally unintelligible as we could easily translate it back into more traditional language. But such translation would reduce the right to justification to

[43] Interestingly, in order to elucidate the main point of his theory, Forst himself develops the thought experiment of a poor, exploited worker who gets the opportunity of bringing her claims of justice before a court that is capable of implementing global distributive justice: Forst, 'Constructions of Transnational Justice' (n 35). That is, he suggests imagining an already existing full-fledged procedure with clearly identified parties and a sufficiently powerful authority.

[44] Forst, 'The Basic Right to Justification' (n 32) 210.

[45] Rainer Forst, 'The Justification of Human Rights and the Basic Right to Justification: A Reflexive Approach' (2010), 120 Ethics 711, 719.

[46] See also Forst, '"To Tolerate Means to Insult"' (n 31) 140.

an aspirational idea and Forstian criticism of modern society to the familiar claim that the system is unjust in terms of decision-making processes as well as in terms of distributive results. The point is not that no basic structure could ever be justified by reasons fulfilling Forst's criteria of reciprocity and generality but rather that it is highly contingent whether there is anybody who *owes* the other ones reasons that not only justify his or her use of authority but also *the basic structure* that lends him or her authority—too contingent for a right that is supposed to ground social justice.

This might look like nitpicking. So let's not harp on about the *right* to justification. Forst is right, one might say, in reminding us that justice is something to be made, and we make justice by justifying. As a matter of fact, Forst often speaks of a 'principle of justification'. But then, Forst's political justification theory of justice often comes across as a theory of legitimacy rather than as a theory of justice. In fact, it also seems more promising as a theory of legitimacy than as a theory of justice. Caney has made the point well:

> Let us distinguish between the justification required for *political legitimacy* (political justification) and the justification required for a view to be *philosophically correct* (philosophical justification). Now the claim that political legitimacy-justification might require a discursive justification through political 'procedures of justification' seems plausible (though not uncontroversial). However, it does not follow from this that my views on justice are only (philosophically) sound and correct if they have gone through the same political process. . . . Distributive justice is one thing and political legitimacy is another and, though I think (with Forst) that the second entails some kind of socio-economic preconditions, that does not undermine the fundamental point that they are conceptually distinct (and moreover they might pull us in different directions).[47]

Indeed, that *legitimacy* (in the normative, not just empirical sense) should be derived primarily or even exclusively from procedures of justification under favourable socio-economic preconditions does not seem outlandish.[48] Much less plausible is the claim that universal acceptance of justifications under favourable preconditions or acceptance of justifications for the procedures of justification and decision-making guarantees or even constitutes *justice*, especially given that Forst is not talking about some 'counterfactual assent but assent based on institutionalized justification procedures'.[49] But Forst has a response. He distinguishes

[47] Caney (n 28) 256f.
[48] Actually, it may be too strong as a theory of (democratic) legitimacy.
[49] Forst, 'Two Pictures of Justice' (n 2) 20f.

between fundamental (minimal) and full (maximal) justice, rather than between legitimacy and justice:

> Whereas the task of fundamental justice is to construct a *basic structure of justification*, the task of full justice is to construct a *justified basic structure*. The former is necessary in order to pursue the latter, that is, a 'putting-into-effect' of justification through constructive, discursive democratic procedures in which 'justificatory power' is distributed as evenly as possible among the citizens. This calls for certain rights and institutions and a multiplicity of means and specific capabilities and information, including real opportunities to intervene and exercise control within the basic structure—hence, not a 'minimalist' structure, yet one justified in material terms solely on the basis of the principle of justification. The question of what is included in this minimum must be legitimized and assessed in accordance with the criteria of reciprocity and generality.[50]

What this makes clear is that there is an element of counterfactuality or idealization in Forst's theory of assent-based justice, even of fundamental (minimal) justice. This *per se*, to be sure, is not a defect. There is no conception of justice without idealization. But it raises again the question of what Forst's theory adds to other conceptions, apart from what appears to be an overly 'rationalist conception of human nature'.[51] For the other—distributive—conceptions of justice (whether resourcist, welfarist, or capabilities-oriented) can be described as nothing else than (controversial) normative explications of what reciprocity and generality amount to in this or that context (with regard to norms yielding and justifying this or that distribution). We can agree (because it's an analytical truth) that injustice is a state of affairs not properly justified in terms of justice. But non-Forstians deny that the injustice of unjust states of affairs always ultimately lies in the fact that no proper justification *has been given*.

As to Forst's account of the distinction between fundamental and full justice, I'm not so sure whether a 'basic structure of justification' should be considered strictly necessary *in order to pursue* full justice, if a basic structure of justification is supposed to consist of 'discursive democratic procedures'. Or rather, changing the basic structure of justification may well be necessary to achieve full justice, but it is not necessarily the first priority on the agenda of a politics of social justice. Thus I would rather treat such procedures as one (essential) element of a just basic structure among others. As a matter of fact,

50 ibid 23.
51 Caney (n 28) 149.

many of today's transnational struggles for economic justice, climate justice, etc. take place outside of democratic procedures and are not driven by the hope for transnational democracy either (if by 'democracy' we understand certain procedures of *collective decision-making*, not just a loose set of forums of deliberation, protests, and other happenings with lots of talking). Though often much is won by creating a pressure for the opponent to come up with justifications beyond the usual rhetoric and 'bullshit',[52] *structures* of justification typically alter as a by-product, following changes of the distribution of certain goods and of patterns of recognition. And there are times (for example, times of right-wing populist upheaval against technocracy and post-democracy) when making political decision-making more responsive to public discourse bears a significant risk of much more maldistribution and misrecognition, and thus of further deteriorating the quality of political debate and decision-making, at least in the short term.

What I have said so far, however, is not meant to deny that egalitarian relations between people are to significant degree justificatory relations. I also agree that structures of justification are structures of power and thus should be of great concern to anybody who deals with social justice, whether theoretically or more practically as a political actor. At least, such 'materialist' view of structures of justification works against the illusion that we could neatly separate issues of production and distribution, exemplified by the motto: 'Let a pretty free market take care of the creation of wealth, and let us correct its distribution afterwards!' For afterwards (whenever that is) economic inequalities may have constituted political power structures that are not conducive to redistribution anymore. Or the motto may, in a sense, undermine itself by giving rise to the further illusion of a justificatory *asymmetry* between 'free markets' and redistributive institutions, ie the idea that the former are more natural, and thus less in need of justification, than the latter.

So perhaps the differences between Forst's and my view of justice and equality boil down to little else than the fact that I'm less of a 'Harvard man' or 'Frankfurt man' than Forst. But I'm not really an 'Oxford man' either. The following should place me somewhere in-between by sketching a way of how to bring the distributive picture and the relational picture of equality closer to each other. I think the notion of (basic and not-so-basic) rights provides a useful conceptual link.

[52] Harry G Frankfurt, *On Bullshit* (Princeton University Press 2005).

IV. Rights, Distributable Goods, Relationships, and Reasons

Relational accounts of justice and equality in general and Forst's theory in particular owe a good part of their appeal to examples from interpersonal relationships and small groups. There is nothing wrong with that, provided they also have something to offer for the normative analysis of larger institutions and de-localized structures of modern society. But at first glance, the distributional language seems to be better suited to complex mass societies consisting of people who stand in abstract relations and do not know each other. It draws less heavily on concepts we use when we deal with personal interactions. Then again, a lot of reasoning within distributive egalitarianism (as well as anti-egalitarian strains of thought) also shows a strong focus on micro-contexts and begs the question of how to get from there to the level of social justice, the level of basic institutions, without major conceptual amendments.

In the following I want to start with distributions and show that many distributional concerns can be described as inherently relational rather than as deriving from relational issues. In turn, many relational concerns can be given a fully adequate distributional characterization. Actually, often a distributional account is the best account available. 'Often' but not always, because social equality and justice is not just about distribution but also includes norms of transactional justice, corrective justice, and political justice.[53] However, the adequacy of these latter norms and their applications partly depends on the justice of the distribution of goods and burdens in the background. In fact, there is an asymmetry: the other forms of justice depend on distributive justice to a larger extent than the latter depends on them. Thus it seems appropriate to think of distributive justice as the core of social justice.[54] As this claim is not particularly controversial among egalitarians I do not need to provide a thorough argument for it here. Even relational egalitarians can accept it. As I said above (in Section II), they just derive the significance of distributions from the ideal of equal social status. What I argue now is that it's extremely difficult to give a non-distributional account of the ideal itself, and it's unnecessary, too.

Let us take a closer look at what is usually distributed under what conditions. Though we habitually speak of goods and burdens to be distributed, we tend to

[53] See Koller, 'Economic Distributive Justice' (n 15) 66.

[54] Peter Koller, 'Recht und soziale Verteilungsgerechtigkeit in soziologischer und ethischer Perspektive' in Gerhard Baumgartner and others (eds), *Verteilungsgerechtigkeit im Recht* (Verlag Österreich 2017).

not distribute the goods themselves but rights to those goods and corresponding duties.[55] After all, normally we do not distribute goods among different people who are permanently present and consume their share immediately; distributional decisions are supposed to be binding for a longer period of time, not just for the time it takes to consume the good. And when we talk about the distribution of income and wealth we obviously do not stand around a pile of money and other material goods and divide it among us.

This is what some social egalitarians aiming at a radical paradigm shift do not accept, for example Iris Young (approvingly quoted by Jürgen Habermas[56]): 'What does distributing a right mean? One may talk about having a right to a distributive share of material things, resources, or income. But in such cases it is the good that is distributed, not the right . . . Rights are not fruitfully conceived as possessions.'[57] But if rights can be transferred and exchanged, why can't they be distributed? The answer might be: 'Because they often do not exist before distribution, ie because it's precisely the distribution of goods that creates rights to those goods'. But then what do we distribute if a good we share (for example, a car or a computer) cannot be divided without destruction? This is another reason why distribution of goods usually means distribution of rights. If rights could not be 'fruitfully conceived as possessions' then very large parts of legal and economic discourse would have no point.

However, we talk about the goods rights *refer to* when dealing with the question of how (through which mechanism) the rights should be distributed and which principles apply, because much depends on the nature and the value of those goods.[58] And we talk about the goods, and the opportunities to achieve the goods, rights refer to when determining whether there is anything to be distributed in the first place, ie whether we *share* certain goods and burdens as a community of possession, cooperation, and/or solidarity. Actually, many political debates are about whether we constitute such a community and who belongs to it rather than about the justice of the distribution of shares in the form of rights and duties. It's about creating a sense of commonality, one of the major aims of egalitarians being to disseminate the idea that, whatever our individual motivations, wealth is produced collectively or cooperatively; that individual actions cause negative externalities and thus problems that can only

[55] To be sure, we also allocate duties not (or, at least, not directly) corresponding to any right, such as duties to pay taxes or to protect the environment. Such duties impose limitations on, and thus contribute to the definition and specification of, our rights (to various liberties).

[56] Jürgen Habermas, *Between Facts and Norms: Contributions to a Discourse Theory of Law and Democracy* (William Rehg tr, MIT Press 1996) 419.

[57] Young (n 13) 25.

[58] Walzer (n 13).

be solved by collective action which, among other things, involve a distribution of burdens (for example, burdens associated with the reduction of greenhouse gas emissions). On the other hand, sometimes the disagreement between egalitarians and non- or anti-egalitarians is not about whether social goods such as liberties and opportunities or costs associated with them should be distributed but about what this is supposed to amount to in terms of allocation of specific rights and duties.

In principle, general as well as special rights constitute objects of distribution. Here the category 'general rights' includes human rights as well as perhaps not so basic rights held by the members of a polity or community, or by the people living in a jurisdiction in which the rights are supposed to exist. The latter include, among others, rights to social benefits and subsidies not clearly and directly derivable from human rights, and are often subject to certain conditions. Notice that such rights are general does not imply that they are necessarily equal or equally weighty rights (regardless of the persons of the right-holders, their wealth, their sex/gender, their ethnicity, their education, their age, etc.). In contrast to general rights, a special right is a right of a particular person. Hence my property rights, my titles to certain things, are special rights while the human right to enjoy one's possessions is a general right; freedom of contract is a general right of normal adults, contractual claims are special rights; there is a general freedom of contract (with gradations according to age and mental condition, and in earlier times also to sex/gender), and there is *my* freedom of contract; the right to spousal support is a right every married person has against his or her partner under certain conditions: if the conditions are fulfilled, I have a special right to spousal support against my wife.[59]

One might concede that some rights may be conceived as distributable goods but ask whether *basic* or *human* rights are among them. Well, at least basic *legal* rights seem to be collectively 'produced' and distributed. Today, typically, we only accept an equal distribution of such rights. And even if what can be properly described as being produced and distributed is not the part that is enjoyed by the right-holder and the duties of others most obviously implied by it (for the

[59] The terminology used here ('general'/'special rights') deviates from the terminology used in more refined analyses of the structure of rights, such as Peter Koller, 'Die Struktur von Rechten' in Georg Meggle (ed), *Philosophy of Mind, Practical Philosophy, Miscellanea* (De Gruyter 1997). Koller distinguishes, according to the right-holders, between universal and particular rights; according to the addressees, between general, general-specific, and special rights; and according to the content of rights (following Hohfeld), between claims, liberties, powers, and immunities. In contrast, I use the distinction between general and special rights as a distinction according to the right-holders. I'm not really happy with that, but I want to avoid any suggestion that a right which is not just the right of a particular person is necessarily a fundamental and equal human right.

right may be conceived as natural, pre-political, or pre-institutional), it is certainly those positive duties that are necessary for the rights to be implemented, protected, and promoted in a complex modern society. We share these duties and have to determine who has to contribute what and how much to the satisfaction of the interests underlying the right. For even if we believe the state to be the primary bearer of the corresponding duties, in addition to allocate the responsibilities among different states, we have to accept duties to financially and otherwise contribute to enabling the states to fulfil their duties with regard to basic rights. The provision of rights is not costless.[60] Not only positive rights but also negative rights raise questions of distribution, even more so if such rights imply duties to create and maintain, or contribute to, costly institutions facilitating the use of rights, let alone if we demand, as egalitarians do, the rights be of roughly equal value to their holders. At any rate, the argument of liberty as a political argument, though often used precisely to suppress concerns about maldistribution, is incomplete without a distributive component.

As Cohen has shown, this also holds for property rights and money, given that the right of interference implied by a property right can be viewed as a burden any addressee of the right has to bear:

> A property distribution just *is* . . . a distribution of rights of interference. If *A* owns *P* and *B* does not, then *A* may use *P* without interference and *B* will, standardly, suffer interference if he attempts to use *P*. *But money serves, in a variety of circumstances (and, notably, when A puts P up for rent or sale), to remove that latter interference. Therefore money confers freedom, rather than merely the ability to use it*, even if freedom is equated with absence of interference.[61]

One might object that, to the degree that economic activities are coordinated by market mechanisms, property rights are not actually distributed but simply exchanged or transferred, and that most of the rules constituting and regulating markets are not rules of distribution but rules of coordination and cooperation. Still, these rules have a distributional function; they provide for distributions, at least, indirectly.[62] After all, it makes perfect sense to speak of the distribution of income and wealth or of the cost of certain kinds of behaviour, and when discussing rules of coordination and cooperation we (should) also take distributional effects into account. Actually, some of these rules, far from just

[60] See Stephen Holmes and Cass R Sunstein, *The Cost of Rights: Why Liberty Depends on Taxes* (W.W. Norton & Company 2000).

[61] Cohen, *On the Currency of Egalitarian Justice* (n 6) 176.

[62] See Stefan Arnold, *Vertrag und Verteilung: Die Bedeutung der iustitia distributiva im Vertragsrecht* (Mohr Siebeck 2014).

regulating terms of exchange, quite directly distribute goods and burdens in the form of rights and duties within relationships that involve strong elements of a community. Just think of relations constituted by labor contracts, relations between employer and employee as well as between employees, collaborating in production. Rules of coordination and cooperation regulate production and, though often less 'recipient-oriented' than rules of secondary distribution (taxation rules and rules about transfers or subsidies), they determine the primary distribution.[63]

In any case, in order to have a distribution of goods, you don't need a central distributor who distributes the goods directly by norms of distribution.[64] By 'distribution' we do not only mean a process. More often we refer to a state.[65] One may say that general rights are directly distributed by a legislator or by way of the members of society recognizing each other as equally or unequally holding such rights, while special rights (again, most notably property rights) use to be distributed qua rules that govern the use of general rights. According to social egalitarianism, general rights, if they reflect fundamental human interests, are to be distributed quite equally *regardless of choice and luck*, or, if they are less fundamental, so that their being subjected to certain conditions does not amount to any discrimination; similarly, special rights may be distributed unequally within certain limits drawn by non-discriminatory principles. Prima facie non-discriminatory reasons for unequal distributions are: contributions, basic needs, and legitimate expectations.[66] For whatever we are precisely, 'each person [has] the right to be something other than an engine for the welfare of other people'.[67]

However, as should be clear from what has been said already, rights are not just goods in the most ordinary sense. Every moral or legal right, whether their content is a claim, a liberty, a power, or an immunity, constitutes a relation between individuals (or groups) as well as between individuals (or groups) and the

[63] Obviously, taxation also influences the primary distribution by creating as well as diminishing incentives and opportunities, for example, by making it pointless to bargain extremely high salaries. See Thomas Piketty, *Capital in the Twenty-First Century* (Arthur Goldhammer tr, The Belknap Press of Harvard University Press 2014) 509f.

[64] See Koller, 'Economic Distributive Justice' (n 15) 68, 72–73; Koller, 'Recht und soziale Verteilungsgerechtigkeit in soziologischer und ethischer Perspektive' (n 54).

[65] To avoid confusion, Jon Elster, *Local Justice: How Institutions Allocate Scarce Goods and Necessary Burdens* (Russell Sage Foundation 1992) 186, uses the term 'allocation' for the process of distribution and 'distribution' *only* for denoting a state.

[66] Koller, 'Economic Distributive Justice' (n 15) 68.

[67] Cohen, *Rescuing Justice and Equality* (n 7) 10. It's quite significant that Cohen continues by saying that 'we are not nothing but slaves to social justice'. ibid. Relational egalitarians certainly agree but would add that the concept of being a 'slave to social justice' is incoherent. Accordingly, the 'personal prerogatives' Cohen (following Scheffler) assumes are not just *external* limitations to equality. They are an essential element of any reasonable conception of (relational) equality.

larger community the formers belong to.[68] For holding a right means that all or particular others have a duty to behave or refrain from behaving towards you in a certain way. This holds for rights supposed to be general that directly and explicitly confer social status such as basic liberty rights, rights to political participation, or freedom of contract. And it equally holds for special rights such as property rights that impose duties of non-interference on every other person. Such rights also contribute to one's social status as an equal or an unequal by adding substance to general rights, ie by adding meaning and value. For example, the wealthier a person, the more valuable the right to protection of property (Article 1 of Protocol No. 1 to the Convention for the Protection of Human Rights and Fundamental Freedoms) is to him or her—which is not to say that there is a strict proportionality all the way down (it's quite clear that we have an interest in the protection not only of our own possessions but also of the property of other, wealthier people).

To be sure, social equality is not just a relation constituted by, or describable as, a certain distribution of rights and corresponding duties. Apart from the fact, already mentioned, that social justice is not just distributive justice, egalitarianism also has a 'cultural dimension'. Egalitarian social relationships require an ethos that goes beyond the acceptance of a few abstract principles of justice and habitual compliance with the rules and conventions allocating rights and duties in accordance with the principles. This ethos consists in a special sense of solidarity with the not so well-off, a certain reluctance (though, of course, not strict refusal) to stress individual responsibility in order to explain and justify considerable inequalities. As it were, the sense of egalitarian justice includes the virtue of 'not-too-sentimental compassion', that is, of a compassion that also tolerates the unpleasant traits of character sometimes displayed especially by those who live in a mean social environment without being able to present themselves as helpless victims of blatant discrimination. Among other things, such an ethos can be expressed by the willingness to develop, finance, and defend reasonably efficient public institutions designed for providing social inclusion and integration of those unable to pay for the required goods (education, health care, pensions, etc.) were they allocated through the market. Another part of the egalitarian ethos is a habit of showing respect or, rather, of not showing disrespect in public for groups prone to discrimination. In short, the egalitarian ethos becomes apparent in the public use of arguments that are supposed to *justify* distributions and specifications of rights.

[68] See, again, Young (n 13) 25.

Still, arguably, anonymous social relations at the societal level are constituted by established rights to a much larger extent than interpersonal relations between people who know each other or interact on a regular basis. Though certainly not reducible to questions of distribution, even issues of 'recognition' at this level, the most obviously relational concerns, are best to be phrased as questions of what moral and/or legal rights people have. More precisely, it's about what general and quite abstract rights that have been distributed already, such as the right to equality before the law, basic liberty rights, and rights to political participation, amount to in a context of diverse life-styles and 'cultural identities'.

Social status itself, whether equal or unequal, is largely a bundle of actually existing (ie mutually acknowledged and implemented) general and special, legal and non-legal rights. As I said before, equality, at least in modern society, requires pretty equal general rights and not too unequal amounts of special rights, especially of property rights (ie income and wealth). In addition to having the potential of quite directly causing several social pathologies at the interpersonal level or within social micro-contexts (neighbourhoods, workplaces, etc.), high inequality of property rights, through a variety of mechanisms, notoriously undermines political equality and eventually even the sense of belonging to one and the same society, let alone of living in a society of *equals*.[69]

Finally, as rights constitute normative social relations, they trigger and organize 'justificatory practices'. I take this to be one of the most important reminders Forst gives us. That is, the claim to have a right, or that another person has a right, typically creates a justificatory burden. More precisely: a social relation as a certain distribution of rights is a state of affairs whose description by the individuals involved implies its justification or, rather, the assumption that there is some justification. When it comes to rights, at least from the perspective of their subjects and addressees (as opposed to detached observers of social conventions), there is no strict distinction between distribution and justification. The statement made by person A or B that A has a right R_A against B implies the claim that there are *reasons* for R_A. Even if R_A is supposed to be merely a positive-legal right, the statement that A has R_A against B cannot be a *pure* description like the description of an empirical entity. Actually, this seems quite obvious. It's even more obvious if R_A is supposed to be a moral right. Depending on the nature, the

[69] As far as I can see, the view of social status as a bundle of general and special rights, particularly of property rights, is one of the major ingredients of relational-egalitarian, certainly not overly recipient-oriented, 'pre-distributive' conceptions of property-owning democracy. See Martin O'Neill and Thad Williamson (eds), *Property-Owning Democracy: Rawls and Beyond* (Wiley-Blackwell 2012); Alan Thomas, *Republic of Equals: Predistribution and Property-Owning Democracy* (Oxford University Press 2017).

content, and the addressee of the right that is claimed, the justificatory burden can be a relatively light one and consist in little else than the requirement to cite a relevant legal rule; yet, especially in the case of some non-legal rights or where the relevant legal grounds are controversial, it may be necessary to dig deeper and refer explicitly to some political ideology and/or moral conception. (Note that all this does not imply a basic right to justification of a complex system of general and special rights. We do not need to assume such a basic right in order to have reason to think about the justifiability of social institutions and structures and to engage in political struggle for more or less radical reform.) But it's not just about justificatory burdens for claimants of rights. Rights trigger justificatory practices also in another way. Once established, they attribute justificatory burdens to the addressees, in the normative sense of creating an obligation to justification and, if the rights are widely recognized and thus socially exist, also in the empirical sense of exerting a pressure to justification.

In addition, rights themselves function as reasons for and against certain behaviours. One may draw on rights in order to show that one's behaviour is right or that it is permissible, ie that is required by the rights of others and/or that it is within one's own rights. As normative constraints, rights prohibit addressees from acting in a certain way or demand weighty reasons for certain types of interference with particular interests. (Modern legal systems typically contain an elaborate set of rules that determine justificatory duties and standards of proof in great detail.) The more specified and well-grounded rights are, the harder it is to justify interference.[70] More abstract rights such as constitutionally guaranteed basic rights preclude interference by public authorities or similarly powerful actors much less definitively but typically require considerations of proportionality. Here egalitarian political philosophy, otherwise dealing with the question of which rights should be accepted and politically implemented as principles in the first place, enters legal debates. It makes a difference whether the balancing of basic rights and public interests is done by an egalitarian of this or that variety, a sufficientarian, a non-egalitarian communitarian, or a free-market-libertarian.[71] Of course, much more is needed than what I have provided here, namely a *conception* of equality that tells us what reasons of interference with interests underlying rights are *compatible with*, or *conducive to*, equality.

By nature, egalitarian *legal* discourse is more concerned with the compatibility-issue. To egalitarian lawyers, equality itself has more of a side-constraint rather

[70] Rights can be more or less abstract or concrete. The right to privacy or the right to equality before the law is more abstract than the right to marry another person regardless of his or her sex, or the right to financial spousal support.
[71] See Alexander Somek, *Rechtliches Wissen* (Suhrkamp 2006) ch 4.

than a value or ideal to be balanced against others. That is, egalitarian legal reasoning focuses on the question of what reasons for interference with rights are reciprocal and generally acceptable (or: not reasonably rejectable) *in the sense of being non-discriminatory.*[72] And it does so largely within an already established system of norms, whereas egalitarian *political* reasoning may address *systems* of norms and rights, thus of equality and inequality, involving considerations (for example, about economic fairness) that cannot be fully translated into the juridical language of non-discrimination. I do not deny that there is a connection between legal justification and political justification. Still, proper equality-compatible legal balancing does not amount to exactly the same as equality-compatible *and* equality-enhancing political balancing, especially if the latter is done with more radical aspiration.

Whatever the details of an egalitarian legal methodology or of a political conception of equality, both in legal and in political thought, equality should be viewed as not only depending on rights under a distributive description but also on justifications of rights, on their contents as well as on their being given in public (thus contributing to what may be called 'societal culture'). This truth appears to be more congenial to relational than to distributive egalitarianism, though the aim of neutralizing some kinds of luck in distribution may be among the reasons for or against rules and the relations between people these rules give rise to.

In any case, it should be clear that the approach outlined in the preceding paragraphs is not vulnerable to an objection often raised against conceptions of justice centering on rights: 'Such conceptions display a much too strong individualist bias and provide for a much too legalistic framework for political reasoning.' The rights-focused approach to social equality, I believe, does nothing of that. For it is rights-focused, but not rights-based. To be sure, it does not preclude rights-based arguments, but neither does it suggest that we proceed from the assumption of some natural right or an even more basic right to justification. Rather, its point is that abstract relations between members of a highly complex mass society can hardly be conceived of other than as allocations of moral and, even more importantly, legal rights. One's social status, whether equal or unequal, is not just an *effect* of having rights, but largely *consists* in a bundle of (equal or unequal) general and special rights. The grounding and distribution of such rights and the determination of their content and relative weight may well involve considerations of public interests, the common good, and collective history or identity, though, clearly, not all of them are compatible with, or conducive to, social equality. For egalitarianism, even its relational variety, is

[72] See Alexander Somek, *Rationalität und Diskriminierung: Zur Bindung der Gesetzgebung an das Gleichheitsrecht* (Springer 2001).

basically an individualistic paradigm. It just does not rely on an atomistic conception of society and the individuals in it. Actually, taking rights as relations between people that are supposed to be equals seriously implies being highly sceptical of social-theoretical atomism and its political cousin libertarianism. This should be quite obvious. Less obvious, yet nonetheless true, I believe, would be the claim that sufficientarian theories of social justice also become either quite egalitarian or less persuasive once they are being reformulated in the language not of goods in general but of rights and the relations rights constitute in particular. However, even if sufficientarian theories proved unpersuasive as theories of social justice, sufficientarian arguments, just like luck-egalitarian concerns, could have some force in this or that social micro-context sphere. Put differently, sufficientarianism as well as luck egalitarianism might provide us with useful theories of local justice, rather than of more comprehensive social justice.

V. Conclusion

The aim of this chapter was to outline how rights constitute a link between distributive and relational (including justification-based) accounts of equality and justice. I've argued that rights do this due to their triple nature. They are goods to be distributed in so far as they, or the goods they refer to, are in a sense cooperatively produced or possessed in common. Even if we conceive of some rights as pre-institutional or natural, the question of who has to contribute what exactly to the fulfilment of the rights is a question of distribution. At the same time, socially existing rights are relations between right-holders and addressees triggering and structuring justificatory practices as well as providing reasons relevant to legal and political discourse.

The focus on rights and corresponding duties in egalitarian thinking thus allows us to combine the advantages of both paradigms without having to tackle their respective main problems: the danger of remaining stuck in quasi-platonic, sociologically sterile conceptual analysis typical of luck-egalitarian approaches and the difficulty of finding a non-distributional language capable of adequately identifying and describing egalitarian or inegalitarian relationships at the societal level, ie beyond personal interactions.

References

Anderson ES, 'What Is the Point of Equality?' (1999), 109 Ethics 287.

Anderson ES, 'Equality' in David M Estlund (ed), *The Oxford Handbook of Political Philosophy* (Oxford University Press 2012).

Arnold S, *Vertrag und Verteilung: Die Bedeutung der iustitia distributiva im Vertragsrecht* (Mohr Siebeck 2014).
Arneson R, 'Justice Is Not Equality' (2008) 21 Ratio 371.
Arneson R, 'Luck Egalitarianism—A Primer' in Carl Knight and Zofia Stemplowska (eds), *Responsibility and Distributive Justice* (Oxford University Press 2011).
Barry B, *Culture and Equality: An Egalitarian Critique of Multiculturalism* (Polity Press 2001).
Caney S, 'Justice and the Basic Right to Justification' in Rainer Forst, *Justice, Democracy and the Right to Justification: Rainer Forst in Dialogue* (Bloomsbury Academic 2014).
Cohen GA, *Rescuing Justice and Equality* (Harvard University Press 2008).
Cohen GA, *Why Not Socialism?* (Princeton University Press 2009).
Cohen GA, *On the Currency of Egalitarian Justice, and Other Essays in Political Philosophy* (Princeton University Press 2011).
Dworkin R, *Sovereign Virtue: The Theory and Practice of Equality* (Harvard University Press 2000).
Elster J, *Local Justice: How Institutions Allocate Scarce Goods and Necessary Burdens* (Russell Sage Foundation 1992).
Forst R, 'Zu einer kritischen Theorie transnationaler Gerechtigkeit' in Rainer Forst, *Das Recht auf Rechtfertigung: Elemente einer konstruktivistischen Theorie der Gerechtigkeit* (Suhrkamp 2007).
Forst R, 'The Justification of Human Rights and the Basic Right to Justification: A Reflexive Approach' (2010), 120 Ethics 711.
Forst R, 'Constructions of Transnational Justice: Comparing John Rawls's *The Law of Peoples* and Otfried Höffe's *Democracy in the Age of Globalisation*' in Rainer Forst, *The Right to Justification: Elements of a Constructivist Theory of Justice* (Jeffrey Flynn tr, Columbia University Press 2011).
Forst R, 'Introduction: The Foundation of Justice' in Rainer Forst, *The Right to Justification: Elements of a Constructivist Theory of Justice* (Jeffrey Flynn tr, Columbia University Press 2011).
Forst R, 'Practical Reason and Justifying Reasons: On the Foundation of Morality' in Rainer Forst, *The Right to Justification: Elements of a Constructivist Theory of Justice* (Jeffrey Flynn tr, Columbia University Press 2011).
Forst R, 'The Basic Right to Justification: Toward a Constructivist Conception of Human Rights' in Rainer Forst, *The Right to Justification: Elements of a Constructivist Theory of Justice* (Jeffrey Flynn tr, Columbia University Press 2011).
Forst R, *The Right to Justification: Elements of a Constructivist Theory of Justice* (Jeffrey Flynn tr, Columbia University Press 2011).
Forst R, 'Toward a Critical Theory of Transnational Justice' in Rainer Forst, *The Right to Justification: Elements of a Constructivist Theory of Justice* (Jeffrey Flynn tr, Columbia University Press 2011).
Forst R, 'Introduction: On the Idea of a Critique of Relations of Justification' in Rainer Forst, *Justification and Critique: Towards a Critical Theory of Politics* (Ciaran Cronin tr, Polity Press 2013).
Forst R, '"To Tolerate Means to Insult": Toleration, Recognition, and Emancipation' in Rainer Forst, *Justification and Critique: Towards a Critical Theory of Politics* (Ciaran Cronin tr, Polity Press 2013).
Forst R, *Toleration in Conflict: Past and Present* (Ciaran Cronin tr, Cambridge University Press 2013).

Forst R, 'Justifying Justification: A Reply to My Critics' in Rainer Forst, *Justice, Democracy and the Right to Justification: Rainer Forst in Dialogue* (Bloomsbury Academic 2014).

Forst R, 'Two Pictures of Justice' in Rainer Forst, *Justice, Democracy and the Right to Justification: Rainer Forst in Dialogue* (Bloomsbury Academic 2014).

Fourie C, Schuppert F, and Wallimann-Helmer I (eds), *Social Equality: On What It Means to be Equals* (Oxford University Press 2015).

Frankfurt HG, *On Bullshit* (Princeton University Press 2005).

Gilens M, *Affluence and Influence: Economic Inequality and Political Power in America* (Princeton University Press 2012).

Habermas J, *Between Facts and Norms: Contributions to a Discourse Theory of Law and Democracy* (William Rehg tr, MIT Press 1996).

Hausman DM and McPherson MS, *Economic Analysis, Moral Philosophy, and Public Policy* (Cambridge University Press 2002).

Heyd D, 'Justice and Solidarity: The Contractarian Case against Global Justice' (2007), 38 Journal of Social Philosophy 112.

Hinton T, 'Must Egalitarians Choose Between Fairness and Respect?' (2001), 30 Philosophy & Public Affairs 72.

Holmes S and Sunstein CR, *The Cost of Rights: Why Liberty Depends on Taxes* (W.W. Norton & Company 2000).

Koller P, 'Die Struktur von Rechten' in Georg Meggle (ed), *Philosophy of Mind, Practical Philosophy, Miscellanea* (De Gruyter 1997).

Koller P, 'Economic Distributive Justice' in Sonja Puntscher Riekmann, Alexander Somek, and Doris Wydra (eds), *Is There a European Common Good?* (Nomos 2013).

Koller P, 'Recht und soziale Verteilungsgerechtigkeit in Soziologischer und ethischer Perspektive' in Gerhard Baumgartner and others (eds), *Verteilungsgerechtigkeit im Recht* (Verlag Österreich 2017).

Kymlicka W, *Multicultural Citizenship: A Liberal Theory of Minority Rights* (Clarendon Press 1995).

Miller D, 'Equality and Justice' (1997), 10 Ratio 222.

Nagel T, 'The Problem of Global Justice' (2005), 33 Philosophy & Public Affairs 113.

O'Neill M, 'What Should Egalitarians Believe?' (2008), 36 Philosophy & Public Affairs 119.

O'Neill M, 'Constructing a Contractualist Egalitarianism: Equality after Scanlon' (2013), 10 Journal of Moral Philosophy 429.

O'Neill M and Williamson T (eds), *Property-Owning Democracy: Rawls and Beyond* (Wiley-Blackwell 2012).

Parfit D, 'Equality or Priority?' in Matthew Clayton and Andrew Williams (eds), *The Ideal of Equality* (Palgrave MacMillan 2002).

Piketty T, *Capital in the Twenty-First Century* (Arthur Goldhammer tr, The Belknap Press of Harvard University Press 2014).

Pogge TW (ed), *Freedom from Poverty as a Human Right: Who Owes What to the Very Poor?* (Oxford University Press 2007).

Rawls J, *A Theory of Justice* (Harvard University Press 1971).

Roemer JE, *Equality of Opportunity* (Harvard University Press 1998).

Scanlon T, *The Difficulty of Tolerance: Essays in Political Philosophy* (Cambridge University Press 2003).

Scheffler S, 'What Is Egalitarianism?' (2003), 31 Philosophy & Public Affairs 5.

Scheffler S, 'The Practice of Equality' in Carina Fourie, Fabian Schuppert, and Ivo Wallimann-Helmer (eds), *Social Equality: On What It Means to Be Equals* (Oxford University Press 2015).

Sen A, *Inequality Reexamined* (Harvard University Press 2002).

Somek A, *Rationalität und Diskriminierung: Zur Bindung der Gesetzgebung an das Gleichheitsrecht* (Springer 2001).

Somek A, *Rechtliches Wissen* (Suhrkamp 2006).

Taylor C, 'The Nature and Scope of Distributive Justice' in Charles Taylor, *Philosophical Papers*, vol 2 (Cambridge University Press 1985).

Temkin LS, *Inequality* (Oxford University Press 1993).

Thomas A, *Republic of Equals: Predistribution and Property-Owning Democracy* (Oxford University Press 2017).

Walzer M, *Spheres of Justice: A Defense of Pluralism and Equality* (Basic Books 1983).

Wolff J, 'Fairness, Respect, and the Egalitarian Ethos' (1998), 27 Philosophy & Public Affairs 97.

Wolff J, 'Fairness, Respect and the Egalitarian Ethos Revisited' (2010), 14 The Journal of Ethics 335.

Young IM, *Justice and the Politics of Difference* (Princeton University Press 1990).

5

Practical Justice

Bernhard Schlink

I.

'There can be no right life within the false one', Adorno stated in *Minima Moralia*,[1] as the concluding assertion to a reflection that was explicitly directed only against living in a particular place and against ownership or property as illusions, or rather as an ideology of being at home with oneself. These considerations, however, actually targeted all undertakings in which people wish to shape and keep what is theirs, in the false world, with a bad conscience.

Yet it is precisely this which constitutes the ethos of practice: engaging in one's own particular activities in the false world, doing something good, yet with a bad conscience, for it inevitably entails simply patching up flaws, and the world remains false. The architect builds his house, even if the other houses in the city, as Adorno asserts, 'are good only to be thrown away, like old tin cans';[2] the doctor treats his patients, even if public health generally is in a dreadful state; the teacher instructs pupils in a particular subject despite realizing that the school is poor and leaves pupils ill-equipped to face life's challenges. The judge hands down rulings; he or she strives to take fair decisions in disputes between parties or to determine a just punishment for a particular deed, yet is aware that the society in which he or she serves as a judge is full of injustice. There is no right life within the false one? The right life exists only within the false one; a just life exists only within the injustice of life.

Our world is not just, our society is not just: if there is no justice within this unjust world and within this unjust society, there is no justice at all. That does not mean that our society and our world could not become more just; there are many areas where there is room for improvement, where more justice is possible. Nor does it mean that there is no need for conceptions of a just society or a just world, as addressed in the philosophical debate on justice since Rawls;[3] such

[1] Theodor W Adorno, *Minima Moralia: Reflexionen aus dem beschädigten Leben* (Band 4, Suhrkamp 2003) 43.
[2] ibid 42.
[3] John Rawls, *A Theory of Justice* (Harvard University Press 1971).

Bernhard Schlin, *Practical Justice* In: *Constitutionalism Justified: Rainer Forst in Discourse.* Edited by: Ester Herlin-Karnell and Matthias Klatt, Oxford University Press (2020),
DOI: 10.1093/oso/9780190889050.003.0005

ideas can help us find our bearings as we work towards more justice in the many areas where there is room for improvement. It does, however, mean that efforts to achieve more justice must be undertaken wherever there is room for improvement, even if the situation in the world and in society is far from being how it should rightly be.

That is why the following considerations examine practical justice, the practice of solving problems that we generally understand as problems pertaining to justice, wherever these arise. I shall address practical justice in the light of the current philosophical discussion of justice. Philosophy of law is an intermediate discipline, situated between doctrinal and practical, and historical and philosophical modes of engagement with the law; the specific and particular contribution it can offer lies in the way in which it views the practice of justice in the light of the philosophical discussion on justice, whilst at the same time shedding light on that debate through reflections on how justice is practiced.

II.

The paradigm of distributive justice[4] is the paradigm traditionally deployed to discuss and resolve problems pertaining to justice. A mother is just if she shares out a cake correctly between her children; an employer is just if he takes the correct decision on the wages paid to employees; the state is just if it responds correctly to citizens with their demands and good deeds, with the term 'correctly' signifying that each individual receives 'what is his (or her) own'. The point that has long been, and remains, controversial is whether what each individual should receive as 'his (or her) own' is determined in terms of worthiness, of performance and merit, or of need. In any event there has been an evolution through the course of history, with a shift from status to contract, from a state under the rule of law to the welfare state, from poor relief to social security benefits. In the course of this evolution, the focus on worthiness has been superseded by an emphasis on performance and merit, with neediness assuming an increasingly important role as a criterion alongside performance and merit. When appraising neediness, we no longer draw distinctions based on its causes, analyzing whether it is the fault of the individual concerned or not; there is now a legal right to social security benefits even in cases where generosity and charity once offered the only hope. Determining methods to set the level of social benefits means addressing

[4] Going back to Aristotle's *Nicomachean Ethics*, book V on justice in general; on distributive justice in particular see book V, 1130b30ff, 1131a25ff, 1131b. For an overview over various concepts of distributive justice, see among others John E Roemer, *Theories of Distributive Justice* (Harvard University Press 1996); Samuel Fleischacker, *A Short History of Distributive Justice* (Harvard University Press 2004).

the question of what constitutes each individual's 'share', what he or she needs for subsistence and to participate, in his or her own way, in social and cultural life.

The paradigm of distributive justice is increasingly rejected nowadays due to its purported shortcomings, even though it has proved adaptable and viable as these historical developments unfold. It is rejected as functioning only for the distribution of material goods and ceasing to function when no greater and smaller quantities are involved; as failing when we turn to rights and opportunities, self-realization, cooperation, and participation;[5] as ignoring the organization of fair social and political institutions and procedures.[6] But this critique objectifies and curtails the distributive paradigm. In actual fact, the distributive paradigm is concerned neither with material goods nor with anything else of which more or less may be available.

The distributive paradigm demands respect for the notion of *suum cuique*—to each his (or her) own. In this context, the share accorded to each individual is the same, unless it is possible to give the reasons and make intelligible to those involved why this share should not be the same for all, but should be configured differently.[7] If we shift the focus away from the idea that each individual's 'own share' is determined on the basis of worthiness, or of performance and merit, and instead concentrate increasingly on needs,[8] this also entails shifting the way in which reasons are given to substantiate inequality and make it intelligible. The notion that individuals in need, whether due to external causes or due to an individual's own fault, may not be treated equally by the state—in terms of providing for their essential needs and offering scope for each individual to participate in their own way in social and cultural life—is no longer tenable today, nor can it be justified to those concerned.

The needy, of course, also receive goods, material goods, as well as immaterial goods in the case of participation in social and cultural life, and perhaps even an opportunity to acquire self-confidence, self-respect, and recognition. That is however the consequence of a line of argument based on the reasoning provided

[5] Axel Honneth, *Das Ich im Wir: Studien zur Anerkennungstheorie* (Suhrkamp 2010) 59ff with further references; Rainer Forst, 'Two Pictures of Justice' in Rainer Forst, *Justice, Democracy and the Right to Justification: Rainer Forst in Dialogue* (Bloomsbury Academic 2014) 6, 10f, 13; Rainer Forst, 'A Kantian Republican Conception of Justice as Non-Domination' in Andreas Niederberger and Philipp Schink (eds), *Republican Democracy: Liberty, Law and Politics* (Edinburgh University Press 2013); Jürgen Habermas, 'Diskursethik—Notizen zu einem Begründungsprogramm' in Jürgen Habermas, *Moralbewusstsein und kommunikatives Handeln* (Suhrkamp 1983); Jürgen Habermas, 'Moralbewusstsein und kommunikatives Handeln' in Jürgen Habermas, *Moralbewusstsein und kommunikatives Handeln* (Suhrkamp 1983). See also from a somewhat different perspective Michael Walzer, *Spheres of Justice: A Defense of Pluralism and Equality* (Basic Books 1983) especially 3ff.

[6] Forst, 'Two Pictures of Justice' (n 5) 4f, with further references, 8f, 17, 22; Honneth, *Das Ich im Wir* (n 5) 65f.

[7] John Rawls, *A Theory of Justice* (revised edn, Oxford University Press 1999) especially 52ff.

[8] ibid 347ff.

and the effort of rendering decisions intelligible that the distributive paradigm demands and opens up, but it is not a direct consequence of the distributive paradigm per se. The distributive paradigm does not distribute goods, but instead it distributes the burden of argumentation. Within the frame of the distributive paradigm, the onus is on anyone who holds that unequal treatment is just to demonstrate the reasoning that substantiates this, and to make this unequal treatment intelligible to those affected.

Unequal treatment assumes two main forms. There is in a certain sense a classical form of unequal treatment where it is apparent that individuals, although they fall under the same overarching category and are thus comparable, are treated differently in terms of interventions or benefits, in proceedings or decisions. Examples include differing treatment of refugees seeking asylum, refugees fleeing war or civil war, and economic refugees; wage differentials between women and men; differences in financing for newly founded and long-established private schools.

However, if someone's freedom is removed or curtailed, for example, if a sentence is imposed, a demonstration is broken up, or a book is banned, this is also an instance of unequal treatment, and the distributive paradigm demands reasons to substantiate this and render it intelligible. Restrictions on freedom can be reformulated as unequal treatment (and vice-versa) as it is always possible to identify comparable individuals whose freedom is not constrained. Evidence for this is furnished by the German and the Austrian constitutions, which explicitly enshrine specific freedoms, yet also seek to protect freedoms that are not explicitly individually enshrined in the constitutions. This general protection of liberty is assured by the German Federal Constitutional Court by guaranteeing general freedom of action, and by the Austrian Constitutional Court through the general precept of equality.

The notion that reasons must be put forward to substantiate unequal treatment references the rationality standards of the time and place in which the unequal treatment occurs. Standards of rationality differ, and such standards are different today than they were in the past, are different here and elsewhere. It is foolish to lambast discrimination against women in the nineteenth century as if it were occurring today, or to condemn discrimination against homosexuals in Russia as if such discrimination had not been rampant here until recently. That does not, however, mean that being able to provide reasons to substantiate unequal treatment is somehow an arbitrary matter.

An evolution can be detected on this front too; there has been a move away from substantiation in terms of what a person is towards substantiation in terms of what they do, a shift away from reasoning grounded in assertions about the essence of concepts to reasoning based on the finality of such concepts, a move away from reasoning vis-à-vis one's immediate audience to reasoning vis-à-vis other audiences too, and, against the backdrop of globalization, vis-à-vis the world. It no longer suffices to assert that women are treated unequally because they are different, that citizens must do everything for the state because that is the essence of citizenship, or that genital mutilation of women is justified where a tribe or a country accepts it.

Arbitrariness is also precluded by the fact that, although the questions addressed are normative, the answers examine empirical considerations. Justifications given for unequal treatment generally claim that it is proportionate, which means that it serves a legitimate purpose, is not merely suitable but necessary to attain that purpose, and that the objective pursued is sufficiently important to compensate, in a certain sense, for the loss of quality of life associated with the unequal treatment.

Appraising the suitability and necessity of a measure is a matter for empiricism; either a connection exists, and can be demonstrated by tried-and-tested hypotheses about reality, linking the unequal treatment and the circumstances in which the purpose can be considered to be attained, or such a connection does not exist. Data retention is either a viable and necessary measure to combat crime, in particular organized crime, or it is not. Of course there is often uncertainty about the empirical method deployed, which raises the question of who bears the burden of proof in such cases: Is it the person providing reasons to substantiate unequal treatment or the person seeking to prevent such treatment? The answer to the question is different depending on the degree of uncertainty and the nature and import of the unequal treatment—a vast topic.

As it is essential that unequal treatment be made intelligible to those affected, such treatment cannot simply be imposed upon people without any regard for their expectations, nor must their expectations simply be satisfied. Even before deciding on and enforcing unequal treatment, there must be comprehensible communication about it to those affected, also providing the reasons put forward; those affected should have an opportunity beforehand to express their views and proposals, and, if the unequal treatment can easily be made acceptable by making modifications or arranging compensation, this should be done. Often however those affected will not accept unequal treatment but simply submit to it. In this scenario, unequal treatment is less problematic the more widely it is accepted in similar situations by others similarly affected.

Who decides whether the requirement imposed by the distributive paradigm, namely, that reasoning must be given, has been met? Is it those who suffer from unequal treatment, or also those who benefit from it, or even all those who belong to the community in which the unequal treatment occurs? What happens if they cannot reach an agreement? Is a vote taken, and if so, which procedural rules are applied? Should an absolute, a relative, or a qualified majority be needed to win the vote?

This too is a vast topic. However, irrespective of how these questions are answered from case to case, it is obvious that the decision should, whenever feasible, be preceded by a debate conducted by and with the people affected. This debate must address the unequal treatment and also, unless this point has already been resolved, the institutions and procedures involved in discussing and deciding about the reasoning put forward for the unequal treatment and whether it can be explained to those involved.

Providing reasons and explaining the grounds for the unequal treatment to the people it affects will be more successful the more this process functions within established institutions and tried-and-tested procedures, integrating the perspective of those affected, responding to their needs and interests, and justifying the unequal treatment to them as proportionate. In this sense, discussions between and with those affected can be termed a discourse of justification, and providing reasons and substantiating the grounds can be described as justifiability; this, therefore, also means that we can raise the question of how this relates to the philosophical conception of justice, which since Habermas has viewed justice as justifiability.[9]

III.

How does the paradigm of distributive justice relate to the paradigm of justice as justifiability? How does it relate to the idea that what is required first and foremost is a fundamental structure of justification: a structure that affords citizens justificatory power through co-deliberation and co-determination in institutions and procedures, and thus ensures that all other aspects, including in particular the production, procurement, and distribution of societal goods, can be justified in subsequent discursive-constructive exercise of justificatory power?

The allure of the idea of justice as justifiability is that it does not seem to presuppose knowledge concerning what is just. It promises to produce such knowledge, not in a conceptual operation that envisions human beings as a construct behind a veil of ignorance, or in the guise of the egoistic *homo economicus* or the altruistic *homo politicus*, but in the genuine discourses of justification of those

[9] See especially Jürgen Habermas, *Faktizität und Geltung: Beiträge zur Diskurstheorie des Rechts und des demokratischen Rechtsstaats* (Suhrkamp 1992); Jürgen Habermas, *Wahrheit und Rechtfertigung: Philosophische Aufsätze* (Suhrkamp 1999); Jürgen Habermas, *Erläuterungen zur Diskursethik* (Suhrkamp 1991); see also Rainer Forst, *The Right to Justification: Elements of a Constructivist Theory of Justice* (Jeffrey Flynn tr, Columbia University Press 2011), especially ch 4; in general Stephen K White (ed), *The Cambridge Companion to Habermas* (Cambridge University Press 1995); comparing Adorno and Habermas, Romand Coles, 'Identity and Difference in the Ethical Positions of Adorno and Habermas' in Stephen K White (ed), *The Cambridge Companion to Habermas* (Cambridge University Press 1995).

who are really affected: if something is justifiable and is justified by citizens in discourse, it is just—first of all, the fundamental social structure, the institutions and procedures of co-deliberation and co-determination, and subsequently everything else, including in particular the production, procurement, and distribution of societal goods.

Yet many things are justifiable, and justifications are put forward for many things. The entrepreneur justifies floating his firm on the stock exchange, the general justifies an attack or retreat of his troops, the teacher justifies the choice of the book that she reads with the class, and the cook justifies the dishes he has chosen for the festive menu. When actions are called into question, justifications are given: economic arguments for the stock market flotation, strategic and tactical reasons for the attack or retreat, pedagogical justifications for a school's reading choices, and culinary arguments for the festive menu. In this context, the justification of the company's stock market flotation can only function because we know when a company is ready for flotation, and are aware of what might constitute good and bad reasons for a stock market flotation. Similarly, the general, the teacher, and the cook can only justify their actions because military science, pedagogical, and culinary experiences and standards exist. Justifications relate to something about which there is certainty, and they succeed if and because we share in that certainty.

It is no different when it comes to justifying something as just. Such justifications can only function if there is certainty about justice or at least some notion of what justice means to help us find our bearings. The process of seeking a justification for something as just within the discourse of those affected may begin without a shared conception of justice, but it cannot begin without individual conceptions of justice, and it cannot succeed if these individual conceptions do not have enough in common.[10] It is illusionary to suggest that justification of something does not presuppose any knowledge of justice[11] but instead generates such knowledge.

This, however, also makes it untenable to assume that a just fundamental structure is the pre-requisite for just production, acquisition, and distribution of goods, or indeed for other just solutions to social problems.[12] The justice of

[10] cf Raz's critique on Rawls: Joseph Raz, *The Morality of Freedom* (Clarendon Press 1986) 124ff.

[11] cf Rawls, *A Theory of Justice* (n 7) 348: 'But to establish these principles it is necessary to rely on some notion of goodness, for we need assumptions about the parties' motives in the original position.'

[12] As Habermas insinuates eg in *Faktizität und Geltung* (n 9) especially 13, 17ff, 24ff, 78ff; furthermore, Habermas, 'Diskursethik—Notizen zu einem Begründungsprogramm' (n 5); Habermas, 'Moralbewusstsein und kommunikatives Handeln' (n 5). See also Axel Honneth, 'The Other of Justice: Habermas and the Ethical Challenge of Postmodernism' in Stephen K White (ed), *The Cambridge Companion to Habermas* (Cambridge University Press 1995); Rainer Forst, *Contexts of Justice: Political Philosophy Beyond Liberalism and Communitarianism* (John MM Farrell tr, University of California Press 2002) 238.

the fundamental structure can be a pre-requisite for just solutions to societal problems only if justice as justifiability is procedurally determined in such a fashion that discourses of justification on societal problems that make it possible to find justifiable, and just solutions cannot exist without a discursively justifiable fundamental structure with discursively justified institutions and procedures.

However, if justice is not justifiability, and if it is not manifested only when citizens' democratic, discursive-constructive justificatory power is exercised, if instead justification always exists already prior to this step, the question of justice can be raised independently in each instance—and indeed it is absolutely essential that it is raised to ensure that citizens seek the justification for solutions to problems in terms of justice rather than in terms of efficiency, advantages, or any other considerations.

As a conception of justice always precedes exercise of citizens' discursive-constructive justificatory power, exercising this justificatory power is not a sufficient condition for justice, and it is also not a necessary condition. It is important; generally speaking, the knowledge and discourses of the citizens affected, as well as of all interested and engaged citizens, are indispensable in finding a just solution to a social problem, that is to say, in resolving the question of whether reasons can be given for unequal treatment and whether it can be made intelligible to those affected. However, the importance of exercising justificatory power does not make this a precondition of justice—just as the discursively justified fundamental structure is not the precondition for justice.

In practice, reaching an agreement about just solutions to societal problems anyway only occasionally draws on the fundamental structure of society. Development projects try to meet the needs of those they are aimed at, even in countries with structures that are anything but just and democratic; passing a verdict on genital mutilation of women does not require waiting until justice and democracy prevail in the countries where it is practiced; judging whether a mother has divided the cake fairly between her children is possible even if the mother is a tyrant.

Certainly, discourses of justification are, again and again, compelled to move from the idea of having a share of something to the notion of participating in something; again and again, configuring one social constellation in a just fashion demands that other social constellations must be configured in a just manner too, and in places where repression prevails, enclaves of justice cannot give citizens what they are entitled to as autonomous subjects. At the same time, the huge variety of social functions, contexts, and constellations in our highly differentiated society within which specific forms of unequal treatment occur and where specific reasons are required means that the justice and justifiability 'big picture' fades into the background.

The relationship between the paradigm of distributive justice and the paradigm of justice as justifiability is multifaceted. Being able to substantiate and to explain convincingly to those affected, which are issues central to the former paradigm, and justifiability, the crux of the latter, rely on the knowledge, perceptions, and considerations of those affected; in terms of the distributive paradigm, it is crucial that substantiation and convincing explanations be found for, to, and if possible, with those affected, whereas the paradigm of justifiability envisions justification only with and through those affected; in both paradigms, the discourses associated with this process play a role, which in one case is significant, and in the other paradigm is utterly indispensable. However, in relying solely on discursive justification by those affected, the paradigm of justifiability overreaches itself. Without a guiding notion of justice, discursive justifications may head off in many different directions—and run into the sand.

IV.

It is certainly true that the distributive paradigm, in contrast to the paradigm of justification, does not make the justice of society's fundamental structure a prerequisite for all other steps. Yet in this respect it does not deny the validity of enquiring about the justice of the fundamental structures of state and society. The justice of the distributive paradigm is practical justice, because it makes it possible to raise the question of justice on a situation-by-situation basis and to provide answers on this basis. What kind of practical answers can the distributive paradigm offer when the question of justice is raised in relation to structural problems within the state and society?

In this context, as in other realms, the distributive paradigm offers only a procedure for developing the kind of arguments that must be used to seek answers. Equality must be taken as the initial assumption in this procedure for developing arguments, and it must be shown that reasons can be given for unequal treatment and that it can be made intelligible. In the distributive paradigm, justice does not demand unequal treatment; it permits unequal treatment if reasons can be given and if it is intelligible—just as Rawls's difference principle does not demand unequal treatment but merely establishes conditions under which unequal treatment is acceptable.[13] Social justice is not simply justice developed for the social realm, but rather a framework of reasoned and intelligible forms of unequal treatment. This also applies to electoral justice, tax justice, educational justice, equal treatment for all those liable for military service, and all other specific

[13] Rawls, *A Theory of Justice* (n 7) 57ff.

forms of justice. The focus is always on equality and on additional arguments that seek to justify unequal treatment, on arguments concerning how citizens should live, participate in decision-making and burden-sharing, have access to education, or assume responsibility for national defence.

The equality that forms the initial assumption must however first of all be ascertained. Our notion of social justice works on the premise that all citizens must be equal in terms of provision for subsistence and scope to participate in social and cultural life, if need be with the state's assistance if this is not possible through citizens' own efforts. Our notion of tax justice imposes an equal progressive tax burden on all citizens. Our notion of electoral justice gives each citizen's vote the same numerical weight and the same effectiveness through the representational voting system. These types of equality that form the initial assumption could also be determined in a different fashion; social justice could be based on basic material needs and leave immaterial needs out of the equation; tax justice could simply envisage a flat-rate percentage for taxing all citizens; electoral justice, under the absolute majority system, could simply accord the same numerical value to votes, leaving the effectiveness of each vote out of the picture.

The equality posited by the conception of justice in each case can be called into question, and reasons for it must then be provided; when such reasoning is laid out, the form of equality that forms the point of departure often turns out to be tantamount to unequal treatment that, with its substantiation and explanations, has become self-evident. In the case of the initial equality underpinning social justice, it has become self-evident that those who cannot meet their basic needs through their own efforts receive something that others do not receive. In the case of progressive taxation, it is accepted as self-evident that citizens with different income levels are affected by taxation to an unequal degree. In the case of the initial assumption of equality that determines the equal numerical value and equal effectiveness of votes in the proportional representation voting system, it is not the parties or individuals that win an election that are treated equally, as in the majority voting system, but instead all voters are given equal treatment. One of these two voting systems has become self-evident, for all that both have their own democratic traditions and can be defended with arguments pertaining to representation, stability, and effectiveness. All these self-evident points can be called into question, and the reasoning underpinning such issues can and must then be given.

Based on these initial assumptions of equality, politicians, legislators, and the administration create structures that include unequal treatment, which, provided that the reasoning is given and that such unequal treatment can be made intelligible, is also just. Social security legislation accordingly stipulates what various people in various situations need for subsistence and to participate in social and cultural life; electoral legislation stipulates the voting age, how voters cast their vote, and what value is accorded to each vote; tax law determines the tax brackets for progressive taxation of various income levels.

Different categories of people encounter different legal provisions: within each of the various categories, however, there must be equality, for unequal treatment within a category, unless it is substantiated and explained as an exception to the general rule, would be an instance of arbitrariness. Disproportionate regulations and decisions cannot be defended by reasoning nor rendered intelligible; in legal and judicial oversight of laws and regulations, administrative and court decisions, proportionality is a small-scale manifestation of justice.

The just order of the state and society thus proves to be a structure of assumptions concerning equality that build one upon another, together with forms of unequal treatment that can be substantiated and explained. The basic assumption that all citizens are equal forms the foundation underpinning social, tax, and voting-related assumptions about equality, assumptions that de facto are forms of unequal treatment that have become self-evident; in social security legislation, tax law, or electoral law, categories are formed and are treated unequally, which in turn must be substantiated and must be explicable; within each category, however, the tenet of equality once again applies, affording scope for instances of unequal treatment only as exceptions that can be substantiated and explained.

Much that is regulated and decided is justice-neutral. Policy goals encompass a wide spectrum of objectives. Justice does not essentially demand that particular goals are pursued nor that particular forms of unequal treatment shall arise in pursuing those goals; it simply requires that if unequal treatment does occur, it must occur in a just fashion. Justice demands that the principle of *suum cuique* be respected, meaning to each the same unless we give a reason and provide an explanation why someone should be treated differently; such different treatment may take many and varied forms, yet still be just.

Justice does not, in all this, create a just order for the state and society, but merely determines the conditions that the state and societal order must satisfy in order to be just. Justice only rarely provides an answer to pressing political questions. The fact that refugees that come to Germany are equal to Germans as human beings does not provide an answer to the question of whether refugees should be taken in, and if so, how many: a country does not bear the same responsibility for people from elsewhere as it does for its own people. That is not tantamount to saying that there is no responsibility for people from other countries; to the extent that a country is involved in creating poverty and adversity in other countries due to global political and economic interconnections, that country also owes a contribution to overcoming that poverty and adversity. It is not possible to provide reasoning for excluding people from other countries from our obligation to compensate for damage caused for which we are responsible, nor would it be possible to render such an exception intelligible. Making good such damage may also include taking in people in need from other countries.

However, the current situation bursts the bounds of that scenario, and justice does not offer a way to unravel the tangle of demographic self-interest, selfless willingness to help, treaty obligations, European considerations, and a sheer sense of being overwhelmed that accompanies the influx of refugees. Nonetheless, to the extent that criteria are applied to manage and control migratory movements, such criteria must be formed and administered in keeping with the principle of equality.

V.

Justice demands equality, and it develops explosive, transformative force by demanding justifications for unequal treatment and condemning unequal treatment that cannot be substantiated by reasoning and made intelligible. Justice is directed against unexamined traditions and unquestioned assumptions, just as it is directed against privileges, exclusion, discrimination, and prejudices. It underpins the demand for democracy; constitutions that do not allow all citizens to decide upon the path to be taken but reserve this right to a certain class, race, religion, or party are virtually impossible to substantiate through reasoning or to explain, even in places where abolishing such constitutions remains a pipedream.

Membership-based institutions, such as chambers, universities, and churches, can no longer exclude those members from decisions either; the only restriction it is possible to substantiate involves allowing members to participate to varying degrees in decision-making power as a function of their skills, or as a function of how involved or affected members would be by the decisions taken. The European Union's attempt to square the circle by striking a balance between the principles of equality of the Member States and equality of citizens gives rise to compromises that should be able to be substantiated and explained to both Member States and citizens, but which do not pass this litmus test, thus keeping an unresolved constitutional problem simmering.

The critical potential of justice is greater than its constructive power. With its explosive, transformative force, justice is at the forefront of the struggle against heteronomy, oppression, and arbitrariness, but it does not lead so unambiguously to a just social order, a just taxation and electoral system, a just system of military service, or a just educational system. In order to take up this struggle, all that is required is to demand justice, and of course courage, vigour, and tenacity. Shaping the state and society means taking into account and reconciling many different positions, interests and conflicts, concerns, finances, and resources. In this process, justice can function only as a permanent corrective force.

Justice is in any case not the only factor that ensures there is a right life within the wrong one. Friendliness, wisdom, and beauty also play a part. Justice cannot tell us how to respond to the current influx of refugees. However, compassion does call on us to help, out of respect for our own dignity and other people's dignity, even where justice does not impose a responsibility or obligation upon us.

Justice and compassion are no strangers, although neither can be transposed into the other. The practical force of both justice and compassion stems from the fundamental experience of equality, namely, that we encounter ourselves in others and vice-versa. Although equality is justified as a precondition for justice simply because equality is a weaker hypothesis than a hypothesis of inequality, the truly vital prerequisite if we are to delight in justice and in defending justice, and indeed if we are to practice compassion with a joyful heart, is solidarity, which draws its life-force from the fundamental experience of equality.

References

Adorno TW, *Minima Moralia: Reflexionen aus dem beschädigten Leben* (Band 4, Suhrkamp 2003).

Coles R, 'Identity and Difference in the Ethical Positions of Adorno and Habermas' in Stephen K White (ed), *The Cambridge Companion to Habermas* (Cambridge University Press 1995).

Fleischacker S, *A Short History of Distributive Justice* (Harvard University Press 2004).

Forst R, *Contexts of Justice: Political Philosophy Beyond Liberalism and Communitarianism* (John MM Farrell tr, University of California Press 2002).

Forst R, *The Right to Justification: Elements of a Constructivist Theory of Justice* (Jeffrey Flynn tr, Columbia University Press 2011).

Forst R, 'A Kantian Republican Conception of Justice as Non-Domination' in Andreas Niederberger and Philipp Schink (eds), *Republican Democracy: Liberty, Law and Politics* (Edinburgh University Press 2013).

Forst R, 'Two Pictures of Justice' in Rainer Forst, *Justice, Democracy and the Right to Justification: Rainer Forst in Dialogue* (Bloomsbury Academic 2014).

Habermas J, 'Diskursethik—Notizen zu einem Begründungsprogramm' in Jürgen Habermas, *Moralbewusstsein und kommunikatives Handeln* (Suhrkamp 1983).

Habermas J, 'Moralbewusstsein und kommunikatives Handeln' in Jürgen Habermas, *Moralbewusstsein und kommunikatives Handeln* (Suhrkamp 1983).

Habermas J, *Erläuterungen zur Diskursethik* (Suhrkamp 1991).

Habermas J, *Faktizität und Geltung: Beiträge zur Diskurstheorie des Rechts und des demokratischen Rechtsstaats* (Suhrkamp 1992).

Habermas J, *Wahrheit und Rechtfertigung: Philosophische Aufsätze* (Suhrkamp 1999).

Honneth A, 'The Other of Justice: Habermas and the Ethical Challenge of Postmodernism' in Stephen K White (ed), *The Cambridge Companion to Habermas* (Cambridge University Press 1995).

Honneth A, *Das Ich im Wir: Studien zur Anerkennungstheorie* (Suhrkamp 2010).

Rawls J, *A Theory of Justice* (Harvard University Press 1971).

Rawls J, *A Theory of Justice* (revised edn, Oxford University Press 1999).
Raz J, *The Morality of Freedom* (Clarendon Press 1986).
Roemer JE, *Theories of Distributive Justice* (Harvard University Press 1996).
Walzer M, *Spheres of Justice: A Defense of Pluralism and Equality* (Basic Books 1983).
White SK (ed), *The Cambridge Companion to Habermas* (Cambridge University Press 1995).

6

Noumenal Power, Reasons, and Justification

A Critique of Forst

*Sameer Bajaj and Enzo Rossi**

I. Introduction

1. Forst on Power and Justification

In recent years, under the banner of a 'right to justification' (or *Recht auf Rechtfertigung*, in the pithier German version), Rainer Forst has put forward a novel and distinctive project in normative political theory. One could say that Forst's overall aim is to reconcile some insights from Frankfurt School critical social theory—notably an awareness of the potential for ideological distortions in power-justifying discourse—with a set of broadly liberal first-order normative commitments. While at first blush that combination may be reminiscent of Habermas's later work, Forst's contribution is distinctive in both its influences and its central philosophical underpinnings. In terms of influences, as the present discussion will make clear, Forst is much more directly and constructively engaged with contemporary Anglophone political philosophy. More importantly, his foundational philosophical commitments are in some ways both more diffident of power and more thoroughgoingly Kantian that those of the later Habermas—in a word, they are more *critical*. As in the original Frankfurt School usage, 'critical' refers to the Kantian project of investigating knowledge, experience, and morality transcendentally, ie in terms of their conditions of possibility. Forst's project can be understood as an inquiry into the conditions of possibility of normativity—an account of the features of the human condition that make us subject to normative considerations. That, in turn, illuminates what it takes for particular normative considerations to apply to particular agents, and what that entails for the purposes of regulating human interaction through social norms and political institutions.

* Enzo Rossi's research for this essay was supported by the Dutch National Science Organisation's (NWO) Vidi project 'Legitimacy Beyond Consent' (grant n. 016.164.351).

Sameer Bajaj and Enzo Rossi, *Noumenal Power, Reasons, and Justification: A Critique of Forst* In: *Constitutionalism Justified: Rainer Forst in Discourse*. Edited by: Ester Herlin-Karnell and Matthias Klatt, Oxford University Press (2020), © Ester Herlin-Karnell and Matthias Klatt.
DOI: 10.1093/oso/9780190889050.003.0006

The specific aspect of Forst's project that we wish to focus on is his attempt to draw a connection between power and justification. Forst draws this connection primarily conceptually, though we will also consider whether a normative connection may be drawn within his framework. At any rate, Forst's key insight is this. If we understand power as operating by furnishing those subjected to it with reasons, then we create a space for the normative contestation of any exercise of power. He calls this the *noumenal* understanding of power. It is noumenal in the Sellarsian sense of being located in the 'space of reasons':

> ... in characterizing a situation as an exercise of power, we do not merely give an empirical description of a state of affairs or a social relation; we also, and primarily, have to place it in the space of reasons, or the normative space of freedom and action.[1]

That passage neatly encapsulates the critical nature of Forst's approach: notice the rejection of a positivist approach that would seek to reduce power to an observable behaviour. Rather, Forst maintains, power is a relation brought about by a specific class of reasons some agents may give others, and they are reasons in so far as others may recognize them. More precisely, for Forst power is '*the capacity of A to motivate B to think or do something that B would not have thought or done*'.[2] And that motivation is, conceptually, the product of the recognition of one or more reasons (to think or do) that A implicitly or explicitly provided to B. Reason-recognition, importantly, is more than a mere external stimulus—hence the rejection of behavioural, empirical accounts of power. Furthermore, Forst draws an important distinction between the use of force and the use of power, where the former is not an instance of the latter (as in many empirical accounts), but rather a product of its failure: 'In contrast to the exercise of physical force or violence, power rests on recognition'.[3] If a state jails me for violating its laws, it is not exercising power over me; it is acting as a consequence of the realization of a failure in its exercise of power:

> ... if, as sometimes happens, the threat by the blackmailer or the kidnapper is no longer taken seriously, their power disappears. They can still use brute force and kill the kidnapped person, but that is rather a sign of having lost power ... The exercise and effects of power are based on the recognition of a reason—or better, and more often, of various reasons—to act differently than one would have acted without that reason.[4]

[1] Rainer Forst, 'Noumenal Power' (2015), 23 Journal of Political Philosophy 111, 112.
[2] ibid 115 (emphasis in original).
[3] ibid.
[4] ibid 116.

Setting aside, for now, whether that distinction between power and force can adequately capture the role of coercion in the exercise of power in politics (as opposed to other contexts), we can now lay out what we take to be the bare bones of Forst's argument as follows:

1. To be a subject of power is to be moved by reason(s).
2. Reasons cannot move subjects without recognition.
3. Therefore, power requires recognition.

---

4. Recognition requires justification.

---

5. Therefore, power requires justification.

2. Plan for the Chapter

This chapter's argument is in two main parts. In the next section we will try to show how, while that is clearly a valid argument, it is unsound, and so that (5) is not warranted. Our main contention will be that (4) is false, though we will also cast some doubt on (1). But our objections to (1) will only be exploratory, so we do not think we can undermine the inference to (3), which in itself is a significant achievement, and one with potentially fruitful offshoots other than (5), as we will briefly touch upon later. The gist of our arguments is this. Against (1), we try to show that on most plausible accounts of political freedom, some freedom-restrictions commonly attributed to the successful exercise of power would perplexingly count as failures of power on Forst's view (sub-section 1). Against (4), we argue that on the most plausible account of reason-recognition, namely, an appropriateness of response account, a justification relation is only a sufficient but not necessary condition for recognition (sub-section 2).

In the final section of this essay, we consider whether Forst might defend (5) not by appeal to a conceptual connection between power and justification, but by appeal to the *normative* connection that his theory of the right to justification posits. Roughly, Forst argues that a universal right to justification of power in terms of reciprocal and general reasons can be established by reconstructing the presuppositions of rational discourse in moral contexts. We respond that Forst can establish the existence of such a right only if he reconsiders the transcendental aspirations of his theory. The upshot, then, is in an invitation to Forst to reframe his otherwise illuminating project of transcendentally establishing a necessary connection between power and justification.

II. Does Power Require Justification?

1. Subjects of Power and the Recognition of Reasons

Why think that to be a subject of power is to be moved by reasons? One appealing feature of that view of Forst's is that, on most plausible construals of reasons and reason-giving, it necessarily makes power an object of normative enquiry. The space of reasons is a space in which competing sets of considerations must be balanced against one another. In the context of contemporary Anglophone political philosophy that may not even seem something we need to establish—after all, the field is customarily characterized as a normative inquiry into the justifiability of exercises of political power and of our attitudes towards them. But notice how on that construal of normative political theory—the prevalent one in Anglophone philosophy—power is but an accidental object of study. As Bernard Williams put it, much contemporary (Anglophone) political philosophy is a form of applied ethics, concerned either with implementing moral ideals through political instruments ('enactment model'), or with setting moral boundaries to what one may do in politics ('structural model').[5] Either way, power is just a contingent instrument or even an unfortunate occurrence in need of constraining, rather than a conceptually indispensable focus of politico-philosophical enquiry. Forst's approach, on the other hand, restores power to its central place, thus reconnecting critical theory's longstanding preoccupation with power structures with the normative concerns of contemporary analytic political philosophy (for the former often eschews prescription for diagnosis-critique, and the latter, as we have seen, tends to be oblivious to the importance of power relations—a problem highlighted in much recent realist literature).

Given that context, it is even more striking that Forst should try to develop 'a normatively neutral notion of power'.[6] It would arguably have been easier to build his view around an explicitly moralized notion such as domination or oppression. Those concepts are indeed usually characterized as subsets of power, specifically problematic kinds of social relations. Forst's project is more ambitious. From a normatively neutral account of power Forst wants to derive which features of power are suitable objects for normative judgment. And, as we have touched upon earlier, that feature is the justificatory, reason-giving nature that Forst ascribes to power. Before examining that move in detail, it may be worth stopping to briefly consider starting with the broader picture of power, as

[5] Bernard Williams, 'Realism and Moralism in Political Theory' in Bernard Williams, *In the Beginning Was the Deed: Realism and Moralism in Political Argument* (Geoffrey Hawthorn ed, Princeton University Press 2005) 1.

[6] Forst, 'Noumenal Power' (n 1) 111.

opposed to delving directly into an account of what makes particular instances of the exercise of power obligatory, permissible, or impermissible (to borrow the moralizing terminology of contemporary Anglophone political philosophy). One important affordance of this more ambitious strategy is that it makes it impossible to write off any instance of power exercise as 'natural' or 'par for the course' in any sense that would place it above (or beneath) the threshold of normative contestation—hence the rejection of positivist, purely behavioural accounts of power.

Given that motivation, the question then becomes: Is it feasible to provide an account of power that is both plausible and normatively neutral enough to not be reducible to the familiar moralized accounts of domination, exploitation, oppression, and the like? The answer, we suggest, has to do with the account of freedom implicit in Forst's theory of noumenal power. To be sure, it's not as if the very presence of an implicit account of freedom is the problem. As we have seen, Forst explicitly says that the noumenal space of reasons is 'the normative space of freedom and action'.[7] Besides, the freedom literature contains several well-developed normatively neutral accounts of freedom.[8] Rather, our focus should be on spelling out Forst's commitments with regard to freedom, and on assessing whether they are plausible in themselves as well as whether they are well suited to his project.

2. Challenging the Justificatory Recognition View

We now move on to our criticism of what we have identified as the fourth step in Forst's argument, namely, the view that in order to be a subject of power one needs to recognize the power as such. In our reconstruction of Forst's argument, that view depends on the prior premise that recognition is what enables reasons to move subjects; and that, in turn, is motivated by the view that power moves its subjects through reasons—the first premise, which we cast doubt upon in the previous sub-section. It's worth noting, however, that the idea that (reason) recognition requires justification[9] has independent plausibility, and so interesting implications of its own. We shall try to criticize it in ways that do not depend on our earlier argument either, and so without impugning Forst's

[7] ibid 112.

[8] eg Ian Carter, *A Measure of Freedom* (Oxford University Press 1999). We shall set aside the question of whether accounts of freedom such as Carter's, which are intended to be compatible with a broadly behavioural, empirical philosophy of social science (in the tradition inaugurated by Felix Oppenheim and others), can be squared with Forst's anti-positivism.

[9] So, strictly speaking, the object of this sub-section is the conjunction of propositions (2) and (4) in the argument with attribute to Forst.

theoretical motivations for this view, which from now on we will call the justificatory recognition view.

Arguably the prima facie appeal of the justificatory recognition view rests in the intuitive idea that recognizing that reason applies in a given situation is a matter of applying some normative standard, and in turn applying normative standards is a practice of justification—it involves adducing considerations for why a certain belief, feeling, or action conforms to a certain class of criteria. To use a mundane example, I (correctly) recognize that I have reason to feel offended when someone deliberately shows me the soles of their feet only if the context is such that applying the norms of Arab etiquette is appropriate. That is to say, the norms of Arab etiquette justify my taking offence. The person with whom I become offended is owed a justification, and I can provide one by showing that Arab etiquette is appropriate in our context and that it tells us that deliberately showing the soles of one's feet is offensive, and that, therefore, I have reason to feel offended. It doesn't matter, for the purposes of that example, whether adherence to etiquette is connected to any power structures. The example merely illustrates the connection between reason-recognition and (relevant) normative standards, ie between reason-recognition and justification.

Now, what the example shows is that whenever I can provide a justification it is the case that I produce reasons that can be recognized as such. But our contention is that Forst's justificatory recognition view requires a stronger claim, namely, that only justification can provide recognizable reasons. In other words, Forst claims that justification is necessary and sufficient for reason recognition, whereas we claim that it is merely sufficient. Before arguing for our claim, it is worth pointing out its import for Forst's theory of the right to justification. Simply put, if it is possible to recognize reasons in the absence of a justification, then reason-responsiveness of power does not suffice to ground the right to justification. Just because humans can be (and arguably inevitably are) subjects of power, it doesn't follow that they are 'justificatory beings'.[10]

To see why reason recognition does not require justification, we will need a brief detour to distinguish reason giving from reason recognition. Our contention is indeed that Forst lumps them together, whereas they are distinct, and only the former requires justification—even if we assume, as we do for the sake of the argument, that any reason given is ipso facto recognizable.[11] So the question, for us, is whether one can recognize that an agent is providing them with a reason (to

[10] Rainer Forst, 'Kritik der Rechtfertigenden Vernunft: Die Erklärung Praktischer Normativität' in Rainer Forst, *Normativität und Macht: Zur Analyse sozialer Rechtfertigungsordnungen* (Suhrkamp 2015) 37 (our translation).

[11] For a discussion of the difference between the accessibility and the acceptability of justificatory reasons, see Enzo Rossi, 'Legitimacy, Democracy and Public Justification: Rawls' Political Liberalism Versus Gaus' Justificatory Liberalism' (2014), 20 Res Publica 9.

act, say) even though that agent fails to provide—and perhaps couldn't provide—a justification for why that course of action is required, or is a good idea, and so on. To be sure, when Forst talks about 'orders of justification'[12] he doesn't imply that those in power must always do the justificatory labour—literally formulate and offer the reasons why those subjected to their power should comply. Rather, he points out how the noumenal view of power can account for power *structures*.[13] So what matters is not that someone in power possesses—let alone presents—a justification. What matters is that the justification is somehow available to its addressees, the subjects of power. We are talking here of a shared understanding of what Bernard Williams would call a 'legitimation story':[14] 'Every social order in general . . . is based on a certain understanding of its purpose, aims, and rules—in short, it is a normative order as an order of justification'.[15] The question for us, then, becomes: Can there be a functional, compliance-inducing shared understanding of a normative order whose recognition does not depend on its justification? Or, put differently, can subjects of power recognize that they have reason to comply even in the absence of a justification?

We will now try to answer those questions affirmatively while remaining in agreement with Forst on his normative and cognitive understanding of motivation (for compliance with power). An affective rather than cognitive model of motivation[16] would provide a more direct route to a critique of Forst's position, but it would depend on premises we cannot defend here. Without wading too deeply into the quagmire of the debate on reasons, we can say that a compelling way to understand them as normative and cognitive notions is to think of reason relations[17] as eliciting *responses* in human agents. Those responses are not mere stimuli of a mechanistic sort, but rather behaviours—actions, beliefs,

[12] Forst, 'Noumenal Power' (n 1) 117.

[13] ibid 118.

[14] See Bernard Williams, 'From Freedom to Liberty: The Construction of a Political Value' in Bernard Williams, *In the Beginning Was the Deed: Realism and Moralism in Political Argument* (Geoffrey Hawthorn ed, Princeton University Press 2005) 95. On the role of legitimation stories in Williams's theory of legitimacy, see Jan P Beetz and Enzo Rossi, 'The EU's Democratic Deficit in a Realist Key: Multilateral Governance, Popular Sovereignty and Critical Responsiveness' (2017), 8 Transnational Legal Theory 22.

[15] Forst, 'Noumenal Power' (n 1) 119. Notice the consonance, which Forst more or less explicitly acknowledges, with what has come to be known as the practice-dependent approach in normative political theory: Andrea Sangiovanni, 'Justice and the Priority of Politics to Morality' (2008), 16 Journal of Political Philosophy 137.

[16] On this distinction, see John Skorupski, *The Domain of Reasons* (Oxford University Press 2010) 239ff. Relatedly, for an intriguing argument that tries to push Forst away from his rationalism, see Andrea Sangiovanni, 'Scottish Constructivism and the Right to Justification' in Rainer Forst, *Justice, Democracy and the Right to Justification: Rainer Forst in Dialogue* (Bloomsbury Academic 2014).

[17] Here we loosely follow Skorupski (n 16) 35ff. The complex position he defends is compatible with Forst's way of writing about reasons for the purposes of our argument, which at any rate does not depend on Skorupski's cognitive irrealism about reasons (though it is compatible with it).

feelings—with an intentional content we can ascribe to the agent who is answerable to the reason(s) at hand. To say that reason relations are normative in character, then, is to say that we can evaluate the (degree of) appropriateness of a response. And, like Forst, we can be cognitivists about the grounds of that evaluation: that a response is appropriate can be true or false.[18]

With that conceptual apparatus in place, we can now rephrase our questions as follows. Can a subject's response to an instance of the exercise of power be appropriate even in the absence of a justification for the power? It seems to us that, in the light of that reformulation, it is easy to answer affirmatively, pace Forst. Recognizing that someone has power over you just means seeing that you have reason to do as she says—the burden is on Forst to show that such a response would be inappropriate in the absence of a relevant justification. For instance, the deciding factor *for me* may be that I fear the power-holder's secret police, but that is not a justification in Forst's sense of the term. At the end of the day, if the illuminating notion of noumenal power is to remain as neutral as it needs to be but also as realistic as Forst claims it is,[19] it cannot be made to enshrine a right to justification.

III. Can the Right to Justification Normatively Link Power and Justification?

1. Disagreement and the Right to Justification

If the arguments in the previous section are right, then Forst might attempt to defend a necessary connection between power and justification in a different way. While we have argued that his analysis of the idea of noumenal power cannot be made to enshrine the right to justification, he develops a different argument for this right in other parts of his work. The argument we have in mind defends the right to justification as a constitutive principle of practical reason that can be established by reconstructing the presuppositions of rational discourse in moral contexts. This argument differs from the argument considered in Section I in that it is a *practical* transcendental argument—it aims to ground the right to justification in the presuppositions of a certain kind of practice, namely, the practice of rational moral discourse.

The problem with the argument is that, so far as we can see, it cannot satisfy two of Forst's core aims in developing it, and thus cannot establish connection

[18] We will remain neutral as to whether that truth-value depends on a truthmaker (or not, as in Skorupski's irrealist cognitivism).

[19] Forst, 'Noumenal Power' (n 1) 118.

between power and justification that Forst seeks. First, Forst rejects 'ideal theory' approaches to theorizing about justice that aim to articulate a model of a perfectly just society in favour of a 'practice-immanent' approach that employs the right to justification to offer emancipatory critiques of actually existing relations of rule and domination.[20] Second, Forst aims to develop a critical theory of justice that is 'reflexive' in the sense it contains the resources to critique its own limitations and shortcomings. This capacity for self-scrutiny is essential if a theory of justice is to avoid a 'metaphysical slumber' that arbitrarily privileges its own normative recommendations over the competing 'narratives of justification' undergirding relations of rule and domination.[21]

The challenge for Forst's theory arises once we consider attempts to make the right to justification socially effective in an existing political community. The right to justification requires that relations of power 'must be justified in a reciprocal and general manner, where one side many not simply project its reasons onto the other but has to justify itself discursively'.[22] According to Forst, the right to justification generates a requirement of 'fundamental' justice to secure the political rights, institutions, capabilities, information, and opportunities necessary for 'all those who are subjected to a normative order [to] be its co-authors as equal participants and normative authorities in adequate justificatory practices that critically reflect on and constitute that order'.[23] Once a just 'basic structure of justification' that respects all relevant individuals' right to justification has been established, citizens can work through its discursive participatory mechanisms to achieve a 'maximally' just distribution of goods.[24]

[20] Rainer Forst, 'Realisms in International Political Theory' in Rainer Forst, *Normativity and Power: Analyzing Social Orders of Justification* (Ciaran Cronin tr, Oxford University Press 2017) 151. Rawls's *A Theory of Justice*, of course, is generally taken to exemplify the ideal theory approach in political philosophy: John Rawls, *A Theory of Justice* (Harvard University Press 1971). For more on the distinction between ideal and non-ideal theory, see Zofia Stemplowska and Adam Swift, 'Ideal and Non-ideal Theory' in David M Estlund (ed), *The Oxford Handbook of Political Philosophy* (Oxford University Press 2012).

[21] Rainer Forst, 'Einleitung: Ordnungen der Rechtfertigung. Zum Verhäaltnis von Philosophie, Gesellschaftstheorie und Kritik' in Rainer Forst, *Normativität und Macht: Zur Analyse sozialer Rechtfertigungsordnungen* (Suhrkamp 2015) 11. Forst explicitly adopts this ideal of reflexive self-scrutiny from Kant, who famously says: 'Reason must subject itself to critique in all its undertakings, and cannot restrict the freedom of critique through any prohibition without damaging itself . . . The very existence of reason depends upon this freedom, which has no dictatorial authority, but whose claim is never anything more than the agreement of free citizens, each of whom must be able to express his reservations, indeed even his veto, without holding back'. Immanuel Kant, *Critique of Pure Reason* (Paul Guyer and Allen W Wood eds and trs, Cambridge University Press 1998) A:738f, B:766f.

[22] Rainer Forst, 'Two Pictures of Justice' in Rainer Forst, *Justification and Critique: Towards a Critical Theory of Politics* (Ciaran Cronin tr, Polity Press 2013) 34.

[23] Forst, 'Noumenal Power' (n 1) 117.

[24] Rainer Forst, 'Toward a Critical Theory of Transnational Justice' in Rainer Forst, *The Right to Justification: Elements of a Constructivist Theory of Justice* (Jeffrey Flynn tr, Columbia University Press 2011) 262.

In line with Forst's practice-immanent approach to theorizing about justice, suppose that we consider a political community in which many citizens' right to justification has not been secured by their basic political structure. This is true of most existing political communities, including most liberal democracies. Consider the United States, where the instrumentalizing influence of money, widespread political disenfranchisement of minority voters (bolstered by deep structural racism), relative lack of women representatives in Congress (bolstered by deep structural sexism), and many other phenomena pose significant barriers to realizing the kind of deliberative equality the right to justification requires. Forst's theory implies that individuals ought to reform the basic structure of such a political community so that it respects all individuals' right to justification. Of course, what political reforms the right to justification requires will depend on the nature of the existing relations of domination in a given community; in the case of the United States, for example, plausible candidates for reform include campaign finance reform, criminal justice reform, significant wealth redistribution, policies addressing the gendered division of labor, and so on.

Now, it is a fact about all existing liberal democracies that citizens deeply and pervasively disagree about moral and philosophical matters. Indeed, John Rawls famously argues that such disagreement is the inevitable result of the good-faith use of reason under the very conditions of freedom of thought and expression that all liberal democracies protect.[25] Whether or not we accept Rawls's view here, it is obvious that Forst's argument for the right to justification and his view of the political recommendations it generates will be intensely controversial in all existing liberal democracies. As such, individuals who attempt to reform their basic structure so that it respects all subjects' right to justification will be doing so in face of deep and pervasive disagreement. For example, when individuals appeal to the right to justification to advocate for political reforms that limit wealth inequality or keep wealth inequality from influencing democratic politics, they will be pushing for policies that are intensely controversial in the United States on the basis of arguments that are themselves intensely controversial.

The problem is that it is difficult to see how individuals who push for such policies can avoid arbitrarily privileging the right to justification and the arguments for it over competing narratives of justification. Recall that the right to justification requires that 'one side many not simply project its reasons onto the other but has to justify itself discursively.' Yet, individuals who advocate for the political recommendations the right to justification generates in the face of widespread disagreement appear to be projecting their reasons onto those who reject that principle. Specifically, such individuals fail to satisfy the requirement that

[25] John Rawls, *Political Liberalism* (expanded edn, Columbia University Press 2005) 144.

relations of power be justifiable *to* all individuals subject to that power based on reasons they can appreciate as reasons. Of course, if all individuals in a given liberal democracy were to accept the right to justification as the correct standard for evaluating how political power ought to be exercised, then perhaps the political recommendations the principle generates would be interpersonally justifiable. However, to theorize about a political community in which all individuals accept the right to justification as the correct standard for evaluating political power would be a paradigmatic instance of the sort of ideal theorizing that Forst rejects. In existing liberal democracies—the very liberal democracies that Forst's practice-immanent approach seeks to theorize about—many individuals will reject Forst's argument for the right to justification. The point we want to emphasize here is that advocating for policies based on the right to justification in the face of such disagreement appears to involve arbitrarily privileging that right and the argument for it over competing narratives of justification found in diverse liberal democracies.[26]

2. Reflexivity and the Normative Status of the Right to Justification

It might seem that this objection ignores the capacity for reflexive self-scrutiny that Forst builds into his theory.[27] In so far as his theory contains the resources to critique its own limitations and shortcomings, the response goes, then individuals who advocate for the policies the right to justifications recommends are not *arbitrarily* privileging that principle and the argument for it over competing narratives of justification. Rather, they are *justifiably* doing so, since that principle and the argument for it are licenced by the foundational critical standard the theory advances—namely, the right to justification itself. But we do not think that this response is convincing. The problem is that the response presupposes that the right to justification is the correct standard for evaluating political power. The fact that the right to justification passes self-inspection licences its use as a justificatory grounds for political power only if the right to justification is the correct standard for evaluating justificatory grounds for political power.

To illustrate the point, consider a deliberative exchange between two members of an existing liberal democracy: Maxine—who accepts the right

[26] This objection bears similarities to the so-called self-defeat objection to public reason theories of political legitimacy. See Steven Wall, 'Is Public Justification Self-Defeating?' (2002), 39 American Philosophical Quarterly 385; Steven Wall, 'Rawlsian Perfectionism' (2013), 10 Journal of Moral Philosophy 573.

[27] For an incisive critique on this point, see Lois McNay (in this volume).

to justification as the correct standard for evaluating political power—and Shivani—who endorses a utilitarian standard for evaluating political power. Suppose that Maxine publicly advocates for a particular tax policy because that policy is the best way of respecting individuals' right to justification. Shivani rejects the policy because it fails to satisfy the utilitarian standard she endorses. If Maxine continues to press for the policy in the face of Shivani's utilitarian objections, then it appears Shivani can rightly accuse Maxine of projecting Maxine's reasons onto Shivani and thus arbitrarily privileging Maxine's preferred narrative of justification over Shivani's preferred utilitarian narrative of justification. If Maxine then goes on to defend herself by arguing that she is not arbitrarily privileging the right to justification and her argument for it because the right to justification passes the test of reflexive self-scrutiny, Shivani can complain that she rejects the very standard that Maxine employs to licence her use of the right to justification as a grounds for political power: namely, the right to justification itself.

The most promising response to this objection gets us to the metaethical core of Forst's theory. Forst might argue that the right to justification is *inescapable* in a way that renders it appropriate to privilege itself over competing standards in justifying the use of political power. Recall that Forst defends the right to justification as a constitutive principle of practical reason, one that can be established by reconstructing the presuppositions of rational discourse in moral contexts. Forst might thus argue that the right to justification represents the context-transcending normative bedrock of all interpersonal moral deliberation and, as such, individuals cannot discursively challenge it without presupposing it. So, when Shivani discursively challenges Maxine's appeal to the right to justification as a justificatory ground for the use of political power, Maxine can observe that Shivani herself is presupposing the very critical standard she seeks to challenge and, as such, is caught in a kind of performative contradiction. Shivani is, in this respect, guilty of irrationality.

The problem with this response is that it appears to be inconsistent with how Forst thinks of the normative status right to justification, and Forst's reasons for thinking of the normative status of that principle as he does are compelling. In order to see what we have in mind, notice the similarity between the response articulated in the previous paragraph and Habermas's well-known attempt to ground a universalization constraint on moral norms. Habermas argues that such a constraint can be found in the rational presuppositions of interpersonal deliberation, in particular in the conditions for discursively redeeming a validity claim to how we ought to act in planning contexts. When we make such claims, Habermas argues, we presuppose that they are justified only if they 'meet (or could meet) with the approval of all affected in their capacity as participants in a practical discourse.'[28] Forst famously argues that Habermas fails to demonstrate the objective normativity of the universalization constraint he seeks to ground. While Habermas arguably shows how individuals are to justify moral claims if they are to be engaged in genuine interpersonal planning, Forst argues, Habermas does not show *that* individuals ought to justify such claims in accordance with a universalization constraint.

How does Forst's own view escape this problem? According to Forst, while the right to justification is a constitutive principle of rational discourse in moral contexts, individuals must have a higher-order practical 'insight' that there is a moral duty to comply with that principle.[29] Having such an insight is what it means to regard others as ends in themselves rather than as means. We find the nature of insight somewhat obscure. But putting this worry aside, the deeper problem is that one does not have to have this insight in order to engage in rational moral discourse—one can fully engage in rational moral discourse without having the moral insight that Forst believes is essential to establishing the normativity of the right to justification. And if one does not have this insight—if one believes, instead, that a competing standard for evaluating political power is correct—then individuals who employ the right to justification as a justificatory ground for political power appear to be projecting their reasons onto others. So, individuals cannot vindicate privileging that principle over competing standards in justifying political power by appeal to the idea that the principle is an escapable presupposition of rational moral discourse. Even if this is true, it does not show that appreciating the reasons to comply with that principle is an escapable presupposition of rational moral discourse. So, we believe that Forst must do more to show that his theory can satisfy his own conditions for a successful critical theory of justice. Ultimately, it appears that individuals who accept the right to justification cannot escape privileging that right in justifying political power—at least if they want to bring about a political order that secures that right.

References

Beetz JP and Rossi E, 'The EU's Democratic Deficit in a Realist Key: Multilateral Governance, Popular Sovereignty and Critical Responsiveness' (2017), 8 Transnational Legal Theory 22.

Carter I, *A Measure of Freedom* (Oxford University Press 1999).

[28] Jürgen Habermas, 'Discourse Ethics: Notes on a Program of Philosophical Justification' in Jürgen Habermas, *Moral Consciousness and Communicative Action* (Christian Lenhardt and Shierry Weber Nicholsen trs, Polity Press 1990) 66.

[29] Rainer Forst, 'Practical Reason and Justifying Reasons: On the Foundation of Morality' in Rainer Forst, *The Right to Justification: Elements of a Constructivist Theory of Justice* (Jeffrey Flynn tr, Columbia University Press 2011) 35.

Forst R, 'Practical Reason and Justifying Reasons: On the Foundation of Morality' in Rainer Forst, *The Right to Justification: Elements of a Constructivist Theory of Justice* (Jeffrey Flynn tr, Columbia University Press 2011).
Forst R, 'Toward a Critical Theory of Transnational Justice' in Rainer Forst, *The Right to Justification: Elements of a Constructivist Theory of Justice* (Jeffrey Flynn tr, Columbia University Press 2011).
Forst R, 'Two Pictures of Justice' in Rainer Forst, *Justification and Critique: Towards a Critical Theory of Politics* (Ciaran Cronin tr, Polity Press 2013).
Forst R, 'Einleitung: Ordnungen der Rechtfertigung. Zum Verhäaltnis von Philosophie, Gesellschaftstheorie und Kritik' in Rainer Forst, *Normativität und Macht: Zur Analyse sozialer Rechtfertigungsordnungen* (Suhrkamp 2015).
Forst R, 'Kritik der Rechtfertigenden Vernunft: Die Erklärung Praktischer Normativität' in Rainer Forst, *Normativität und Macht: Zur Analyse sozialer Rechtfertigungsordnungen* (Suhrkamp 2015).
Forst R, 'Noumenal Power' (2015), 23 Journal of Political Philosophy 111.
Forst R, 'Realisms in International Political Theory' in Rainer Forst, *Normativity and Power: Analyzing Social Orders of Justification* (Ciaran Cronin tr, Oxford University Press 2017).
Habermas J, 'Discourse Ethics: Notes on a Program of Philosophical Justification' in Jürgen Habermas, *Moral Consciousness and Communicative Action* (Christian Lenhardt and Shierry Weber Nicholsen trs, Polity Press 1990).
Kant I, *Critique of Pure Reason* (Paul Guyer and Allen W Wood eds and trs, Cambridge University Press 1998).
Rawls J, *A Theory of Justice* (Harvard University Press 1971).
Rawls J, '*Political Liberalism* (expanded edn, Columbia University Press 2005).
Rossi E, 'Legitimacy, Democracy and Public Justification: Rawls' Political Liberalism Versus Gaus' Justificatory Liberalism' (2014), 20 Res Publica 9.
Sangiovanni A, 'Justice and the Priority of Politics to Morality' (2008), 16 Journal of Political Philosophy 137.
Sangiovanni A, 'Scottish Constructivism and the Right to Justification' in Rainer Forst, *Justice, Democracy and the Right to Justification: Rainer Forst in Dialogue* (Bloomsbury Academic 2014).
Skorupski J, *The Domain of Reasons* (Oxford University Press 2010).
Stemplowska Z and Swift A, 'Ideal and Non-ideal Theory' in David M Estlund (ed), *The Oxford Handbook of Political Philosophy* (Oxford University Press 2012).
Wall S, 'Is Public Justification Self-Defeating?' (2002), 39 American Philosophical Quarterly 385.
Wall S, 'Rawlsian Perfectionism' (2013), 10 Journal of Moral Philosophy 573.
Williams B, 'From Freedom to Liberty: The Construction of a Political Value' in Bernard Williams, *In the Beginning Was the Deed: Realism and Moralism in Political Argument* (Geoffrey Hawthorn ed, Princeton University Press 2005).
Williams B, 'Realism and Moralism in Political Theory' in Bernard Williams, *In the Beginning Was the Deed: Realism and Moralism in Political Argument* (Geoffrey Hawthorn ed, Princeton University Press 2005).

7

The Limits of Justification

Critique, Disclosure, and Reflexivity

Lois McNay

I. Introduction

One of the defining premises of Frankfurt School critical theory is that, given the situated nature of all thought, emancipatory political critique necessarily has immanent foundations. Critique is politically effective when it is guided not by transcendental principles but by existing values and norms embedded within the practices and struggles of a given age. The task of critique is to identify these endogenous normative resources, reconstructing them in such a way as to establish the evaluative emancipatory perspective from which it diagnoses a particular social order. Although he aligns himself with the Frankfurt School tradition, the critical theory of Rainer Forst is distinctive because it rejects this founding premise of immanence on the grounds that it deprives critique of the independent normative foundations necessary to support truly emancipatory claims. To be universally binding, critique must have the context transcending validity that can only be derived from free-standing principles. Forst finds such autonomous grounds in the principle of justification which he maintains represents the transcendental core of practical reason. Mindful however of the 'metaphysical slumber' that may ensue from this idealizing move, Forst also insists, in line with the Frankfurt School approach, that to be genuinely radical, critique must be concerned above all to develop a critical theory of existing injustice and to build into itself the capacity for reflexive self-scrutiny. Power is the 'first question' of justice, and normative theory is empty unless accompanied by a disclosing focus on oppressive, dominating, and other unwarranted social hierarchies. Attentiveness to power also implies that critique understand itself as a type of reflexive practical knowledge that critically evaluates its conceptual limitations and blind spots in response to changing social practices. Justification critique's inherent capacities for disclosure and reflexive self-scrutiny are indispensable in ensuring its radical trajectory and avoiding the pre-democratic, prescriptive tendencies that Forst finds so problematic in mainstream ideal theorizing.

Lois McNay, *The Limits of Justification: Critique, Disclosure, and Reflexivity* In: *Constitutionalism Justified: Rainer Forst in Discourse.* Edited by: Ester Herlin-Karnell and Matthias Klatt, Oxford University Press (2020),

DOI: 10.1093/oso/9780190889050.003.0007

In this chapter, I argue that Forst's paradigm is less radical than claimed in so far as it fails to establish an immanent connection between the role of justification as a transcendental principle and as tool of disclosing, reflexive critique. My primary concern is with the feasibility of the critical rather than ideal side of his project, and I maintain that the construal of justification as a trans-historical principle, by definition, shields it from systematic criticism and consequently constrains critique's capacity for reflexive self-scrutiny. In a general sense, reflexivity is ignited by disclosure to the degree that it is reflection on the non-identical elements of social life, on that which doesn't fit in, that may prompt critical re-evaluation of a theory's conceptual framework. Justification critique's capacity for disclosure, and hence reflexivity, is crucially limited, however, by Forst's reliance on a tendentious concept of noumenal power, which does not satisfactorily explain the complex, material dynamics through which major structural inequalities are reproduced. Its normative scope is further stymied by a disregard of the latent power dynamics often at work in the actual conversation about justice that subvert formally equal relations of justification and make it difficult for certain individuals to be taken seriously as democratic interlocutors. In short, the lack of reflexivity is evident in Forst's failure to adequately consider how entrenched asymmetries of power may require him to advance beyond an abstract, one-dimensional account of mutually owed justifications. Vacillating inconsequently between transcendent and immanent perspectives, I conclude that justification critique is in fact a self-undermining theoretical enterprise.

II. Immanent and Transcendent Foundations

Despite considerable divergences in their respective accounts of critical theory, thinkers of the Frankfurt School share one underlying intellectual premise, namely, that, given the situated nature of all thought, emancipatory theory should necessarily take the form of immanent social critique. Radical critique is most effective when it is guided not by transcendental moral principles but by values and norms that are already embodied, in an incomplete form, in the core institutions, practices, and beliefs that structure social life. The task of critique is to reconstruct these normative resources in such a way as to establish the evaluative perspective on which to base social criticism and make proposals for change. Although critical theorists have differed widely in their approach to the reconstruction of socially embedded norms—arguably the thinkers of the second and third generation being more successful in this reconstructive effort than those of the first—they all can be said to share a common commitment to the tenet of critique's immanent foundations.

What sets the work of Rainer Forst apart from the Frankfurt tradition with which he otherwise strongly identifies is his rejection of the necessary presumption of critique's immanent foundations. He maintains that the grounding of critique in socially internal values deprives it of the impartial perspective from which its evaluative insights may be systematically justified. Lacking external standards, critique is reduced to an unsystematic and parochial relativism where 'we would just replace one form of justification with another more to our liking'.[1] To ensure irrefutable emancipatory force, critique must be based in principles and standards that transcend particular contexts and that, in so far as they are genuinely independent, all subjects can recognize as morally binding. Theorists such as Habermas and Honneth are well aware that their rejection of thought's morally freestanding status has troubling relativist implications, and they aim to circumvent this by basing critique in principles that, although immanent, have a generalizable or 'quasi-transcendent' validity by virtue of their social omnipresence. Such principles of intra-mundane transcendence are found in seemingly foundational features of social interaction identified by Habermas as the universal pragmatics of communication and, by Honneth, as the primary role that recognition plays in healthy individuation processes. But, for Forst, these attempts to derive a 'rational universal' from social ontology are either too biased to deliver a sufficiently impartial foundation for critique or too procedurally thin to have binding moral force.[2] Against Honneth, Forst maintains that the recognition paradigm lacks impartiality because it erroneously generalizes a thick ethical good, qua a substantive anthropology of self-realization, as the basis for inclusive political structures. As complex and open as a formal theory of the good or flourishing life might be, it will always fail to encompass the plurality of possible ethical ways of life and will unavoidably yoke respect for persons as 'ends in themselves' to 'particular ends or ways of pursuing ends that are supposed to characterise a good life'.[3] Forst concludes that a comprehensive theory of social justice can only do justice to the good, 'the less it rests on particular conceptions of the good'.[4] Although Habermas avoids such a conflation of the just with the good, the difficulty with communicative ethics is that it rests on a justificatory procedure that is too formal to prevent non-democratic outcomes. Forst identifies a 'normative gap between the pragmatically derived and hence weak transcendental "must" of discourse ethics and the stronger, normatively

[1] Amy Allen, Rainer Forst, and Mark Haugaard, 'Power and Reason, Justice and Domination: A Conversation' (2014), 7 Journal of Political Power 7, 11.

[2] Axel Honneth, 'A Social Pathology of Reason: On the Intellectual Legacy of Critical Theory' in Fred Rush (ed), *The Cambridge Companion to Critical Theory* (Cambridge University Press 2004).

[3] Rainer Forst, 'The Justification of Justice: Rawls's Political Liberalism and Habermas's Discourse Theory in Dialogue' in Rainer Forst, *The Right to Justification: Elements of a Constructivist Theory of Justice* (Jeffrey Flynn tr, Columbia University Press 2012) 118.

[4] ibid.

justified "must" that he holds is crucial for a binding political theory of justice and its essential components, such as a theory of human rights'.[5]

To avoid the relativism and formalism that hamper the critical theories of his contemporaries, Forst consequently concludes that critique must have autonomous moral grounds and such a *fundamentum inconcussum* can be established though constructivist reflection on the essential nature of practical reason. If we reconstruct what it means to reason practically, then we discern at the very heart of the process, a shared basic practice of justification. In answering fundamental questions such as 'what should I do?' or 'why did I believe that a certain course of action was permissible or necessary?', the individual is required to 'provide reasons that can justify actions according to criteria that are valid in a moral context'.[6] Valid criteria in this sense of moral justification are not subject relative but inter-subjective in nature; the point of justification is not to explain actions as the most rational way of realizing personal ends and goals, but rather to provide reasons for actions that others, who are morally affected, cannot reasonably refuse. Practical reason is, at its core, 'the ability to answer a moral question with a morally justifiable answer that can be supported intersubjectively. It is reasonably justified if no moral reasons speak against it'.[7] This inter-subjective formulation highlights a further defining feature of reasonable justification that, for a normative claim to be accepted as valid, it must meet the criteria of *reciprocity* and *generality*. Reciprocity is defined in terms of content—'no one may refuse the particular demands of others that one raises for oneself'—and reasons—'no one may simply assume that others have the same values and interests as oneself or make recourse to "higher truths" that are not shared'.[8] Generality means that reasons for generally valid basic norms must be sharable by all those affected, that is they must not exclude the objections of anyone affected.[9] The criteria of general and reciprocal justification generate a binding normative force that is stronger, according to Forst, than comparable ideas of de facto accord, like-mindedness, or assent that rest on weaker notions of moral reasoning as intersubjective acceptability or agent neutrality. At the same time, by making the regulative principle of deliberation that which cannot be reasonably rejected rather than the demanding notion of consensus, Forst's model overcomes a

[5] Rainer Forst, 'Moral Autonomy and the Autonomy of Morality: Toward a Theory of Normativity after Kant' in Rainer Forst, *The Right to Justification: Elements of a Constructivist Theory of Justice* (Jeffrey Flynn tr, Columbia University Press 2012) 59.

[6] Rainer Forst, 'Practical Reason and Justifying Reasons: On the Foundation of Morality' in Rainer Forst, *The Right to Justification: Elements of a Constructivist Theory of Justice* (Jeffrey Flynn tr, Columbia University Press 2012) 15.

[7] ibid.

[8] Rainer Forst, 'Introduction: The Foundation of Justice' in Rainer Forst, *The Right to Justification: Elements of a Constructivist Theory of Justice* (Jeffrey Flynn tr, Columbia University Press 2012) 6.

[9] ibid.

problem with the Habermasian one, namely, it shows us how a claim can be justified even if agreement cannot be achieved. Moreover, by accommodating a degree of disagreement in this way, justification critique is arguably better able to deal with the 'diversity of evaluative approaches' that should characterize truly inclusive deliberation. Forst maintains that the principle of justification is unconditional in so far as it is not dependent on any prior notion of the good or other extraneous social criterion. Moral constructivism reveals justification to be the essence of practical reason; there is no other entity that can be appealed to beyond reason because reason constitutes its own grounds, as he puts it: 'there are no external derivations that can trump the construction'.[10] This autonomy establishes that 'moral persons have a fundamental *right to justification* and corresponding unconditional *duty to justify* morally relevant actions'.[11]

Forst argues that the a priori of justification establishes incontestable normative foundations for a binding concept of justice: 'moral constructivism form[s] the normative core of *political* constructivism'.[12] Justification is a basic moral right in the sense that all humans have the right not to be subjected to norms and institutions that cannot be adequately justified. The first task of justice is accordingly to guarantee a 'basic structure of justification', that is, one in which all affected subjects have an irrevocable right to collectively deliberate and decide about the institutions that they are to live under and veto any arrangements that cannot be reciprocally and generally justified to her. The basic structure of justification is not intended to provide a complete blueprint for a fair society, but rather to establish the 'minimally' just conditions and principles upon which further discussion about a 'maximally' just society can be realized. In succeeding discussions about maximal justice, the criteria of general and reciprocal justification provide the independent standards for judging whether particular social arrangements have legitimate foundations or not. The criteria provide a morally rigorous 'normative grammar' that 'works like a filter to sort out justifiable from unjustifiable claims, one that opens up and at the same time restricts the possibility of justice claims'.[13]

III. Disclosure and Reflexivity

While the a priori of justification appears to provide a way out of the relativist dilemmas of immanent critique, it seems, at first glance, that Forst has moved

[10] ibid 7.
[11] Forst, 'Practical Reason and Justifying Reasons' (n 6) 21.
[12] Forst, 'Introduction: The Foundation of Justice' (n 8) 6.
[13] Forst, 'The Justification of Justice' (n 3) 113.

some distance from the type of approach usually understood to typify critical theory. Indeed, a number of commentators hold that his claim that critique 'needs' transcendental foundations pushes the justification paradigm closer towards the style of political reasoning that Bernard Williams famously termed political philosophy as applied ethics.[14] On this view, Forst's attempt to transcendentalize the justification principle replicates the ideological errors of ideal theory where contingent social practices are reified as free-floating universal norms.[15] Forst emphatically rejects such comparisons with ideal theory arguing that justification critique offers a far more radical approach to justice because of its inherent capacity for disclosure and reflexivity. With this claim, Forst explicitly re-connects justification critique to Frankfurt School critical theory and its premise of the inescapable dialectic of power and reason. The dialectic implies, inter alia, that to be politically effective, thought about emancipation must proceed through a critical theory that exposes existing injustice and domination. Accordingly, Forst states that power must be the 'first question' of justice and 'a critical theory of (in) justice has to be above all a critique of the existing *relations of justification*'.[16] It is not that ideal theorists are uninterested in how moral principles might bear on unwarranted social hierarchies, but for them, this is an extrinsic and derivative matter of 'application', whereas, for Forst, the critique of power lies at the very heart of normative reasoning. Emancipatory political thought is most effective when it disrupts settled norms and assumptions through the unmasking of injustices: 'every theory of justice requires a complex theory of injustice, not just as a normative account, but also in the form of a social analysis'.[17] Justification critique enacts its disclosing function not only through radical social criticism but also through its recursive structure. What Forst finds particularly troubling about ideal theory are the 'pre-democratic', prescriptive tendencies that flow from its method of antecedent justification. This has the effect, albeit unintended, of undermining democratic sovereignty by rendering it an organ for executing pre-given moral principles rather than treating it as the autonomous political body that actively determines the content of a just social structure.[18] Forst circumvents the problematic imposition of 'teleological values' because his constructivist method is 'discursive' rather than 'metaphysical' meaning that,

[14] Amy Allen, 'The Power of Justification' in Rainer Forst, *Justice, Democracy and the Right to Justification: Rainer Forst in Dialogue* (Bloomsbury Academic 2014) 84; Kevin Olson, 'Complexities of Political Discourse: Class, Power and the Linguistic Turn' in Rainer Forst, *Justice, Democracy and the Right to Justification: Rainer Forst in Dialogue* (Bloomsbury Academic 2014) 100.

[15] eg James Tully, 'Dialogue' (2011), 39 Political Theory 145.

[16] Rainer Forst, 'First Things First: Redistribution, Recognition and Justification' in Rainer Forst, *Justification and Critique: Towards a Critical Theory of Politics* (Ciaran Cronin tr, Polity Press 2013) 120.

[17] ibid 114.

[18] Forst, 'The Justification of Justice' (n 3) 106–10.

other than 'a certain conception of the person and particular criteria of reasonable practical justification', everything else is determined by the discursive practice itself.[19] Discursive thinness permits genuine democratic self-determination in the public use of reason because it is not the political philosopher but citizens themselves who autonomously determine the normative content of justice and revise it when appropriate.[20] Contra Rawls, the conversation about justice can never be finished; if it is to retain emancipatory relevance it must be ceaselessly taken up and given renewed meaning by each successive generation and constituency to whom it pertains. The radical bite of justification critique emanates therefore from the way it positions individuals as co-authors of the fundamental norms that guide society, replacing passive, 'principle interpreting' accounts of justice with an emancipatory 'principle-generating' account.[21] Combined with the critique of power, its recursive structure enhances democratic inclusivity by eschewing normalizing constructions of 'reasonable' deliberators and opening itself to voices from below, in particular, those of disempowered and marginalized groups, permitting them to challenge the status quo and to dispute settled notions of justice, affectedness, and subjection.[22]

The dialectic of reason and power also demands that critique build into itself a heightened capacity for reflexive self-scrutiny in order to guard against theoretical bias and conceptual reification. Critical theory has always understood itself as a highly self-reflexive form of evaluative thought that necessarily builds into itself a capacity to test and revise its values and principles in the light of what political practice might reveal about their emancipatory relevance. Forst endorses this by taking up Kant's well-known notion of the 'critique of critique', that no aspect of social practice should be immune from critical scrutiny, including critique itself. Immanent grounds may be normatively insufficient for emancipatory critique but it is just as unsatisfactory to resort to notions of 'otherworldly transcendence' to fill this foundational gap. This would be to fall into a 'metaphysical slumber' which neglects thought's own social preconditions: 'no social critic, no matter how radical, is not also an "immanent critic"'.[23] A theory can only count as critical and radical, in Forst's eyes, in the extent to which it

[19] ibid 111.

[20] Rainer Forst, 'Introduction: On the Idea of a Critique of Relations of Justification' in Rainer Forst, *Justification and Critique: Towards a Critical Theory of Politics* (Ciaran Cronin tr, Polity Press 2013) 8.

[21] Rainer Forst, 'The Rule of Reasons: Three Models of Deliberative Democracy' in Rainer Forst, *The Right to Justification: Elements of a Constructivist Theory of Justice* (Jeffrey Flynn tr, Columbia University Press 2012) 184.

[22] Rainer Forst, 'Justifying Justification: A Reply to My Critics' in Rainer Forst, *Justice, Democracy and the Right to Justification: Rainer Forst in Dialogue* (Bloomsbury Academic 2014) 178.

[23] Allen, Forst and Haugaard (n 1) 21.

understands itself as 'an activity that reflects back on itself and its own blind spots and exclusions in a self-critical manner'.[24]

It is in relation to the issue of reflexivity, however, that Forst's assertion that justification is simultaneously a principle of transcendence and immanence, of autonomy and critique, becomes perplexing. Put bluntly, how exhaustive can critique's reflection upon its own presumptions, blind spots and potential exclusions be if its animating core supposedly floats free of particular configurations of power? If the principle of justification is a universal constant, then, by definition, there must be a limit to the extent to which it is open to critical evaluation and rethinking should it be found to be less inclusive than it initially seems. By removing the justificatory essence of critique from the hermeneutic circle, Forst appears to drastically curtail the scope of the supposedly 'indispensable' tenet of the 'critique of critique'. The reflexive capacity of critique is not unrelated to its disclosing function for it is the unmasking of suppressed, negative aspects of social experience that frequently serves as the catalyst for critical self-scrutiny. Reflexivity entails not just acknowledgment of alterity and non-identity but the capacity to respond as fully as possible to the potentially destabilizing implications that this other perspective may have for one's previously settled view of the world.[25] But, if reflexive examination is prompted in part by a theory's ability to disclose and engage with the non-identical elements of social life—as Adorno puts it, the 'cross-grained, opaque, unassimilated material'—then justification critique is further undermined because of Forst's reliance on a tendentious account of power as a noumenal force.[26] Its central premise that social relations are secured through justificatory narratives that rest on the 'acceptance of reasons' forecloses an adequate understanding of the materiality of power and the complex, often indirect ways in which inequality and oppression are perpetuated. As I argue in the following sections, the inadequacies of Forst's account of power, qua disclosing critique, foreshadow an inability to advance beyond an empty formalism when thinking about how, in the conversation about justice, deep discrepancies of power between democratic interlocutors might be mitigated.

[24] Forst, 'Introduction: On the Idea of a Critique of Relations of Justification' (n 20) 8.

[25] eg James Bohman, 'Critical Theory as Practical Knowledge: Participants, Observers and Critics' in Stephen P Turner and Paul A Roth (eds), *The Blackwell Guide to the Philosophy of the Social Sciences* (Blackwell 2003).

[26] Theodor W Adorno, *Minima Moralia: Reflections from Damaged Life* (EFN Jephcott tr, New Left Books 1974) 151.

IV. Noumenal Power

Forst claims that in order to understand power, it is necessary to understand justification and accordingly proposes that social relations are conceptualized as relations of justification.[27] By conceptualizing society as multiple, overlapping orders of justification, the task of radical critique is to examine the legitimacy of existing justifications for social hierarchies and to expose the *lack* of justificatory practice in other settled and seemingly inevitable areas of social practice. The overall aim is an exhaustive analysis of 'all those more or less institutionalized social relations and structures which . . . are marked by forms of exclusion, by privileges and domination'.[28] The correlate of Forst's linguistic construal of sociality is the idea that power is essentially a noumenal, discursive, cognitive, or intellectual force—he uses the terms interchangeably—that operates through control over the 'space of reasons'.[29] Power is the capacity of some individuals to get others to think or do something they would otherwise not have thought or done, it is the ability to: 'determine the limits of what can be said and thought and . . . of what is accepted and acceptable, of what is justified'.[30] Power is emphatically not a matter of strength or will, nor a material state of affairs, but one of convictions and beliefs: 'To be a subject of power is to be moved by reasons that others have given me and that motivate me to think or act in a certain way intended by the reason-giver'.[31] This cognitivist construal does not mean that the reasons given for a particular state of affairs need be fully justified and coherent, they may be false or misleading and used to justify relations of oppression, subordination, and inequality. But, in essence, even in cases of extreme social disparity, power always acts upon 'cognitively motivated subjects' and rests on the recognition and 'acceptance of reasons'.[32]

If 'power is what goes on in the head', then an issue that immediately confronts Forst's rarefied conception is how to explain types of power whose impact is more immediately 'material', whose modus operandi is not primarily the manipulation of consciousness and the acceptance of reasons but the shaping of the socio-structural and practical conditions of existence. Such types of material power not only follow very different logics but arguably are prior to and constitutive of noumenal forms in so far as they create the underlying social conditions

[27] Rainer Forst, 'A Critical Theory of Politics: Grounds, Method and Aims: Reply to Simone Chambers, Stephen White and Lea Ypi' (2015), 41 Philosophy & Social Criticism 225.

[28] Forst, 'Introduction: On the Idea of a Critique of Relations of Justification' (n 20) 8.

[29] ibid 9.

[30] Rainer Forst, 'The Ground of Critique: On the Concept of Human Dignity in Social Orders of Justification' in Rainer Forst, *Justification and Critique: Towards a Critical Theory of Politics* (Ciaran Cronin tr, Polity Press 2013) 103.

[31] Rainer Forst, 'Noumenal Power' (2015), 23 Journal of Political Philosophy 111, 112.

[32] ibid 119.

in which specific reasons and justifications only become intelligible in the first place. Material power can be conceptualized in a number of ways, including, notably those ideas of disciplinary embodiment, theorized by Foucault, Bourdieu, and others, which provide a powerful explanation, inter alia, of the persistence of inequalities of race, gender, and class in formally equal democracies. On these accounts, inequalities endure not so much because individuals buy into justifications (good or bad) about their conventional social role but rather because objective asymmetries of power are internalized in the body as a cluster of naturalized subjective dispositions (habitus). In terms of gender, the practical living through of normalizing bodily tendencies reproduces wider social inequalities and renders women (and men) unconsciously complicit with their own subordination. Thus, at a rational level, individuals may be conscious of the shortcomings of conventional hierarchies of gender, but, at the level of emotional and psycho-sexual dispositions, they may be deeply invested in their continuing subjection in the sense captured by Butler's notion of 'passionate attachments'.[33] This kind of embodied power appears to have little to do with justification precisely because it operates beneath the radar of reason through the shaping of corporeal being in accordance with the tendencies of the world.

Forst insists, however, that ideas of disciplinary bio-power do not seriously challenge his concept because, ultimately, to be efficacious all types of power necessarily possess a noumenal essence: 'material means . . . only serve their function if they are seen as reason giving'.[34] Thus, the material power of money can only be properly explained, according to Forst, with reference to its noumenal effects for 'money only motivates those who see its use as justified and who have aims which make money necessary'.[35] If people do not recognize the justification for money, then it ceases to have power over people. This seems questionable, however, if we think about how the lack of money, in the form of maldistribution of material resources, imposes brute constraints on the life chances of individuals regardless of whether they recognize its use as 'justified' or not. Analogously, hegemonic gender norms would not cease to have an influence on women if they chose not to recognize the patriarchal arguments conventionally used to justify them. Nonetheless, Forst maintains that a Foucauldian notion of disciplinary embodiment that bypasses reason represents a 'super-Cartesian' separation of the symbolic realm from the material one with the untenable implication that there is a corporeal reality 'beyond justification'.[36]

[33] Judith Butler, *The Psychic Life of Power: Theories in Subjection* (Stanford University Press 1997).
[34] Forst, 'Justifying Justification: A Reply to My Critics' (n 22) 180f.
[35] ibid.
[36] Forst, 'Noumenal Power' (n 31) 123.

The disclosing potential of a notion of power that turns around the acceptance of reasons is further compromised if we consider another way of thinking about the materiality of power, namely, the systemic mechanisms that maintain structural inequalities. Take the case of gender; most feminists concur that women's subordination in advanced democracies no longer relies, in any significant sense, on patriarchal justifications (although they undoubtedly exist), but rather on entrenched systemic dynamics that disadvantage women regardless of whether they accept conventional norms or not. Susan Okin famously described this impersonal mode of subordination as 'a cycle of socially caused and distinctly asymmetric vulnerability by marriage' denoting the combined effects of a skewed domestic division of labour, especially as it relates to child-rearing, interacting with the operations of a gender-segregated labour market.[37] This impersonal cycle has an effect on all women, even those who are unmarried and childless, rendering them 'vulnerable to subordination and deprivation in most societies in the world'.[38] Forst concedes that such 'subjectless' modes of oppression present a challenge to his cognitivist notion to the extent that they appear to function on another level entirely to that of the acceptance of reasons. He insists nonetheless that social structures do still depend upon noumenal power but that, in this impersonal form, it takes hold of individuals through the mechanism of narrative inculcation rather than that of interpersonal influence. Moreover, noumenal power in this structural sense is defined very broadly including not just direct appeals to reason but unconscious socialization processes, false narratives, ideological distortions, emotional investments, and so on. On his account, imperfect social structures are often accepted because it is felt that nothing else is available; acquiescence is generated by naturalizing narratives that make a particular order seem inevitable and thereby socialize individuals into a conformist 'frame of mind'.[39] Gender inequality persists because, although the person of the patriarch may no longer be present in western democracies, patriarchal narratives continue to exert an enduring influence over women who conform to its rules for 'reasons of love, admiration, self-interest, convention, religious upbringing, fear, or despair'.[40]

Sexist rationales may well be socially entrenched, but Forst's suggestion that women's subordination persists primarily because of the widespread acceptance of patriarchal narratives rather than because of structurally generated gendered vulnerabilities is not convincing. Women's subordination has little to do with

[37] Susan M Okin, *Justice, Gender, and the Family* (Basic Books 1989) 4.
[38] Iris M Young, 'The Gendered Cycle of Vulnerability in the Less Developed World' in Debra Satz and Rob Reich (eds), *Toward a Humanist Justice: The Political Philosophy of Susan Moller Okin* (Oxford University Press 2009) 228.
[39] Forst, 'Noumenal Power' (n 31) 120.
[40] ibid 126.

the acceptance of false narratives or ill-informed choices so much as a structural lack of opportunities. Poor women, for instance, are frequently placed in situations where they have few options and where these options may be organized to provide few gains, often even to be 'no win'. In such situations, the only rational course is often for women to accept low-paid domestic and sex-work as well as unpaid responsibilities.[41] Likewise there is considerable sociological evidence to suggest that nowadays, many women and men do not unthinkingly buy into traditional 'narratives' of gender; they see marriage and parenting in terms of a shared partnership rather than fixed roles and have expectations of equal treatment in education and work. Yet, despite these expectations, gender inequality persists, suggesting that a convincing explanation lies not in the enduring noumenal force of patriarchal narratives but rather in structural dynamics that have a determining effect regardless of individual beliefs. The persistence of labour markets that disadvantage women combined with lack of state attention to domestic work and child care mean that even less conventional, egalitarian minded couples are often compelled to adopt a traditional gender division of labour against their best intentions. It makes sense to choose to develop the husband's professional skills rather than the wife's because, in most cases, this ensures greater economic security.[42] In short, it is not evident that inequalities of gender persist primarily because of justificatory narratives but rather because of systemic dynamics that auto-poetically reproduce them. As Amy Allen puts it:

> systemic relations of dominance and subordination . . . are probably always connected to . . . hegemonic narratives of justification—but this does not mean that they are inculcated in individuals through or by means of . . . such justifications or even that they are recognized by their targets as reasons to act in a certain way.[43]

In sum, Forst's assertion that it is only when we understand justification that we understand power is doubtful. The orientation of social critique around a logic of justification in fact initiates a discursive reduction upwards where relations of power that do not operate according to a one-dimensional linguistic rationale are occluded.[44] At points, Forst attempts to mitigate this symbolic occlusion by

[41] eg Alison M Jaggar, 'Transnational Cycles of Gendered Vulnerability: A Prologue to a Theory of Global Gender Justice' in Alison M Jaggar (ed), *Gender and Global Justice* (Polity Press 2014) 34.

[42] Young (n 38) 228.

[43] Allen, Forst, and Haugaard (n 1) 18f.

[44] This occlusion is evident in the way in which Forst treats the issue of violence which, by being conceptually disconnected from that of power, limits an understanding of the structural causes of certain dysfunctional social phenomena. Take, for instance, the problem of domestic violence endemic to intimate heterosexual relations in all societies, traditional or democratic. Noumenal power provides few conceptual resources for understanding its persistence because the rationale of justification imposes a conceptual hiatus between the phenomenon and the general context of masculine

stating that justificatory power does not work only through the recognition of reasons but encompasses broader non-cognitive socializing dynamics. This gesture is unsupported, however, by further conceptual elaboration, and the concept of power becomes overly diffuse and emptied of diagnostic bite. At other points, Forst retreats from this capacious stance, insisting on a narrow essentialist definition where: 'to be a subject of power is to be moved by reasons that others have given me and that motivate me to think or act in a certain way intended by the reason-giver'.[45] This hyper-rationalist notion is critically limited when it comes to explaining complex dynamics of embodiment, structural causation, and other material forces. Forst's vacillation between inclusive and restricted concepts remains unresolved and forestalls the development of the differentiated, multidimensional account of power necessary for effective social critique. As I discuss in the next section, the limited disclosing capacity of Forst's concept of power is symptomatic of a more general shortcoming in his thought, namely, the failure to integrate transcendent and immanent perspectives in such a way as to engender a form of radical, self-reflexive critique.

V. Justification and Justice

The radical bite of justification critique is ensured not just by a critical theory of injustice but also by the recursive structure that, in principle, renders it sensitive to the perspectives of those citizens not normally included in the conversation about justice. The justification principle has an explicitly maieutic function intended to bring to the fore un-noticed forms of social suffering and injustice.[46] It is, according to Forst, ignited by 'the claims of individuals themselves' and bestows paramount importance on 'their concrete experiences of . . . political powerlessness and social exclusion'.[47] It is one thing, however, to assert an equal

domination. Following Arendt, Forst maintains that violence is the opposite of power because the agency of the victim, qua the capacity to accept reasons, is negated by the perpetrator of violence: the free subject becomes a mere object. The erasure of agency is of course an undeniable effect of violence but this does little to develop understanding of how, in a domestic context, violence does not so much represent the end of patriarchal power but rather one of its symptoms. It is truistic to say with Forst that domestic violence is beyond the scope of reasonable justification, for this does not explain why it arises, how it might be a pathological expression of other asymmetrical social dynamics, and what might be done to prevent it. Given that it is a pervasive feature of intimate relations, male violence must be connected to the larger societal context of masculine 'scripts' of entitlement, aggression, and independence, on the one side, and female passivity and feminine scripts of dependence, sacrifice, and duty to care, on the other: Nancy J Hirschmann, *The Subject of Liberty: Toward a Feminist Theory of Freedom* (Princeton University Press 2002) 128.

[45] Forst, 'Noumenal Power' (n 31) 112.

[46] Stanley Cavell, *Conditions Handsome and Unhandsome: The Constitution of Emersonian Perfectionism* (University of Chicago Press 1990) 108.

[47] Forst, 'The Justification of Justice' (n 3) 121.

right to justification in an abstract recursive sense and another to ensure that equality will be realized in practice in the actual conversation about justice. It may well be that, in the idealized space of practical reason, where subjects are disembodied justificatory agents, they do indeed understand themselves as 'reasonable, autonomous and moral beings who must be able to account for their actions to one another'.[48] But, in the situated deliberative encounter, individuals frequently fail to treat each other as reasonable and morally autonomous beings. Latent dynamics of power and authority may subvert formally equal relations, making it far more difficult for certain individuals and groups to be taken seriously as justificatory agents than others. As Miranda Fricker reminds us, 'testimonial injustice' disproportionately effects subordinate groups who are often subtly stigmatized and de-legitimated as speakers, their speech frequently discounted, trivialized, or ignored.[49] History provides numerous examples of politically marginal and oppositional groups (suffragettes, civil rights activists, environmental campaigners) who, as a result of such processes of symbolic de-authorization, have had to resort eventually to coercive forms of civil action to be taken seriously as democratic interlocutors.[50]

This problem of the gap between formal and actual justificatory equality is potentially acute for Forst given the transcendental grounds of his theory. What he deems to be the universal practice of justification may turn out to be a contingent socio-cultural practice that is less inclusive then he presumes. The hegemonic imposition that flows from this discursive universalism takes effect not through the direct prescription of Western ideals but through the insidious naturalization of the linguistic and epistemic habits of dominant classes. In a cross-cultural context, for instance, the idea of reasonable justification may reflect the depersonalized sensibility and linguistic habitus of Western elites which are, if not wholly inaccessible to less privileged, non-Western groups may nonetheless be deeply estranging and hence tacitly exclusionary. Such occluded status quo bias is a difficulty frequently associated with Habermas's communicative ethics largely because of its attempt to stringently confine speech acts to their supposedly rational core. A consequence of this delimitation is that disempowered groups may find that their experiences of injustice are de facto excluded from consideration in discourse ethics. Certain experiences of oppression and disempowerment are by their very nature confusing, inchoate, or fragmenting and hence are inherently difficult to reconstruct in the rational terms that Habermasian validation

48 Forst, 'Practical Reason and Justifying Reasons' (n 6) 22.

49 Miranda Fricker, *Epistemic Injustice: Power and the Ethics of Knowing* (Oxford University Press 2007).

50 eg John Medearis, 'Social Movements and Deliberative Democratic Theory' (2005), 35 British Journal of Political Science 53; Marc Stears, *Demanding Democracy: American Radicals in Search of a New Politics* (Princeton University Press 2010).

requires.[51] Forst claims to circumvent such status quo bias by invoking the thinness of his discursive constructivism, which, unlike the Habermasian rationale, does not impose conditions of any kind upon the manner or content of the justificatory process. The definition of what counts as 'reasonable' justification is left entirely open and must be determined by participants in debate according to the demands of their specific context: 'only reason—constantly reflecting on what counts as reasonable and whether that is deserved—can provide a solution here'.[52] The parsimony of justificatory monism creates the space for 'evaluative pluralism' and consequently for disempowered and marginal groups to be heard and thus enables Forst to rebut criticisms of ethnocentrism and other types of status quo bias. Indeed he makes the counter-charge that it is, in fact, those who level such criticisms who are guilty of ethnocentrism because they reify cultural difference as an insuperable barrier to understanding and thereby deny the 'other's' capacity for justification: '[they] homogenize non-Western societies as frameworks in which no radical critique asking for new or better reasons was either possible or legitimate'.[53] It is imperative, in Forst's view, to cut through the superficial appearance of unbridgeable difference in the cross-cultural encounter in order to discern the basic demand for justification that always underlies political claims no matter how seemingly diverse.

Yet although Forst upholds the sensitivity of justification critique to context, that it takes account of the 'normative reality' of political demands emanating from disempowered groups, it is hard to see how, in practice, he makes good on such claims. If the abstract right to justification is to be truly inclusive then it behoves Forst to address the precise nature of its internal connection to situated forms of rationality and speech. But the theory rarely moves beyond the assertion of a speculative justificatory equality to consider seriously what participatory parity requires given entrenched asymmetries of power between democratic interlocutors. For example, permitting citizens themselves to define the nature of the justificatory process is not really a satisfactory solution to status quo bias because it simply displaces the problem unaddressed from the hypothetical scenario to that of the actual conversation. No indication is given as to what concrete safeguards might be put in place in the actual scenario to prevent powerful citizens from defining reasonable justification in a way that continues to favour their interests over those of the less powerful. In any case, the justificatory process is not necessarily as open as Forst presumes in so far as the 'criteria' of general and reciprocal acceptability potentially pose considerable barriers to the inclusion of marginal and oppressed voices. Although it supposedly ignites

51 eg Axel Honneth, *Disrespect: The Normative Foundations of Critical Theory* (Polity Press 2007).
52 Allen, Forst, and Haugaard (n 1) 21.
53 ibid.

the justificatory scenario, the testimony of oppressed groups can only be fully vindicated by passing the threshold of general and reciprocal acceptability to all participants in the conversation: 'experiences of disrespect and exclusion need to be transformed into generally and reciprocally justifiable claims to legal, political or social respect and inclusion'.[54] Given that, by virtue of their intrinsic negativity, many experiences of injustice, are marked by 'structured heterogeneities and discontinuities', it is not clear how this transformation into homogenous and generally acceptable justificatory claims is supposed to occur.[55] It may be uncontentious in the frictionless, symmetrical world of the ideal conversation, to claim that all perspectives, those of privileged and suffering interlocutors alike, be redeemed in such a standardized manner. In the actual situation of polemical and unequal debate, however, it is unlikely that many deep injustices could in fact pass such an unchanging justificatory threshold. One only has to think of the contentious nature of contemporary discussions over migrant rights to see that even cases of intense humanitarian concern, that seem to possess a prima facie justifiability in Forstian terms, are often far from commanding general and reciprocal assent.

Forst tries to smooth over this discrepancy between ideal and actual scenarios of justification through the circular argument that real world situations of injustice must always be answered through the counterfactual thought experiment that, under ideal epistemic conditions, democratic citizens would not find them justifiable. For example, he maintains that, on his definition of justification, it would not be possible for gay individuals to be denied an equal right to marriage because this would involve relying on 'thick' religious and traditional notions of the meaning of marriage that are deeply contested and therefore reciprocally non-generalizable.[56] But, this seems to overlook the fact that, beyond the hypothetical scenario of justification, the right to marriage for gays continues to be highly disputed on precisely these terms even where it has been legally recognized by the state. Moreover, in pre-determining the outcome of the justificatory process in this way, Forst seems to tacitly draw on substantive, but unarticulated principles of equality, freedom, tolerance, solidarity, and so on, in a manner that he explicitly rejects in his criticism of the pre-democratic nature of antecedent justification. In short, he appears to want to have his cake and eat it too; asserting, on the one hand, that the conversation about justice is always situated, that there can never by a perspective outside of it, but, repeatedly affirming, on the other, the moral priority of an ideal perspective over a situated one.

[54] Rainer Forst, 'Justice, Reason and Critique: Basic Concepts of Critical Theory' in David M Rasmussen (ed), *The Handbook of Critical Theory* (Blackwell 1996) 157f.
[55] Charles W Mills, *Blackness Visible: Essays on Philosophy and Race* (Cornell University Press 1998) 28.
[56] Forst, 'First Things First' (n 16) 113.

Differently put, the justification paradigm fails to reflexively enact the dialectic of transcendence and immanence that Forst regards as a vital element of emancipatory critique. If it turns out that the criteria of general and reciprocal acceptability do disadvantage disempowered interlocutors in the conversation about justice, then, on his own definition of reflexivity, it follows that Forst should think more carefully about how to amend the formal process of justification. But this self-reflection is foreclosed by Forst's prioritization of the abstract procedure of justification over the situated encounter. For instance, issues of interpretative incommensurability and testimonial injustice are bypassed by reliance on an undifferentiated notion of affectability which holds that 'in moral contexts the community of justification may not be arbitrarily restricted, but rather must include all those affected by actions or norms in morally relevant ways'.[57] The unqualified term moral relevance does not distinguish adequately, however, between the deep discrepancies that may exist between individuals in terms of 'intensity of affectability' where a given state of affairs may have a far more prolonged and harmful impact upon some individuals than on others. Individuals who have suffered directly from chronic or severe injustice may justifiably feel that a greater urgency and moral weight attaches itself to their view than to those of citizens less directly affected and that this should somehow be acknowledged in deliberation. From this perspective, Forst's stipulation that all groups, regardless of experiential discrepancies, meet the unchanging threshold of justificatory acceptability may constitute a supervening form of epistemic or hermeneutical injustice that compounds the original injustice. In short, the practical enactment of concern for others might require us on occasions to consider whether, with certain types of injustice, it is in fact appropriate to insist on reciprocally acceptable justifiability: 'affectability brings with it an excess over rational justifiability'.[58] This is the view of Adorno, for instance, who is sceptical about the possibility of establishing discursive foundations for morality because he believes that our moral responses rest largely on immediate, intuitive reactions to suffering. It is an 'outrage', in his view, to demand that we justify our response to the evil of Auschwitz when it is our spontaneous reactions to the event that should be our normative guide. We instinctively recognize oppression when we see it and grounding morality in a priori theories and principles is neither desirable or necessary since it entangles us in an infinite chain of argument.[59] Adorno famously

[57] Rainer Forst, 'The Basic Right to Justification: Toward a Constructivist Conception of Human Rights' in Rainer Forst, *The Right to Justification: Elements of a Constructivist Theory of Justice* (Jeffrey Flynn tr, Columbia University Press 2012) 214.

[58] Matthias Fritsch, 'Rational Justification and Vulnerability: On the "All-Affected" Principle in Rainer Forst's Right to Justification' (2015), 43 Political Theory 805, 813.

[59] Fabian Freyenhagen, *Adorno's Practical Philosophy: Living Less Wrongly* (Cambridge University Press 2013) 198f.

prefers a negativist construal of morality, namely, that our normative responses to possible injustices should be directed not by comprehensive principles of the good or the right but by concrete knowledge of social suffering and other 'bads' and what might be done practically to overcome them.

It is not necessary to endorse an epistemic negativism akin to Adorno's to recognize that in some cases there may be a profound disconnection between the lived reality of suffering, on the one side, and the demand, on the other, that such experiences be vindicated according to pre-given criteria, no matter how seemingly thin. The paradox of equal treatment for all is that sometimes the perspective of what is equally good for all be abandoned temporarily for the sake of its other perspective, that of singular-oriented treatment.[60] In principle, Forst recognizes the significance of this dilemma when, for instance, he invokes Levinas's claim that moral law derives its authority from 'the face' or singular presence of the other. Yet, concerted exploration of how normative receptivity to the vulnerable subject of injustice may be practically enacted is curtailed by Forst's categorical assertion that empathy generates amoral results. In a circular fashion, he concludes that if there is a role for empathy in the encounter with vulnerable others, it can only be the 'reasonable empathy' generated by the criterion of justification.[61]

By cleaving to the unyielding formalism of mutually owed justifications, Forst is in danger of doing what he explicitly denies, namely, treating 'injustice as a 'surprising abnormality' from the norm of justice.[62] If a theory of normative validity is to provide a viable internal point of justification for oppressed groups then it must be more responsive than Forst's formal paradigm to the effects of social position on epistemic and linguistic capacity. This need not entail abandonment of the principle of justification so much as the development of notions with greater contextual sensitivity oriented not necessarily towards achieving universally acceptable validation but towards what Azamova calls 'giving reasons for having reasons'.[63] Justification, on this alternative account, would be grounded in personal experience and the narration of how one has come to one's view and reasons that prompted one to form it. Instead of imposing a normative threshold of acceptability, it would allow oppressed subjects to explain their experiences in their own terms and thereby hopefully generate enhanced understanding of their normative stance as well as shedding light on connections and commonalities with the position of others. Alternatively, responsibility to others might demand a recalibration of the burden of the conversation about

[60] eg Fritsch (n 58) 810.
[61] Forst, 'Justifying Justification: A Reply to My Critics' (n 22) 176f.
[62] Judith N Shklar, *The Faces of Injustice* (Yale University Press 1990) 17.
[63] Albena Azmanova, *The Scandal of Reason: A Critical Theory of Political Judgment* (Columbia University Press 2012).

justice so that it falls more heavily on privileged than vulnerable interlocutors. Instead of focusing one-sidedly on the formal vindication of the latter's experience and, consequently, tacitly limiting how they can appear to others, it may be more equalizing to require the former to cultivate an ethos of 'epistemic responsibility' for others.[64] This would involve combatting the inherited cognitive and discursive habits that sustain the hermeneutically marginalizing effects of the supposedly impartial perspective. The cultivation of such a sensibility would of course not be easy in the face of the deeply entrenched linguistic habitus of privilege but might involve such measures as, inter alia, renunciation of fixed principles of interpretation, willingness to render oneself vulnerable to others, embracing rather than smoothing over experiential disruption and complexity, and the use of imagination and sympathy in interactions with others rather than fixed categorizations.[65] In short, challenging epistemic 'meta-blindness' and 'meta-insensitivity' to injustice and oppression might require the development of communicative and interpretative virtues quite different to the standardized norms implied in Forst's justificatory process.

VI. Conclusion: Reconciliation or Vacillation?

It is difficult to demur from a hypothetical principle that accords the right to justification to all affected, but, on closer inspection, it seems to be such a socially weightless notion that its precise relevance to the correction of actual injustices is unclear. At best, the syntax of justification is what Nancy Fraser terms a 'circuitous route' to dealing with unwarranted disparities of power between individuals that may be more effectively dealt with by a direct focus on the nature of the specific injustice in question.[66] Forst's inability to advance beyond a one-dimensional formulation of justification speaks to the contradictory nature of his enterprise where instead of establishing an immanent connection between critical and ideal perspectives, he vacillates inconsequently between the two in a manner that is ultimately self-undermining. No sooner does he establish the universal status of justification as the core of practical reason, then he appears to back track from this by stating repeatedly that there can be no truly objective perspective, that all reasoning is situated and perspectival. But when faced with challenges from the perspective of social practice, he prioritises the a priori of justification over a contextually embedded response. The undermining effects of

[64] Fricker (n 49).

[65] José Medina, *The Epistemology of Resistance: Gender and Racial Oppression, Epistemic Injustice, and Resistant Imaginations* (Oxford University Press 2013) 112ff.

[66] See Nancy Fraser, 'Prioritizing Justice as Participatory Parity: A Reply to Kompridis and Forst' in Kevin Olson (ed), *Adding Insult to Injury: Nancy Fraser Debates Her Critics* (Verso 2008).

this vacillation permeate Forst's work and are evident, for example, in the uncertain status of the criteria of reciprocity and generality. Neither first order moral principles or socially derived norms, they lack determinate content and are unsatisfactory from both ideal and critical stances. Hence, for the ideal theorist concerned with grounding justice in independent foundations, the criteria are insufficient because they are not substantive moral principles. As we have seen, this thinness is a deliberate strategy on Forst's part because he wishes to avoid making metaphysical claims and replicating the 'pre-democratic' error of ideal theory. Any normative content the criteria possess must necessarily come to them from the outside, from the deliberations of citizens in a given justificatory scenario. But this thinness inevitably weakens the unconditional moral force that Forst wishes to confer on justification critique. Consequently the criteria are vulnerable to such criticisms from ideal theorists as they are tautologous (generality implies reciprocity), too vague (a more precise idea of all affected principle needs to be worked out), or require supplementing with other criteria (such as that of priority) to render them normatively effective.[67] To pre-empt such criticisms, Forst implicitly draws on thick norms of tolerance, solidarity, freedom, and so on, to demonstrate the criteria's supposed moral rigour. However, as we have seen, this violates the premise that it is citizens who are the rightful authors of democratic principles, not the theorist.

Equally, however, for the critical theorist concerned with immanent social critique, the criteria are just as empty but in the different sense of being abstractions that repress awareness of their social conditions of possibility. According to Honneth, for instance, the criteria would be devoid of normative bite if they did not implicitly presuppose that 'social norms and corresponding roles already exist and determine the elements of justification'.[68] In his view, Forst is only able to establish justification as the universal core of practical reason by fictitiously bracketing off the social context in which dialogue always takes place and which gives it substantive content. Context does not simply constitute the post hoc setting to transcendental practice but rather is its necessary pre-condition. It is only ever in a given social context that the criteria of justification make sense, for in considering whether particular social relations are just or not, individuals invariably encounter each other as situated beings who draw on their accumulated knowledge of social roles, norms, and practices to make such judgments.

[67] eg Simon Caney, 'Justice and the Basic Right to Justification' in Rainer Forst, *Justice, Democracy and the Right to Justification: Rainer Forst in Dialogue* (Bloomsbury Academic 2014); Fernando Suárez Müller, 'Justifying the Right to Justification: An Analysis of Rainer Forst's Constructivist Theory of Justice' (2013), 39 Philosophy & Social Criticism 1049.

[68] Axel Honneth, 'Rejoinder' in Danielle Petherbridge (ed), *Axel Honneth: Critical Essays* (Brill 2011) 416.

In the end, this vacillation between critical and ideal perspectives throws into question where exactly the supposed moral and analytical rigour of the justification paradigm actually lies. But, above all, Forst's methodological indecision undermines the very capacity for reflexive self-scrutiny that he regards as an indispensable feature of emancipatory critique, preventing its lapse into metaphysical slumber, on the one side, and parochial relativism, on the other. The effect of according justification a transcendental status is to immunize it against systematic critical scrutiny since an invariant principle, *eo ipso*, cannot be subject to extensive revision. There are several grounds, however, on which we might want to subject the justification principle to precisely such critical scrutiny particularly when it comes to questioning its foundational status as the invariant essence of practical reason. From a historical perspective, for instance, Forst's uniform, de-historicized interpretation of all political struggles, regardless of context, as expressions of the self-same demand for the right to justification is dubious. As Jeffrey Flynn argues, for instance, when Muslim women around the world struggle against patriarchy in Islam, they may be asking for equal treatment as Muslims on the basis of a certain interpretation of their rights and duties in the Qur'an, but whether this can be construed in the strong terms as a claim about their moral right to justification is moot:

> It does not seem to be the case that whenever people demand reasons from others or even when they demand that they no longer be ignored, that they necessarily enter into a kind of dynamic that implicates a moral right to justification.[69]

It is possible to partially agree with Forst that what distinguishes certain struggles as political is some kind of universal claim, but it remains questionable whether this is most appropriately conceptualized as an assertion of the right to justification rather than, in the more politically germane terms, as an assertion of the right to equality or freedom as Ranciere[70] and Honneth[71] respectively hold.

Even on the constructivist scenario set out by Forst, it is doubtful whether justification emerges as the fundamental characteristic of practical reasoning rather than some other inter-subjective dynamic principle of, say, dialogue, or recognition. After all, the reason that the need to justify one's position arises in the first place is as a response to the demand emanating from an 'other' who has already

[69] Jeffrey Flynn, 'On the Nature and Status of the Right to Justification' (2015), 43 Political Theory 793, 801.

[70] Jacques Rancière, *Disagreement: Politics and Philosophy* (Julie Rose tr, University of Minnesota Press 1999).

[71] Axel Honneth, *Freedom's Right: The Social Foundations of Democratic Life* (Joseph Ganahl tr, Columbia University Press 2014).

been recognized as a partner in dialogue. If reason was not already presumed to be dialogical, there would be no duty to justify oneself in a general, reciprocally acceptable fashion. Forst asserts the inter-subjective nature of reason but fails to pursue the potentially de-stabilizing implications that this presumption has for the supposedly foundational status of the justification principle. If it is dialogue with the other that precedes and creates the demand for justification, then, as Honneth points out, recognition must be the more fundamental principle: 'mutual recognition always precedes discourse, and the mutual ascription of normative capacities . . . always precedes justification'.[72] Indeed, according to Honneth, the antecedence of recognition emerges 'unnoticed' in Forst's work—in, for instance, the idea of 'contexts' of justification—and does a lot of unacknowledged work to make the idea of justification operable. Likewise, Muller concludes from Forst's presumption of the intersubjective nature of practical reason that there is a 'deeper root of justice' and more fundamental right than that of justification, namely, the right to participate in dialogue. It is only in the context of a right to participate in dialogue that a subsequent right to justification makes sense: 'dialogue does not take place because there is a need of justification, but the other way round, there is a need of justification because reason is, in its own dynamic and inner life, dialogical'.[73] This is not necessarily to endorse the argument that recognition is in fact the more fundamental principle but rather to draw attention to the way in which the conferral of a transcendental status on justification prevents Forst from effectively implementing the type of reflexive self-scrutiny that he regards as essential to emancipatory critique.

In the end, Forst's vacillation is perhaps inevitable in so far as his goals of establishing independent moral grounds for critique, on the one side, and of developing a penetrating critical theory of injustice, on the other, have greater contradictory entailments for political reasoning than he is prepared to acknowledge. In so far as they cannot be reconciled, they represent what Adorno calls torn halves which, when brought together, do not add up to a unified whole.[74] A solution to Forst's difficulties, given his stated allegiance to Frankfurt School critique, would be to let go of the transcendental side of his project and construe the right to justification as a contingent historical achievement albeit one that is akin to what other critical theorists term an immanent universal. Historicizing justification in this manner would enhance reflexive elaboration of the concept although it would undoubtedly mean giving up on a certain type of strong universalism. But, contra Forst, it doesn't follow that, by de-transcendentalizing its governing principle, critique loses the capacity for systematic social criticism

72 Honneth, 'Rejoinder' (n 68) 416.
73 Suárez Müller (n 67) 1057.
74 Adorno (n 26) 123.

and generalizable normative relevance. Indeed, perhaps the real underlying difficulty with Forst's work is the misleading presumption that animates it, namely, that if critique cannot find incontestable foundations and a way out of the hermeneutic circle, it must inevitably fall prey to a parochial relativism. This false antithesis between transcendence and immanence forecloses exploration of the complicated middle ground where there are better and worse interpretations of the world and a variety of methodological indices, standards of evidence and conceptual logics with which to test any given theory's respective explanatory and normative merits. Accepting the inescapably situated nature of critique would mean, however, that the validity of its diagnoses and proposals will always be a matter for argumentation and that the critic must be prepared to justify her critical insights without resort to a transcendental guarantee. Critique must be 'guided by a concern for an answer that is right in a context transcending sense and that proceeds in a historicist, comparative, open-ended, and concrete way'.[75] The attempt to de-historicize the justification principle forecloses what many would regard as the essential strength of an effective critical theory, namely, a dialogical, contextually sensitive, and cumulative style of political reasoning. Moreover, Forst is arguably misguided in thinking that constructivist 'moral invention' can provide a definitive frame for matters of social justice because, as Michael Walzer reminds us, there are always an infinite number of possible 'inventions' and because every invention requires interpretation.[76]

References

Adorno TW, *Minima Moralia: Reflections from Damaged Life* (EFN Jephcott tr, New Left Books 1974).

Allen A, 'The Power of Justification' in Rainer Forst, *Justice, Democracy and the Right to Justification: Rainer Forst in Dialogue* (Bloomsbury Academic 2014).

Allen A, Forst R, and Haugaard M, 'Power and Reason, Justice and Domination: A Conversation' (2014), 7 Journal of Political Power 7.

Azmanova A, *The Scandal of Reason: A Critical Theory of Political Judgment* (Columbia University Press 2012).

Bohman J, 'Critical Theory as Practical Knowledge: Participants, Observers and Critics' in Stephen P Turner and Paul A Roth (eds), *The Blackwell Guide to the Philosophy of the Social Sciences* (Blackwell 2003).

Butler J, *The Psychic Life of Power: Theories in Subjection* (Stanford University Press 1997).

Caney S, 'Justice and the Basic Right to Justification' in Rainer Forst, *Justice, Democracy and the Right to Justification: Rainer Forst in Dialogue* (Bloomsbury Academic 2014).

[75] Maeve Cooke, *Re-presenting the Good Society* (MIT Press 2006).

[76] Michael Walzer, *Interpretation and Social Criticism* (Harvard University Press 1987) 26.

Cavell S, *Conditions Handsome and Unhandsome: The Constitution of Emersonian Perfectionism* (University of Chicago Press 1990).

Cooke M, *Re-presenting the Good Society* (MIT Press 2006).

Flynn J, 'On the Nature and Status of the Right to Justification' (2015), 43 Political Theory 793.

Forst R, 'Justice, Reason and Critique: Basic Concepts of Critical Theory' in David M Rasmussen (ed), *The Handbook of Critical Theory* (Blackwell 1996).

Forst R, 'Introduction: The Foundation of Justice' in Rainer Forst, *The Right to Justification: Elements of a Constructivist Theory of Justice* (Jeffrey Flynn tr, Columbia University Press 2012).

Forst R, 'Moral Autonomy and the Autonomy of Morality: Toward a Theory of Normativity after Kant' in Rainer Forst, *The Right to Justification: Elements of a Constructivist Theory of Justice* (Jeffrey Flynn tr, Columbia University Press 2012).

Forst R, 'Practical Reason and Justifying Reasons: On the Foundation of Morality' in Rainer Forst, *The Right to Justification: Elements of a Constructivist Theory of Justice* (Jeffrey Flynn tr, Columbia University Press 2012).

Forst R, 'The Basic Right to Justification: Toward a Constructivist Conception of Human Rights' in Rainer Forst, *The Right to Justification: Elements of a Constructivist Theory of Justice* (Jeffrey Flynn tr, Columbia University Press 2012).

Forst R, 'The Justification of Justice: Rawls's Political Liberalism and Habermas's Discourse Theory in Dialogue' in Rainer Forst, *The Right to Justification: Elements of a Constructivist Theory of Justice* (Jeffrey Flynn tr, Columbia University Press 2012).

Forst R, 'The Rule of Reasons: Three Models of Deliberative Democracy' in Rainer Forst, *The Right to Justification: Elements of a Constructivist Theory of Justice* (Jeffrey Flynn tr, Columbia University Press 2012).

Forst R, 'First Things First: Redistribution, Recognition and Justification' in Rainer Forst, *Justification and Critique: Towards a Critical Theory of Politics* (Ciaran Cronin tr, Polity Press 2013).

Forst R, 'Introduction: On the Idea of a Critique of Relations of Justification' in Rainer Forst, *Justification and Critique: Towards a Critical Theory of Politics* (Ciaran Cronin tr, Polity Press 2013).

Forst R, 'The Ground of Critique: On the Concept of Human Dignity in Social Orders of Justification' in Rainer Forst, *Justification and Critique: Towards a Critical Theory of Politics* (Ciaran Cronin tr, Polity Press 2013).

Forst R, 'Justifying Justification: A Reply to My Critics' in Rainer Forst, *Justice, Democracy and the Right to Justification: Rainer Forst in Dialogue* (Bloomsbury Academic 2014).

Forst R, 'A Critical Theory of Politics: Grounds, Method and Aims: Reply to Simone Chambers, Stephen White and Lea Ypi' (2015), 41 Philosophy & Social Criticism 225.

Forst R, 'Noumenal Power' (2015), 23 Journal of Political Philosophy 111.

Fraser N, 'Prioritizing Justice as Participatory Parity: A Reply to Kompridis and Forst' in Kevin Olson (ed), *Adding Insult to Injury: Nancy Fraser Debates Her Critics* (Verso 2008).

Freyenhagen F, *Adorno's Practical Philosophy: Living Less Wrongly* (Cambridge University Press 2013).

Fricker M, *Epistemic Injustice: Power and the Ethics of Knowing* (Oxford University Press 2007).

Fritsch M, 'Rational Justification and Vulnerability: On the "All-Affected" Principle in Rainer Forst's Right to Justification' (2015), 43 Political Theory 805.
Hirschmann NJ, *The Subject of Liberty: Toward a Feminist Theory of Freedom* (Princeton University Press 2002).
Honneth A, 'A Social Pathology of Reason: On the Intellectual Legacy of Critical Theory' in Fred Rush (ed), *The Cambridge Companion to Critical Theory* (Cambridge University Press 2004).
Honneth A, *Disrespect: The Normative Foundations of Critical Theory* (Polity Press 2007).
Honneth A, 'Rejoinder' in Danielle Petherbridge (ed), *Axel Honneth: Critical Essays* (Social and Critical Theory, vol 12, Brill 2011).
Honneth A, *Freedom's Right: The Social Foundations of Democratic Life* (Joseph Ganahl tr, Columbia University Press 2014).
Jaggar AM, 'Transnational Cycles of Gendered Vulnerability: A Prologue to a Theory of Global Gender Justice' in Alison M Jaggar (ed), *Gender and Global Justice* (Polity Press 2014).
Medearis J, 'Social Movements and Deliberative Democratic Theory' (2005), 35 British Journal of Political Science 53.
Medina J, *The Epistemology of Resistance: Gender and Racial Oppression, Epistemic Injustice, and Resistant Imaginations* (Oxford University Press 2013).
Mills CW, *Blackness Visible: Essays on Philosophy and Race* (Cornell University Press 1998).
Okin SM, *Justice, Gender, and the Family* (Basic Books 1989).
Olson K, 'Complexities of Political Discourse: Class, Power and the Linguistic Turn' in Rainer Forst, *Justice, Democracy and the Right to Justification: Rainer Forst in Dialogue* (Bloomsbury Academic 2014).
Rancière J, *Disagreement: Politics and Philosophy* (Julie Rose tr, University of Minnesota Press 1999).
Shklar JN, *The Faces of Injustice* (Yale University Press 1990).
Stears M, *Demanding Democracy: American Radicals in Search of a New Politics* (Princeton University Press 2010).
Suárez Müller F, 'Justifying the Right to Justification: An Analysis of Rainer Forst's Constructivist Theory of Justice' (2013), 39 Philosophy & Social Criticism 1049.
Tully J, 'Dialogue' (2011), 39 Political Theory 145.
Walzer M, *Interpretation and Social Criticism* (Harvard University Press 1987).
Young IM, 'The Gendered Cycle of Vulnerability in the Less Developed World' in Debra Satz and Rob Reich (eds), *Toward a Humanist Justice: The Political Philosophy of Susan Moller Okin* (Oxford University Press 2009).

PART II
CONSTITUTIONAL THEORY

8

Proportionality and Justification

*Matthias Klatt**

I. Introduction

Among the most vital problems in both the theory and the practice of human rights, proportionality analysis occupies a top position. Proportionality is the dominant technique of rights adjudication in the world.[1] It is not just a test or a method among many others. Rather, proportionality is the main means that allows to structure justificatory processes in rights reasoning to the utmost possible degree of rationality.[2] Its worldwide and rapid dissemination has made the proportionality test one of the most successful legal transplants ever.[3] Several descriptive accounts have sought to explain this development from a socio-legal or historical perspective.[4] Cohen-Eliya and Porat, for example, have linked this development to a 'culture of justification'. They state:

> The global move toward proportionality is . . . a global move toward justification . . . The global spread of proportionality is therefore *explained* by the

* This contribution is based upon my inaugural lecture delivered to the Law Faculty in Graz on 20 May 2016. Later drafts were presented, inter alia, at conferences in London and Barcelona, and they profited from the comments and questions raised on these occasions. I wish, in particular, to thank my commentator in Barcelona, Juan Carlos Bayón, as well as Samantha Besson, Cristina Lafont, and Mattias Kumm.

[1] This is acknowledged eg by Kai Möller, who includes proportionality analysis in the four central features of his global model of constitutional rights; see Kai Möller, *The Global Model of Constitutional Rights* (Oxford University Press 2012) 21, 3–15.

[2] Matthias Klatt and Moritz Meister, *The Constitutional Structure of Proportionality* (Oxford University Press 2012) 167–71.

[3] ibid 1–3.

[4] Aharon Barak, *Proportionality: Constitutional Rights and Their Limitations* (Doron Kalir tr, Cambridge University Press 2012) 175–210; the German genealogy and the international diffusion are also explained by Alec Stone Sweet and Jud Mathews, 'Proportionality Balancing and Global Constitutionalism' (2008) 47 Columbia Journal of Transnational Law 72, 97–159. Carlos Bernal, albeit ultimately engaging in a normative justification of proportionality's migration, distinguishes and describes six migration moves of proportionality across Europe: Carlos Bernal Pulido, 'The Migration of Proportionality across Europe' (2013) 11 New Zealand Journal of Public and International Law 483, 489–503. For proportionality's migration to Brazil, see João Andrade Neto, *Borrowing Justification for Proportionality: On the Influence of the Principles Theory in Brazil* (Springer 2018). For an empirical account, see also Niels Petersen, *Proportionality and Judicial Activism: Fundamental Rights Adjudication in Canada, Germany and South Africa* (Cambridge University Press 2017).

Matthias Klatt, *Proportionality and Justification* In: *Constitutionalism Justified: Rainer Forst in Discourse.* Edited by: Ester Herlin-Karnell and Matthias Klatt, Oxford University Press (2020), © Ester Herlin-Karnell and Matthias Klatt.
DOI: 10.1093/oso/9780190889050.003.0008

> global spread of a constitutional *culture* which puts justification at its centre. Proportionality is the central legal device to ensure the flourishing of this legal culture.[5]

Such *descriptive* accounts link the advance of the proportionality test to mere factual processes of migration of constitutional ideas. In contrast, this contribution takes issue with the *normative* basis of the proportionality test. Irrespective of whether the empirical explanations of the worldwide spread of the proportionality test are correct, I would like to object to the idea that the proportionality test was merely a matter of culture. The latter idea would suggest that different cultures could have different means of rights reasoning. In consequence, the 'triumphant advance'[6] of proportionality would have merely been a contingent process reflecting a particular tradition or convention, thus lending the proportionality relative validity only.[7] Ultimately, this line of thought would support sceptical accounts of proportionality, which criticize proportionality (in its 'orthodox' form) for being 'just a piece of unsophisticated doctrinal jargon about legal rights' devoid of any deeper philosophical basis.[8] In sharp contrast to these ideas of cultural relativity, I would like to defend the view that the link between proportionality and justification is closer than the descriptive accounts assume. My main aim is to provide a deep normative justification of proportionality as a universally valid analytical tool in rights adjudication.

One way to approach this aim would be to point to the close relation between the structure of rights and proportionality, and then to extend this relation to the notion of justification. This way could proceed on the basis that proportionality analysis embodies fundamental standards of justification, lending the relation between justification and proportionality a conceptual, necessary, and universal

[5] Moshe Cohen-Eliya and Iddo Porat, 'Proportionality and the Culture of Justification' (2011) 59 American Journal of Comparative Law 463, 474, 482 (emphases added); see also Moshe Cohen-Eliya and Iddo Porat, *Proportionality and Constitutional Culture* (Cambridge University Press 2013); Barak, *Proportionality* (n 4) 458–60; but cf Gardbaum's claim that proportionality was contingent even within the paradigm of justification, Stephen Gardbaum, 'Positive and Horizontal Rights: Proportionality's Next Frontier or a Bridge Too Far?' in Vicki C Jackson and Mark V Tushnet (eds), *Proportionality: New Frontiers, New Challenges* (Cambridge University Press 2017) 222.

[6] cf Martin Borowski, 'Limiting Clauses: On the Continental European Tradition of Special Limiting Clauses and the General Limiting Clause of Art 52(2) Charter of Fundamental Rights of the European Union' (2007) 1 Legisprudence 197, 210.

[7] On the notion of relative validity, cf Robert Alexy, 'The Absolute and the Relative Dimension of Constitutional Rights' (2017) 37 Oxford Journal of Legal Studies 31, 32. The problem of a mere relative validity of proportionality was discussed in the Alexy-Jestaedt-debate on proportionality's contingency: Matthias Jestaedt, 'The Doctrine of Balancing: Its Strengths and Weaknesses' in Matthias Klatt (ed), *Institutionalized Reason: The Jurisprudence of Robert Alexy* (Oxford University Press 2012) 159, 172; and Alexy's answer: Robert Alexy, 'Comments and Responses' in Matthias Klatt (ed), *Institutionalized Reason: The Jurisprudence of Robert Alexy* (Oxford University Press 2012) 332f; also in favour of the contingency thesis is Gardbaum (n 5) 222.

[8] George Letsas, 'Rescuing Proportionality' in Rowan Cruft, SM Liao, and Massimo Renzo (eds), *Philosophical Foundations of Human Rights* (Oxford University Press 2015) 324.

character. Robert Alexy has defended such a view.[9] I label this way the *analytical defence* of an absolute validity of proportionality. While I concur with this analytical defence, I would like to submit that the case for the absolute validity of proportionality could be made even stronger by adding to the analytical defence a *normative defence*, which I will elaborate on here.

My central argument for the normative defence of proportionality's absolute validity will be that proportionality is one of the central rules that establish the space of reasons. Proportionality enables us to construct a justified and well-founded basis for the rational application of human rights.[10] The normative basis of proportionality lies in a moral right to justification.

In order to explore this idea, I will start by explaining in more detail what is meant by a right to justification (section II). Next, I will explore how it relates to the proportionality test (section III). This will include an analysis of the relation between law's claim to correctness and the notions of justification and argumentation. I will demonstrate how justification qua proportionality analysis integrates both form and substance of rights reasoning, thus institutionalizing a space of reasons. Building upon the distinction between internal and external justification of rights reasoning, I will also address the universality problem that consists in doubts about the global validity of the right to justification. I defend the international and transnational validity of the right to justification against claims to cultural relativity by discussing the application of human rights.[11] This, in turn, will allow me to defend Forst's right to justification as a robust fundament of discursive global constitutionalism (section IV).

II. The Right to Justification

1. Justificatory Beings and the Space of Reasons

Rainer Forst develops a right to justification as the central element of justice:

> [The basis of the demand for justice] is the claim to be respected as an agent of justification, that is, in one's dignity as a being who can ask for and give

[9] Alexy, 'The Absolute and the Relative Dimension of Constitutional Rights' (n 7) 36–42.

[10] Forst refers to these rules that are conceptualized by a theory of reason: Rainer Forst, 'Practical Reason and Justifying Reasons: On the Foundation of Morality' in Rainer Forst, *The Right to Justification: Elements of a Constructivist Theory of Justice* (Jeffrey Flynn tr, Columbia University Press 2011) 14.

[11] The proportionality test is the most important means concerning the *application* of human rights. The right to justification plays also a vital role in justifying the *existence* of human rights. The present contribution concerns the relation between justification and the application of human rights only. I explore the relation between the right to justification and the justification of human rights in a different article: Matthias Klatt, Human Rights and the Concept of Law, unpublished manuscript.

> justification. . . . I argue for the thesis that we should understand political and social justice on the basis of a single right—the right to justification . . .[12]

Forst bases the right to justification on a certain anthropology. He characterizes human beings as discursive animals and 'justificatory beings'.[13] Humans not only have the ability to justify their own beliefs and actions by giving reasons to others. They also see this as a duty in certain contexts and expect that others will do the same. Human actions and beliefs necessarily claim to be based on reasons. The space of reasons, however, is inevitably a social space. The claim that one's actions are based on reasons is raised vis-à-vis other human beings. In the same way, we demand from others that their actions towards us are based on reasons as well. Actions that affect us and our legitimate interests must not be arbitrary. According to Forst, what is just is ascribed to what is justified.

Whenever humans talk or act, they are necessarily talking and acting within a 'game of giving and asking for reasons' in the sense introduced by Robert Brandom.[14] '[A]ll concrete legitimations of given social relations [are constantly being] provided, questioned, revised, or rejected . . .'[15] Brandom's normative pragmatics and Forst's discourse-theoretic approach perfectly match together in this respect. We live and act in a complex normative net of mutual commitments and entitlements.[16] A central mechanism in this net of normative relations is the right to justification, which originates in our mutual recognition that we are socially situated in 'a space of justification'.[17]

2. Reciprocity and Generality

In order that attempts to justify an action in the social space of reasons be successful, it is not sufficient to state just any reason. A dictator may have

[12] Rainer Forst, 'Introduction: The Foundation of Justice' in Rainer Forst, *The Right to Justification: Elements of a Constructivist Theory of Justice* (Jeffrey Flynn tr, Columbia University Press 2011) 2.

[13] ibid 1.

[14] Robert B Brandom, *Articulating Reasons: An Introduction to Inferentialism* (Harvard University Press 2000) 189–96.

[15] Forst, 'Introduction' (n 12) 3.

[16] On Brandomian normative pragmatics and the reciprocal mechanisms of commitments and entitlements, see Matthias Klatt, *Making the Law Explicit: The Normativity of Legal Argumentation* (Jörg Rampacher and Neil Mussett trs, Hart Publishing 2008) 117–34.

[17] Rainer Forst, 'Moral Autonomy and the Autonomy of Morality: Toward a Theory of Normativity after Kant' in Rainer Forst, *The Right to Justification: Elements of a Constructivist Theory of Justice* (Jeffrey Flynn tr, Columbia University Press 2011) 59. Cf Sellars' 'logical space of reasons', Wilfrid Sellars, *Empiricism and the Philosophy of Mind* (Harvard University Press 1997) 76.

reasons for employing oppressing measures, like preserving his personal wealth and position of power, but we do not accept that these measures are justified on account of these reasons. It is hence required to provide a normative theory capable of delineating legitimate reasons from illegitimate ones. Forst uses two criteria in this respect, namely, reciprocity and generality. According to Forst, 'the very right to reciprocal and general justification [is] the most basic right . . . to be treated as a reason-giving and reason-deserving being'.[18]

Reciprocity requires '. . . that the normative claim to validity really can be upheld reciprocally (ie without some of the addressees claiming certain privileges over others and without one's own needs or interests being projected onto others)'.[19] The criterion of generality is fulfilled if no objection of anyone affected is excluded.[20] It requires 'that all those affected have an equal right to demand justifications',[21] they 'must have equal chances to advance their claims and arguments'.[22] In consequence, 'the "justification community" must be identical with the "validity community"'.[23] Since the normative claim to validity of moral norms and actions is necessarily raised in a discursive context, the principle of reciprocal and general justification makes any justification a discursive process whose primary participants are those affected by the norm or action in question.[24]

3. Justification qua Discourse

Forst's discourse-theoretic and constructivist account of justification is contrasted from a Kantian approach.[25] The latter would focus on whether the action can be willed generally without contradiction, or whether the agent can will

[18] Rainer Forst, 'Toward a Critical Theory of Transnational Justice' in Rainer Forst, *The Right to Justification: Elements of a Constructivist Theory of Justice* (Jeffrey Flynn tr, Columbia University Press 2011) n 43.

[19] Forst, 'Practical Reason and Justifying Reasons' (n 10) 20.

[20] cf ibid.

[21] Forst, 'Toward a Critical Theory of Transnational Justice' (n 18) 258.

[22] Rainer Forst, 'The Rule of Reasons: Three Models of Deliberative Democracy' in Rainer Forst, *The Right to Justification: Elements of a Constructivist Theory of Justice* (Jeffrey Flynn tr, Columbia University Press 2011) 173f.

[23] ibid.

[24] Forst, 'Practical Reason and Justifying Reasons' (n 10) 20.

[25] 'Forst's view is non-Kantian in its substitution of the intersubjective practice of rational discourse for Kant's individualistic method'. William J Talbott, 'The Right to Justification: Elements of a Constructivist Theory of Justice' (2013) 123 Ethics 750, 754.

that each person decide as she would in the given situation.[26] In contrast, Forst's theory seeks to turn Kant 'from his transcendental head onto his social feet . . .'[27] Reasons only exist in a practice of mutual and general justification. The practice of reasoning constitutes a space of justification, which does not draw from a stock of settled moral truths. Rather, we constantly reactualize and newly validate our reasons in concrete practices of justification.[28] In consequence, the right to justification demands not merely a hypothetical test, but a real one: 'Ultimately, only those affected can themselves carry out the justification of their *own* basic social structures'.[29] In that way, Forst links critical theory with the claims raised by the participants in concrete social contexts. It is our concrete practices of justification in which the strength of the better argument legitimizes itself.

The anchoring of any justification of norms, actions, and beliefs in concrete social contexts and actual discourse, rather than in a fixed reservoir of settled moral truths, makes the construction of procedures that allow for reciprocal and general justification 'the first task of justice'.[30] This is why the right to justification is so well suited to clarify the concept of deliberative democracy: deliberative democracy institutionalizes a rule of reasons. The central feature of democracy is 'a political practice of argumentation and reason-giving among free and equal citizens . . . Only those norms, rules, or decisions that result from some form of reason-based agreement among the citizens are accepted as legitimate'.[31] That way, moral justification and political justification are integrated with each other.[32]

[26] cf Jürgen Habermas, 'Discourse Ethics: Notes on a Program of Philosophical Justification' in Jürgen Habermas, *Moral Consciousness and Communicative Action* (Christian Lenhardt and Shierry Weber Nicholsen trs, Polity Press 1990) 66f.

[27] Forst, 'Moral Autonomy and the Autonomy of Morality' (n 17) 48.

[28] Forst, 'Practical Reason and Justifying Reasons' (n 10) 21–22.

[29] Forst, 'Toward a Critical Theory of Transnational Justice' (n 18) 258f.

[30] Rainer Forst, 'Social Justice, Justification, and Power' in Rainer Forst, *The Right to Justification: Elements of a Constructivist Theory of Justice* (Jeffrey Flynn tr, Columbia University Press 2011) 189.

[31] Forst, 'The Rule of Reasons' (n 22) 155. For a critical view on Forst's attempt to explain collective decision-making in a democracy in terms of individual rights to justification, see Eva Erman, 'The Right to Justification: Elements of a Constructivist Theory of Justice' (24 May 2012) <https://ndpr.nd.edu/news/31035-the-right-to-justification-elements-of-a-constructivist-theory-of-justice> accessed 17 January 2019.

[32] cf Rainer Forst, 'The Basic Right to Justification: Toward a Constructivist Conception of Human Rights' in Rainer Forst, *The Right to Justification: Elements of a Constructivist Theory of Justice* (Jeffrey Flynn tr, Columbia University Press 2011) 218.

4. Constructivism and the Is-Ought-Problem

The right to justification is based upon an anthropologic-existentialist basis. Its normativity ultimately stems from the *fact* that human beings are discursive beings. Humans are both capable of and in need of reasons. This argument seems to be vulnerable to the naturalistic fallacy objection.[33] What ought to be cannot be justified by what is.[34] From the mere fact that humans engage in a practice of justifying it does not follow that they ought to do so. Exactly this ought, however, must be justified if a right to justification is to exist—and not just a practice of justifying. Höffe has hence raised the objection from the is-ought-problem against the right to justification.[35]

This objection, however, looks for the source of moral normativity at a wrong site. It rests on the premise that the right to justification has to be justified externally, from the outside of our moral practices. However, the very point of giving the right to justification a constructivist basis is to justify its normativity from the inside of our practices, recursively, as Forst puts it. The justification of the right to justification originates from our internal, participant perspective, when we ask context-immanently for the conditions of satisfying the claim for correctness which is necessarily raised in our discursive practices.[36]

This recursive reconstruction has a very important consequence: the normativity of our discursive justifications cannot be separated from the practices of justifying because it arises from these very practices in the first place. We construct the normative moral world intersubjectively in our practices. The binding force of our moral norms is instituted 'by virtue of the fact that no good reasons . . . can be adduced against them'.[37] Robert Brandom has labelled and explained this intersubjective process of establishing the normative world qua discourse in his normative pragmatics.[38] This explanation of the right to justification makes explicit what is implicitly present whenever we ask for and give each other reasons. In this way the right to justification is dependent upon our *social* practices of justification. This is an important departure from Kantian thought which would ground the normativity of moral norms in the individual moral person alone and her reflection on her own dignity. In contrast to this

33 cf GE Moore, *Principia Ethica* (Cambridge University Press 1903) para 10.

34 David Hume, *A Treatise of Human Nature* (David Fate Norton ed, Oxford University Press 2009) book III, part I, section I.

35 Otfried Höffe, 'Kant ist kein Frankfurter: Rainer Forst begründet das Recht auf Rechtfertigung, allerdings nicht ganz zureichend' *Die Zeit* (Hamburg, 1 November 2007) <https://www.zeit.de/2007/45/ST-Forst> accessed 17 January 2019.

36 Forst, 'Practical Reason and Justifying Reasons' (n 10) 19, and n 29.

37 Forst, 'Moral Autonomy and the Autonomy of Morality' (n 17) 50 (emphasis added).

38 Robert B Brandom, *Making It Explicit: Reasoning, Representing, and Discursive Commitment* (Harvard University Press 1998) 3–66; cf Klatt, *Making the Law Explicit* (n 16) 117–22.

'monological fashion',[39] the right to justification is reconstructed as a discursive, intersubjective process concerned with the dignity of other persons.[40]

Qua sociality, the right to justification is dependent upon our ability to reciprocally cognize and recognize each other as justificatory beings:

> [H]umans recognize themselves and each other reciprocally as members of the moral community of justification that includes all human beings . . . , as autonomous and responsible beings, endowed with reason, who are members of a shared (and commonly constructed) space of justifying reasons.[41]

Cognizing and recognizing are cognitive and volitive acts by which we enter the space of reasons spontaneously and by ourselves. The right to justification depends on our disposition to want both ourselves and others to be discursive creatures. It is hence reliant on existentialist decisions on our identities, on constructive acts of self-interpretation and self-formation.

This dependency of normativity on sociality and on existentialist decision, however, does not imply that normativity can be reduced to social facts, as the objection from the natural fallacy assumes. Normativity is created in the social space, but it does not collapse to mere intersubjective consensus. Rather, what is being created in the social space of reasons is a distinct normative status.

Thus, while the normativity of any justification exists only in the consensus achieved in the social practices, it is not true that just about any consensus is sufficient, as the objection from the natural fallacy is bound to argue. The brute de facto consensus is not the final criterion of legitimate normative claims. If it were otherwise, the distinctive characteristic of normativity, ie its anti-reductionist supervenience, would be lost.[42] The consensus 'must be such that it *could* gain the support of free and equal persons'.[43] That way, the validity of moral norms, though grounded in the de facto claims made by social actors in concrete social contexts, still links up with a Habermasian theory of counterfactual, ideal presuppositions of rational discourse.[44] Normativity exhibits a dual nature, comprising both a real, factual, social dimension and an ideal dimension.

Brandomian normative pragmatics can help to bring the decisive difference between a mere de facto validity and authentic moral validity grounded in social practice to light. Brandom shows that moral norms are products of our practical

39 Erman (n 31) 2.

40 Forst, 'Moral Autonomy and the Autonomy of Morality' (n 17) 48.

41 Forst, 'Practical Reason and Justifying Reasons' (n 10) 37f. Cf Brandom, *Making It Explicit* (n 38) 5, 50–55, 243–53.

42 On anti-reductionist supervenience as condition of normativity, see Matthias Klatt, *Making the Law Explicit* (n 16) 98f.

43 Forst, 'Moral Autonomy and the Autonomy of Morality' (n 17) 48.

44 Forst, 'Toward a Critical Theory of Transnational Justice' (n 18) 259, n 39.

normative attitudes. These attitudes are expressed in our activities, whenever we impose normative significances and acknowledge them in our practices of assessments.[45] Normative attitudes sanction performances as correct or incorrect. Sanctioning, however, cannot be understood as purely factual reactions, since sanctioning itself can be done correctly or incorrectly.[46] Sanctions and normative attitudes cannot be reconstructed in purely naturalistic terms. Brandom elucidates this problem by considering an archaic community in which a valid practical norm requires everyone to display a leaf from a certain sort of tree whenever one enters a specific hut. Any violation of this norm is sanctioned by refusing the admission to the hut and beating the transgressor with sticks. While this sanction can be fully described in non-normative terms, this is not true of a different assessing response: the sanction may also consist of making other actions inappropriate, eg by refusing permission to attend the weekly festival:

> In such a case, the normative significance of transgression is itself specified in normative terms (of what is *appropriate*, of [scil. what] the transgressor is *entitled* to do). The punishment for violating one norm is an alteration in other normative statuses. Acting incorrectly alters what other performances are correct and incorrect.[47]

The decisive point here is that the normative attitudes relating to one kind of normative status (eg correctness of hut entering) are made explicit by normative internal sanctions which are construed in terms of another sort of normative status (eg correctness of festival attending). This kind of normative internal sanctions is specifiable only in normative terms.[48] In result, normativity is instituted by social practice.[49] It is 'generated by a discursive justification procedure that equips norms with reasons that cannot be rejected'.[50] Without the practical acknowledgment of participants in the game of giving and asking for reasons, performances would not have any normative properties.[51] Performances can only be reconstructed as correct or incorrect by reference to their assessment as such by the participants of a practice in which the norms are implicit.

[45] Brandom, *Making It Explicit* (n 38) 49; cf Klatt, *Making the Law Explicit* (n 16) 117–22. On the relevance of reciprocal recognition by means of normative attitudes shared in a social space, see Robert B Brandom, 'A Hegelian Model of Legal Concept Determination: The Normative Fine Structure of the Judges' Chain Novel' in Graham Hubbs (ed), *Pragmatism, Law, and Language* (Routledge 2014) 26–30.

[46] Brandom, *Making It Explicit* (n 38) 36.

[47] ibid 43.

[48] ibid 44.

[49] cf Klatt, *Making the Law Explicit* (n 16) 122.

[50] Forst, 'Moral Autonomy and the Autonomy of Morality' (n 17) 51.

[51] Brandom, *Making It Explicit* (n 38) 63.

Practical rationality is hence socialized. It remains 'a specifically human institution that is founded on the practice of human beings mutually *according* each other the status of moral persons . . .'[52] The normative practical attitudes of the participants who acknowledge the normative significances of actions have a social structure. Any description of normativity, therefore, must include regularities in conduct and dispositions. Yet Brandom's account of normativity remains to be non-reductionist in nature, since the regularities of normative dispositions are not part of what is being claimed by the norms, and the normative is not reduced to the dispositional.[53] That way, regularity is made a necessary, but not a sufficient condition for normativity. Normativity depends on sociality; it is instituted socially, and hence without social settings there cannot be normativity. Still, the normative cannot be conflated with mere social regularity of normative dispositions.[54] The decisive point in the present context is, that if mere conformity cannot constitute correctness, then the objection from the natural fallacy is mistaken.

5. The Relative Necessity of Normativity

In contrast to Forst's account, I should like to stress that the right to justification is relativized by grounding practical rationality in the social practice of human beings recognizing each other as justificatory beings and subscribing themselves and each other to the force of the better argument. It is relativized to a certain practice, namely, to the practice of giving and asking for reasons. The necessity of normativity is not absolute, but relative to our discursive practice as justificatory beings.[55] It is dependent upon our existential decisions to accept each other as discursive persons competent in asserting, asking, and arguing.[56]

Does this relativization of the right to justification mean that its justification is ultimately unconvincing? I do not think so. The relative necessity of justification

[52] Forst, 'Moral Autonomy and the Autonomy of Morality' (n 17) 60 (emphasis added).
[53] Brandom, *Making It Explicit* (n 38) 46.
[54] ibid 37–42.
[55] For the concept of relative necessity, of necessity 'within any conceptual scheme we adopt or use", see HP Grice and PF Strawson, 'In Defense of a Dogma' (1956) 65 The Philosophical Review 141, 157f.
[56] cf Robert Alexy, 'Menschenrechte ohne Metaphysik?' (2004) 52 Deutsche Zeitschrift für Philosophie 15, 24; Robert Alexy, 'Law, Morality, and the Existence of Human Rights' (2012) 25 Ratio Juris 2, 11; Robert Alexy, 'Coherence and Argumentation or the Genuine Twin Criterialess Super Criterion' in Aulis Aarnio and others (eds), *On Coherence Theory of Law* (Juristförlaget 1998) 43. On the relevance of decision for justifying normativity, see Robert Alexy, 'Normativity, Metaphysics and Decision' in Stefano Bertea and George Pavlakos (eds), *New Essays on the Normativity of Law* (Hart Publishing 2011) 226–28; for a similar critique, see Fernando S Müller, 'Justifying the Right to Justification: An Analysis of Rainer Forst's Constructivist Theory of Justice' (2013) 39 Philosophy & Social Criticism 1049, 1053–56, 1062–66.

means that justification is conditional upon the game of giving and asking for reasons. This is not a very demanding condition, and hence the relativization is not a problem we should worry much about. Furthermore, the relativization is only of an external character. From the internal perspective of the participant, the necessity of normativity remains absolute.[57] Furthermore, since the right to justification is a necessary element of any concept of rational discourse, and since the scenario to forgo completely the idea of rational discourse is not a very tempting proposal, this relativization is hardly a great problem. At any rate, any attempt to *argue* in favour of such a scenario is a *contradictio in adiecto*.

III. The Right to Proportionality

We owe the insight on the relation between the right to justification and the proportionality test to Mattias Kumm. In his contribution to *Institutionalized Reason*, he remarked that judicial review with the help of the proportionality test can be interpreted as the attempt to institutionalize a right to justification.[58] 'Both the structure and the scope of rights that Alexy defends fit perfectly with the function to provide a test to be used to establish whether or not actions by public authorities are justifiable in terms that the burdened party might reasonable accept'.[59] Alexy highlighted specifically this point in his response.[60] Each constitutional right includes a right to justification. It follows that judicial review can be regarded as the institutionalization of a right to justification.

Proportionality analysis translates the right to justification into constitutional practice. Yet we may ask how exactly the relation between the right to justification and the proportionality test can be reconstructed. In order to explore this relation problem in detail, I will first clarify the relationship between correctness, justification, and argumentation (sub-section 1). Second, I will establish that proportionality integrates the form and the substance of justification (sub-section 2). This analysis will, third, amount to institutionalizing the space of reasons in constitutional law (sub-section 3), which, fourth, allows for both internal and external justification in rights reasoning (sub-section 4). Fifth, I will address the problem of the universality of proportionality in a culturally diverse world (sub-section 5).

[57] cf Robert Alexy, 'Hans Kelsens Begriff des relativen Apriori' in Robert Alexy and others (eds), *Neukantianismus und Rechtsphilosophie* (Nomos 2002) 201.

[58] Mattias Kumm, 'Alexy's Theory of Constitutional Rights and the Problem of Judicial Review' in Matthias Klatt (ed), *Institutionalized Reason: The Jurisprudence of Robert Alexy* (Oxford University Press 2012) 213–17; cf Aharon Barak, *Proportionality* (n 4) 458–60.

[59] Kumm, 'Alexy's Theory of Constitutional Rights and the Problem of Judicial Review' (n 58) 214.

[60] Alexy, 'Comments and Responses' (n 7) 340.

1. Correctness, Justification, and Argumentation

The proportionality test is the central means to establish whether infringements with human rights are justified. It is the main instrument to assess whether the state's duty to 'justify its decisions to those who raise . . . grievances' has been fulfilled.[61] The proportionality test is an element of legal argumentation used in the context of justifying decisions in rights cases. It is important to note the vital difference between the normative problem of justification and the empirical problem of stating the causes for the genesis or discovery of a legal decision.[62] Justifying a decision is an argumentative exercise, whereas discovering it is a mental activity. Despite the fact that many relations between these two activities exist, the theory of legal argumentation focuses on the problem of justification. In contrast to the discovery of a legal decision, the public use of reason in the argumentative exercise is intersubjectively testable. The quality of the justification process is entirely independent of the real empirical causes of a decision. Bad motives do not disqualify good arguments, and acceptable motives do not transform wrong arguments into true arguments.[63]

Based on this normative understanding of the context of justification, proportionality analysis faces the challenges of incommensurability and of the necessity of value judgments and balancing.[64] Many scholars claim that, in the light of these challenges, a rational justification of legal decisions in rights cases was impossible. For Habermas, 'weighing takes place either arbitrarily or unreflectively, according to customary standards and hierarchies'.[65] In a similar vein, Schlink criticizes balancing as decisionism,[66] and both Somek and Poscher quite bluntly trace back balancing to intuitionistic[67] prejudices. The common core of these sceptical approaches is that balancing propositions were not intersubjectively testable, even though they could perhaps be explained in sociological

[61] Alon Harel, *Why Law Matters* (Oxford University Press 2014) 8.

[62] On the context of justification, in contrast to the context of discovery, see Richard A Wasserstrom, *The Judicial Decision: Toward a Theory of Legal Justification* (Stanford University Press 1961) 25–31; Jerzy Wróblewski, 'Legal Syllogism and Rationality of Judicial Decision' (1974) 5 Rechtstheorie 33, 35–37; Hans-Joachim Koch and Helmut Rüßmann, *Juristische Begründungslehre: Eine Einführung in die Grundprobleme der Rechtswissenschaft* (C.H. Beck 1982) 115–18; Bernhard Schlink, 'Bemerkungen zum Stand der Methodendiskussion in der Verfassungsrechtswissenschaft' (1980) 19 Der Staat 73, 87–91.

[63] cf Koch and Rüßmann (n 62) 1, 116.

[64] cf Klatt and Meister, *The Constitutional Structure of Proportionality* (n 2) 3, 49–73.

[65] Jürgen Habermas, *Between Facts and Norms: Contributions to a Discourse Theory of Law and Democracy* (William Rehg tr, MIT Press 1996) 259.

[66] Bernhard Schlink, 'Freiheit durch Eingriffsabwehr: Rekonstruktion der klassischen Grundrechtsfunktion' (1984) 11 Europäische Grundrechte-Zeitschrift 457, 462.

[67] Alexander Somek, *Rechtliches Wissen* (Suhrkamp 2006) 135; Ralf Poscher, 'The Principles Theory: How Many Theories and What Is Their Merit?' in Matthias Klatt (ed), *Institutionalized Reason: The Jurisprudence of Robert Alexy* (Oxford University Press 2012) 241.

or psychological terms. This conclusion would have devastating consequences for both the legitimacy of judicial decision-making and the scientific character of normatively oriented legal dogmatics, even though the scepticists rarely acknowledge these consequences.

In sharp contrast to these sceptical views, the discourse-theoretical approach to rights reasoning that I follow here highlights that the cornerstone of any rational analysis of legal argumentation is the claim of law to correctness.[68] The justification of propositions used in rights reasoning is necessarily connected with the concept of correctness, because what is justifiable is correct. The claim to correctness is key to reconstructing the relation between proportionality and justification.[69] The claim to correctness represents the overarching argumentation-theoretic framework in which the relation between proportionality and justification must be reconstructed.

Legal propositions and their reasons necessarily claim to be correct. Any legal assertion necessarily contains a discursive commitment in Brandom's sense that the judgment be substantially and procedurally correct.[70] This discursive commitment to correctness has three elements.[71] The first element is the assertion of correctness. Since correctness implies justifiability, this assertion is supplemented by a claim to justifiability. Legal argumentation is a game of giving and asking for reasons in the sense of Brandomian normative pragmatics.[72] Therefore, as a third element of the claim to correctness, every legal assertion implies the expectation that its correctness will be accepted by others. It is easy to see how this relates to Forst's right to justification. The right to justification concerns the second element of the claim to correctness, the claim to justifiability. The two neatly fit together. In addition, there is a more important insight: the claim to correctness is more fundamental than the right to justification, because justification is only one element of the wider concept of correctness in law.

To say that justification is embedded in the wider context of law's claim to correctness does not in itself state anything as to the criteria of correctness. The

[68] Robert Alexy, *A Theory of Legal Argumentation: The Theory of Rational Discourse as Theory of Legal Justification* (Neil MacCormick and Ruth Adler trs, Oxford University Press 1989) 214; Matthias Klatt, 'Robert Alexy's Philosophy of Law as System' in Matthias Klatt (ed), *Institutionalized Reason: The Jurisprudence of Robert Alexy* (Oxford University Press 2012) 5f, 15f.

[69] cf TRS Allan, 'Democracy, Legality, and Proportionality' in Grant Huscroft, Bradley W Miller, and Grégoire CN Webber (eds), *Proportionality and the Rule of Law: Rights, Justification, Reasoning* (Cambridge University Press 2014) 205: '*Because* justice consists in the *correct* regulation of affairs or resolution of disputes, according to the moral principles applicable, it invokes the notion of proportionality" (emphases added).

[70] Robert Alexy, 'Law and Correctness' (1998) 51 Current Legal Problems 205, 208; Brandom, *Making It Explicit* (n 38) 157; Klatt, *Making the Law Explicit* (n 16) 127–29; cf Klatt, 'Robert Alexy's Philosophy of Law as System' (n 68) 5f, 12f, 15f.

[71] Alexy, 'Law and Correctness' (n 70) 208.

[72] Klatt, *Making the Law Explicit* (n 16) 117–22; Brandom, *Making It Explicit* (n 38) 20.

openness of the criteria for correctness is a condition for the general validity of the claim to correctness in all legal systems and in all areas of the law.[73] Different legal systems have different criteria for correctness, and even within one and the same legal system different criteria of correctness may apply, eg for the various institutional acts, like statutes, administrative acts, and court decisions.

The decisive question is whether for all diversity something common exists which can justify the universality of the claim to correctness in law. Rainer Forst's right to justification operates with two criteria, generality and reciprocity. The three elements of law's claim to correctness fulfil these criteria. They endorse generality because in the game of giving and asking for reasons, anyone is entitled to raise objections against an asserted claim to correctness, anyone can bring forward arguments that challenge the entitlement of the person who raised this claim about a specific institutional act. According to the rules of general practical discourse, no asserted claim to correctness is sacrosanct. 'Everyone may problematize any assertion'.[74] If anyone challenges an assertion, the speaker must give reasons for what she asserts, according to the general justification rule.[75] This is so since the claim to correctness entails a claim to justifiability, which normatively commits the speaker to state reasons. This furthers the reciprocity of the discursive process since it prevents any privileges for specific speakers. Reciprocity is also secured by the rule of general practical discourse stating that no speaker may be prevented from exercising her discursive rights by any kind of coercion.[76] Lastly, the normative expectation that the addressees will accept the correctness of an institutional act also underlines the reciprocal orientation of any assertion of correctness. The claim to correctness in both general practical and legal discourse thus has a general and reciprocal character. It fits perfectly well with the two criteria of the right to justification.

The above argument demonstrates that even though the detailed criteria for correctness may be different in various contexts, across different legal systems or even within a legal system, the elements that are constitutive for the fact that if these criteria are fulfilled, then the legal act is correct, are universally valid. This universal validity also underlines that the claim to correctness is key to reconstructing the relation between proportionality and justification. The internal connections between correctness, justification, and argumentation provide a firm basis for the possibility to rationally justify the legal propositions used

[73] Alexy, 'Law and Correctness' (n 70) 209.
[74] Alexy, *A Theory of Legal Argumentation* (n 68) 193.
[75] ibid 192.
[76] cf ibid 193.

in proportionality analysis. The integration of proportionality and argumentation lends the proportionality test as such its absolute character.[77]

2. Integrating Form and Substance

The fact that the right to justification is embedded in the wider discourse-theoretical claim to correctness also clears the way for some criticism of Forst's account of the right to justification. This is so because correctness is a more complex and more demanding concept than the two criteria of reciprocity and generality indicate.[78] Reciprocity and generality are necessary conditions for the correctness of legal assertions—but they are not sufficient conditions, as Forst claims. The claim to correctness embraces both formal and material correctness, both the formal rules of discourse and the substance of justification. In contrast, Forst's right to justification seems to be limited to the rather formal requirements of reciprocity and generality. Hence, the substantial aspects of justification must be added to his theory in order to comply completely with the fully- fledged claim to correctness that comprises substantive correctness. Substantive correctness is mainly determined by human rights. Therefore, human rights must be added to reciprocity and generality as an additional criterion to determine the right to justification.

In fact, Forst himself recognizes that a theory of justice cannot be purely procedural. He characterizes the right to justification as a '*substantive* individual moral right'.[79] This characterization, however, is misleading. It is more accurate to characterize the human right to justification as a formal human right, since it prescribes a specific form of legal discourse, that of giving and asking for reasons. Still, this does not render the whole theory purely formal, because the formal right to justification necessarily relates to substantial considerations of justice—the latter are simply the objects of the former.

The integration between the form and the substance of justification can be demonstrated with the help of three distinct elements. First of all, it is vital to note that the claim to correctness and the right to justification presuppose some, though not all substantial human rights. Rational justificatory discourse presupposes, eg the freedom of expression and the freedom of information.

[77] Alexy, 'The Absolute and the Relative Dimension of Constitutional Rights' (n 7) 39. The validity of this statement is dependent upon a second thesis, namely, that no alternative form of argumentation exists that is more rational than the proportionality test.

[78] cf Talbott (n 25) 754.

[79] Forst, 'Introduction' (n 12) 5.

These substantive human rights constrain the democratic process significantly.[80] Even more importantly, these substantial human rights are not artificially added to the right to justification.[81] Rather, they follow directly from the idea of free and rational discourse as a necessary condition of any general and reciprocal practice of justification. Second, the substance of justification is part and parcel of the right to justification to the degree that the two criteria of reciprocity and generality allow to distinguish better from worse arguments. The 'criterial strength of these requirements' for grading the material quality of arguments is a substantive implication of the right to justification.[82] Thirdly, the substance of justification is necessarily fed into the discourse when a political community sets out to establish its basic social structure. This process is necessarily a collective, internal, and discursive construction in intersubjective practice, rather than a cognitive access to some external principles of justice or natural law truths. No political community can avoid this constructive process, since 'there are no external "derivations" that can trump the construction'.[83]

In consequence, moral constructivism is a necessary part of political constructivism, and hence the latter cannot be separated from the former.[84] This is the reason why rights reasoning qua legal discourse is a special case of general practical discourse.[85] The internal connections between moral and political constructivism, between legal and general practical discourse, bring about an intrinsic integration between the form and the substance of justification: 'the right to justification can always assume the form of a substantive objection or argument as well as the procedural form of demand for discourses of justification . . . A general recursive and reflexive context is thereby set up, which overcomes old divisions between procedural and substantive approaches not only in moral philosophy but also in democratic theory'.[86] All of this sounds very familiar to anyone acquainted with the debate on the proportionality test. Proportionality as well is incorrectly accused of being purely formal and of

[80] Forst, 'The Rule of Reasons' (n 22) 185; Joshua Cohen, 'Procedure and Substance in Deliberative Democracy' in James Bohman and William Rehg (eds), *Deliberative Democracy: Essays on Reason and Politics* (MIT Press 1997) 415.

[81] Forst, 'The Rule of Reasons' (n 22) 185.

[82] cf Forst, 'Introduction' (n 12) 6.

[83] ibid 7.

[84] ibid 6.

[85] Alexy, *A Theory of Legal Argumentation* (n 68) 212–20; Klatt, 'Robert Alexy's Philosophy of Law as System' (n 68) 4f, 14. For a critical discussion, see Habermas, *Between Facts and Norms* (n 65) 204, 206, 233ff; Klaus Günther, 'Critical Remarks on Robert Alexy's Special Case Thesis' (1993) 6 Ratio Juris 143. For Alexy's replies, see Robert Alexy, 'The Special Case Thesis' (1999) 12 Ratio Juris 374; Robert Alexy, 'Justification and Application of Norms' (1993) 6 Ratio Juris 157. See also George Pavlakos, 'The Special Case Thesis. An Assessment of R. Alexy's Discursive Theory of Law' (1998) 11 Ratio Juris 126; Ingrid Dwars, 'Application Discourse and the Special Case Thesis' (1992) 5 Ratio Juris 67.

[86] Forst, 'Introduction' (n 12) 7.

trying to avoid substantive discussions of justice. Indeed, the proportionality test perfectly represents the dual nature of justice and the integration of form and substance in rights reasoning.[87]

That the right to justification implies some, but not all, human rights indicates that the right to justification is not a sufficient basis to justify the existence of all human rights. This is a strong reason against acknowledging an analytical priority of the right to justification. It is more convincing to reconstruct the derivative relation between man rights and the right to justification such that substantial human rights are analytically prior. Human rights demand to be institutionalized and applied correctly, and this correctness implies a right to justification. The right to justification, in turn, implies a right to proportionality. The right to proportionality, on the other hand, requires reasoning with the substantial content of human rights. That way, the analytical circle is closed: it starts and ends with substantial human rights, and it has two formal elements—the right to justification and the right to proportionality—in the middle. The four elements are not detached from each other, but tied to each other with strong derivative bonds of necessary character. Furthermore, it becomes clear that the right to justification functions as a normative bridge concept: it bridges the move from human rights to proportionality.

3. Institutionalizing the Space of Reasons

It is important to note that neither the claim to correctness nor the right to justification say anything about the objects for correctness and for justification. These objects have to be established separately. In rights cases, they follow from the structure of rights. The structure of rights tells us that the objects of justification are threefold: first, the existence of a right with a specific scope. Second, that there is or was an infringement with the right. Third, that the infringement is or was justified.

The proportionality test relates to the third element. It is the central means to establish whether or not actions by public authorities are justified infringements. What Forst says about transnational justice is also true for justice within a state legal order: the institutions-theoretic task is to establish sufficient structures of justification that serve to realize the force towards the better argument. By this means, no relevant aspect remains hidden behind a veil of non-justification. These structures of justification are discursive provisions for heading for higher levels of rights reasoning.[88] The proportionality test simply is one of these

[87] See below, Section III.4 Internal and External Justification.

[88] Rainer Forst, 'Dialektik der Moral: Grundlagen einer Diskurstheorie Transnationaler Gerechtigkeit' in Rainer Forst, *Das Recht auf Rechtfertigung: Elemente einer konstruktivistischen*

structures and provisions. It fulfils all the functions just mentioned, thus enhancing transparency, inclusiveness, and general quality of reasoning.[89]

On an even more basic level, the proportionality test can be interpreted as a formal rule which serves to establish the space of reasons which is inhabited in common by human beings as justificatory beings.[90] That way, the proportionality test is not a specific feature of rights reasoning, but bears upon more fundamental characteristics of a shared practice of reasoning in general. As Forst has aptly put it:

> An intentional . . . action can be characterized as rationally grounded if the practical deliberation leading up to it is oriented toward specific rules that refer both to the consideration of ends and to the choice of means.[91]

The proportionality is precisely a specific rule in this sense.[92]

The space of reasons operated by means of the proportionality test is necessarily an open-ended space. Discourse never comes to a definite stop; justification is potentially infinite. I label this the *diachronic dimension* of the right to justification.[93] Ronald Dworkin prominently suggested reconstructing the development of the law by analogy to writing a chain novel.[94] My suggestion is that this metaphor does not only apply to the interpretation of legal rules but also to applying legal principles by means of proportionality analysis.[95] Each judge inherits a corpus comprising earlier applications of the proportionality test, which have been submitted by other judges or legal scholars. The new decision made by the judge is meant to extend this corpus and to fit into the chain in a way that 'makes the work more significant or otherwise better'.[96]

Theorie der Gerechtigkeit (Suhrkamp 2007) 355f. I cite the German edition here because the English translation misses out the parts relevant to my point.

---

[89] Klatt and Meister, *The Constitutional Structure of Proportionality* (n 2) 167–71.

[90] Forst, 'Practical Reason and Justifying Reasons' (n 10) 14.

[91] ibid.

[92] cf Kumm's characterization of proportionality as establishing 'a test of public reason': Mattias Kumm, 'Is the Structure of Human Rights Practice Defensible? Three Puzzles and Their Solution' in Vicki C Jackson and Mark V Tushnet (eds), *Proportionality: New Frontiers, New Challenges* (Cambridge University Press 2017) 65.

[93] A similar argument can be found in Brandom, 'A Hegelian Model of Legal Concept Determination' (n 45) 31; Alexy, 'Coherence and Argumentation or the Genuine Twin Criterialess Super Criterion' (n 56) 48f.

[94] Ronald Dworkin, *Law's Empire* (Fontana 1986) 228–38.

[95] On the norm-theoretic distinction between rules and principles, and the related legal methods of subsumption and balancing, see Robert Alexy, 'On Balancing and Subsumption' (2003) 16 Ratio Juris 433. Cf Klatt, 'Robert Alexy's Philosophy of Law as System' (n 68) 7f, 19–21.

[96] Dworkin (n 94) 233.

Judges deciding rights cases operate on a basis of chain novels containing prima facie answers to questions like 'What public interest counts as a legitimate aim?', 'What kind of means is suitable to foster a goal?', etc. Arguably the most important part of the diachronic dimension of the right to proportionality are chain novels on the outcome of previous balancing exercises, ie on conditional preference-relations between colliding fundamental rights and other constitutional principles.[97] This does not mean that the judge could not divert from, modify, or rewrite the answers given previously to these kind of questions by other judges. Nevertheless, it does mean that some kind of default-and-challenge structure is a place that lends considerable legal certainty to proportionality analysis. It makes the law foreseeable to a certain degree and shifts the burden of argument to any proposition that wants to challenge these answers.[98] Following Brandom's deontic-scorekeeping model of normativity, specific answers to the questions of the proportionality test are considered to have a prima facie entitlement. This is precisely what is behind Alexy's statement that proportionality 'rests on a massive fundament of clear cases'.[99] For any of these default propositions on proportionality, it is true what Forst stresses for interpretations of basic rights in general: '[n]one of the formulations or interpretations of basic rights is "absolute"; yet the justificatory threshold of unpacking and criticizing them is high'.[100] The prima facie status can be challenged by doubts, but these doubts must re reasoned. In making a decision on any of the four prongs of proportionality, a judge undertakes a normative commitment, according to the implicit claim to correctness. This new commitment is fitted into a 'constellation of prior commitments', by means of a 'process of sequential rational integration', thus instituting 'normative statuses of authority and responsibility according to the model of reciprocal recognition'.[101]

In this way, over time repeated applications of proportionality analysis create an evolving specification of fundamental rights.[102] The diachronic dimension of the right to justification leads to chains of arguments. Any link in these chains can be taken as a new initial statement, which again can be challenged

[97] On conditional preference relations between constitutional principles, see Robert Alexy, *A Theory of Constitutional Rights* (Julian Rivers tr, Oxford University Press 2002) 50–54. The diachronic nature of these judicial processes resembles the processes of contestation and deliberation leading towards specific constitutional settlement which Benhabib has labelled 'iterative democratic processes': Seyla Benhabib (ed), *Another Cosmopolitanism* (Oxford University Press 2006) 45–80.

[98] On the concept of default-and-challenge structure, see Klatt, *Making the Law Explicit* (n 16) 149f, 217.

[99] Alexy, 'The Absolute and the Relative Dimension of Constitutional Rights' (n 7) 47.

[100] Rainer Forst, 'The Justification of Basic Rights: A Discourse-Theoretical Approach' (2016) 45(3) Netherlands Journal of Legal Philosophy 7, 22.

[101] Brandom, 'A Hegelian Model of Legal Concept Determination' (n 45) 33.

[102] Julian Rivers, 'The Presumption of Proportionality' (2014) 77 The Modern Law Review 409, 409f.

by counter-arguments, thus starting a new chain of argument. In this way, clusters of arguments evolve in the discursive interplay of giving and asking for reasons. Such clusters of arguments have important characteristics: contrary to what Raz claims,[103] they have to be consistent, comprehensive, and connected. It follows that 'the concept of justification . . . implies the core of the concept of coherence'.[104] The necessary connection between justification and coherence establishes another important relation between justification, correctness, and proportionality: proportionality is the best justificatory instrument to foster coherence in rights reasoning, and hence the principle of constitutional coherence demands applying the proportionality test.

4. Internal and External Justification

The right to justification integrates the form and the substance of justificatory discourse.[105] Nothing demonstrates this integration better than the proportionality test. Its four prongs enable reciprocal and general justifications in rights reasoning. Recent studies on proportionality have introduced the distinction between the internal and the external justification.[106] The proportionality test per se provides a formal structure, a formal set of five questions that have to be answered in order to develop correct decisions in rights cases. Any legal decision that follows this structure by posing and answering these five questions is internally justified. Many scholars, however, mistake the proportionality test for this pure formality.[107] Luc Tremblay, for example, argues that 'for the purposes of judicial review, the judges do not need to postulate the validity or truth of one substantive theory . . . and do not need to use the process of constitutional interpretation to this end'.[108]

[103] Joseph Raz, 'The Relevance of Coherence' (1992) 72 Boston University Law Review 273.

[104] Alexy, 'Coherence and Argumentation or the Genuine Twin Criterialess Super Criterion' (n 56) 44.

[105] See above, Section III.2 Integrating Form and Substance.

[106] Matthias Klatt and Johannes Schmidt, 'Epistemic Discretion in Constitutional Law' (2012) 10 International Journal of Constitutional Law 69, 74; Matthias Klatt, 'An Egalitarian Defense of Proportionality-Based Balancing: A Response to Luc B. Tremblay' (2014) 12 International Journal of Constitutional Law 891; Matthias Klatt and Moritz Meister, 'Proportionality—A Benefit to Human Rights? Remarks on the ICon Controversy' (2012) 10 International Journal of Constitutional Law 687; Klatt and Meister, *The Constitutional Structure of Proportionality* (n 2).

[107] cf Letsas who states that 'the orthodox understanding of proportionality as a human rights doctrine is *vacuous*': Letsas (n 8) 340 (emphasis added). The opposite mistake (interpreting proportionality as 'unconstrained moral reasoning') is likewise present in the literature, see Francisco J Urbina, *A Critique of Proportionality and Balancing* (Cambridge University Press 2017) 9, 198ff.

[108] Luc B Tremblay, 'An Egalitarian Defense of Proportionality-Based Balancing' (2014) 12 International Journal of Constitutional Law 864, 869. I have presented the following argument previously in Klatt, 'An Egalitarian Defense of Proportionality-Based Balancing: A Response to Luc B. Tremblay' (n 106).

Tremblay's normative defence of proportionality boils down to a relief thesis: the proportionality test, in his view, offers judges relief from the burden of engaging in far-reaching normative assumptions: '[t]he judges can avoid almost all difficult epistemological and normative questions [. . . .] and the courts are not compelled to impose certain controversial, moral, political or philosophical substantive views'.[109] By using balancing, judges could, so Tremblay hopes, escape the slippery slope of substantial, politically contested moral argument.

The relief thesis represents a commonly held misunderstanding of the proportionality test, which claims that it were purely formal.[110] However, the proportionality test is not detached from substantial reasoning. Any decision of a rights case must employ a general theory of legal argumentation. In its most developed form, proportionality analysis and balancing are supplemented by a discursive theory of legal argumentation.[111] The application of rights is an argumentative exercise requiring substantial argument.[112] According to the special case thesis, legal discourse is a special case of general practical discourse.[113] Hence, 'balancing is an instance of moral reasoning'.[114] When determining the degrees of satisfaction and non-satisfaction of the colliding principles, in accordance with the law of balancing, judges have to engage in contested moral and political considerations.[115]

The formality and substantial neutrality of the proportionality goes only as far as its formal structure, in just the same way as the legal syllogism is formal and neutral. Nevertheless, the claim to correctness and the right to justification require more than pure formality.[116] This is the reason why any decision of a rights case must also be externally justified, in addition to its internal justification.

[109] Tremblay (n 108) 23.

[110] Grégoire CN Webber, 'Proportionality, Balancing, and the Cult of Constitutional Rights Scholarship' (2010) 23 Canadian Journal of Law and Jurisprudence 179, 191; Stavros Tsakyrakis, 'Proportionality: An Assault on Human Rights?' (2009) 7 International Journal of Constitutional Law 468, 474. For a response to that argument, see Klatt and Meister, 'Proportionality—A Benefit to Human Rights? Remarks on the ICon Controversy' (n 106) 694f. For a detailed discussion of the impact of morals on balancing, see Klatt and Meister, *The Constitutional Structure of Proportionality* (n 2) 51–56.

[111] cf Klatt, 'Robert Alexy's Philosophy of Law as System' (n 68).

[112] cf Virgílio Afonso da Silva, 'Comparing the Incommensurable: Constitutional Principles, Balancing and Rational Decision' (2011) 31 Oxford Journal of Legal Studies 273, 288.

[113] Alexy, *A Theory of Legal Argumentation* (n 68) 212–20; Klatt, 'Robert Alexy's Philosophy of Law as System' (n 68) 4–5, 14. For a critical discussion of the special case thesis, see Habermas, *Between Facts and Norms* (n 65) 204; Günther (n 85). For Alexy's replies, see Alexy, 'The Special Case Thesis' (n 85); Alexy, 'Justification and Application of Norms' (n 85). See also Pavlakos (n 85); Dwars (n 85).

[114] Klatt and Meister, *The Constitutional Structure of Proportionality* (n 2) 53.

[115] Afonso da Silva (n 112) 288.

[116] cf Dimitrios Kyritsis, 'Whatever Works: Proportionality as a Constitutional Doctrine' (2014) 34 Oxford Journal of Legal Studies 395, 414: 'Formal rationality will not do'.

Judges must justify externally that, for instance, the intensity of an interference with a right was serious or that the weight of a competing principle was light. Such evaluations can only be externally justified by means of practical reasoning and substantial argument.[117] In its consideration of substantive political morality, the balancing of legal principles in proportionality analysis resembles very much the justificatory process of 'law as integrity' according to Dworkin's interpretive theory.[118] I label this the *proportionality as integrity model.*

This integrative account of moral and legal discourse received criticism. It has been objected that it would turn balancing into a 'microcosm of all the disagreements found within contemporary political philosophy'.[119] I subscribe to that description to the degree that follows from the first part of the special case thesis, which states that legal argumentation is a case of general practical reasoning.[120] As far as balancing qua legal argumentation is a case of moral reasoning, it necessarily inherits the rational disagreement and epistemic unreliability of moral reasoning. However, the integrative account of rights reasoning I want to defend does not at all conflate moral and legal argument. On the contrary, it acknowledges that legal discourse does not aim at answering practical questions in a general or absolute sense, but rather within the framework of a specific legal system. This framework imposes restrictions on practical discourse, by means of binding norms, precedents, and legal doctrine.[121] It is hence vital to note that the proportionality as integrity model does not lead to 'unconstrained moral reasoning'.[122] Rather, the special cases thesis acknowledges the constraints stemming from the authoritative-institutional nature of the law. Proportionality, while depending upon moral reasoning, does not collapse into politics and personal morality. The combination of these authoritative elements with the ideal and critical elements of legal discourse is best captured in the thesis that legal argumentation has a dual nature.[123] The objection from a purported conflation

[117] cf Mattias Kumm, 'Political Liberalism and the Structure of Rights: On the Place and Limits of the Proportionality Requirements' in George Pavlakos (ed), *Law, Rights and Discourse: Themes from the Legal Philosophy of Robert Alexy* (Hart Publishing 2007) 148f; Mattias Kumm, 'Constitutional Rights as Principles: On the Structure and Domain of Constitutional Justice' (2004) 2 International Journal of Constitutional Law 574, 575. Alexy, *A Theory of Constitutional Rights* (n 97) 105; Robert Alexy, 'Thirteen Replies' in George Pavlakos (ed), *Law, Rights and Discourse: Themes from the Legal Philosophy of Robert Alexy* (Hart Publishing 2007) 344; see also TRS Allan, *Constitutional Justice: A Liberal Theory of the Rule of Law* (Oxford University Press 2001) 315; Allan, 'Democracy, Legality, and Proportionality' (n 69); Allan, 'Democracy, Legality, and Proportionality' (n 69) 233.

[118] cf Dworkin (n 94) 225–75. Cf Kumm, 'Constitutional Rights as Principles' (n 117) 575: '... such a structural account is compatible with the kind of strong substantive commitments that characterize normative theories ...'

[119] Tremblay (n 108) 16.

[120] Alexy, 'The Special Case Thesis' (n 85).

[121] Klatt, 'Robert Alexy's Philosophy of Law as System' (n 68) 4f, 14.

[122] Urbina (n 107) 9, 198ff.

[123] Matthias Klatt, 'The Rule of Dual-Natured Law' in ET Feteris and others (eds), *Legal Argumentation and the Rule of Law* (Eleven International Publishing 2016) 31, 35f.

of moral and legal discourse is wrong because it misses the institutional and authoritative character of rights reasoning.

Understood in the sense of the dual nature thesis, the connection between moral and legal discourse is unavoidable. Tremblay suggests that 'no court should read a constitution in terms that take side on fundamental controversial substantive issues'.[124] In contrast, the dual-nature of proportionality analysis insists that judges cannot confine themselves to some purely formal egalitarian handling of rights conflicts. In deciding rights cases on the basis of proportionality and balancing, they establish a conditional relation of preference between the colliding interests by stating which principle prevails in the concrete case. This inevitably amounts to taking sides.

Balancing, the last prong of the proportionality test, can be characterized by a relation of inheritance between the premises and the conclusion. The balancing result will inherit all unreliabilities and imponderabilia of those substantial, political, moral, contested propositions that are used as normative premises in applying the law of balancing. It is precisely due to this relation of inheritance that Tremblay's relief thesis is unconvincing.

Two additional points are worth mentioning. First, external justification in proportionality analysis must not be misunderstood as providing an objective epistemic standpoint of some eternal moral or political truth.[125] Rather, proportionality and justification have a discursive nature. Ultimately, we decide upon the correctness of constitutional propositions in our concrete practices of justification. The practices of justification by means of proportionality analysis never come to a definite ending.[126] This is the diachronic dimension of the proportionality analysis.[127]

Second, one of the most frequently made objections against the principles-theoretical account of proportionality and against the theory of balancing is that it did not provide a theory on the external justification and did not answer the question as to the criteria of moral importance in that process.[128] This objection is true only if one looks for these criteria in constitutional rights theory, thus neglecting the general theory of legal argumentation. As I have laid down elsewhere, constitutional rights theory and the general theory of legal argumentation complement one another.[129] The latter provides a detailed discourse-theoretical account of moral and legal reasoning.[130]

124 Tremblay (n 108) 18.
125 cf Forst, 'Practical Reason and Justifying Reasons' (n 10) 21f.
126 cf Forst, 'The Rule of Reasons' (n 22) 185; cf Klatt, 'The Rule of Dual-Natured Law' (n 123) 41.
127 See page 176 above.
128 Urbina (n 107) 27.
129 Klatt, 'Robert Alexy's Philosophy of Law as System' (n 68) 18–21.
130 cf Alexy, *A Theory of Constitutional Rights* (n 97) 386f.

5. The Universality Problem

That external justification is at the same time necessary and external to the proportionality test per se has very important consequences for the problem of the universality of proportionality. If the proportionality test is the main criterion for justified infringements with human rights, the important question arises whether the validity of this criterion is limited to the particularistic framework of specific legal systems or whether it is a universal criterion applicable on a global scale. This is heavily contested.[131] If proportionality is an important element of global constitutionalism, as I have claimed elsewhere, its universality needs to be defended.[132]

I would like to submit that the distinction between the internal and the extern justification leads way to a precise solution to this puzzle. The distinction between internal and external justification can explain why and to what degree proportionality can be at the same time universally valid and open to cultural variations. The internal justification qua formal structure is of universal applicability and culturally neutral. The structure of internal justification qua proportionality analysis stems from the necessary connection between principles and proportionality.[133] The external justification, however, is culturally sensitive and admits different cultural perspectives as to what, eg, counts as a legitimate aim, or what amounts to a serious infringement. The external justification in proportionality analysis perfectly explains why it is so exceptionally well suited to be applied in diverse concrete social and legal contexts. The concept of external justification underlines that proportionality is capable of doing 'justice to the plurality of ethical values and to various social spheres and communities'.[134]

[131] See Barak's request that '[w]e should ensure that the legal construction of proportionality allows the realization of various and conflicting social theories', a request that presupposes the possibility to do so: Aharon Barak, 'A Research Agenda for the Future' in Vicki C Jackson and Mark V Tushnet (eds), *Proportionality: New Frontiers, New Challenges* (Cambridge University Press 2017) 335. See also João Andrade Neto, 'The Debatable Universality of the Proportionality Test and the Wide-Scope Conception of Fundamental Rights' (2016) 12(1) Revista Brasileira de Direito 4; Urbina (n 107) 8.

[132] Klatt and Meister, *The Constitutional Structure of Proportionality* (n 2) 1–4, 171; Matthias Klatt and Moritz Meister, 'A Proporcionalidade como Princípio Constitucional Universal' (2015) 1 Revista Publicum 30; Matthias Klatt and Moritz Meister, 'Verhältnismäßigkeit als universelles Verfassungsprinzip' in Matthias Klatt (ed), *Prinzipientheorie und Theorie der Abwägung* (Mohr Siebeck 2013) 104. For a critical view of 'foundational constitutionalism' beyond the state, see Nico Krisch, *Beyond Constitutionalism: The Pluralist Structure of Postnational Law* (Oxford University Press 2010) 27–68; Martin Loughlin, 'What Is Constitutionalization?' in Petra Dobner and Martin Loughlin (eds), *The Twilight of Constitutionalism?* (Oxford University Press 2010); Dieter Grimm, 'The Constitution in the Process of Denationalization' (2005) 12 Constellations 447.

[133] Alexy discusses this point as the 'absoluteness of the principle of proportionality'', see Alexy, 'The Absolute and the Relative Dimension of Constitutional Rights' (n 7) 36f.

[134] cf Forst, 'Introduction' (n 12) 7.

However, it would be a far too rough picture if we equated internal justification with universality and external justification with particularism. If beyond internal justification there was only culture-relativity, proportionality could be universal only in a very weak sense. Yet the integration between external justification in proportionality analysis, on the one hand, and rational argumentation, on the other, enables universally valid propositions in external justification also. The distinction between the discursively necessary, impossible, and possible is key here. The scope of particularistic cultural diversity stretches as far as the discursively possible. It consists precisely in those areas in which two incompatible normative propositions can be justified without violating any of the rules of rational discourse.[135] This can be called the relative dimension of proportionality. Nonetheless, the scope of discursive possibility is limited. Several normative propositions are 'stringently required' or 'flatly excluded' by the rules of rational discourse.[136] It is precisely these discursively necessary and discursively impossible propositions that represent an absolute dimension of proportionality within external justification.[137] In result, the universality of proportionality analysis is present not only in internal justification, but to a certain degree also in external justification.

Proportionality as a general standard of legal rationality shares this most important reconciliation of universalism and particularism with the moral right to justification. Both the right to justification and proportionality are universally valid standards, which are interculturally nonrejectable. At the same time, however, they remain culturally sensitive and applicable to particular cases and contexts.[138] Justification qua proportionality provides a universal structure of justice capable of framing a great diversity of rights discourse. The external justification required for any proportionality analysis has a socially relative character. Proportionality's external justification is sensitive to the pluralism of specific and local accounts of justice.[139]

Still, a critic may object that the universality of proportionality was limited to a certain understanding of rights, namely, to the view that interprets rights as principles and principles as optimization requirements. We could label this the dependency objection. Proportionality would be dependent upon a specific understanding of rights—and hence not applicable in legal systems that adopt different rights conceptions. It is worth noting that this objection challenges the universality of proportionality's internal justification, rather than only its external justification. The dependency objection, however, is mistaken because any

[135] cf Alexy, *A Theory of Legal Argumentation* (n 68) 207.
[136] ibid.
[137] cf Alexy, 'The Absolute and the Relative Dimension of Constitutional Rights' (n 7) 45f.
[138] Forst, 'The Basic Right to Justification' (n 32) 204.
[139] cf Forst, 'Introduction' (n 12) 8.

alternative rights conception can be demonstrated to be either included in the optimization model or to be less convincing. This is true, in particular, of the trias of the most important rights conceptions discussed as alternative to the optimization model, namely, rights as trumps, rights as deontological constraints, and absolute rights. Proportionality is able to reconstruct trumping effects and the absoluteness of rights to a sufficient degree.[140] The notion of deontological constraints, on the other hand, provided they can be rationally justified, can be accounted for in the external justification. External justification is not limited to consequentialist arguments. The dependency objection does, therefore, not successfully challenge the universality of proportionality's internal justification.

Proportionality is a central means to integrate moral constructivism with legal constructivism, in accordance with the special case thesis and the dual nature of law. The rights that moral persons can claim and justify as moral rights can 'only be *concretely* justified, interpreted, institutionalized, and *realized* in social contexts, that is to say, only within a legally constituted political order'.[141] This is precisely what proportionality analysis enables us to achieve. Proportionality provides a universal structure to a plurality of internal moralities, leaving it to the participants of each specific social or cultural context to determine which substantial reasons are adequate, or which infringements can be justified.[142] That the proportionality test is at the same time a universal and necessary element of rights reasoning *and* sensitive to concrete circumstances and cultural contexts explains why it enables us to go 'beyond both particularistic bias and context-indifferent globalism'.[143] Proportionality analysis provides the best combination of universal-monistic and relative-contextualist features of justification.[144] It is precisely this capacity of reconciling universalism and particularism that makes the proportionality test so well suited as an element of global constitutionalism.[145]

Its specific capacity to reconcile universalism and particularism, in turn, can explain the factual success of proportionality, its worldwide spread and triumphant advance as a legal transplant.[146] In this light, the proportionality test can be characterized as a core example of integrative jurisprudence, ie of an account of law that combines analytic-normative and historical or social-scientific

140 cf Klatt and Meister, *The Constitutional Structure of Proportionality* (n 2) 23–44.

141 Forst, 'The Basic Right to Justification' (n 32) 218.

142 cf ibid 212.

143 cf ibid 228.

144 ibid 227.

145 Klatt and Meister, 'Verhältnismäßigkeit als universelles Verfassungsprinzip' (n 132); Klatt and Meister, 'Proportionality—A Benefit to Human Rights? Remarks on the ICon Controversy' (n 106).

146 On this development, see above, Section I Introduction.

perspectives.[147] The integration between the observer's and the participant's perspectives unfolds the full dynamic of justification inherent in proportionality analysis, and it underlines that proportionality represents the deep normative grammar of constitutional justice.[148] Most importantly, the integrative account emphasizes that both the right to justification and proportionality analysis are not just rationalistic chimaera but powerful ideas that are effective in the real world.[149]

IV. Discursive Global Constitutionalism

Discursive constitutionalism is a theory that integrates the four elements of constitutional rights, proportionality analysis, constitutional review, and justification, qua discourse.[150] Discursive constitutionalism institutionalizes the moral right to justification in a specific form of deliberative democracy that allows for practices of reciprocal and general justification. It provides the best framework for reconstructing the rule of law as a rule of reason, in accordance with the dual nature of legal argumentation, which integrates real and normative elements.[151] Discursive constitutionalism best accounts for 'the argumentativeness of legal practice'.[152] This, in turn, allows constituting a legitimate form of global constitutionalism.[153]

The right to justification provides a middle way between liberalism and communitarianism, offering 'a better combination of universal moral and particular political-ethical components of the ethos of democracy'.[154] This middle way, in turn, is of vital importance for a mixed account of global constitutionalism that unite the liberal ideas of universal fundamental values with republican virtues of deliberation, contestation, and participation.[155]

Proportionality analysis is a central means to achieve this unification.[156] Some scholars have claimed that the rise of proportionality as a general standard of

[147] On the concept of integrative jurisprudence, see Matthias Klatt, 'Integrative Rechtswissensc haft: Methodologische und wissenschaftstheoretische Implikationen der Doppelnatur des Rechts' (2015) 54 Der Staat 469.

[148] For a similar argument, see Forst, 'Introduction' (n 12) 3.

[149] cf ibid.

[150] cf Robert Alexy, 'Balancing, Constitutional Review, and Representation' (2005) 3 International Journal of Constitutional Law 572.

[151] Klatt, 'The Rule of Dual-Natured Law' (n 123) 31; cf C Mac Amhlaigh, 'Harmonising Global Constitutionalism' (2016) 5 Global Constitutionalism 173, 177.

[152] John Finnis, 'On Reason and Authority in "Law's Empire"' (1987) 6 Law and Philosophy 357, 358.

[153] Mac Amhlaigh, 'Harmonising Global Constitutionalism' (n 151) 189–92.

[154] Forst, 'The Rule of Reasons' (n 22) 179.

[155] Mac Amhlaigh, 'Harmonising Global Constitutionalism' (n 151) 192–95, 205.

[156] On the challenge to combine unity and totality with variety and pluralism in a Kantian sense, see Arthur Ripstein, 'Reclaiming Proportionality' (2017) 34 Journal of Applied Philosophy 1, 11.

rationality had detached the normativity of constitutional law from its local origins. Somek finds the constitution was 'no longer firmly tied to the history of a particular community', and he blames the prominence of proportionality for this.[157] The real dimension of discursive constitutionalism disproves this claim.[158] The real dimension of discursive constitutionalism is in accordance with the dual-nature of legal argumentation, and it shapes the external justification of proportionality analysis. That way, and contrary to Somek's claim, it allows giving proper weight to authoritative, real, and community-related considerations.[159]

The control of proportionality by means of judicial review exercised by a constitutional court is a central element of a model of discursive constitutionalism that institutionalizes the right to justification properly.[160] This is due to the fact that every constitutional right is 'a basic human interest of sufficient importance that any limitation of it by a public authority warrants formal checking for correctness by a court'.[161] The right to justification demands a form of constitutional review that controls whether the criteria of reciprocity and generality have been satisfied.[162] Constitutional review 'requires deliberation concerning the justifiability of the decision in light of the specific circumstances'[163] and 'grants right-holders an opportunity to participate in rights-based reasoning or deliberation'.[164]

The discursive nature of constitutional review, however, does not exhaust its character. There is also an institutional or authoritative element, because constitutional review typically involves the competence of a constitutional court to invalidate unconstitutional legislation.[165] Constitutional review has a dual nature,

[157] Alexander Somek, 'The Cosmopolitan Constitution' in Miguel Maduro, Kaarlo Tuori, and Suvi Sankari (eds), *Transnational Law: Rethinking European Law and Legal Thinking* (Cambridge University Press 2014) 105.

[158] Constitutionalism 'emerges from a series of convergent' local practices, see Mac Amhlaigh, 'Harmonising Global Constitutionalism' (n 151) 190.

[159] Klatt, 'The Rule of Dual-Natured Law' (n 123) 31–36; see also Mac Amhlaigh, 'Harmonising Global Constitutionalism' (n 151) 189.

[160] cf Robert Alexy, 'Die Institutionalisierung der Menschenrechte im demokratischen Verfassungsstaat' in S Gosepath and G Lohmann (eds), *Philosophie der Menschenrechte* (Suhrkamp 1998) 262–64. Cf Allan, 'Democracy, Legality, and Proportionality' (n 69) 210: 'Although the judicial enforcement of constitutional rights imposes significant limits on the scope of legislative and governmental decision making, it provides a necessary guarantee of individual autonomy. Freedoms of speech, conscience, and association are basic ingredients of any liberal democratic polity; judicial protection of their core requirements safeguards citizens' moral independence, ensuring their continuing ability to challenge the exercise of power'.

[161] Rivers (n 102) 432; see also Vicki C Jackson, 'Proportionality and Equality' in Vicki C Jackson and Mark V Tushnet (eds), *Proportionality: New Frontiers, New Challenges* (Cambridge University Press 2017) 174.

[162] Forst, 'The Rule of Reasons' (n 22) 182.

[163] Harel (n 61) 206.

[164] ibid 209.

[165] Alexy, 'Balancing, Constitutional Review, and Representation' (n 150) 578.

consisting of both an ideal or discursive dimension and a real or authoritative dimension. The real dimension is of likewise importance: contrary to what Somek claims in Luhmann's terms, the real dimension of constitutionalism does bring the 'open-ended assessment of the rationality of the system' to an end.[166]

It is vital to give the control competence on rights issues over to a constitutional court, and not merely to some special chamber of the legislature or some other authority. It is not sufficient to follow Kyritsis's interpretation of the right to justification and limit its impact to participation in democratic processes of establishing political-legal rights regimes, and denying its relevance for the judicial forum.[167] Only the judicial forum will ensure a truly discursive conception of authority as a reason-giving practice.[168] Only courts are capable of adding sustainably reason to will, of supplementing 'a mere act of the will by adding reasons to it'.[169] It is justified to assign judges this central task because 'only by fitting the willed statutory law into such a broader framework of "reason" does it become fully right, that is to say, authoritative'.[170] Only in the judicial forum is it cognizable whether or not acts of an authority really possess the 'potentiality of reasoned elaboration' which makes them 'worthy of acceptance'.[171]

Critics object to this concept of constitutional review that it amounted to transforming democracy into 'juristocracy'.[172] There are two elements of critique entailed in this objection. The first is the claim that constitutional review per se was violating the principle of democracy.[173] It is worth noting that this objection does not address, and even less discredit, the fully-fledged conception of democracy that accepts the dual nature of democracy, eg deliberative democracy.[174]

The second objection in this critique raises concerns of competence. Any account of the relation between justification and proportionality would be

[166] Somek, 'The Cosmopolitan Constitution' (n 157) 100.

[167] cf Dimitrios Kyritsis, *Where Our Protection Lies: Separation of Powers and Constitutional Review* (Oxford University Press 2017) 65.

[168] David Dyzenhaus, 'Constitutionalism in an Old Key: Legality and Constituent Power' (2012) 1 Global Constitutionalism 229, 258.

[169] Carl J Friedrich, 'Authority, Reason, and Discretion' in Carl J Friedrich (ed), *Authority* (Harvard University Press 1958) 30.

[170] ibid 31.

[171] ibid 35.

[172] Ran Hirschl, *Towards Juristocracy: The Origins and Consequences of the New Constitutionalism* (Harvard University Press 2004); Jeremy Waldron, 'A Right-Based Critique of Constitutional Rights' (1993) 13 Oxford Journal of Legal Studies 18, 42; Katharine G Young, *Constituting Economic and Social Rights* (Oxford University Press 2012) 134; Ernst-Wolfgang Böckenförde, 'Grundrechte als Grundsatznormen: Zur gegenwärtigen Lage der Grundrechtsdogmatik' in Ernst-Wolfgang Böckenförde (ed), *Staat, Verfassung, Demokratie: Studien zur Verfassungstheorie und zum Verfassungsrecht* (Suhrkamp 1991) 190.

[173] Jeremy Waldron, 'The Core of the Case Against Judicial Review' (2006) 115 Yale Law Journal 1346, 1353.

[174] Matthias Klatt, 'Positive Rights: Who Decides? Judicial Review in Balance' (2015) 13 International Journal of Constitutional Law 354, 374–76; Alexy, 'Balancing, Constitutional Review, and Representation' (n 150) 579.

incomplete if it failed to address the competence issue. The competence issue is due to a conflict between formal principles. Modern constitutions aim to protect the competence of the democratically elected legislature, but they also strive at protecting rights by means of a control competence exercised by courts. Both competences are constitutional principles and, hence, must be realized to the greatest extent possible.

In the principles-theoretical account of judicial review I have defended elsewhere,[175] the question is not, whether the judiciary should determine the definite scope of rights protection or, alternatively, this is the task of the legislature. The problem of constitutional review is not a matter of either-or, but a matter of degree. If it is correct that the institutional problem of judicial constitutional is a conflict of formal principles, rather than of rules, than the solution of that problem is neither to be found by interpreting competence norms nor by means of unconditional preference relations. Rather, a balancing procedure has to be employed.

Many scholars aim at some sort of abstract balancing exercise that would settle an unconditional preference relation between the colliding competences. This is the case with all proposals suggesting a fixed control intensity in proportionality analysis. Dixon, eg, has proposed a general establishment of weak review by means of dialogue.[176] Harel, in contrast, argues in favour of what he calls 'constrained judicial review' which applies a moderate, or intermediate, degree of scrutiny to all cases. Such unconditional solutions to the competence problem have one major advantage: they best institutionalize the principle of legal certainty. All participants of the legal system will be able to determine beforehand the control intensity any controlling authority will apply. If the principle of legal certainty was the only criterion which mattered for determining the correct intensity of control, the problem would be solved: we would have to adopt a unconditional solution to the competence problem. Yet this premise is not true. There are all sorts of different principles that also influence the correct intensity of control: epistemic considerations, the intensity of an infringement with a human right, the quality of the primary decision, to name but a few. Unlike the principle of legal certainty, these additional criteria call for a more flexible approach. It allows for a variable solution to the competence problem by applying flexible control intensities that also need to be justified.[177] It needs to be stressed

[175] Matthias Klatt, 'Balancing Competences: How Institutional Cosmopolitanism Can Manage Jurisdictional Conflicts' (2015) 4 Global Constitutionalism 195; Klatt, 'Positive Rights: Who Decides? Judicial Review in Balance' (n 174).

[176] Rosalind Dixon, 'Creating Dialogue about Socioeconomic Rights: Strong-form versus Weak-form Judicial Review Revisited' (2007) 5 International Journal of Constitutional Law 391, 393.

[177] Klatt, 'Positive Rights: Who Decides? Judicial Review in Balance' (n 174) 364–81; Klatt, 'Balancing Competences' (n 175) 209–17.

the combination of proportionality analysis and judicial review does not necessarily and in all cases amount to a strict control intensity which annuls any deference. Rather, this combination is well capable of accommodating the whole range of control intensities and deference. By balancing formal principles, the competence problem of constitutional review can be solved in constitutionalist terms, contrary to what Somek claims.[178]

In discursive constitutionalism, the right to justification applies not only to the substantial questions of material justice but also to the institutional questions of competence.[179] Discursive constitutionalism institutionalizes reason and correctness with respect to both, the authoritative and the substantive dimension of constitutional law.

Discursive constitutionalism is not limited to the sphere of the state. Its characteristics are also valid beyond the state. In particular, discursive constitutionalism qua global constitutionalism enables dynamic and reflexive justificatory processes of reason-giving for the legitimacy of an authority in the international arena.[180] It can provide normative guidance by means of balancing competences, sovereignties, and authorities.[181]

V. Conclusion

In contrast to descriptive accounts, which explain the worldwide dissemination of proportionality by referring to a culture of justification, I have sought to establish a normative basis for proportionality analysis by referring to a moral right to justification. This normative defence of proportionality supplements Alexy's analytical defence and thereby strengthens the case for an absolute validity of proportionality while still ensuring an integrative combination with relative and cultural-sensitive properties of proportionality justification.

The moral right to justification rests on an understanding of humans as justificatory beings. Based on the two criteria of generality and reciprocity, it is situated in a discourse-theoretic and constructivist understanding of justification which underlines that moral propositions have to be validated in concrete social practices of justification. This enables an understanding of deliberative democracy as providing an institutionalized space of reasons. Justificatory normativity

[178] According to Somek, constitutionalism (in the particular variant he labels '1.0') is 'incapable of arriving at a conclusive answer' to the competence problem of constitutional review: Somek, 'The Cosmopolitan Constitution' (n 157) 97. The model of balancing competences proves the opposite.

[179] Klatt, 'Robert Alexy's Philosophy of Law as System' (n 68) 21.

[180] Mac Amhlaigh, 'Harmonising Global Constitutionalism' (n 151) 178, 194.

[181] Klatt, 'Balancing Competences' (n 175); Matthias Klatt, *Die praktische Konkordanz von Kompetenzen: Entwickelt anhand der Jurisdiktionskonflikte im europäischen Grundrechtsschutz* (Mohr Siebeck 2014).

still depends on sociality and existentialist decision. The moral right to justification is relative to the practice of giving and asking for reasons.

The moral right to justification is a necessary part of any fundamental right. This is the reason why constitutional review by means of proportionality analysis can be conceived as institutionalizing the right to justification. Proportionality analysis enables us to construct justified and rational applications of fundamental rights. I have objected to sceptical approaches, which claim that such rational application was impossible, by exploring the intertwining relationships between law's claim to correctness, the right to justification, and discursive argumentation. In particular, justification is one important element of the claim to correctness, and the latter has a general and reciprocal character, which fits well with the two criteria of the right to justification. The internal connection between correctness, justification, and argumentation provides a firm basis for the absolute character and universal validity of proportionality analysis.

Still, correctness is a more complex concept demanding an integration of form and substance of justification. Proportionality analysis qua establishing a space of reasons for rights reasoning provides this integration, according to the principle of coherence. We may call this *proportionality as integrity*, transferring Dworkin's interpretive theory to the realm of legal principles. As a structure of reasoning, it serves to realize the force towards the better argument by enhancing transparency, inclusiveness, and general quality of rights reasoning. Owing to the diachronic dimension of justification, the argumentative practice of proportionality analysis produces a chain novel. Despite the fact that modifications of any element in this chain is always possible, if better argument arises, a default-and-challenge-structure operates that allows for strong prima facie entitlements and, hence, for legal certainty.

The vital integration of internal and external justification in proportionality analysis rests on the dual nature of law. It disproves criticism of both too much and too little morality in rights reasoning. It also helps to understand why and to what extent proportionality is an absolute, universally valid principle. It is the universal core of every internal morality. At the same time, proportionality remains sensitive to a wide degree of cultural variation. It thus reconciles universalism and particularism in the best possible way.

Owing to the particular features explained in this chapter, proportionality analysis is an important element discursive global constitutionalism. Its control by means of judicial review gives rise to institutional problems of competence that can be solved by employing a balancing of formal principles. The right to justification does not refer to material correctness only but also to formal correctness of competence and authority, both within and beyond the state.

It would be wrong to assume that the combination of justification and proportionality led only to a thin constitutionalism, characterized by pure formality and detachment from substantial considerations of justice. This assumption would be correct if the right to justification related to proportionality's internal justification only. However, the right to justification is a comprehensive concept integrating both internal and external justification and embracing the whole range of factual, normative, universal, and local elements of rights adjudication. It thus lays the basis for constructing thick constitutionalism properly so called. The moral right to justification is a robust fundament of discursive global constitutionalism. Following this theory of discursive constitutionalism, law's claim to correctness implies a claim to proportionality. The right to justification is a right to proportionality, and the former is the moral basis of the latter. The right to proportionality, in turn, is controlled in the judicial forum, by means of constitutional review. Therefore, the right to justification is the normative fundament not only of proportionality analysis, but of constitutional review as well.

One may wonder whether the move from a *moral* right to justification to proportionality as a *legal* principle was well founded. Some kind of bridge mechanism seems to be required to justify the move from the moral to the legal world. This bridge mechanism can be found in human rights themselves, because they carry an inherent drive into the legal world: human rights qua moral rights demand to be institutionalized, and hence they demand constitutional rights. Constitutional rights, in turn, necessarily imply the proportionality principle. Therefore, human rights qua moral rights demand the proportionality principle qua legal principle. Constitutional rights qua legal rights institutionalize human rights qua moral rights. And the proportionality principle qua legal principle institutionalizes the moral right to justification. This is the strongest conceivable normative defence of proportionality.

References

Afonso da Silva V, 'Comparing the Incommensurable: Constitutional Principles, Balancing and Rational Decision' (2011) 31 Oxford Journal of Legal Studies 273.

Alexy R, *A Theory of Legal Argumentation: The Theory of Rational Discourse as Theory of Legal Justification* (Neil MacCormick and Ruth Adler trs, Oxford University Press 1989).

Alexy R, 'Justification and Application of Norms' (1993) 6 Ratio Juris 157.

Alexy R, 'Coherence and Argumentation or the Genuine Twin Criterialess Super Criterion' in Aulis Aarnio and others (eds), *On Coherence Theory of Law* (Juristförlaget 1998).

Alexy R, 'Die Institutionalisierung der Menschenrechte im demokratischen Verfassungsstaat' in S Gosepath and G Lohmann (eds), *Philosophie der Menschenrechte* (Suhrkamp 1998).

Alexy R, 'Law and Correctness' (1998) 51 Current Legal Problems 205.

Alexy R, 'The Special Case Thesis' (1999) 12 Ratio Juris 374.

Alexy R, *A Theory of Constitutional Rights* (Julian Rivers tr, Oxford University Press 2002).

Alexy R, 'Hans Kelsens Begriff des relativen Apriori' in Robert Alexy and others (eds), *Neukantianismus und Rechtsphilosophie* (Nomos 2002).

Alexy R, 'On Balancing and Subsumption' (2003) 16 Ratio Juris 433.

Alexy R, 'Menschenrechte ohne Metaphysik?' (2004) 52 Deutsche Zeitschrift für Philosophie 15.

Alexy R, 'Balancing, Constitutional Review, and Representation' (2005) 3 International Journal of Constitutional Law 572.

Alexy R, 'Thirteen Replies' in George Pavlakos (ed), *Law, Rights and Discourse: Themes from the Legal Philosophy of Robert Alexy* (Hart Publishing 2007).

Alexy R, 'Normativity, Metaphysics and Decision' in Stefano Bertea and George Pavlakos (eds), *New Essays on the Normativity of Law* (Hart Publishing 2011).

Alexy R, 'Comments and Responses' in Matthias Klatt (ed), *Institutionalized Reason: The Jurisprudence of Robert Alexy* (Oxford University Press 2012).

Alexy R, 'Law, Morality, and the Existence of Human Rights' (2012) 25 Ratio Juris 2.

Alexy R, 'The Absolute and the Relative Dimension of Constitutional Rights' (2017) 37 Oxford Journal of Legal Studies 31.

Allan TRS, *Constitutional Justice: A Liberal Theory of the Rule of Law* (Oxford University Press 2001).

Allan TRS, 'Democracy, Legality, and Proportionality' in Grant Huscroft, Bradley W Miller and Grégoire CN Webber (eds), *Proportionality and the Rule of Law: Rights, Justification, Reasoning* (Cambridge University Press 2014).

Andrade Neto J, 'The Debatable Universality of the Proportionality Test and the Wide-Scope Conception of Fundamental Rights' (2016) 12(1) Revista Brasileira de Direito 4.

Andrade Neto J, *Borrowing Justification for Proportionality: On the Influence of the Principles Theory in Brazil* (Springer 2018).

Barak A, *Proportionality: Constitutional Rights and Their Limitations* (Doron Kalir tr, Cambridge University Press 2012).

Barak A, 'A Research Agenda for the Future' in Vicki C Jackson and Mark V Tushnet (eds), *Proportionality: New Frontiers, New Challenges* (Cambridge University Press 2017).

Benhabib S (ed), *Another Cosmopolitanism* (Oxford University Press 2006).

Bernal Pulido C, 'The Migration of Proportionality across Europe' (2013) 11 New Zealand Journal of Public and International Law 483.

Böckenförde E-W, 'Grundrechte als Grundsatznormen: Zur gegenwärtigen Lage der Grundrechtsdogmatik' in Ernst-Wolfgang Böckenförde (ed), *Staat, Verfassung, Demokratie: Studien zur Verfassungstheorie und zum Verfassungsrecht* (Suhrkamp 1991).

Borowski M, 'Limiting Clauses: On the Continental European Tradition of Special Limiting Clauses and the General Limiting Clause of Art 52(2) Charter of Fundamental Rights of the European Union' (2007) 1 Legisprudence 197.

Brandom RB, *Making It Explicit: Reasoning, Representing, and Discursive Commitment* (Harvard University Press 1998).

Brandom RB, *Articulating Reasons: An Introduction to Inferentialism* (Harvard University Press 2000).

Brandom RB, 'A Hegelian Model of Legal Concept Determination: The Normative Fine Structure of the Judges' Chain Novel' in Graham Hubbs (ed), *Pragmatism, Law, and Language* (vol 53, Routledge 2014).

Cohen J, 'Procedure and Substance in Deliberative Democracy' in James Bohman and William Rehg (eds), *Deliberative Democracy: Essays on Reason and Politics* (MIT Press 1997).

Cohen-Eliya M and Porat I, 'Proportionality and the Culture of Justification' (2011) 59 American Journal of Comparative Law 463.

Cohen-Eliya M and Porat I, *Proportionality and Constitutional Culture* (Cambridge Studies in Constitutional Law, Cambridge University Press 2013).

Dixon R, 'Creating Dialogue about Socioeconomic Rights: Strong-form versus Weak-form Judicial Review Revisited' (2007) 5 International Journal of Constitutional Law 391.

Dwars I, 'Application Discourse and Special Case Thesis' (1992) 5 Ratio Juris 67.

Dworkin R, *Law's Empire* (Fontana 1986).

Dyzenhaus D, 'Constitutionalism in an Old Key: Legality and Constituent Power' (2012) 1(2) Global Constitutionalism 229.

Erman E, 'The Right to Justification: Elements of a Constructivist Theory of Justice' (2012) <http://ndpr.nd.edu/news/31035-the-right-to-justification-elements-of-a-constructivist-theory-of-justice/> accessed 14 March 2016.

Finnis J, 'On Reason and Authority in "Law's Empire"' (1987) 6(3) Law and Philosophy 357.

Forst R, 'Dialektik der Moral: Grundlagen einer Diskurstheorie transnationaler Gerechtigkeit' in Rainer Forst, *Das Recht auf Rechtfertigung: Elemente einer konstruktivistischen Theorie der Gerechtigkeit* (Suhrkamp 2007).

Forst R, 'Introduction: The Foundation of Justice' in Rainer Forst, *The Right to Justification: Elements of a Constructivist Theory of Justice* (Jeffrey Flynn tr, Columbia University Press 2011).

Forst R, 'Moral Autonomy and the Autonomy of Morality: Toward a Theory of Normativity after Kant' in Rainer Forst, *The Right to Justification: Elements of a Constructivist Theory of Justice* (Jeffrey Flynn tr, Columbia University Press 2011).

Forst R, 'Practical Reason and Justifying Reasons: On the Foundation of Morality' in Rainer Forst, *The Right to Justification: Elements of a Constructivist Theory of Justice* (Jeffrey Flynn tr, Columbia University Press 2011).

Forst R, 'Social Justice, Justification, and Power' in Rainer Forst, *The Right to Justification: Elements of a Constructivist Theory of Justice* (Jeffrey Flynn tr, Columbia University Press 2011).

Forst R, 'The Basic Right to Justification: Toward a Constructivist Conception of Human Rights' in Rainer Forst, *The Right to Justification: Elements of a Constructivist Theory of Justice* (Jeffrey Flynn tr, Columbia University Press 2011).

Forst R, 'The Rule of Reasons: Three Models of Deliberative Democracy' in Rainer Forst, *The Right to Justification: Elements of a Constructivist Theory of Justice* (Jeffrey Flynn tr, Columbia University Press 2011).

Forst R, 'Toward a Critical Theory of Transnational Justice' in Rainer Forst, *The Right to Justification: Elements of a Constructivist Theory of Justice* (Jeffrey Flynn tr, Columbia University Press 2011).

Forst R, 'The Justification of Basic Rights: A Discourse-Theoretical Approach' (2016) 45(3) Netherlands Journal of Legal Philosophy 7.

Friedrich CJ, 'Authority, Reason, and Discretion' in Carl J Friedrich (ed), *Authority* (Nomos vol 1, Harvard University Press 1958).

Gardbaum S, 'Positive and Horizontal Rights: Proportionality's Next Frontier or a Bridge Too Far?' in Vicki C Jackson and Mark V Tushnet (eds), *Proportionality: New Frontiers, New Challenges* (Cambridge University Press 2017).

Grice HP and Strawson PF, 'In Defense of a Dogma' (1956) 65 The Philosophical Review 141.

Grimm D, 'The Constitution in the Process of Denationalization' (2005) 12 Constellations 447–63.

Günther K, 'Critical Remarks on Robert Alexy's Special Case Thesis' (1993) 6 Ratio Juris 143.

Habermas J, 'Discourse Ethics: Notes on a Program of Philosophical Justification' in Jürgen Habermas, *Moral Consciousness and Communicative Action* (Christian Lenhardt and Shierry Weber Nicholsen trs, Polity Press 1990).

Habermas J, *Between Facts and Norms: Contributions to a Discourse Theory of Law and Democracy* (William Rehg tr, MIT Press 1996).

Harel A, *Why Law Matters* (Oxford University Press 2014).

Hirschl R, *Towards Juristocracy: The Origins and Consequences of the New Constitutionalism* (Harvard University Press 2004).

Höffe O, 'Kant ist kein Frankfurter: Rainer Forst begründet das Recht auf Rechtfertigung, allerdings nicht ganz zureichend' *Die Zeit* (1 November 2007) <https://www.zeit.de/2007/45/ST-Forst>.

Hume D, *A Treatise of Human Nature* (David Fate Norton ed, Oxford University Press 2009).

Jackson VC, 'Proportionality and Equality' in Vicki C Jackson and Mark V Tushnet (eds), *Proportionality: New Frontiers, New Challenges* (Cambridge University Press 2017).

Jestaedt M, 'The Doctrine of Balancing: Its Strengths and Weaknesses' in Matthias Klatt (ed), *Institutionalized Reason: The Jurisprudence of Robert Alexy* (Oxford University Press 2012).

Klatt M, *Making the Law Explicit: The Normativity of Legal Argumentation* (Jörg Rampacher and Neil Mussett trs, Hart Publishing 2008).

Klatt M, 'Robert Alexy's Philosophy of Law as System' in Matthias Klatt (ed), *Institutionalized Reason: The Jurisprudence of Robert Alexy* (Oxford University Press 2012).

Klatt M, 'An Egalitarian Defense of Proportionality-Based Balancing: A Response to Luc B. Tremblay' (2014) 12 International Journal of Constitutional Law 891.

Klatt M, *Die praktische Konkordanz von Kompetenzen: Entwickelt anhand der Jurisdiktionskonflikte im europäischen Grundrechtsschutz* (Jus publicum vol 232, Mohr Siebeck 2014).

Klatt M, 'Balancing Competences: How Institutional Cosmopolitanism Can Manage Jurisdictional Conflicts' (2015) 4 Global Constitutionalism 195.

Klatt M, 'Integrative Rechtswissenschaft: Methodologische und wissenschaftstheoretische Implikationen der Doppelnatur des Rechts' (2015) 54 Der Staat 469.

Klatt M, 'Positive Rights: Who Decides? Judicial Review in Balance' (2015) 13 International Journal of Constitutional Law 354.

Klatt M, 'The Rule of Dual-Natured Law' in ET Feteris and others (eds), *Legal Argumentation and the Rule of Law* (Eleven International Publishing 2016).

Klatt M and Meister M, 'Proportionality—A Benefit to Human Rights? Remarks on the ICon Controversy' (2012) 10 International Journal of Constitutional Law 687.

Klatt M and Meister M, *The Constitutional Structure of Proportionality* (Oxford University Press 2012).

Klatt M and Meister M, 'Verhältnismäßigkeit als universelles Verfassungsprinzip' in Matthias Klatt (ed), *Prinzipientheorie und Theorie der Abwägung* (Mohr Siebeck 2013).

Klatt M and Meister M, 'A Proporcionalidade como Princípio Constitucional Universal' (2015) 1 Revista Publicum 30.

Klatt M and Schmidt J, 'Epistemic Discretion in Constitutional Law' (2012) 10 International Journal of Constitutional Law 69.

Koch H-J and Rüßmann H, *Juristische Begründungslehre: Eine Einführung in die Grundprobleme der Rechtswissenschaft* (Schriftenreihe der Juristischen Schulung, C.H. Beck 1982).

Krisch N, *Beyond Constitutionalism: The Pluralist Structure of Postnational Law* (Oxford University Press 2010).

Kumm M, 'Constitutional Rights as Principles: On the Structure and Domain of Constitutional Justice' (2004) 2 International Journal of Constitutional Law 574.

Kumm M, 'Political Liberalism and the Structure of Rights: On the Place and Limits of the Proportionality Requirements' in George Pavlakos (ed), *Law, Rights and Discourse: Themes from the Legal Philosophy of Robert Alexy* (Hart Publishing 2007).

Kumm M, 'Alexy's Theory of Constitutional Rights and the Problem of Judicial Review' in Matthias Klatt (ed), *Institutionalized Reason: The Jurisprudence of Robert Alexy* (Oxford University Press 2012).

Kumm M, 'Is the Structure of Human Rights Practice Defensible? Three Puzzles and Their Solution' in Vicki C Jackson and Mark V Tushnet (eds), *Proportionality: New Frontiers, New Challenges* (Cambridge University Press 2017).

Kyritsis D, 'Whatever Works: Proportionality as a Constitutional Doctrine' (2014) 34 Oxford Journal of Legal Studies 395.

Kyritsis D, *Where Our Protection Lies: Separation of Powers and Constitutional Review* (Oxford University Press 2017).

Letsas G, 'Rescuing Proportionality' in Rowan Cruft, SM Liao, and Massimo Renzo (eds), *Philosophical Foundations of Human Rights* (Oxford University Press 2015).

Loughlin M, 'What Is Constitutionalization?' in Petra Dobner and Martin Loughlin (eds), *The Twilight of Constitutionalism?* (Oxford University Press 2010).

Mac Amhlaigh C, 'Harmonising Global Constitutionalism' (2016) 5 Global Constitutionalism 173.

Möller K, *The Global Model of Constitutional Rights* (Oxford University Press 2012).

Moore GE, *Principia Ethica* (Cambridge University Press 1903).

Müller FS, 'Justifying the Right to Justification: An Analysis of Rainer Forst's Constructivist Theory of Justice' (2013) 39 Philosophy & Social Criticism 1049.

Pavlakos G, 'The Special Case Thesis. An Assessment of R. Alexy's Discursive Theory of Law' (1998) 11 Ratio Juris 126.

Petersen N, *Proportionality and Judicial Activism: Fundamental Rights Adjudication in Canada, Germany and South Africa* (Cambridge University Press 2017).

Poscher R, 'The Principles Theory: How Many Theories and What Is Their Merit?' in Matthias Klatt (ed), *Institutionalized Reason: The Jurisprudence of Robert Alexy* (Oxford University Press 2012).

Raz J, 'The Relevance of Coherence' (1992) 72 Boston University Law Review 273.

Ripstein A, 'Reclaiming Proportionality' (2017) 34 Journal of Applied Philosophy 1.

Rivers J, 'The Presumption of Proportionality' (2014) 77 The Modern Law Review 409.

Schlink B, 'Bemerkungen zum Stand der Methodendiskussion in der Verfassungsrechtswissenschaft' (1980) 19 Der Staat 73.
Schlink B, 'Freiheit durch Eingriffsabwehr: Rekonstruktion der klassischen Grundrechtsfunktion' (1984) 11 Europäische Grundrechte-Zeitschrift 457–68.
Sellars W, *Empiricism and the Philosophy of Mind* (Harvard University Press 1997).
Somek A, *Rechtliches Wissen* (Suhrkamp 2006).
Somek A, 'The Cosmopolitan Constitution' in Miguel Maduro, Kaarlo Tuori, and Suvi Sankari (eds), *Transnational Law: Rethinking European Law and Legal Thinking* (Cambridge University Press 2014).
Stone Sweet A and Mathews J, 'Proportionality Balancing and Global Constitutionalism' (2008) 47 Columbia Journal of Transnational Law 72.
Talbott WJ, 'The Right to Justification: Elements of a Constructivist Theory of Justice' (2013) 123 Ethics 750.
Tremblay LB, 'An Egalitarian Defense of Proportionality-Based Balancing' (2014) 12 International Journal of Constitutional Law 864.
Tsakyrakis S, 'Proportionality: An Assault on Human Rights?' (2009) 7 International Journal of Constitutional Law 468.
Urbina FJ, *A Critique of Proportionality and Balancing* (Cambridge University Press 2017).
Waldron J, 'A Right-Based Critique of Constitutional Rights' (1993) 13 Oxford Journal of Legal Studies 18.
Waldron J, 'The Core of the Case Against Judicial Review' (2006) 115 Yale Law Journal 1346.
Wasserstrom RA, *The Judicial Decision: Toward a Theory of Legal Justification* (Stanford University Press 1961).
Webber GCN, 'Proportionality, Balancing, and the Cult of Constitutional Rights Scholarship' (2010) 23 Canadian Journal of Law and Jurisprudence 179.
Wróblewski J, 'Legal Syllogism and Rationality of Judicial Decision' (1974) 5 Rechtstheorie 33.
Young KG, *Constituting Economic and Social Rights* (Oxford University Press 2012).

9

Republicanizing Rights?

Proportionality, Justification, and Non-Domination

Eoin Daly

I. Introduction

For the most part, republican political thought has been hostile, or at least ambivalent, towards the very concept of judicially enforceable constitutional rights, or of rights-based judicial review of parliamentary legislation. Republican thinkers—with notable exceptions—have tended to regard judicial review as a site of unaccountable power or of political domination, or as diminishing the virtues associated with, and undercutting the legitimacy of, representative democracy. For leading republican philosophers like Richard Bellamy, procedural democracy—in a context of social disagreement about rights—is the preeminent institutional expression of republican freedom. Other republicans bemoan the promotion of an individualist culture of rights, at the expense of social solidarity and the common good.

A further, critical objection concerns the nature of 'rights' themselves: in contrast with liberals, republicans will typically resist any understanding of 'rights' as limits on politics, or as boundaries against state activity based on transcendent or ahistorical criteria. Rights-claims, instead, are contextual and contingent, and therefore, any attempt to hive off particular areas of policy against politics—in the name of rights—is simply a futile attempt to depoliticize something that remains stubbornly and intrinsically political. And republicans will resist rights-based judicial review, then, because they will understand that it will counterproductively obscure the political nature of rights-claims and the intractability of political and social conflict concerning matters of 'right' as well as questions of the 'good'. In so far as constitutional adjudication depoliticizes rights, it obscures and occludes intractable conflicts and disagreements intrinsic to politics. And based on this insight, republicans will tend to believe that political freedom is best realized through the constitutional structure and procedure through which conflicting rights-claims are reconciled—rather than through any definite concept of rights that might be captured in a constitutional text (or indeed in the practice of adjudication itself).

Eoin Daly, *Republicanizing Rights? Proportionality, Justification, and Non-Domination* In: *Constitutionalism Justified: Rainer Forst in Discourse.* Edited by: Ester Herlin-Karnell and Matthias Klatt, Oxford University Press (2020),

DOI: 10.1093/oso/9780190889050.003.0009

While I am sympathetic to many aspects of the republican argument against judicial review, I will argue that this particular aspect of the critique is misplaced. In particular, I will illustrate this argument by reference to the doctrine of proportionality. Whereas constitutional rights are often understood as placing fixed limits on politics, transcending historical and political contingencies, the doctrine of proportionality in particular enables us to understand constitutional adjudication as accounting for the instability, the contestability, and even the indeterminacy of rights.[1] In short, the doctrine is consistent with an understanding of rights as falling within the 'circumstances of politics'. In particular, constitutional rights can be understood not as guaranteeing spheres of presumptive immunity for particular kinds of activities presumed as essential to human dignity or autonomy, but rather as requiring public authorities to provide special kinds of justifications for specific kinds of acts (just as Forst, in particular, suggests). That is to say, constitutional rights can be understood as controlling the arbitrariness of state actions, rather than as placing particular kinds of individual interests beyond any social calculus or compromise. Accordingly, constitutional rights can be understood, in a republican sense, as controls on the predicates of state power, rather than as definite guarantees of non-interference as per the dominant liberal understanding.

II. Rights are 'Political': The Republican Case Against ('Strong') Judicial Review

Before outlining a republicanized interpretation of constitutional-rights adjudication, first I will outline one particular aspect of the republican critique of the practice—namely, that in purporting to settle rights-claims using specifically legal standards, it occludes their intractably 'political' character.

According to republican critics, the dominant liberal doctrines conceive of 'rights' as being both antecedent to politics, and beyond the scope of political calculus or compromise. And indeed, there is ample basis for this view within liberal philosophy. We may think, for example, of Dworkin's influential understanding of 'rights as trumps'—in other words, as antecedent limits upon the pursuit of 'policy' or ordinary politics. Equally, Rawls, as the dominant liberal philosopher of the past half-century, states that basic liberties must be 'taken off . . . the political agenda'.[2]

[1] This in no sense assumes that there is any connection between the proportionality principle per se and the existence of a competence of strong-form judicial review.

[2] John Rawls, *Justice as Fairness: A Restatement* (Harvard University Press 2001) 115.

According to most liberal doctrines, rights, on the one hand, typically consist of guarantees of *non-interference*, in certain choices and activities. Thus they operate to limit state power. As Pettit points out, Bentham, for example, understands that all coercive laws are intrinsically abrogative of freedom *prima facie*.[3] On the other hand, such doctrines suggest that the scope of rights is relatively fixed, in the sense that they transcend any contextually specific balancing process or the 'calculus of social interests'[4]—that is, the 'actual preferences and interests'[5] prevailing in society at a given time. As Rawls puts it, 'the priority of liberty . . . means that a basic liberty can be limited or denied only for the sake of one or more other basic liberties, and never for a greater public good understood as a net sum of social and economic advantages for society as a whole'.[6] In other words, it is in the nature of 'rights' that they are exempt from the ordinary calculations and trade-offs that characterize political reasoning in general.

Much has been written about how, for republicans, freedom consists not of non-interference, but rather non-domination—where domination consists of unchecked power of the kind that entails a fear or apprehension of arbitrary interference. Unfreedom, then, may arise from the mere fact of disparate power, without interference of whatever kind actually ever being suffered.[7] This in itself may lead republicans to reject judicially enforced constitutional rights as instruments of freedom, because they fail to capture the socially embedded and polycentric nature of domination across various sites of asymmetric social power relations.[8] Perhaps a more fundamental republican objection to constitutionalized rights, however (or perhaps, admittedly, to juridical rights in general) is that rights-claims are intrinsically 'political', and so cannot be transferred or divested to a purely juridical domain.[9]

What is meant, specifically when it is said that rights are 'political'?[10] On the one hand, this refers to the *content* and scope of rights. For many republicans, that is to say, questions of rights—questions as to what rights are, how they are protected in practice, how they are weighted against each other and against competing moral and social claims—inevitably involve prominent elements of *political* judgment and appraisal. That is to say, when we *reason* about rights, we inevitably reason in ways that must be understood as 'political'. Similarly, critical

[3] Philip Pettit, 'Law and Liberty' in Samantha Besson and José L Martí (eds), *Legal Republicanism: National and International Perspectives* (Oxford University Press 2009).
[4] John Rawls, *A Theory of Justice* (revised edn, Oxford University Press 1999) 181.
[5] Rawls, *Justice as Fairness* (n 2) 106.
[6] ibid 111.
[7] For an exposition of this idea, see Pettit, 'Law and Liberty' (n 3).
[8] For discussion, see Eoin Daly, 'Freedom as Non-Domination in the Jurisprudence of Constitutional Rights' (2015), 28 Canadian Journal of Law & Jurisprudence 289.
[9] See generally Richard Bellamy, *Political Constitutionalism* (Cambridge University Press 2007).
[10] For further discussion of the relation of constitutional rights to the political, see generally Martin Loughlin, *Foundations of Public Law* (Oxford University Press 2010).

legal thinkers reject the Dworkinian idea that conflicting political agendas or ideals can be adjudicated under a 'principled' mode of juridical reasoning that can itself avoid some element of 'political' decision.[11] In turn, then, any effort to bring rights within a purely juridical frame, beyond legislative appraisal or interference, is not only futile, but counterproductive and misleading.

On the other hand, the claim that rights are 'political' also refers, more fundamentally, to their historical and philosophical foundations. That is to say, republicans in general believe that rights are not only interpreted and reasoned out in ways that are intractably political but also that, conceptually and historically, rights are *founded* in political community itself—not something prior to, beyond or outside it. Modern liberalism, and especially the contractarian tradition, often depicted rights as antecedent to politics, using the justificatory and expositive device of the 'state of nature'. Rights, in other words, are antecedent to politics and citizenship. Philip Pettit and Quentin Skinner, in particular, depict this as a decisive historical *rupture*—one tinged with nostalgia and regret—in which a once dominant republican account of freedom, linked intrinsically with citizenship, was supplanted by an ideal of bourgeois freedom centring on the value of non-interference.[12]

In the ancient ideal, by contrast, freedom is realized through participation in politics, either because politics, in the Aristotelian vein, is essential to self-realization, or alternatively, because it is only *through* citizenship, as per the neo-Roman account, that we are meaningfully secured against domination. In both variants, crucially, freedom has no sense or meaning outside of, or prior to the political association itself. Rousseau gave an early-modern expression to this republican tradition in insisting that man, through the social contract, completely relinquished 'natural' freedom to constitute a new kind of freedom—'civil' freedom. This was a kind of freedom, constituted under the rule of the general will, that could only be realized and understood within the political compact itself.[13]

In the Lockean liberal tradition, by contrast, rights are understood and defined by reference to the 'state of nature', an imagined state antecedent to political association. The novelty and specificity in this model is that rights are *preserved*, rather than being constituted, by political society. It follows, in turn, that rights consist largely of guarantees of non-interference, by reference with the freedom that was hypothetically enjoyed in the pre-social or pre-political state. And even

[11] Mark V Tushnet, 'Following the Rules Laid Down: A Critique of Interpretivism and Neutral Principles' (1983), 96 Harvard Law Review 781. For Dworkin's account, see Ronald Dworkin, *Freedom's Law: The Moral Reading of the American Constitution* (Harvard University Press 1996).

[12] See generally Quentin Skinner, *Liberty before Liberalism* (Cambridge University Press 1998); Philip Pettit, *Republicanism: A Theory of Freedom and Government* (Clarendon Press 1997).

[13] Jean-Jacques Rousseau, *Du Contrat Social: Principes de Droit Politique* (ENAG 1988) Book II.

Hobbes, who defended an absolutist state, understood that such a state would provide freedom of a sort—a negative freedom—since its subjects would, by enjoying security, be safeguarded against depredations at the hands of private as much as public tyranny. For Hobbes, then, 'a free man is he that in those things which by his strength and wit he is able to do is not hindered to do what he hath the will to do'.[14] And whether for liberals or authoritarians, this contractarian understanding of freedom (or rights) as securing non-interference gained ascendancy from the early modern period onwards.

Thus Rousseau represented a radical break *within* the social contract tradition, because using the same contractarian device as his liberal and absolutist adversaries, he depicted a radical departure from natural freedom, whereby men constituted a new *kind* of freedom that was not merely a partial preservation of their natural freedoms—that they had entirely alienated—but rather, which depended entirely upon, and which could only be understood by reference to the political community itself.[15] Rousseau's insight, effectively, is that whereas the freedom from dependency that was experienced in the state of nature can never be recovered in civil society, a different species of freedom can nonetheless be recovered in a context of the mutual interdependency experienced in political society. In this reconstituted political freedom, men are dependent not on the arbitrary will of others (or indeed on their recognition and esteem), but rather on the impersonal rule of the general will—a will they can internalise and recognise as their own.[16]

Rousseau's republican insight, then, is that we enter into, and consent to political society not to guarantee ourselves a sphere of non-interference for our private ends, but rather to free ourselves of domination in all its (often insidious) social forms. And this reflects his deeper insight as to the deep-rooted and insidious structure that domination itself may assume within legally ordered and ostensibly consensual social relations—and thus as to the insufficiency of bourgeois liberties under the rule of law, which, he understands, will simply entrench social domination in ostensibly innocent forms. The republican insight, then, is that freedom is not negated by coercive interference as such, but rather by dependency in a variety of forms—psychic and affective, as well as material and economic. In turn, crucially, freedom cannot be secured through piecemeal guarantees of non-interference within a social order that remains marked by pervasive dependency; rather, it could only be recovered, Rousseau conjectures, by transitioning to a fuller or more complete phase of social and political

14 Thomas Hobbes, *Leviathan: Or, the Matter, Forme and Power of a Commonwealth Ecclesiasticall and Civil* (Ian Shapiro ed, Yale University Press 2010) ch XXI.

15 See generally Rousseau, *Du Contrat Social: Principes de Droit Politique* (n 13).

16 See generally David Gauthier, *Rousseau: The Sentiment of Existence* (Cambridge University Press 2006).

integration—and specifically, through a form of mutual interdependency in a self-governing political community.[17] A simulacrum of 'natural' freedom in the guise of piecemeal negative liberties will only perpetuate and obscure the dependency and thus the unfreedom running through the totality of social relations.[18] The bourgeois liberties might protect against some of the most obvious forms of physical coercion and depredation, but are ineffective against, and possibly serve to entrench, those complex forms of domination that are embedded in various social and symbolic hierarchies.

What this republican perspective suggests is that 'rights', as we understand them now, may provide only an illusion of security and freedom in a universe of insidious social domination. The salient point is that once the freedom of the state of nature is lost, it cannot meaningfully be recovered, in some partial or compromised form, within political society: rather, a new kind of freedom can only be constituted by and within the framework of political community itself. This explains why, through the social contract, we renounce natural freedom completely and constitute a new form of freedom as self-rule in political community.[19]

Crucially, Pettit argues that beyond and after Hobbes' contractarian absolutism, a similar *concept* of freedom as non-interference—one that came to dominate late-modern thought—was embraced in particular by Bentham and his followers, ultimately providing a somewhat awkward philosophical basis for the later politics of social liberalism.[20] While 'freedom', for Bentham, was simply instrumental to utility understood as net social happiness, most utilitarians assumed this would be best achieved under a regime in which freedom as non-interference was widely observed.[21] It appeals to the value of being 'left alone' generally to pursue one's own happiness or pleasures, subject to the demands of net social utility. And crucially, freedom defined in this sense is dissociated from any particular form or

[17] In *Emile*, Rousseau notes: 'natural man is wholly for himself; he is numerical unity, the absolute entirety which is relative only to itself or its kind. Civil man is only a fractional unity dependent on the denominator; his value is determined by his relation to the entirety, which is the social body. Good social institutions are those that best know how to denature man, to take his absolute existence from him in order to give him a relative one, and transport the I into the common unity, with the result that each individual believes himself no longer one but a part of the unity and no longer feels except within the whole'. Jean-Jacques Rousseau, *Emile: Or, on Education* (Allan Bloom tr, Basic Books) 39f.

[18] Patrick Riley, 'A Possible Explanation of Rousseau's General Will' (1970), 64 American Political Science Review 86.

[19] Rousseau's innovation, then, was to repurpose and adapt the device of the social contract during a period where 'the ideals of classical republicanism had largely been swallowed up by the rising tide of contractarian political thought'. Quentin Skinner, 'The Republican Ideal of Political Liberty' in Michael Rosen and Jonathan Wolff (eds), *Political Thought* (Oxford University Press 1999) 168.

[20] Pettit, *Republicanism* (n 12) chapters 1 and 2.

[21] ibid. See John S Mill, *On Liberty* (John Parker and Son 1859); Henry R West, *An Introduction to Mill's Utilitarian Ethics* (Cambridge University Press 2004).

structure of government, whether democratic or otherwise. Freedom as non-interference is undermined, at least in an initial sense, by all forms of external coercion, of whatever provenance. And coercive laws, as Bentham argues, all carry an 'initial cost' for freedom, even where they are justified in overall terms.[22]

Freedom, then, acquired quite an individualistic, and somewhat depoliticized understanding which denied any intrinsic value in politics, citizenship, or political community.[23] Freedom, in this sense requires *no more* than the absence of interference: it is silent as to the various aptitudes and resources individuals might need to exercise some measure of directive control over their lives, whether this is achieved through collective political action or otherwise.[24] The contrast is captured in the metaphors of the 'liberty of the heath'—understood by analogy with natural independence as the regulatory ideal—and the 'liberty of the city', one that is constituted relationally through an appropriate configuration of power and recognition within political community itself.[25]

Since the content of rights, in the liberal account, is defined by reference to the freedoms of the state of nature, crucially, we can understand how for republicans, the 'political' character of rights in the first sense outlined—the interpretive and substantive sense—is intrinsically linked with the second sense outlined, the genealogical and conceptual claim.

In this vein, in turn, contemporary republicans (and others) will tend to argue that the dominant juridified culture of rights obscures both the intractably political character of rights-claims as well as the conceptual interdependency of rights and citizenship. Richard Bellamy, as perhaps the most influential contemporary republican exponent of political constitutionalism, argues that rights cannot be understood as spheres of non-interferences—and thus as limits upon politics—because, on the one hand, this misconceives the analytical structure of rights-claims. Claims to freedom as non-interference imply a triadic relationship ('a three-way relation') whereby the subject of the claimed right calls upon a public authority to prevent 'interference' by a third party.[26] The state, then, interferes

[22] Jeremy Bentham, 'Anarchical Fallacies' in Jeremy Bentham, *The Works of Jeremy Bentham: Published under the Superintendence of His Executor, John Bowring*, vol 2 (William Tait 1843) 503, cited in Pettit, 'Law and Liberty' (n 3) 39.

[23] In this respect it is worth noting Rainer Forst's observations concerning the relation between political freedom and ethical individualism: 'No unquestioned ethical, objective values are available a priori to determine the legitimate uses of personal freedom in a political community . . . It is a fallacy to see ethical and legal contexts connected in that way; individual rights are not based on the idea of individualistic or "atomistic" life plans'. Rainer Forst, 'Political Liberty: Integrating Five Conceptions of Autonomy' in Rainer Forst, *The Right to Justification: Elements of a Constructivist Theory of Justice* (Jeffrey Flynn tr, Columbia University Press 2011) 134.

[24] Isaiah Berlin, *Two Concepts of Liberty* (Clarendon Press 1958); Pettit, *Republicanism* (n 12) 18.

[25] Anthony Laden, 'Republican Moments in Political Liberalism' (2006), 237 Revue Internationale de Philosophie 341.

[26] Bellamy, *Political Constitutionalism* (n 9) 30.

to prevent interference, leaving open the question of how competing claims of non-interference are weighted. And the range of interests, activities, or choices that are to be specially protected against interference is intractably contested and historically contingent. Any adjudication of such competing claims cannot transcend some substantive account of autonomy based on a thicker sense of freedom embedded in relations of power—or indeed, which rests on some set of interests or agendas or conceptions of good that inevitably, in itself, violates the supposed 'neutrality' of the liberal state.[27]

Equally, Bellamy argues, rights belong within the 'circumstances of politics' partly because there is intractable disagreement, amongst reasonable citizens, as to the ordering and reconciliation of competing rights-claims under varying historical and social circumstances. This is distinct from any relativist stance as to the indeterminate content of moral claims as such. Yet appraisals or interpretations of rights fail, ultimately, to transcend a social or political calculus, as per the Rawlsian canon, because there is no fair metric for ordering conflicting rights-claims. Any attempt at distinguishing between 'rights' and mere interests ultimately collapses in incoherence. Rather than understanding rights as apolitical, Bellamy suggests that citizenship comprises a 'continuously reflexive process, with citizens reinterpreting the basis of their collective life in new ways that correspond to their evolving needs and ideals'.[28] Thus he argues that we cannot realise freedom, in the republican sense, by somehow settling, in advance, on a concept of rights that is to be placed beyond politics and hived off from the ordinary procedures of contestation. Inevitably, such determinations prove *ad hoc* and historically arbitrary: a state cannot be built on a durable consensus about 'rights'. *Contra* Rawls, then the starting point for political philosophy is the fact that reasonable citizens disagree, in a permanent and intractable way, not only on the *good* but also questions of *right*. Therefore, freedom as non-domination is not realized by enshrining any specific *concept* or *content* of rights; rather, it is realized in the institutional *process* for reconciling competing rights-claims. And it is realized specifically, he claims, through a majoritarian parliamentary politics which, by according equal weight to each vote, enshrines 'equal concern and respect' for citizens who, quite reasonably, disagree as to the content and scope of rights.[29]

Liberal theories of rights, then, ignore those dimensions of freedom that reside in political participation—that is to say, the value in defining the content of

[27] See generally Richard Bellamy, *Liberalism and Modern Society: An Historical Argument* (Penn State University Press 1992).

[28] Richard Bellamy, 'Constitutive Citizenship versus Constitutional Rights: Republican Reflections on the EU Charter and the Human Rights Act' in Tom Campbell, KD Ewing, and Adam Tomkins (eds), *Sceptical Essays on Human Rights* (Oxford University Press 2001) 15.

[29] Bellamy, *Political Constitutionalism* (n 9).

rights—especially in a context of uncertainty or disagreement concerning the content or scope of rights in practice.[30] In a sense, then, Bellamy's republican account of procedural democracy is an institutional interpretation of Griffith's claim that 'rights' are best understood as political claims rather than as objective moral propositions.[31] Political freedom requires a right of contestation concerning the meaning of rights, such that nothing can be put 'off the agenda' in advance.[32] Indeed, the 'right to democracy' is, both in Bellamy's and Waldron's work, itself a paramount right.[33] For Waldron, moreover, 'the right to democracy is a right to participate on equal terms in social decisions on issues of high principle and that it is not to be confined to interstitial matters of social and economic policy'.[34] By contrast, it is the very attempt to determine a-politically a substantive concept of rights, to demarcate the limits of politics using rights, that leads to political domination in the guise of arbitrary rule—as 'a juridified culture of rights freezes the debate on their contents'.[35] In short, Bellamy argues, 'depoliticisation can fuel domination'.[36]

Beyond the specific democratic objection, republicans will tend to argue that 'rights talk' generally, or a juridified culture opposing legal rights against democratic process, tends to 'depoliticise' freedom both conceptually and institutionally, depicting it as a 'boundary around the individual . . . against the state'.[37] Since

[30] In this respect it is worth noting Forst's linking of rights with democratic participation. He argues that human rights 'are also constructive rights, rights to be part of processes of political justification . . . In other words, there is a basic right to be part of a political construction of a legitimate and generally acceptable basic structure through processes of public justification'. Rainer Forst, 'The Justification of Human Rights and the Basic Right to Justification: A Reflexive Approach' (2010), 120 Ethics 711, 721.

[31] John AG Griffith, 'The Political Constitution' (1979), 42 The Modern Law Review 1. Alternatively, strong-form judicial review has equally been challenged from within rights-centred liberalism, see eg James Allan, 'Bill of Rights and Judicial Power: A Liberal's Quandary' (1996), 16 Oxford Journal of Legal Studies 337. In contrast with Bellamy's instrumental justification of democracy (on republican grounds), see Christian F Rostbøll, 'Non-domination and Democratic Legitimacy' (2015), 18 Critical Review of International Social and Political Philosophy 424.

[32] Forst refers to 'procedures of "public justification" among citizens as authors of the law . . . as participants in these justificatory procedures . . . citizens are politically autonomous'. Forst, 'Political Liberty' (n 23) 135.

[33] Richard Bellamy, 'Rights as Democracy' (2012), 15 Critical Review of Social and Political 449.

[34] Jeremy Waldron, 'A Right-Based Critique of Constitutional Rights' (1993), 13 Oxford Journal of Legal Studies 18, 20.

[35] Marco Goldoni, 'Constitutional Reasoning According to Political Constitutionalism: Comment on Richard Bellamy' (2013), 14 German Law Journal 1053, 1058.

[36] Bellamy, *Political Constitutionalism* (n 9) 152.

[37] Duncan Ivison, 'Republican Human Rights?' (2010), 9 European Journal of Political Theory 31, 32. Forst argues that 'the concept of justice . . . possesses a core meaning to which the essential contrasting concept is that of *arbitrariness*, understood in a social and political but not a metaphysical sense'. Rainer Forst, 'Two Pictures of Justice' in Rainer Forst, *Justification and Critique: Towards a Critical Theory of Politics* (Ciaran Cronin tr, Polity Press 2013) 20f. For an exposition of the treatment of arbitrariness in republican and democratic thought, see also Rainer Forst, 'A Kantian Republican Conception of Justice as Non-Domination' in Andreas Niederberger and Philipp Schink (eds), *Republican Democracy: Liberty, Law and Politics* (Edinburgh University Press 2013).

freedom consists of security from arbitrary power, it is constituted (rather than caused) *through* politics—not against or despite it (as reflected in Forst's thought, in particular).[38] Thus in sum, the republican objection centres not only on the familiar debate over procedural democracy versus substantive rights, or the content versus the authorship of rights. Equally, it centres both on the concrete analytical structure of rights as well as their conceptual relation to citizenship and political community.

III. 'Republican' Rights?

While republican critics are correct in identifying a body of liberal thought that posits rights as antecedent to and transcendent of politics, I argue that they err in assuming the same view is institutionally translated within rights-based constitutional adjudication.

If Rousseau is correct in understanding 'freedom' as freedom from dependency upon arbitrary power—across all social relations—then there are many good reasons for understanding constitutional adjudication, as an elite-led endeavour, as being as likely to entrench as much as alleviate social domination. And indeed, republicans such as Bellamy have argued that the very attempt to define and adjudicate 'rights' a-politically is itself a source of domination. Political freedom, in this view, arises from the political *procedure* used to reconcile competing rights claims—a procedure that treats citizens as equals in a context of intractable conflict about rights—and not in any definite set of constitutionalized rights that are to be protected and adjudicated non-politically. Moreover, if freedom consists of non-domination rather than non-interference, it is difficult to see how the distributive and polycentric character of non-domination can be captured within the adversarial, individualized format of rights-based judicial review.[39] Since non-domination depends on people's 'relative' powers [40]—and thus, the opportunities and resources they enjoy relative to others—it requires a strong commitment to social and distributive justice of a kind that cannot be captured or realized as a set of judicially enforced individual rights, and indeed, which might even be thwarted by it.

In summary, once 'rights' are understand as boundaries against politics rather than as being constituted by and within it, institutional mechanisms of judicial review will likely be ineffective, at best, against the most potent and intractable forms of social, political and economic domination. Yet crucially, it is

[38] Forst, 'A Kantian Republican Conception of Justice as Non-Domination' (n 37).
[39] Daly (n 8).
[40] Pettit, *Republicanism* (n 12) ch 2.

wrong to assume that the institution and practice of constitutional-rights adjudication reflects such liberal understandings of rights as antecedent to or beyond politics.

It is true that—historically, at least—constitutional adjudication has operated by guaranteeing areas of immunity, for individuals, against state interference. And it is true, in turn, that this may render it relatively ineffective in addressing complex, polycentric, and distributive forms of domination, whether public and private. The mere existence of a power differential, the sort of which may cause domination, cannot easily be framed as 'interference' in fundamental rights, the sorts of which lends itself to judicial analysis.[41]

On the other hand, however, the individualized and adversarial format of judicial review—the fact that it considers the rights of isolated individuals rather than wider social power relations—does not mean that constitutional adjudication cannot nonetheless account, at least in some ways, for the contingent and indeterminate, that is, the intrinsically *political* character, of rights-claims.

One of the core claims of contemporary republican theory is that, *contra* Bentham and the liberal tradition, *interference* per se carries no intrinsic costs for freedom, even in a *prima facie* sense. This is the thesis of 'interference without domination'—the idea being that non-dominating interference does not diminish freedom at all, and therefore does not need to be accounted for in any calculus of freedom.[42] Only *arbitrary* interference (or the capacity for arbitrary interference) undermines freedom properly speaking.[43]

Ostensibly at least, this does not seem to be reflected in the standard structure of judicial rights analysis, which establishes, first, an 'interference' in the relevant right, and secondly, (usually) considers whether this particular interference is justified, based, say, on proportionality analysis. On the surface, this seems to impose a duty on the state at least to justify particular kinds of 'interference'—in a way that reflects the liberal understanding of freedom as non-interference. It seems to create a *prima facie* presumption against particular kinds of interference. Complaints of domination, by contrast, can be captured only indirectly or inadvertently.

However, what counts as 'interference' in a right, in say, the methodology of the European Court of Human Rights (ECtHR), has a far narrower and more specific meaning that 'interference' as it is used, quite widely, in the political-philosophical sense. For example, where a religiously motivated practice is

[41] Daly (n 8).
[42] Pettit, 'Law and Liberty' (n 3).
[43] See generally Forst, 'A Kantian Republican Conception of Justice as Non-Domination' (n 37).

prohibited by virtue of the general application of an otherwise legitimate law that is not itself targeted at religious practice, arguably there is no 'interference' in religious freedom at the first stage of analysis. Nor, then, does such a measure have to be subject to any special justification or proportionality test at the second stage. Effectively, the US Supreme Court endorsed a similar conceptual schema, in relation to religious freedom, in *Employment Division v Smith*, because the mere fact of state impediment upon religious activity triggered no particular onus of justification (as long as the restriction remained 'neutral' and 'generally applicable').[44]

In this light, it is possible to reconceptualise fundamental rights—not as immunities, or guarantees of non-interference, for privileged areas of activity (eg religious practice)—but rather as controlling the criteria of state action in particular domains. In this lens, constitutional rights may appear not as guarantees of non-interference for individuals *as such*, but rather as controls on the predicates and grounds of state action, and specifically, then, as bulwarks against *arbitrariness* in its republican sense, with republican thought having historically juxtaposed freedom against arbitrary government. Forst, indeed, offers a similar 'republican' interpretation of rights, emphasizing their social-relational rather than pre-political character—arguing that 'human rights . . . are rights not to be subjected to tyrannical rule or to be deprived of one's liberty and social standing'.[45]

This may seem an attractive stance because, in focusing on the predicates of state action and particularly its arbitrariness—rather than on the individual interests being protected—it seems less *ad hoc* than any determination as to those areas of activity that are to remain presumptively free of regulation or control, and indeed as to the relative weight to be assigned to the relevant interests. In the United States, for example, the US Supreme Court shifted to an analysis of the 'neutrality' and general applicability of laws impacting on religious practice, which seemed preferable in some ways to the prior test focused on appraising the relative importance or weight of the affected religious interests, relative to competing public concerns. In reviewing, instead, the procedural and justificatory basis for administrative and legislative coercion, judges might avoid such ad hoc determinations. Relatedly, and more pertinently, this position seems to reflect the republican intuition as to the 'political' character of 'rights', because the question of what 'rights' individuals enjoy relative to competing concerns—that is, the degree of immunity or non-interference they enjoy in respect of particular

44 494 US 872 (1990).

45 Forst, 'The Justification of Human Rights and the Basic Right to Justification' (n 30) 716. Similarly, he refers to 'a political notion of dignity as a relational concept, referring to the social and political standing of human beings as agents of justification who are equal to one another'. ibid 718.

activities—is recognized as being politically contingent and negotiable. What constitutional rights demand, then, is not definite 'rights' for individuals, but rather, special kinds of justifications for certain categories of state actions. This helps to show, indeed, how the institution of constitutional adjudication can be better understood as institutionalizing something approximate to Forst's concept of a 'right to justification', rather than a more classically 'liberal' idea of freedom as non-interference. The very phraseology of constitutional rights, moreover, is potentially misleading, and potentially explains much republican hostility towards mechanisms of rights-based judicial review.

Of course, rights are ostensibly defined in relation to specific *activities* (religion, expression, association, and so on), which seems to accord more with the liberal logic of non-interference than the republican project of non-domination. However, on the one hand, Pettit, for example, acknowledges that the state will entrench and protect only certain *choices* against domination (the domain of the 'fundamental liberties').[46] On the other hand, more importantly, such 'rights' arguably do not serve primarily to protect non-interference for particular kinds of activity (religion, association, etc.), but rather to protect against arbitrary state activity undertaken in relation to such areas of activity. The focus, then, can be placed on the predicates of intervention, rather than the relative value or harm of the activity as such. Of course, these rights still protect citizens, but they do not protect them from interference as such, but only *arbitrary* interference, albeit within specific domains of activity. In this light, they can be understood as *instrumental* guarantees of non-arbitrary government rather than safeguarding privileged activities as such.[47]

Adler, in this vein, argues that American constitutional law is not concerned, primarily, with the moral rights of individuals, but rather the 'predicates of Government action'.[48] This is given expression, as already argued, in the Supreme Court's jurisprudence on religious liberty, which focuses not on the religious harm caused by government actions (say, with reference to the spiritual importance of the restricted practices) but rather on whether laws restricting such practices are 'neutral and generally applicable'.[49] Similarly, Kagan has argued that free-speech doctrine is focused primarily on the purpose rather than the

[46] Philip Pettit, *On the People's Terms: A Republican Theory and Model of Democracy* (Cambridge University Press 2012) 83.

[47] Pettit insists that a broad range of activities and choices, but not 'any old choices', must be protected by the basic liberties; they 'need resources and protection in a range of choice where all can operate at once without getting in another's way . . . [this is] the domain of the fundamental liberties'. ibid.

[48] Matthew D Adler, 'Rights against Rules: The Moral Structure of American Constitutional Law' (1998), 97 Michigan Law Review 1.

[49] *Employment Division v Smith* 494 US 872 (1990).

effects of state action.[50] And in turn, if constitutional review focuses on the 'pattern, purpose or context of government action' rather than 'some specific aspect of one's liberty or welfare',[51] this illustrates, again, that constitutional rights are not concerned primarily with preserving, for individuals, a pre-defined sphere of non-interference, but rather with checking arbitrariness in state power. And particularly, we can understand that checking arbitrariness in this way is instantiated by triggering a special institutional expression of the *right to justification* at least in particular domains of state activity.[52]

This is reflected in standards of review other than proportionality. For example, it has been argued that the American 'compelling state interest' test ('strict scrutiny') 'requires courts to determine the scope of rights with reference to the justifications government offers for limiting them'—precisely because 'rights are better understood as means of realizing certain collective interests'[53] rather than as definite, 'pre-political' spheres of non-interference for individuals. Similarly, the concept of 'balancing' limits on rights against common interests can be interpreted as an attempt to define those *reasons* or criteria that constitute 'impermissible justifications for state actions in different spheres'—and thus, again, as a means of realizing 'those specific common goods the pursuit of which is the point of recognizing particular constitutional rights'.[54] In short, then, constitutional rights 'police the kinds of justifications government can act on in different spheres rather than protecting atomistic interests in autonomy, or liberty, or dignity'.[55] Pildes argues that if rights are understood as 'channelling the kinds of reasons government can invoke when it acts in certain arenas',[56] they are not, then, 'trumps' on the common good—as Dworkin argues—but rather its conduits and its signposts. Put slightly differently, rights need not be placed, a priori, in a definitionally antagonistic relationship with concepts of public interest, common good, even 'majority rule', etc. Again, this feature gives constitutional rights a potentially republican flavour. In a not dissimilar analysis, Forst, linking rights to an overarching right to justification, suggests that 'human rights

[50] Elena Kagan, 'Private Speech, Public Purpose: The Role of Governmental Motive in First Amendment Doctrine' (1996), 63 University of Chicago Law Review 413. Richard H Pildes, 'Why Rights Are Not Trumps: Social Meanings, Expressive Harms, and Constitutionalism' (1998), 27 The Journal of Legal Studies 725.

[51] Christopher Eisgruber and Lawrence Sager, 'Religious Liberty and the Moral Structure of Constitutional Rights' (2000), 6 Legal Theory 253.

[52] Forst argues: 'one claim underlies all human rights, namely, human beings' claim to be respected as autonomous agents who have the right not to be subjected to certain actions or institutional norms that cannot be adequately justified to them'. Forst, 'The Justification of Human Rights and the Basic Right to Justification' (n 30) 712.

[53] Pildes (n 50) 731.

[54] ibid 734.

[55] Ibid 725.

[56] ibid 729 (emphasis added).

are not immediate claims to certain substantive "goods", but to a certain social and political standing of persons'.[57]

What this suggests, then, is that constitutional rights can be understood not, primarily, as promoting non-interference *per se*, but rather as a mechanism for checking arbitrary government power. This has been obscured, in large part, by the fact that such constraints are generally shoe-horned in terminologies of 'rights'. In this view, the starting point for 'rights' is not a moral or ethical concept of rights—one that yields, in turn, certain immunities or spheres of non-interference—but rather a particular concept of government[58]—in which the duty of justification, in Forst's sense, is paramount. Rights, in this sense, are merely 'linguistic or rhetorical tools the law deploys for pragmatic reasons and aims' and 'techniques by which courts police the kinds of purposes government can offer to justify its action'.[59] Of course, such normative concepts of government—say, non-arbitrary rule—are not unconnected to moral understandings of individual 'rights'. Yet 'rights'-based constitutional adjudication does not necessarily take, as its starting point, some idea of defined areas of 'non-interference' for individuals: it is consistent, then, with an idea of rights as 'political' or even as essentially indeterminate. And this accords in particular with an alternative republican historiography of American constitutional concepts, championed by Pocock and others, which suggests that the revolutionaries were inspired by renaissance and ancient republicanism as much as by liberal and Lockean natural-law theory.[60] In particular, Pildes suggests: 'The American idea of constitutionalism did not begin with philosophical conceptions of the person and reason out from there to rights. It began rooted in the experience of government, both English colonial administration and state governments after the Revolution'.[61]

If we take this view to its seemingly natural conclusion, perhaps constitutional rights, then, are not 'subjective' rights at all,[62] and citizens are 'rights-holders', only in a highly abstract, procedural, and instrumental way, in that they may challenge the predicate, criteria, or purpose of state action in some domain where they happen to be affected. This may well still be understood, philosophically speaking, in terms of a 'right to justification' (whether as per Forst's account or otherwise), but based on the foregoing argument, we may rethink the *subject* or recipient of justification in constitutional-rights adjudication. This is not to bring into question the centrality or importance of the right to justification *per*

[57] Forst, 'The Justification of Human Rights and the Basic Right to Justification' (n 30) 721.
[58] ibid.
[59] ibid 730.
[60] JGA Pocock, *The Machiavellian Moment: Florentine Political Thought and the Atlantic Republican Tradition* (Princeton University Press 2003).
[61] Pildes (n 50) 730.
[62] See Raymond Geuss, *Philosophy and Real Politics* (Princeton University Press 2008).

se, but rather to consider how it is mapped on to, or institutionalized in the guise of constitutional-rights adjudication.

Some constitutional provisions ostensibly relating to the structure, predicates and purpose of government—for example, the American prohibition on 'establishment' of religion—have been understood as being nothing more than corollaries of individual rights, such as religious freedom.[63] However, on a republican view, the reverse idea is more compelling: constitutional 'rights' are not definite moral rights, for individuals—and certainly not *natural* rights—but rather signposts for government power.

For Pildes, again: 'Rights discourse need not, and in much of American practice does not, protect the atomistic interests of individuals. Instead, the work that rights rhetoric actually does is to constrain the kind of reasons that government can act on when it seeks to regulate or intervene in some sphere of activity'.[64] In the religious-establishment example as much as in others, 'the primary role of constitutional rights is not to protect individual aspects of conscience. Instead, their role is to secure a common good'.[65]

The fact that such rights-provisions are, in the Anglophone world, invoked through judicial review by *individuals* can lead to confusion concerning their scope and moral structure. That a constitutional injunction on state power is phrased in 'rights' terms may be little more, then, than linguistic and procedural accident. Again, this suggests that the institutional edifice of constitutional rights is not inconsistent with Bellamy's insistence that 'rights' in the narrow sense—the sense, that is, of what legal immunities people enjoy—must be left open to on-going political contestation as part of the 'circumstances of politics'.

IV. Proportionality and the 'Circumstances of Politics'

I have argued that constitutional rights can be understood as protecting not against interference as such, but only against arbitrary interference in particular areas of state activity, and so that they can be reconceptualized, in a republican sense, as guarantees of non-arbitrary government rather than as antecedent limits on politics. But how is this reflected in proportionality doctrines, specifically?

While I have argued that an 'interference' in its analytic-philosophical sense does not necessarily count as 'interference' in a constitutional right doctrinally speaking, equally I argue that the permissibility of *proportionate* interference in

63 See *Lee v Weisman* 505 US 577, 591 (1992).
64 Pildes (n 50) 730f.
65 ibid 750.

rights, in constitutional-rights doctrine, roughly corresponds to the philosophical idea of *non-arbitrary interference* or *interference without domination*. For republican theorists such as Philip Pettit, a non-arbitrary, non-dominating interference must pursue a legitimate aim connected to a common public good—that is, an interest shared at some level by all those affected—rather than say, a factional or sectional interest.[66] And this quintessentially republican concern is captured, at least in part, in the existing methodologies of constitutional and human-rights courts. For example, Articles 8–11 of the ECtHR define the criteria based on which freedom of expression, religion, assembly, etc., may legitimately be limited. These arguably echo the republican concept of arbitrariness in many respects—for example, in the requirements that interferences are 'prescribed by law' (rather than based on administrative discretion)—a formula echoed in the Canadian Charter[67]—and that they must be 'necessary in a democratic society (. . .) or for the protection of the rights and freedoms of others'. National constitutions are often less specific. The rights encompassed by the First Amendment to the US Constitution (religion, association, expression, assembly, 'petition' of government) offer no definition of limiting criteria.[68] The Irish Constitution uses vague formulae such as 'public order and morality' (Article 44) or 'the exigencies of the common good' (Article 43), while the Canadian Charter refers to the 'such reasonable limits . . . as can be demonstrably justified in a free and democratic society' (Article 1). Yet irrespective of textual and stylistic variations, the two-stage structure of much of constitutional-rights doctrine—within the framework of proportionality doctrine—arguably shows that the function of constitutional judges is to safeguard against *arbitrary* interferences in rights specifically (and indeed, to trigger a special duty to *justify* the non-arbitrariness of interferences in certain domains). Thus, their role can ultimately be understood in light of freedom as non-domination rather than the more familiar liberal concept.

The idea that constitutional rights protect against arbitrary interference, rather than interference as such, is also reflected in the structure of proportionality doctrine. Generally speaking, proportionality analysis requires that legislative restrictions on rights pursue a legitimate aim, and that rights are impaired no further than is necessary to realise such aims.[69] Since limitations on rights must be 'rationally connected to the objective and not be arbitrary, unfair or

[66] Pettit, *Republicanism* (n 12) ch 3.

[67] Canadian Charter of Rights and Freedoms, 1982, Article 1.

[68] The first amendment provides: 'Congress shall make no law respecting an establishment of religion, or prohibiting the free exercise thereof; or abridging the freedom of speech, or of the press; or the right of the people peaceably to assemble, and to petition the Government for a redress of grievances'.

[69] For discussion, see generally Tom Hickman, 'The Substance and Structure of Proportionality' [2008] Public Law 694.

based on irrational considerations',[70] this can be interpreted as a mechanism for ensuring that coercive state interference remains non-*arbitrary* in the republican sense, in that it tracks 'commonly avowable' public interests.[71] It is true that in some variants, the proportionality test will effectively require judges to make substantive, even perhaps, intuitive appraisals as to the relative merits of competing claims of public and private right—that is, to assess whether the impact on rights is out of proportion to the benefit obtained by the relevant measure. This seemingly implicates judges in a more far-reaching normative endeavour—involving elements of characteristically 'political' reasoning—going beyond any narrower assessment as to arbitrariness in its republican sense.[72] However, the more technical-rational aspects of the proportionality doctrine—particularly the requirements of necessity and of a rational connection between the means and end of a restriction on rights—helps to show, again, that constitutional rights are not moral rights, institutionalized, but rather, controls on the predicates of state power. In turn, this makes rights-based constitutional adjudication seem quite consistent with a 'political' concept of rights, and cognisant of the reasonable uncertainty and disagreement that pertains concerning the content and scope of specific rights in particular circumstances.

Rivers argues that there are two distinct senses in which we can understand proportionality. In one account (the 'state-limiting' conception), dominant in the Anglosphere, proportionality analysis is a means through which judges police the boundary between rights against public interest, effectively limiting the reach of state power over rights. In an alternative understanding however, the 'optimising conception', predominant in Germany and closely associated with Alexy's thought, there can be no firm formal distinction between 'rights' and the other normative goals pursued by the state—such that proportionality, instead, is a means of optimizing the pursuit of principles as normative goals. It proceeds, then, on the 'assumption that rights and other interests are formally indistinguishable'.[73]

[70] *Heaney v Ireland* [1994] 3 IR 593, 607.

[71] Pettit, *On the People's Terms* (n 46) chapters 4 and 5.

[72] For Kumm, 'The metaphor of "balancing" should not obscure the fact that the last prong of the proportionality test will, in many cases, require the decision maker to engage in theoretically informed practical reasoning, as opposed to mere intuition-based classification. In evaluating the relative importance of the general interest in relation to the liberty interest at stake, such weights may be assigned and priorities established as required by the correct substantive theory of justice. The last prong of the proportionality test, then, provides a space for the reasoned incorporation of an understanding of liberties that expresses whatever priority over collective goods is substantively justified'. Mattias Kumm, 'Constitutional Rights as Principles: On the Structure and Domain of Constitutional Justice. A Review Essay on *A Theory of Constitutional Rights* by Robert Alexy' (2004), 2 International Journal of Constitutional Law 574, 592.

[73] Julian Rivers, 'Proportionality and Variable Intensity of Review' (2006), 65 The Cambridge Law Journal 174. He notes: 'European proportionality is first and foremost about identifying the rational

While the former conception seems more in tune with liberal ideology, in fact neither account posits rights, however conceived, either as being conceptually antecedent to political association, nor as being immune from any balance or calculus of social interests. Whereas Alexy insists 'principles are norms which require that something be realised to the greatest extent possible given their legal and factual possibilities',[74] this obviously admits of the social and historical contingency of specific rights-claims. All that having a 'right' guarantees to the rights-holder is not that any particular range of rights-claims will be vindicated, but only that the infringement of the right will be justified according to a standard that closely resembles the political-theoretical notion of arbitrariness. As Kumm puts it: 'Since relatively little is decided by acknowledging that a measure infringes a right, the focus of rights adjudication is generally on the reasons that justify the infringement . . . the structure of proportionality analysis provides little more than a checklist for the individually necessary and collectively sufficient conditions that determine whether the reasons marshaled to justify an infringement of a right are good reasons under the circumstances'.[75]

On the other hand, however, nothing in the alternative structure, pitting private rights against public interests, posits any incommensurability in terms of a trade-off between these, in the sense that Rawls in particular claims. In this conception, equally, a rights-claim triggers only a right to justification, along similar lines. The same feature is present within the 'compelling interests' test used in US constitutional law. The terminologies used, echoing liberal philosophy, ostensibly suggest that the very idea of qualifying rights is problematic, when 'rights are supposed to set limits to the public interest'.[76] Yet as Rivers notes: 'All the court does is maintain an efficiency-based oversight to ensure that there are no unnecessary costs to rights, that sledgehammers are not used to crack nuts, or rather, that sledgehammers are only used when nutcrackers prove impotent'.[77] Nothing within such a scheme precludes, then, that 'rights' could be trumped by common goals based on what is quintessentially 'political' form of reasoning. The *content* of rights remains firmly open-ended—falling still, decisively, within the 'circumstances of politics'. This apparently 'liberal' understanding of proportionality is still a long way from the concept of 'rights as trumps' that has been so influential in liberal political philosophy.

optimisation of the common good, which includes both rights as protected interests and other interests'. ibid 181.

---

[74] Robert Alexy, *A Theory of Constitutional Rights* (Julian Rivers tr, Oxford University Press 2002) 45.

[75] Kumm (n 72) 582.

[76] Rivers (n 73) 179.

[77] ibid 180.

V. Conclusion

I have not aimed at offering a full normative defence of rights-based judicial review, whether on republican grounds or otherwise. Many of the objections remain compelling. Rather, I have aimed to elucidate one aspect of the republican objection to constitutional-rights adjudication, and to show how this critique of liberal rights as depoliticized is not borne out in the structure and practice of judicial review itself. The most decisive point, perhaps, is the divergence between the concept of rights, ethical or moral, that is prevalent in liberal philosophy, and the quite different concept that—despite appearances and perceptions—predominates within what is often taken as its institutional expression.

References

Adler MD, 'Rights against Rules: The Moral Structure of American Constitutional Law' (1998), 97 Michigan Law Review 1.
Alexy R, *A Theory of Constitutional Rights* (Julian Rivers tr, Oxford University Press 2002).
Allan J, 'Bill of Rights and Judicial Power: A Liberal's Quandary' (1996), 16 Oxford Journal of Legal Studies 337.
Bellamy R, *Liberalism and Modern Society: An Historical Argument* (Penn State University Press 1992).
Bellamy R, 'Constitutive Citizenship versus Constitutional Rights: Republican Reflections on the EU Charter and the Human Rights Act' in Tom Campbell, KD Ewing and Adam Tomkins (eds), *Sceptical Essays on Human Rights* (Oxford University Press 2001).
Bellamy R, *Political Constitutionalism* (Cambridge University Press 2007).
Bellamy R, 'Rights as Democracy' (2012), 15 Critical Review of Social and Political 449.
Bentham J, 'Anarchical Fallacies' in Jeremy Bentham, *The Works of Jeremy Bentham: Published under the Superintendence of His Executor, John Bowring*, vol 2 (William Tait 1843).
Berlin I, *Two Concepts of Liberty* (Clarendon Press 1958).
Daly E, 'Freedom as Non-Domination in the Jurisprudence of Constitutional Rights' (2015), 28 Canadian Journal of Law & Jurisprudence 289.
Dworkin R, *Freedom's Law: The Moral Reading of the American Constitution* (Harvard University Press 1996).
Eisgruber C and Sager L, 'Religious Liberty and the Moral Structure of Constitutional Rights' (2000), 6 Legal Theory 253.
Forst R, 'The Justification of Human Rights and the Basic Right to Justification: A Reflexive Approach' (2010), 120 Ethics 711.
Forst R, 'Political Liberty: Integrating Five Conceptions of Autonomy' in Rainer Forst, *The Right to Justification: Elements of a Constructivist Theory of Justice* (Jeffrey Flynn tr, Columbia University Press 2011).
Forst R, 'A Kantian Republican Conception of Justice as Non-Domination' in Andreas Niederberger and Philipp Schink (eds), *Republican Democracy: Liberty, Law and Politics* (Edinburgh University Press 2013).

Forst R, 'Two Pictures of Justice' in Rainer Forst, *Justification and Critique: Towards a Critical Theory of Politics* (Ciaran Cronin tr, Polity Press 2013).
Gauthier D, *Rousseau: The Sentiment of Existence* (Cambridge University Press 2006).
Geuss R, *Philosophy and Real Politics* (Princeton University Press 2008).
Goldoni M, 'Constitutional Reasoning According to Political Constitutionalism: Comment on Richard Bellamy' (2013), 14 German Law Journal 1053.
Griffith JAG, 'The Political Constitution' (1979), 42 The Modern Law Review 1.
Hickman T, 'The Substance and Structure of Proportionality' [2008] Public Law 694.
Hobbes T, *Leviathan: Or, the Matter, Forme and Power of a Commonwealth Ecclesiasticall and Civil* (Ian Shapiro ed, Yale University Press 2010).
Ivison D, 'Republican Human Rights?' (2010), 9 European Journal of Political Theory 31.
Kagan E, 'Private Speech, Public Purpose: The Role of Governmental Motive in First Amendment Doctrine' (1996), 63 University of Chicago Law Review 413.
Kumm M, 'Constitutional Rights as Principles: On the Structure and Domain of Constitutional Justice. A Review Essay on *A Theory of Constitutional Rights* by Robert Alexy' (2004), 2 International Journal of Constitutional Law 574.
Laden A, 'Republican Moments in Political Liberalism' (2006), 237 Revue Internationale de Philosophie 341.
Loughlin M, *Foundations of Public Law* (Oxford University Press 2010).
Mill JS, *On Liberty* (John Parker and Son 1859).
Pettit P, *Republicanism: A Theory of Freedom and Government* (Clarendon Press 1997).
Pettit P, 'Law and Liberty' in Samantha Besson and José L Martí (eds), *Legal Republicanism: National and International Perspectives* (Oxford University Press 2009).
Pettit P, *On the People's Terms: A Republican Theory and Model of Democracy* (Cambridge University Press 2012).
Pildes RH, 'Why Rights Are Not Trumps: Social Meanings, Expressive Harms, and Constitutionalism' (1998), 27 The Journal of Legal Studies 725.
Pocock JGA, *The Machiavellian Moment: Florentine Political Thought and the Atlantic Republican Tradition* (Princeton University Press 2003).
Rawls J, *A Theory of Justice* (revised edn, Oxford University Press 1999).
Rawls J, *Justice as Fairness: A Restatement* (Harvard University Press 2001).
Riley P, 'A Possible Explanation of Rousseau's General Will' (1970), 64 American Political Science Review 86.
Rivers J, 'Proportionality and Variable Intensity of Review' (2006), 65 The Cambridge Law Journal 174.
Rostbøll CF, 'Non-domination and Democratic Legitimacy' (2015), 18 Critical Review of International Social and Political Philosophy 424.
Rousseau J-J, *Emile: Or, on Education* (Allan Bloom tr, Basic Books).
Rousseau J-J, *Du Contrat Social: Principes de Droit Politique* (ENAG 1988).
Skinner Q, *Liberty before Liberalism* (Cambridge University Press 1998).
Skinner Q, 'The Republican Ideal of Political Liberty' in Michael Rosen and Jonathan Wolff (eds), *Political Thought* (Oxford University Press 1999).
Tushnet MV, 'Following the Rules Laid Down: A Critique of Interpretivism and Neutral Principles' (1983), 96 Harvard Law Review 781.
Waldron J, 'A Right-Based Critique of Constitutional Rights' (1993), 13 Oxford Journal of Legal Studies 18.
West HR, *An Introduction to Mill's Utilitarian Ethics* (Cambridge University Press 2004).

10
Constitutionalism and Justice

Alon Harel

I. Introduction

This chapter is founded on the conviction that legal institutions and legal procedures are not mere means to achieve some desirable contingent outcomes: the protection of rights, the flourishment of democracy, coherence and stability, and so forth. Instead, often institutions which are typically justified on these grounds are valuable as such.[1] More specifically, I maintain that constitutionalism can be justified not merely as a contingent means to bring about justice (or other desirable ends) but as a necessary component of a just polity.

This chapter disputes the methodological starting point of what I have labelled in the past 'instrumentalist constitutionalism' and defends *robust constitutionalism.*[2] Robust constitutionalism denotes a justificatory approach which does not justify constitutions merely by pointing out the desirability of the contingent desirable outcomes of constitutions. It maintains that in addition to such desirable contingent outcomes, constitutionalism restructures the relationships between the state and its citizens in ways that protect and promote human dignity.

Robust constitutionalism may seem at first sight strange. How could constitutionalism possibly be justified other than by specifying its beneficial effects, namely, the effects that constitutionalism is likely to have on the merit of decisions? Is not it mere constitutional fetishism to cherish constitutionalism *as such* independently of its desirable effects? Should not constitutions and judicial review be conducive to some extrinsic ends such as justice? Support for this instrumentalist view comes for instance from the great Austrian legal theorist—Hans Kelsen—who maintained that 'Law is a means . . . not an end', and this view applies to constitutions as well.[3]

While it seems strange, there are in contemporary liberal theory indications that support such a view. In describing contemporary liberalism, Forst

[1] I defended this view in Alon Harel, *Why Law Matters* (Oxford University Press 2014) 2.

[2] See ibid 133–45.

[3] Hans Kelsen, *General Theory of Law and State* (Anders Wedberg tr, Harvard University Press 1949) 20.

Alon Harel, *Constitutionalism and Justice* In: *Constitutionalism Justified: Rainer Forst in Discourse.* Edited by: Ester Herlin-Karnell and Matthias Klatt, Oxford University Press (2020), © Ester Herlin-Karnell and Matthias Klatt.
DOI: 10.1093/oso/9780190889050.003.0010

argues: 'For apart from a mere instrumental or strategic view of the political community or a Hobbesian modus vivendi there has to be a "civic bond" between liberal citizens who consider their social and political framework as a "common project" for which they are responsible.'[4] It seems that contemporary liberal tradition rejects the view that the polity is a mere instrument; instead, it maintains that the political community can serve to transform human beings from mere individuals to members of a community and consequently constrain the extremity of individualism by creating a 'civic bond' and 'a common project'. Ironically, this chapter reaches an opposite conclusion; constitutionalism gives expression to individualistic sentiments rather than to collective or communal sentiments. It does so in two ways. First, by imposing duties on the legislature, constitutionalism facilitates a public recognition that the protection of rights is the state's duty rather than a mere whim or a voluntary gesture on its part. Second, by protecting judicial review, constitutionalism grants individuals a right to a hearing which is nothing but a stringent and robust version of Forst's right to justification. Let me briefly discuss these two points.

Mandatory or binding constitutional directives impose duties on the legislature. The duties discussed later are ones designed to protect fundamental rights. The constitutional entrenchment of directives protecting rights implies that the rights of individuals are not *at the mercy* of the legislature and are not subject to its discretion; they are mandatory. Hence, constitutional directives are emblematic of the mandatory force of rights.

Judicial review implies that an individual can challenge decisions which she believes (justly or unjustly) violate her rights. Such a right to judicial review is nothing but a right to a hearing—a right of a person to challenge or question a decision when such a decision is perceived by her to be a violation of her rights. The desirability of judicial review does not hinge merely on the question of whether it is more likely to bring about justice. Instead, judicial review is in itself a deliberative right—a right to participate in the deliberation of the state when its decisions impinge or may impinge on one's rights.

The primary end of this chapter is to inverse the order of the reasoning characterizing contemporary constitutional theory. Instead of stating (as advocates of constitutional instrumentalism do): human rights ought to be protected and therefore we ought to establish institutions that are most likely to effectively protect these rights, I argue (as robust constitutionalists ought to do): certain institutions ought to be established because only they have the legitimacy to engage in the enterprise of legislating and protecting rights. It is therefore

[4] See Rainer Forst, 'The Rule of Reasons: Three Models of Deliberative Democracy' in Rainer Forst, *The Right to Justification: Elements of a Constructivist Theory of Justice* (Jeffrey Flynn tr, Columbia University Press 2011) 160.

legitimacy rather than usefulness, utility, or pragmatic considerations that drive the urge for constitutionalism. I further argue that the traditional instrumental justifications of legal and political theorists are often mere rationalizations, and they do not reflect the convictions of those who cherish the institutions, support them, or even oppose them.

Section II exposes some of the difficulties in traditional constitutional instrumentalism. Section II defends two aspects of constitutionalism on non-instrumentalist grounds: sub-section 1 binding constitutional directives; sub-section 2 judicial review.

II. The Case against Constitutional Instrumentalism

Constitutional instrumentalism regards constitutions as a contingent means to bring about desirable consequences, eg the protection of rights, democracy, or other valuable states of affairs.[5] Under this view, which dominates the field of constitutionalism, constitutionalism is desirable to the extent that it serves some extrinsic end. Most typically, it is claimed that constitutionalism improves the substantive merit of the resulting decisions.[6]

This view is part of a more general view which can be labelled legal instrumentalism under which all legal institutions are valuable by virtue of some contingent effects they may have. Thomas Aquinas has famously argued: law 'is nothing else than an ordinance of reason *for the common good*, made by him who has care of the community, and promulgated.'[7] Hans Kelsen has also maintained that 'Law is an end . . . not a means' and, last in discussing the conflict between constitutionalism and democratic procedures, Ronald Dworkin saw 'no alternative but to use a result-driven rather than a procedure-driven standard for deciding them. The best institutional structure is the one best calculated to produce the best answers to the essentially moral questions of what the democratic conditions actually are, and to secure stable compliance with these conditions.'[8] The difference among different theorists is primarily in identifying what the extrinsic end that justifies the constitution is. Some believe it is the common good;[9] others maintain it is the

[5] For a description of the various versions of constitutional instrumentalism, see Harel, *Why Law Matters* (n 1) 194–202.

[6] ibid 136f.

[7] Thomas Aquinas, *Summa Theologica* (Fathers of the English Dominican Province trs, Christian Classics 1981) question 90.

[8] Ronald Dworkin, *Freedom's Law: The Moral Reading of the American Constitution* (Harvard University Press 1996) 34.

[9] Aquinas (n 7).

protection of rights or democracy;[10] others point to the consistency and coherence which characterize the decisions of courts as opposed to legislatures.[11]

Constitutional instrumentalism maintains that the authoritativeness of constitutions must be *instrumentally* justified.[12] Let me focus attention on two features which are sufficient to shed doubt on constitutional instrumentalism: empirical concerns and the insincerity objection.

Constitutional instrumentalism rests on empirical or quasi-empirical claims such as that constitutions bring about better protection of rights or better democratic institutions. Empirical claims are of course legitimate in various contexts. Yet the type of claims made by constitutional instrumentalists are too general and sweeping to be empirically validated. Anecdotal evidence also does not support the view that constitutionalism or judicial review are conducive to the protection of rights. In the US context, for instance, courts made notorious constitutional decisions during the slavery era; much later courts declared that the internment of Japanese does not violate the US Constitution. Needless to say, in other periods such as during the fifties and sixties, the US Supreme Court made important contributions to the protection of rights, and these contributions rested upon its interpretation of the Constitution. Yet, it is difficult to evaluate whether in the United States rights would be less or more protected in the absence of a constitution. It is not surprising therefore that many jurists who examined the effects of constitutionalism on decision-making question the claim that US constitutionalism has been instrumentally desirable.[13]

It is easy to see why claims concerning the instrumental value of constitutionalism are so immensely difficult to establish empirically. The question whether constitutions or judicial review are conducive to valuable ends depends upon the identity of judges, the broad sentiments in the public, the system of elections, the system for appointing judges, and so forth. The considerations that determine whether judges protect rights effectively change from time to time and from place to place. On the one hand, legislators are typically subject to public hysteria, and the daily urgent concerns may distract them from protecting rights. On the other hand, judges are often selected from privileged segments of the society, and they may be less sensitive to minorities' concerns than legislators. Given that constitutions typically are documents that are designed to last for a long time, the question of whether they are conducive to

10 See Dworkin (n 8); John H Ely, *Democracy and Distrust: A Theory of Judicial Review* (Harvard University Press 1981); Alon Harel, 'Rights-Based Judicial Review: A Democratic Justification' (2003), 22 Law & Philosophy 247.

11 Frederick Schauer and Larry Alexander, 'On Extrajudicial Constitutional Interpretation' (1997), 110 Harvard Law Review 1359.

12 See Harel, *Why Law Matters* (n 1) 136–39.

13 Wojciech Sadurski, 'Reason of State and Public Reason' (2014), 27 Ratio Juris 21; David M Rabban, *Free Speech in Its Forgotten Years* (Cambridge University Press 1997).

desirable ends cannot be empirically tested or determined. The soundness of such claims differ from place to place and from time to time.[14]

Yet, even if such claims could be established, I would maintain that empirical concerns are not the only ones that one should care about. In *Why Law Matters* I identified an additional reason, namely, that instrumental justifications of constitutionalism are insincere or inauthentic.[15] More specifically, these justifications are mere rationalizations of more foundational convictions we have. Precisely as a utilitarian argument that slavery is wrong because it is detrimental to utility sounds artificial and even silly, so I believe an argument that maintains that constitutions are desirable because they bring about better protection of rights is simply not the right argument. The sentiments underlying constitutionalism are different sentiments; they do not rest on the contingent extrinsic consequences of constitutions. Instead, they often have to do with the expressive or symbolic significance of the entrenchment of explicit public norms protecting basic rights. There is a sense of incongruity between the scholarly justifications of constitutionalism (in terms of the merits of the resulting decisions) and the underlying attitudes triggering the passions of those who sustain these institutions, establish them, design them, or simply cherish them.[16] Even perfectly sound contingent arguments for or against constitutionalism may miss the point because they speak in a language which is foreign to those who guide their lives in the shadow of constitutionalism.

Note that I do not deny that empirical arguments favouring political institutions and practices which are insincere, namely, which deviate from the self-understanding of those who establish these institutions or sustain them always lack normative force. I also do not argue that sincere arguments are always superior to non-sincere ones. My argument is much more modest: when an established institution or a practice gains broad popular support; when it also becomes an integral part of the institutional framework of a polity, it is valuable to explore whether there are sound foundations to this practice and to do so in a way that is faithful to the sentiments and passions of those who support it, sustain it, or even challenge it.

Think about democracy and, in particular, the authoritativeness of democratic decisions. There is a broad support for democracy *on the grounds* that democratic decisions are intrinsically valuable. This conviction is also reflected in the scholarly work on democracy. It is broadly accepted that it is not (merely) the correctness (or the likelihood of correctness) of the resulting decision that

[14] For a valuable critique of my argument here, see Leonard Kahn, 'Book Review: *Why Law Matters* by Alon Harel' (2016), 126 Ethics 831, 833–34.

[15] Harel, *Why Law Matters* (n 1) 4–5.

[16] For some doubts concerning this claim, see Kahn (n 14) 834f.

justifies the authoritativeness of democratic decisions.[17] I argue that the authority of constitutions can also be explained in similar terms without speculating whether constitutions or judicial review are in reality effective protectors of human rights or are conducive to democracy or any other values and, further, such an argument is more faithful to the perspectives of those who care about constitutionalism.

III. The Case for Robust Constitutionalism

This section defends the view that constitutionalism is valuable as such. Constitutionalism in this section refers to two distinct phenomena, each of which will be shown to be a necessary component for a just polity. Constitutionalism, as understood in sub-section 1, refers to a set of norms which bind the legislature (mandatory or binding constitutional directives). This set of norms can be written or unwritten, enforceable or unenforceable; it can be grounded in custom or in norms dictated by a constitutional convention. What characterizes these norms is that they guide decision-makers and, in general, are being used by the public and various institutions to evaluate the legitimacy of legislation and the legitimacy of executive orders. Constitutions, under this view, are primarily conventions or shared social understandings as to how public institutions (in particular the legislature) ought to act. On the other hand, constitutionalism as defined in sub-section 2 refers to a set of *enforceable* norms which are used by courts (or other adjudicative institutions) to evaluate the legal validity of legislation. Under this view, constitutional norms are not merely binding directives, but, in addition, they are also enforceable norms. The question of enforceability is also not merely an instrumental question. It is an embodiment of a fundamental right of citizens—the right to a hearing.

1. Constitutions as Binding Directives

The Talmud tells a story of a Gentile who missed a great business opportunity because he did not want to disturb his father by taking a key that was under his father's pillow. The gentile was rewarded by God for honouring his parents. Rabbi Ulla inferred from this story the lesson that if a Gentile, who is not commanded by God to honour his parents, was rewarded so profoundly, a Jew, who is subject to the commandment to honour his parents, would be rewarded even more for

[17] For a defence of the intrinsic value of democracy, see Forst, 'The Rule of Reasons' (n 4).

so doing. Rabbi Ulla based this conclusion on a Talmudic conviction that 'he who is commanded and fulfills [the command] is greater than he who fulfills it though not commanded.'[18] The main claim of this section is that a society in which a legislature is commanded to honour rights is superior to a society in which a legislature has discretionary powers. This is not because of the greater likelihood that the former legislature honours rights but because in the former polity citizens are not 'at the mercy of the legislature'; they do not depend upon its inclinations, and, consequently, they are freer.

There is no controversy that rights need to be effectively protected by the state. The state should design institutions that are conducive to freedom and equality. Under instrumental constitutionalism, the only concern of the state is to design institutions that are most likely to realize this end. It is precisely this conviction, the conviction that constitutionalism has no independent value, that this chapter challenges. While it is undisputable that the state ought to design institutions that are conducive to freedom, equality, and the protection of human rights, it ought not to be indifferent between different institutions, which are equally capable of achieving these ends. More specifically, constitutional directives are valuable independently of their effectiveness in protecting rights.

Constitutional directives as defined above are norms that bind the legislature. In a constitutional polity, the legislature does not merely protect rights; it is constitutionally bound to protect rights. Citizens are not subject to its preferences, judgments, or whims. Even if the legislature is a good-willed legislature and is most likely to honour individual rights, the dependence of citizens on its good will is demeaning. Precisely as it is demeaning to be a slave even if one's master does not exercise his rights of domination, so it is demeaning to be subjected to the whims of the majority even if the majority does not abuse its powers. Citizens ought to be independent of the popular will; their rights ought to be publicly recognized irrespective of what their legislature desires or believes is desirable. If, instead of being constitutionally entrenched, rights are protected by the legislature (even if effectively protected), their force hinges on the sentiments of the majority or on judgments of representatives.

This implies that constitutions matter *as such*; they matter not as means to the protection of rights; they matter as a public confirmation that the protection of rights is mandatory. A legislature that complies with binding constitutional directives is not considered to having made a free choice to comply with them; instead such a legislature does what it must do irrespective of its wishes or judgments as to what is desirable. Constitutional rights differ therefore from mere rights protected by the legislature not because the former are more

[18] See *Talmud*, Avoda Zara 3. For a discussion, see Harel, *Why Law Matters* (n 1) 147f.

stringent or less likely to be violated but because they are not being *voluntarily* given to citizens; instead, it is publicly understood that individuals are entitled to them.

A similar argument can be used to defend global constitutionalism. The appeal of an international or global human rights regime is not grounded merely in its instrumental value; in addition, it is grounded in the belief that rights ought not be 'at the mercy' of the particular polity.[19] States are obliged rather than entitled to protect human rights. International human rights protect rights that ought not to be subject to the will of the different states. The overriding power of international human rights results from the fact that they publicly convey the subordination of the state to human rights concerns and the mandatory supreme normative force of human rights.

While so far I conceptualized the value of constitutionalism in terms of dignity, it can also be conceptualized in terms of freedom, in particular, republican freedom. Both constitutional rights and international human rights are designed to protect freedom. Freedom results not only from the effective protection of rights but also from the public recognition that rights impose duties on the legislature and on the state. Constitutional rights are designed to publicly proclaim that the legislature is subject to rights-based duties, while international human rights are designed to publicly proclaim that the polity itself is subject to such duties. Freedom results not merely from the effective protection of rights but also from the fact that the protection of rights does not hinge on the will of legislators or the will of the polity. Consequently, there is a fundamental difference between constitutional polities and non-constitutional polities. Even if both polities are equally protective of rights, the constitutional polities grant citizens freedom which is not granted in non-constitutional polities. The citizens in constitutional polities do not live 'at the mercy' of their legislature. Freedom is not merely a matter of whether our rights are protected but also a matter of how they are protected. Using a republican terminology, in a non-constitutional polity, individuals are subject to 'domination', namely, to the risk of a potential arbitrary shift in the legislature's judgments or inclinations.[20] Let me illustrate.

It is not disputable of course that the state has a duty to protect individuals from violations of their basic rights to life and liberty. But does the state have a duty *to criminalize* such violations, or is it sufficient that the state prevent such violations in an effective manner, even without criminalizing the violations? Further, if there is a duty on the part of the state to criminalize violations, should

[19] See Eyal Benvenisti and Alon Harel, 'Embracing the Tension Between National and International Human Rights Law: The Case for Discordant Parity' (2017), 15 International Journal of Constitutional Law 36. See also Harel, *Why Law Matters* (n 1) 185–88.

[20] See Philip Pettit, *Republicanism: A Theory of Freedom and Government* (Clarendon Press 1997) 5.

the duty be constitutionally entrenched? Should the legislature be constitutionally required to criminalize?

As I argued in the past, this question was important in the famous decision of the German Constitutional Court concerning abortions. Among the arguments raised in this case, it was argued that the prohibition on abortion would induce desperate women to seek the assistance of greedy, unprofessional, scrupulous doctors who may encourage them to abort. If, in contrast abortion is legal, women will seek the assistance of professional, conscientious doctors and therefore will be less reluctant to abort. It does not seem preposterous to conclude that the prohibition on abortion may increase rather than decrease the number of abortions. Arguably, the Court should have concluded that it is permissible on the part of the Bundestag to eliminate the criminal prohibition on abortion. The Court rejected this conclusion. The right to life requires not merely to *protect life* (by reducing as much as possible the number of abortions or the likelihood that abortion takes place) but also to protect *the right to life* by criminalizing abortion (even when such a criminalization is not conducive as an empirical matter to the protection of life).[21]

2. Why Judicial Review Matters

Constitutional theory has been struggling for many years to justify judicial review. Typically, the justifications rest on constitutional instrumentalism. Judicial review is desirable because it is more likely to result in just decisions. The weaknesses of instrumental justification in this context are evident as there is very little empirical support for this view. It is not surprising therefore that there are numerous voices that either wish to abolish judicial review altogether or to limit or minimize its scope.[22]

An alternative view is that judicial review is an embodiment of the right to a hearing. Under this view, an individual who believes (right or wrongly) that his right is violated can demand a hearing and judicial review is merely a particular instance of a hearing. Judicial review is indispensable because it grants individuals opportunities to challenge decisions that impinge (or may have impinged)

[21] For a discussion, see Harel, *Why Law Matters* (n 1) 182–85. Needless to say that I do not assume that the German Constitutional Court was right in asserting that the fetus has a right to life and that this right overrides the right of the woman over her body.

[22] The most influential contributions include: Jeremy Waldron, *Law and Disagreement* (Oxford University Press 1999); Mark V Tushnet, *Taking the Constitution Away from the Courts* (Princeton University Press 1999); Mark V Tushnet, *Weak Courts, Strong Rights: Judicial Review and Social Welfare Rights in Comparative Constitutional Law* (Princeton University Press 2007); Larry D Kramer, *The People Themselves: Popular Constitutionalism and Judicial Review* (Oxford University Press 2004).

upon their rights, to engage in reasoned deliberation concerning these decisions, and to benefit from a reconsideration of these decisions in light of this deliberation. Under this view, judicial review is not an instrument to promote extrinsic desirable ends; instead, its value is grounded in the fact it is constitutive of the right to a hearing.[23]

As mentioned in the introduction, I see now that the right to a hearing is inextricably connected to Forst's right to justification. As a matter of fact, judicial review can be regarded as a special (strict) mode of justification—one that applies in cases in which a person believes that her rights have been violated. Such cases require a special mode of justification—one that addresses the specific grievance raised by the person. A hearing is the mode of justification that is suitable for cases which involve or at least are believed to involve violations of rights.

Forst argues that the central feature of democracy consists of:

> A political practice of argumentation and reason-giving among free and equal, citizens, a practice in which individual and collective perspectives and positions are subject to change through deliberation and in which only those norms, rules or decision that result from some form of reason-based agreements are accepted as legitimate.[24]

Forst believes that the right to justification is grounded in the status of agents; it therefore 'emancipates' those who are provided with such a right because the right to justification turns individuals into partners to the deliberation that dictates their rights and duties. Forst argues:

> The demand for justice is an emancipatory demand . . . its basis is the claim to be respected as an agent of justification, that is in one's dignity as a being who can ask for and give justifications. The victim of injustice is not primarily the person who lacks certain goods, but the one who does not 'count' in the production and distribution of goods.[25]

This implies that the good that is delivered by honouring the right of justification 'cannot be "delivered" or "received", but must be discursively and collectively

[23] The analysis is based mainly on previous papers: Harel, *Why Law Matters* (n 1) ch 6; Yuval Eylon and Alon Harel, 'The Right to Judicial Review' (2006), 92 Virginia Law Review 991; Alon Harel and Tsvi Kahana, 'The Easy Core Case for Judicial Review' (2010), 2 Journal of Legal Analysis 227. For a defence of 'modest constitutionalism', see Yossi Nehushtan, 'The Case for Modest Constitutional Instrumentalism: Book Review—*Why Law Matters* by Alon Harel' (2015), 30 Constitutional Commentary 639, 652–54.

[24] Forst, 'The Rule of Reasons' (n 4) 155.

[25] Rainer Forst, 'Introduction: The Foundation of Justice' in Rainer Forst, *The Right to Justification: Elements of a Constructivist Theory of Justice* (Jeffrey Flynn tr, Columbia University Press 2011) 2.

constituted.'[26] The beneficiary of the right to a justification is actively engaged in the exercise of this right.

The right to justification primarily serves Frost to resort to deliberative democracy. More specifically it is used by Forst to establish that deliberative democracy is not merely an instrument; it is constitutive of justice. Forst argues:

> What is finally the 'ultimate ground' of deliberative democracy? As opposed to liberal and communitarian answers, which imply that an instrumental understanding of democracy as either one possible or the only means to realize liberal principles or communal values, the ground of deliberative democracy is the basic moral right to justification which—when applied to a political context—calls for the institutionalization of forms of reciprocal and general justification. Democracy is the only appropriate . . . political expression of the basic right to justification and of mutual respect between persons.[27]

I shall argue that deliberative democracy is not sufficient and that in order to effectively protect the right to justification one ought to subject certain decisions resulting from the democratic process to adjudicative scrutiny. The right to a hearing can be conceptualized as a case in which deliberative democracy fails to deliver the good and hence the individual whose right to justification has not been honoured must be provided with an alternative route—raising his grievance in the court.

Under normal circumstances, public deliberation is sufficient to guarantee the efficacious protection of the right to justification. But there are circumstances under which public deliberation is not sufficient, and in such cases special and more stringent forms of justification are needed. To see why, assume that after thorough deliberation Parliament passed legislation which is perceived by some (rightly or wrongly) to violate their rights. The legislation has been thoroughly discussed and deliberated in the public sphere. Yet, needless to say, as thorough as public discourse in a deliberative democracy can be, not every single individual can fully exercise her right to voice her individual grievances. Further, even if the individual had such an opportunity, it is often the case that public deliberation fails to realize the urgency of the grievance of minorities. This is because public deliberation is conducted abstractly, and the force and urgency of grievances is often revealed only concretely. To address this concern, judicial review provides a special and a highly demanding right to justification—which I label 'the right to a hearing'.

[26] ibid 5.
[27] Forst, 'The Rule of Reasons' (n 4) 186.

The right to a hearing is triggered when a person believes that a right of hers was infringed unjustifiably. The right to a hearing presupposes therefore a moral controversy between the alleged right-holder and the state concerning the existence of an all things considered right.

In contrast to the right to justification as practiced in the context of public discourse, the right to a hearing has a very specific rigid structure; it consists of three components:

1. an opportunity to raise a grievance, argue for it, and provide evidence to substantiate it;
2. a duty on the part of the state to address the grievance and provide a justification for its position. This duty can be labelled a deliberative duty which is imposed on the state by the alleged right-holder; and,
3. a duty to reconsider the initial decision giving rise to the grievance. A genuine hearing requires an 'open heart', ie a principled willingness to reconsider one's decision in light of the moral deliberation.

To establish the normative force of the right to a hearing, think of the type of grievances triggered by an act which is perceived by an alleged right-holder to violate a right of his. When a right of a person is infringed, she typically raises either a substantive or a procedural grievance. The substantive complaint can take the form: 'this is my right', eg 'you promised me and you have to honour your promise'. The procedural complaint can take the form: 'you have no right to break your promise *without consulting me first*.' This latter concern rests upon the conviction that even if the act of the promisor is ultimately a justified act, it needs to be justified *to the right-holder*. The promisee should be given an opportunity to articulate his grievance and convince the promisor that the infringement is an unjustified one.

A simple example can illustrate the force of the right to a hearing. [28] Assume that A promises to meet B for lunch, but unexpected circumstances, eg a memorial, disrupts A's plans. The promisor believes that these circumstances justify overriding the promise, while the promisee does not. Even if the promisor is right, she ought to give the promisee an opportunity to convince her otherwise. Needless to say, the circumstances in the political sphere are different in many ways. Let me therefore briefly discuss two differences between the personal context and the political sphere.

The first difference rests on the opportunities that individuals have to voice their grievances in the political sphere. Arguably, while in the personal case,

[28] This example is taken from Harel, *Why Law Matters* (n 1) 205.

the promisee has no opportunity to be provided with a hearing, in the political sphere, typically the victim could have participated in the political deliberation leading to the decision which he wishes to challenge. Hence, it could be argued, that his participation in the democratic process exhausted his right to justification.

For reasons sketched earlier, I disagree. The deliberative democratic process is not sufficient to protect the right to justification. While public discourse in liberal democracies often facilitates some degree of public participatory involvement, the ability of individuals to raise their grievances, to be provided with a justification, and in particular to trigger a reconsideration of their grievance is highly constrained. The 'hearings' conducted through the democratic process are more diffused and less demanding than the hearings characterizing the adjudicative process.

The second difference is an institutional difference; in the personal case, the promisor herself engages in the hearings. In contrast, in the political sphere, it is the courts rather than the legislature that is in charge of honouring the right to a hearing. What can explain the difference?

In principle, there is no reason that *judges* or *courts* protect the right to a hearing. If the legislature itself can protect this right, it ought to do so, and, indeed, the famous 'right to petition' legislative bodies is entrenched in various legal systems. Section 44 of the Charter of the Fundamental Rights of the European Union solemnly declares: Any citizen of the Union and any natural or legal person residing or having its registered office in a Member State has the right to petition the European Parliament. The US constitution similarly protects in the First Amendment 'the right of the people . . . to petition the Government for a redress of grievances'.[29] What characterizes the right to a hearing is not the institution which is in charge of protecting (courts, legislatures, or other institutions) but the reasoning governing it. Hence, at least in principle, it is possible to reinstate legislative review instead of judicial review. Yet, irrespective of *who* protects the right to a hearing, it must be protected by using an adjudicative process. Precisely as Forst argued that deliberative democracy is not a mere means but is conceptually necessary for realizing the right to a justification, so I shall argue that the adjudicative process is not a mere contingent means to protect the right to a hearing. In fact, the adjudicative process *constitutes* a hearing and it is therefore required by a just constitution. There is a special affinity

[29] For a discussion of the right to petition, see James E Pfander, 'Sovereign Immunity and the Right to Petition: Toward a First Amendment Right to Pursue Judicial Claims against the Government' (1997), 91 Northwestern University Law Review 899; Gary Lawson and Guy Seidman, 'Downsizing the Right to Petition' (1999), 93 Northwestern University Law Review 739.

between adjudication and the right to a hearing, such that adjudication is tantamount to protecting the right to a hearing.

To establish it, think about the way courts operate. Courts are designed to investigate individual grievances.[30] The judicial way of assessing individual grievances consists of three components analogous to the ones characterizing the right to a hearing. First, the adjudicative process grants litigators an opportunity to raise their grievances and demand a remedy. Second, it imposes a duty on the part of others to provide a reasoned justification. It imposes deliberative duties on the shoulders of the person or entity which is charged with the violation of a right. Third, courts are obliged to reconsider the decision giving rise to the dispute. The adjudicative process is not a means to an end (the end being protecting the right to a hearing); it is in fact the end itself.

The very same point can be demonstrated by thinking about two types of failures on the part of the courts. Some failures, such as a failure to do justice, do not undermine the status of courts. Judges are fallible, and they may fail to identify what our rights are. But a failure on the part of courts to adjudicate is not a failure *of courts* but a failure *to be a court*. Given the conceptual relation between adjudication and the right to a hearing, it follows that courts are in essence mechanisms to facilitate the exercise of the right to a hearing.

This description is sufficient to establish that the right to a hearing requires adjudicative procedures, but it tells us nothing of the identity of the institutions in charge of performing this task. Whatever institution performs the hearing, it would operate like a court and effectively become a court if it assigned with the task of realizing the right to a hearing. The institution conducting a hearing necessarily operates in a court-like manner and effectively becomes a court. After all, 'if it walks like a duck, quacks like a duck, looks like a duck, it must be a duck.' Similarly, if it provides an opportunity to raise grievances, examines these grievances, and reconsiders the decision giving rise to the grievance, it is nothing but a court irrespective of what its title is. This implies that a tax agency can also in principle be adjudicative. It may be, of course, that administrators as a contingent matter fail to adjudicate fairly, but there is nothing in principle that precludes them from adjudicating.

30 See, eg Alexander Bickel, *The Least Dangerous Brach* (The Bobbs-Merrill Co. 1962) 173; Donald L Horowitz, 'The Judiciary: Umpire or Empire?' (1982), 6 Law and Human Behavior 129, 131; Richard H Fallon Jr, 'Reflections on Hart and Wechsler Paradigm' (1994), 47 Vanderbilt Law Review 953, 958.

IV. Conclusion

This chapter criticizes instrumentalism in constitutional theory and provides a new robust justification to two features of constitutionalism: binding constitutional directives and judicial review (which is nothing but a form of justification). I established why binding constitutional directives matter as such (rather than merely as means for protecting rights or promoting justice). It is only binding constitutional directives which constitute publicly recognized limitations on the powers of the legislature. In the absence of such directives, the legislature's decision not to violate rights is publicly understood to be contingent on the legislature's judgments (or inclinations). I also defended judicial review on the grounds that judicial review is an embodiment of the right to a hearing. Judicial review is not grounded in contingent institutional features; instead, it is grounded in the the right to raise a grievance. This account establishes that what ultimately judicial review is about is not courts or judges but the adjudicative process as such.

Robust constitutionalism contributes to the leveling of the playing field in constitutional theory. Advocates of instrumentalist constitutionalism fight with one hand tied behind their back because they maintain that constitutionalism is valuable only because of its contingent desirable outcomes. While democracy has intrinsic value, constitutionalism is merely instrumental. Hence, principled or legitimacy-based considerations are perceived to be the enemies of constitutionalism. Robust constitutionalism remedies this defect; it establishes that legitimacy requires rather precludes the possibility of constitutionalism.

The potential ambition of this chapter is not merely to challenge instrumentalist constitutionalism but to illustrate how instrumentalism can and should be challenged more generally. The proposed methodology urges legal theorists to abandon instrumentalism and to ground legal and political institutions and procedures in non-instrumental considerations. It is often the case that the real justification for legal and political institutions is not contingent and does not hinge on the contingent prospects that these institutions are conducive to the realization of valuable ends. Instead, various legal institutions and legal procedures that are perceived as contingent means to facilitate the realization of valuable ends matter as such.

References

Aquinas T, *Summa Theologica* (Fathers of the English Dominican Province trs, Christian Classics 1981).

Benvenisti E and Harel A, 'Embracing the Tension Between National and International Human Rights Law: The Case for Discordant Parity' (2017), 15 International Journal of Constitutional Law 36.

Bickel A, *The Least Dangerous Brach* (The Bobbs-Merrill Co. 1962).
Dworkin R, *Freedom's Law: The Moral Reading of the American Constitution* (Harvard University Press 1996).
Ely JH, *Democracy and Distrust: A Theory of Judicial Review* (Harvard University Press 1981).
Eylon Y and Harel A, 'The Right to Judicial Review' (2006), 92 Virginia Law Review 991.
Fallon Jr RH, 'Reflections on Hart and Wechsler Paradigm' (1994), 47 Vanderbilt Law Review 953.
Forst R, 'Introduction: The Foundation of Justice' in Rainer Forst, *The Right to Justification: Elements of a Constructivist Theory of Justice* (Jeffrey Flynn tr, Columbia University Press 2011).
Forst R, 'The Rule of Reasons: Three Models of Deliberative Democracy' in Rainer Forst, *The Right to Justification: Elements of a Constructivist Theory of Justice* (Jeffrey Flynn tr, Columbia University Press 2011).
Harel A, 'Rights-Based Judicial Review: A Democratic Justification' (2003), 22 Law & Philosophy 247.
Harel A, *Why Law Matters* (Oxford University Press 2014).
Harel A and Kahana T, 'The Easy Core Case for Judicial Review' (2010), 2 Journal of Legal Analysis 227.
Horowitz DL, 'The Judiciary: Umpire or Empire?' (1982), 6 Law and Human Behavior 129.
Kahn L, 'Book Review: *Why Law Matters* by Alon Harel' (2016), 126 Ethics 831.
Kelsen H, *General Theory of Law and State* (Anders Wedberg tr, Harvard University Press 1949).
Kramer LD, *The People Themselves: Popular Constitutionalism and Judicial Review* (Oxford University Press 2004).
Lawson G and Seidman G, 'Downsizing the Right to Petition' (1999), 93 Northwestern University Law Review 739.
Nehushtan Y, 'The Case for Modest Constitutional Instrumentalism: Book Review—Why Law Matters by Alon Harel' (2015), 30 Constitutional Commentary 639.
Pettit P, *Republicanism: A Theory of Freedom and Government* (Clarendon Press 1997).
Pfander JE, 'Sovereign Immunity and the Right to Petition: Toward a First Amendment Right to Pursue Judicial Claims against the Government' (1997), 91 Northwestern University Law Review 899.
Rabban DM, *Free Speech in Its Forgotten Years* (Cambridge University Press 1997).
Sadurski W, 'Reason of State and Public Reason' (2014), 27 Ratio Juris 21.
Schauer F and Alexander L, 'On Extrajudicial Constitutional Interpretation' (1997), 110 Harvard Law Review 1359.
Tushnet MV, *Taking the Constitution Away from the Courts* (Princeton University Press 1999).
Tushnet MV, *Weak Courts, Strong Rights: Judicial Review and Social Welfare Rights in Comparative Constitutional Law* (Princeton University Press 2007).
Waldron J, *Law and Disagreement* (Oxford University Press 1999).

11

Democracy as Good in Itself

Three Kinds of Non-Instrumental Justification

Christian F. Rostbøll

I. Introduction

'If the cultivation of the understanding consists in one thing more than in another, it is surely in learning the grounds of one's own opinions', J.S. Mill wrote.[1] A widespread opinion is that political legitimacy requires democracy. What are the grounds of this belief? My aim of exploring the justification of democracy is not only to cultivate the understanding but also to supply a critical standard for assessing our political and social institutions. What kind of justification of democracy we can provide matters for what model of democracy we should adopt, as well as for what we properly regard as the social preconditions of democracy. Thus, the question concerning the justification of democracy has both intellectual interest and practical consequences.

Some political theorists insist that democracy is the right form of government not merely because of its superior consequences but because democracy is good in itself. But what exactly do we mean when we say that democracy is 'good in itself'? What is implied by the notion of a non-instrumental justification of democracy? And is it tenable to say that democracy is non-instrumentally good?

There are two common ways of understanding the idea that democracy is good in itself. First, there is the idea that democracy is constitutively connected to the good and truly human life. Second, there is the idea that democracy is part of the egalitarian relationships that are demanded by justice. I argue that the first view is right to focus on the constitutive value of democracy but that it is wrong to regard the fulfilling human life as the feature, which explains democracy's non-instrumental value. The second view, by contrast, is right to focus on the egalitarian relationships of democracy, but it is wrong to regard democracy as merely expressing a norm that is defined independently of any reference to democracy. I therefore propose a third kind of non-instrumental justification of

[1] John S Mill, 'On Liberty' in John Stuart Mill, *On Liberty and Other Essays* (John Gray ed, Oxford University Press 1991) 41.

Christian F. Rostbøll, *Democracy as Good in Itself: Three Kinds of Non-Instrumental Justification* In: *Constitutionalism Justified: Rainer Forst in Discourse.* Edited by: Ester Herlin-Karnell and Matthias Klatt, Oxford University Press (2020),
DOI: 10.1093/oso/9780190889050.003.0011

democracy, which includes what the other two get right and avoids what they get wrong. Thus, it includes the notion of the constitutive value of democracy and the norm of egalitarian relationships, and it avoids a sectarian idea of the good life and the idea that we can reduce the value of democracy to a norm given independently of the idea of democracy itself. Thus, my proposed non-instrumental justification of democracy regards relationships of equal freedom as the norm which justifies democracy, while it understands the meaning of this norm as constituted—created and made conceivable—by democracy itself, and not as specified in a more fundamental or prior theory of justice.

My argument is that we can only understand why democracy is good in itself, rather than merely instrumentally good, if we acknowledge that it *creates* something morally good, which cannot be fully conceived independently of the idea—the principles and institutions—of democracy itself. And we can only understand that democracy is not merely good to have but obligatory, if its justification does not rely on a conception of the good that it is not unreasonable to reject but on relationships between persons that they ought to have. Moreover, the type of egalitarian relationship that is constituted by democracy is of a specific kind, the meaning and value of which are fully intelligible only in conjunction with the idea of constitutional democracy itself. They are relationships in which every member enjoys a status of independence and co-ruler. The reason why democracy cannot be understood and justified with reference to a norm specified in a prior theory of justice is that this approach fails to take fully into account the political-institutional character of the relationships created by constitutional democracy and the unique nature and non-instrumental value of these.

I shall refer to my preferred account of why we should regard democracy as good in itself as *Kantian non-instrumentalism*, for reasons that will be explained later. I contrast this kind of democratic non-instrumentalism with two other kinds, which I for convenience label *Aristotelian non-instrumentalism*, because it justifies democracy with reference to the idea that it realizes distinctive human capacities, and *justice-first non-instrumentalism*, because it justifies democracy on the basis of a norm that is specified in a theory of justice that is developed independently of the idea of democracy.

My discussion of what counts as a sound justification of democracy is guided by six requirements. First, the justification must recognize and accommodate the fact that citizens of modern societies are committed to different conceptions of the good. I shall refer to this as a requirement of *non-sectarianism*. Second, it must be able to explain standard democratic procedures and institutions, such as the equal vote, the right to run for office, the right to participate in public deliberation, and so on. This is a requirement of *fidelity*. Third, the justification of democracy must be *independent and direct*. On the one hand, the justification must not be analytical or tautological, as if one were to say that democracy is good because it is democratic. On the other hand, there must be a clear and direct connection between the norm that justifies democracy and democratic procedures. Fourth, the justification must be *robust* in the sense of not being dependent on variable circumstances. It does not have to be logically necessary or to hold under all circumstances, but it should be robust in the sense that it applies under most circumstances. Fifth, a justification of democracy must show that democracy is not just good to have but is *obligatory*. It is not sufficient to show that democracy has some valuable features; it must be shown that these are sufficient to explain the authority and legitimacy of democracy. A justification of democracy of the right kind must be able to explain why democratic decision-making is morally binding (authoritative) and permissible to implement (legitimate).[2] Finally, a justification of democracy must cultivate our understanding of democracy in a way that creates a critical perspective on current institutions and practices. That is, it must be able to explain what democracy is (which principles and institutions are democratic and which are not) and supply a critical standard that provides guidance for assessing the democratic legitimacy of our institutions and their social preconditions. This is a requirement of *providing understanding and critical perspective*.

The chapter begins with an investigation of political-legal instrumentalism in general and democratic instrumentalism in particular. This serves as a general foil for non-instrumental accounts of politics, law, and democracy. I also suggest some general drawbacks of political instrumentalism. This is followed by three sections, each of which presents and discusses the three kinds of democratic non-instrumentalism. The argument here proceeds progressively, in the sense that objections to the first kind of justification (Aristotelian non-instrumentalism) lead to the second kind (justice-first non-instrumentalism), and similarly with the transition from the second to the third kind of non-instrumentalism (Kantian non-instrumentalism). I add an extra section on Kantian non-instrumentalism, since this justification of democracy is the main contribution of the chapter. I argue that the Kantian justification is a justification of a specific form of democracy, namely, constitutional democracy. In the proposed Kantian account, democracy is a *constitutional form*, and it is this constitution that creates the right kind of relationship among citizens and government.

[2] On the concepts legitimacy and authority, see David M Estlund, *Democratic Authority: A Philosophical Framework* (Princeton University Press 2008) 2; Rainer Forst, 'Legitimacy, Democracy, and Justice: On the Reflexivity of Normative Orders' in Rainer Forst, *Normativity and Power: Analyzing Social Orders of Justification* (Ciaran Cronin tr, Oxford University Press 2017) 132f; Niko Kolodny, 'Rule Over None I: What Justifies Democracy?' (2014), 42 Philosophy & Public Affairs 195, 197, and 202; Philip Pettit, *On the People's Terms: A Republican Theory and Model of Democracy* (Cambridge University Press 2012) 137f, 140.

II. The Limits of Political-Legal Instrumentalism

Non-instrumental justifications of democracy share a rejection of *purely* instrumental arguments for democracy. They do not necessarily reject that democracy has instrumental value or can be justified partly because of its good consequences, but they all share the view that democracy also has a moral significance that cannot be accounted for merely by appealing to its external consequences.

The instrumental justification of democracy—'democratic instrumentalism'—holds, first, that the form of government that ought to be instituted is the one with the best consequences, and, second, that democracy is the form of government with the best consequences.[3] Thus, on the instrumental justification, the end that justifies democracy can be fully defined and understood, independently of the idea (principles and institutions) of democracy. Democracy is, in this view, a mere means and of secondary importance to a more fundamental end, such as fundamental (not democratic) rights or social justice. If democracy proves not to be the best feasible means for the required end, it lacks (sufficient) justification, according to the instrumentalist view.

We can see democratic instrumentalism as an instance of a more general idea of instrumentalism regarding law, government, and politics, or, for short, of *political-legal instrumentalism*. This instrumentalism perceives political and legal institutions as contingent means for the realization of valuable ends. Moreover, the ends of politics and law can be described in independent terms, that is, without any reference to the institutions that are the means to their realization. In the tradition of legal philosophy, we find such a form of instrumentalism both in the natural law theory of Thomas Aquinas and in the legal positivism of, for example, Jeremy Bentham and Hans Kelsen.[4] There are, of course, differences between different versions of political-legal instrumentalism, among other things, in terms of what contingent or empirical obstacles law is supposed to overcome (eg man's sinful nature, weakness of will) and which ends it promotes (human happiness, predictability, justice, etc.). But instrumentalists share the view that the values that law and government exist to promote are pre-existing or fully intelligible independently of law and politics themselves.

Non-instrumentalists (especially those of a Kantian bend) regard it as a fatal flaw of political-legal instrumentalism that the justification that it can provide is

[3] Richard J Arneson, 'The Supposed Right to a Democratic Say' in Thomas Christiano and John P Christman (eds), *Contemporary Debates in Political Philosophy* (Wiley-Blackwell 2009) 197; Steven Wall, 'Democracy and Equality' (2007), 57 The Philosophical Quarterly 416.

[4] See Alon Harel, *Why Law Matters* (Oxford University Press 2014), and Arthur Ripstein, *Force and Freedom: Kant's Legal and Political Philosophy* (Harvard University Press 2009), who both describe this legal instrumentalism and advance non-instrumental alternatives.

contingent on certain empirical factors holding true. Instrumental arguments are only as strong as the contingent causal relationships that they rely on. In this way, instrumental arguments can be said to lack robustness. This point, however, does not bite democratic instrumentalists who, exactly, are committed to the idea that democracy cannot be given such a robust justification. Democratic instrumentalism is the idea that democracy is only justified contingently. This is a coherent position, even if others might want to explore the prospects of giving a more robust justification of democracy (as I do).

What is more disconcerting is the idea that 'one can favour democracy while rejecting political equality [which] is the position recommended by democratic instrumentalism'.[5] I assume that what is meant here is that one can reject that political equality has fundamental value and still favour democracy for instrumental reasons. Thus, democratic instrumentalists 'are prepared to recommend politically inegalitarian institutions if it can be shown that they yield better political outcomes over time'.[6] However, the fact that democratic instrumentalists reject political equality, which is a defining characteristic of democracy on most accounts, raises the question whether it is a justification of democracy at all.

The limitation of democratic instrumentalism is that it cannot explain by itself which principles and institutions count as democratic and which do not. The good, but contingent, consequences that justify democracy on the instrumental account—fundamental rights and social justice—can perhaps tell us which kind of government to establish, but they cannot tell us whether or how democratic the recommended institutions are. For the latter, it is parasitic on another account of democracy that can explain which procedures and principles are democratic and which are not.[7] In this way, democratic instrumentalism fails not only to explain standard democratic procedures; it also cannot contribute to discussions of the democratic pedigree of more controversial institutions and practices (electoral systems, judicial review, etc.). To be sure, proponents of the instrumental approach can say that we should choose the institutions with the best consequences, but this says nothing about how democratic these institutions are or if they are democratic at all.[8] The fundamental problem, then, is that the instrumentalist justification of democracy fails to cultivate our understanding of

5 Wall, 'Democracy and Equality' (n 3) 436.

6 ibid 416.

7 Christian F Rostbøll, 'Democratic Respect and Compromise' (2017), 20 Critical Review of International Social and Political Philosophy 619.

8 Joshua Cohen suggests that while non-instrumental reasons can supply a rationale for democracy, instrumental concerns can tell which kind of democracy to select. Joshua Cohen, 'For a Democratic Society' in Joshua Cohen, *The Arc of the Moral Universe and Other Essays* (Harvard University Press 2010) 189f. However, I don't think we can separate the rationale for democracy and the kind of democracy to select so easily. Our justification for democracy will and should also say something about what is the right kind of democracy.

that which we believe to be legitimate, because it only has eyes for considerations of its external consequences.

According to the instrumentalist view, the better the outcomes of a form of government the more legitimate it is. This view presupposes agreement on outcome standards that determine how legitimate a form of government is. In other words, in so far as democratic instrumentalists favour democracy over other forms of government only when the former realizes a certain ideal of social justice better than any feasible alternative, this justification of democracy is dependent on agreement on a specific view of social justice. This is a serious drawback if we think that a justification of democracy must accommodate reasonable disagreement. If reasonable people disagree on what is the right theory of distribute justice, we should not ground democracy in its ability to promote a certain, controversial view of outcome justice.[9] The idea of justifying democracy with reference to a theory of distributive justice would also depart in problematic ways from the reason why democratic citizens commonly view democratic decisions as legitimate. Most democratic citizens do not view democratic decisions as legitimate because they are substantively right, I think, but rather because of the way, they were made and because of the standing, they afford citizens.

Another feature of democratic instrumentalism is that it does not claim that democratic decisions in each instance have better outcomes than non-democratic decisions. The idea is that democratic decision-making 'yield better political outcomes over time'.[10] But if it isn't each decision but only the long-term application of democratic procedures that has good consequences, we have a problem in explaining the bindingness of particular decisions. Why should I regard a decision as legitimate and authoritative, if not this decision but only the long term consequences of democratic decision-making are good?[11] Thus, the instrumental justification fails also to meet the obligatoriness requirement of a justification of democracy.

From this review of democratic instrumentalism, we can understand the impetus for going beyond instrumentalism and exploring the prospects of a non-instrumental justification of democracy. First, if we want to find a robust justification of democracy, we must go beyond purely instrumental justifications and consider if democracy can be given a less contingent justification. If democracy can be shown to be good in itself, we have found such a robust justification.[12]

[9] cf Fabienne Peter, *Democratic Legitimacy* (Routledge 2009) 62–64.

[10] Wall, 'Democracy and Equality' (n 3) 416.

[11] See Kolodny, 'Rúle Over None I: What Justifies Democracy?' (n 2) 201f; Niko Kolodny, 'Rule Over None II: Social Equality and the Justification of Democracy' (2014), 42 Philosophy & Public Affairs 287, 314f, on this bridging problem.

[12] However, I don't claim that we can find an unconditional justification of democracy, that is, a justification that applies at any time and place, without any empirical conditions. What I aim to arrive at is a non-instrumental but conditional justification of democracy.

Second, we must go beyond democratic instrumentalism if we are to explain standard democratic principles and procedures, as well as to explain why they (and which of them) are truly democratic. Third, instrumentalism is insufficient to explain the authority and legitimacy of democratic decisions. This is the case both because the justification is contingent on democracy's actually producing valuable outcomes and because it is unclear why one is bound by each single democratic decision, when the alleged good effects are only products of democratic decision-making over the long run or as a rule.

To be sure, democratic non-instrumentalists are not only driven by the failures of instrumentalism just mentioned. We are also driven by the intuition that if democracy is lost, more than the good consequences are lost.[13] That is, the three kinds of non-instrumentalism that I review later share a commitment to the idea that the good of democracy is integral to democratic institutions and not merely an external consequence of them.

III. Aristotelian Non-Instrumentalism

When we say that democracy is 'good in itself', perhaps the first idea that springs to mind is the idea that democracy is good because it involves an activity that is indispensable to a good life. And this, indeed, is the idea of the first kind of democratic non-instrumentalism. Or, to be more precise, the idea here is not just that democracy's goodness stems from the joy that it affords people, but that democratic participation is of *fundamental, primary, and objective* importance to human happiness or a fulfilling human life. Many activities are enjoyable, but the first non-instrumental justification of democracy is committed to the idea that democratic participation is especially important, necessary for, and constitutive of the good life. I call this justification 'Aristotelian non-instrumentalism', because it relies on three Aristotelian ideas: first, that the good of a thing depends on the nature of that thing. Second, that the good of a living being is to be able to exercise its natural, highest, and distinctive capacities. Third, that human beings, as by nature political animals, realize their natural and highest capacities through political participation.[14] This justification is perfectionist, because it is based on

[13] Emanuela Ceva and Valeria Ottonelli, 'Rescuing Democracy from Reductivism', unpublished manuscript.

[14] For a recent Aristotelian defence of democracy as good in itself, see Josiah Ober, 'Natural Capacities and Democracy as a Good-in-Itself' (2007), 132 Philosophical Studies 59. For an overview, see Will Kymlicka, *Contemporary Political Philosophy: An Introduction* (2nd edn, Oxford University Press 2002) 294–99.

an idea of what perfects our nature as human beings: we become what we are supposed to become through participating in common decision-making.[15]

There are different versions of this kind of non-instrumental justification. We find it, to mention some prominent examples, in J.S. Mill's idea that democracy provides individuals with the opportunity to exercise their highest intellectual and moral capacities,[16] and in Hannah Arendt's notion of political action as a form of public happiness.[17] Among contemporary political philosophers, Elizabeth Anderson has advanced the idea that democratic participation is a constitutive part of a good life.[18] There are important differences among these theorists, but they are sufficiently similar to classify them under one label.

One objection to this first kind of non-instrumental justification of democracy is that the happiness involved in participation is an essential by-product, that is, the value of participation is dependent on and evaporates without the instrumental value of participation.[19] However, this objection is only relevant if the idea were that the non-instrumental value of participation was independent of democracy having also instrumental value. There might be tendencies to such a view in Arendt,[20] but the Aristotelian justification could be amended, without difficulty, to the idea that the non-instrumental value of democracy is conditional on its instrumental value. Indeed, this is the view of Anderson, who writes, 'The proper test of the noninstrumental goodness of an activity is not whether we'd prefer to do it, even if it didn't result in desirable consequences. It is rather whether we'd still prefer to engage in it, even if the same consequences could be brought about by other (passive) means'.[21] Thus, I don't think this objection is damaging to the first kind of non-instrumental justification of democracy, as long as it recognizes that the non-instrumental value of democracy is not unconditional. However, Anderson's talk of 'desirable consequences' has the drawback of making her justification of democracy dependent on agreement on substantive outcome standards and, thereby, she loses an alleged advantage

[15] On perfectionism, see Kymlicka (n 14) 190, 294f; Steven Wall, 'Perfectionism in Politics: A Defense' in Thomas Christiano and John P Christman (eds), *Contemporary Debates in Political Philosophy* (Wiley-Blackwell 2009) 99–117.

[16] John S Mill, 'Considerations on Representative Government' in John Stuart Mill, *On Liberty and Other Essays* (John Gray ed, Oxford University Press 1991) ch 3.

[17] Hannah Arendt, *On Revolution* (Penguin Books 1990) 119, 221, 255. See also Hannah Arendt, *The Human Condition* (2nd edn, University of Chicago Press 1998) ch V.

[18] Elizabeth S Anderson, 'Democracy: Instrumental vs. Non-Instrumental Value' in Thomas Christiano and John P Christman (eds), *Contemporary Debates in Political Philosophy* (Wiley-Blackwell 2009) 213–27.

[19] Jon Elster, 'The Market and the Forum: Three Varieties of Political Theory' in James Bohman and William Rehg (eds), *Deliberative Democracy: Essays on Reason and Politics* (MIT Press 1997) 19–26.

[20] But see Christian F Rostbøll, 'Statelessness, Domination, and Unfreedom: Arendt and Pettit in Dialogue' in Christian Dahl and Tue A Nexø (eds), *To Be Unfree: Republicanism and Unfreedom in History, Literature, and Philosophy* (Transcript Verlag 2014).

[21] Anderson (n 18) 225.

of non-instrumental over instrumental arguments for democracy, namely, that only the former are independent of agreement on what counts as good and just outcomes.

The second objection to the Aristotelian justification of democracy is that not everyone finds political participation a constituent part of the good life, and that there is nothing unreasonable in this. Many people find more fulfilment in their work and their private lives than they do in politics, without for this reason being unreasonable. One might have a moral obligation to participate in the common life of the community and one might be blamed for not doing so, but this is a different issue than whether it is unreasonable not to find political participation fulfilling. And the Aristotelian justification depends on the latter. If the Aristotelian justification cannot establish that everyone does (or ought to) find fulfilment in democratic politics, its explanation for why one ought to have the opportunity to partake in politics lacks a foundation. Thus, Aristotelian non-instrumentalism is sectarian and does not meet the first requirement of a justification of democracy.

Here, it might be replied that some people find fulfilment in political activity, and that they should have the same opportunity for pursuing their happiness as others have an opportunity to pursue theirs. The trouble with this idea is that political activity is importantly different from other activities that can be part of a conception of a good and fulfilling life. My opportunity for engaging in democratic politics demands something of my fellow citizens that other, private, activities do not. In order for me to have the opportunity to engage in democratic politics, my fellow citizens must 'lend themselves' to this activity as co-legislators and as subject to the resulting decisions.[22] If we cannot show that everyone shares my end, I will treat my fellow citizens as mere means to my end. Thus, we are still in violation of the requirement that a justification of democracy must be respectful of citizens' diverse conceptions of the good.

Even more critically, it is unclear whether Aristotelian non-instrumentalism can explain the core democratic norm of political equality. For the Aristotelian, what is a constituent element of *eudaimonia* is to use the distinctive human capacity to speak, deliberate, and decide in common with others about public affairs.[23] It seems that this interest in being able to use one's highest capacities does not require opportunity for *equal* influence, which is a core norm of the democratic ideal.[24] Mill, for example, with his plural voting scheme, clearly thinks that it is sufficient for exercising one's deliberative capacities that one has some opportunity for political influence, and not that the opportunity for influence be

[22] Kolodny, 'Rule Over None I: What Justifies Democracy?' (n 2) 216f.

[23] Ober (n 14) 60. For Arendt, 'expressing, discussing, and deciding' are 'in a positive sense . . . the activities of freedom', while having one's interests represented through voting is not. Arendt, *On Revolution* (n 17) 235, 268f.

[24] Kolodny, 'Rule Over None I: What Justifies Democracy?' (n 2) 213, 215.

equal.[25] Similarly, in Arendt, the opportunity for political participation is more important than any ideal of political equality.[26] Thus, Aristotelians fail the second requirement of a justification of democracy, namely, that it be able to explain standard democratic procedures and institutions. Now, this requirement should not be understood in a conservative spirit, as if a justification of democracy cannot be critical of nominally democratic institutions. Rather, the requirement is that a justification of democracy should be able to explain procedures that we can recognize as democratic. There might be a broad range of such procedures, but procedures that fail to provide all citizens equal opportunity for political influence are clearly not among them.

I would like to draw two main conclusions from the assessment of the prospects of an Aristotelian non-instrumental justification of democracy. First, it is unclear that this justification can explain the authority and legitimacy of democracy. Even if it could be shown that political participation were a valuable activity in itself, it is unclear that this is sufficient to show that we are morally bound to obey democratic decisions and that they are legitimate to implement. We must distinguish between an account that can show that democracy has some valuable inherent features and an account that can show that democracy is obligatory and legitimate. I think a justification of democracy must be of the latter kind. Moreover, the problem of authority and legitimacy is exacerbated by the fact of reasonable disagreement. How can I be morally bound by a political procedure that is justified on the basis of a good that I do not share, and that I am not unreasonable to reject? How can it be legitimate to make me part of an activity and subject to its results simply for the sake of that others can fulfil their conception of the good life? Second, Aristotelian non-instrumentalism fails to explain standard democratic norms and procedures such as equal opportunity for influence and the equal vote. As such, it fails to show fidelity to our common understanding of democracy. In short, it is unclear that it qualifies as a justification of democracy at all. Therefore, I now turn to a second kind of democratic non-instrumentalism, which does better on these two counts than the Aristotelian one.

IV. Justice-First Non-Instrumentalism

The second kind of non-instrumental justification of democracy begins with some important value or norm that is part of an independently conceived theory

[25] Mill, 'Considerations on Representative Government' (n 16) 333–41.

[26] Arendt, *On Revolution* (n 17) 279f. Anderson's approach, by contrast, does have a special concern with equality.

of justice and then proceeds, in a second and separate step, to show how this value or norm is expressed by or is part of democracy. The grounding value or norm in this justification stems from an *independently conceived theory of justice* in the sense that this value or norm can be and is fully described independently of any reference to the idea or institutions of democracy.[27] I call this kind of justification of democracy for 'justice-first non-instrumentalism', because it begins with a theory of justice and assesses the value of democracy in light of this theory.[28] It might be thought that this is the natural structure of justification in political philosophy—that is, that we need an independently conceived norm that can ground or justify what we aim to justify—but as we proceed, especially to the discussion of the third kind of justification, it should become clear that this isn't the case.

Sometimes, the very explanation of what an intrinsic theory of democracy is presupposes the justice-first structure of justification. Thus, in a recent article, Laura Valentini explains an intrinsic justification of democracy as one that regards democracy as *a requirement of justice*. That is, 'on the *intrinsic account*, democracy is seen as a demand of justice itself', and lack of democracy 'would undermine the very ideal of equal respect on which justice is based'.[29] This might sound unremarkable, but in fact, it presupposes a quite specific notion of what a non-instrumental justification of democracy amounts to. It is taken for granted that we must begin from a fully defined norm, here the ideal of equal respect, and that the only difference between instrumentalists and non-instrumentalists is that the former regards democracy as only instrumental to the realization of this norm, while democratic non-instrumentalists hold that the norm of equal respect non-incidentally requires democratic procedures.

We find the same justice-first structure of justification in the work of Rainer Forst, who claims to give a non-instrumental justification of democracy.[30] In Forst, 'the moral right to justification' is given prior to and defined independently of any reference to political-legal institutions.[31] For him, any other form of

27 Christian F Rostbøll, 'The Non-instrumental Value of Democracy: The Freedom Argument' (2015), 22 Constellations 267, 270f.

28 There is some similarity between this description of the justice-first approach and the critical reference to 'ethics-first' approaches found in the political realism of Bernard Williams and Raymond Geuss, but my purposes are different. See Christian F Rostbøll, 'Kant and the Critique of the Ethics-First Approach to Politics' [2019] 22 Critical Review of International Social and Political Philosophy 55.

29 Laura Valentini, 'Justice, Disagreement and Democracy' (2013), 43 British Journal of Political Science 177, 181. See also Christopher Griffin, 'Debate: Democracy as a Non-instrumentally Just Procedure' (2003), 11 The Journal of Political Philosophy 111.

30 Rainer Forst, 'The Rule of Reasons: Three Models of Deliberative Democracy' in Rainer Forst, *The Right to Justification: Elements of a Constructivist Theory of Justice* (Jeffrey Flynn tr, Columbia University Press 2011) 163, 172, 186f.

31 Rainer Forst, 'The Justification of Human Rights and the Basic Right to Justification: A Reflexive Approach' in Rainer Forst, *Justification and Critique: Towards a Critical Theory of Politics* (Ciaran Cronin tr, Polity Press 2013) 39.

justification would be 'to put the cart before the horse'.[32] Accordingly, democracy is 'the *political form of justice*',[33] but there is no suggestion of a special or additional value that is constituted and created by democracy itself and not fully conceivable from the point of view of a prior theory of justice.[34]

Some justice-first accounts of the non-instrumental value of democracy are expressivist theories. They begin from a fundamental norm, and then go on to suggest that democratic procedures are valuable because they *express* this norm, for example, that they express respect for the intrinsic equality of persons. In this view, democracy is justified because it expresses something that we know to be of moral importance from a more fundamental, and independently conceived, theory of justice. Conversely, non-democratic regimes lack justification, because they fail to express the proper norm and thus insult citizens.[35]

Many current non-instrumental accounts of democracy are disagreement theories. These theories begin with the fact that people disagree on the justice of outcomes and argue that this is the reason why democracy must be defended non-instrumentally.[36] We cannot defend democracy because of its good outcomes, if we disagree on standards for judging good outcomes. The problem of disagreement does not touch on the justice of democratic procedures, in this view, because democratic procedures are tailored to the fact that people will disagree on the substance of justice.[37] It might seem misleading to call this approach a form of justice-first non-instrumentalism, if it is based on the fact that citizens disagree on justice. However, if we consider one of the most prominent versions of the argument, that of Thomas Christiano, it quite clearly takes outset and is grounded in a theory of justice. Indeed, his defence of the intrinsic value of democracy is based on 'the principle that well-being ought to be distributed equally by the institutions of society'.[38] Indeed, Christiano's justification of democracy relies on democracy's ability to promote the justice-based aim of equal advancement of interests.[39]

[32] ibid 54.

[33] Forst, 'Legitimacy, Democracy, and Justice' (n 2) 135.

[34] cf Ceva and Ottonelli, 'Recusing Democracy from Reductionism' (n 13).

[35] Thomas Christiano, 'Disagreement and the Justification of Democracy' in Steven Wall (ed), *The Cambridge Companion to Liberalism* (Cambridge University Press 2015) 258; Griffin (n 29) 119f.

[36] Thomas Christiano, *The Constitution of Equality: Democratic Authority and Its Limits* (Oxford University Press 2008); Valentini (n 29); Jeremy Waldron, *Law and Disagreement* (Oxford University Press 1999).

[37] Christiano, *The Constitution of Equality* (n 36) 95f, 101f.

[38] ibid 25.

[39] In a recent piece, Christiano responds to the charge that his justification of democracy is not intrinsic but indirectly instrumentalist. Christiano, 'Disagreement and the Justification of Democracy' (n 35) 255–58. However, I don't think his response shows that his justification of democracy is not a justice-first approach in the way I understand it. Thus, he still grounds the value of democracy in some basic principles of social justice that are prior to the idea of democracy itself (at 239, 250, 252). Yet, there are aspects to Christiano's theory that are less squarely justice-first, for example when he argues that the public standpoint of democracy is non-reducible to non-democratic standpoints (at

Compared to the Aristotelian non-instrumental justification of democracy, the justice-first approach *seems* to have three advantages: (1) It begins from disagreement and thus shows respect for diversity. Hence, it is not a sectarian justification that must explain why one must subject oneself to institutions that are justified with reference to a doctrine of the good one rejects. (2) It shows fidelity to democratic norms and institutions, that is, it is based on a fundamental commitment to equality, which can explain standard democratic procedures. (3) Its grounding in norms of public equality and equal respect are plausible candidates for explaining the authority and legitimacy of democracy. In short, what the second non-instrumental justification gets right is its focus on the egalitarian relationships among citizens in democracy. However, I am unconvinced about the non-instrumental credentials of this justification and whether it provides a direct and sufficiently robust justification of democracy.

In the move from the Aristotelian to the justice-first approach, the emphasis on the constitutive dimension of non-instrumental justifications of democracy has vanished. We lose the idea that democracy creates something new and unique, which we can understand only with reference to democratic institutions and practices. While justice-first theories rightly highlight the egalitarian relationships of democracy, they tend to see the value of such relationships as fully explicably without reference to democratic institutions and procedures. In this way, they do not provide a truly constitutive justification of democracy, which is characterized by the idea that the value of democracy is non-reducible, that is, that the latter cannot be based on some value the meaning of which is given independently of democracy.

The problem is the structure of justice-first theories. They begin with some contingent problems that democratic procedures are meant instrumentally to solve. More fundamentally, they assume that citizens have an independently defined *interest* in some X—an interest in equal respect, unbiased decisions, fulfilment of desires, or the like—and suggest that democracy can satisfy this interest. Thus, in this view, democracy is seen as providing some *benefit* to citizens in terms of their interests or well-being.[40] This is not a direct and robust justification of democracy, but is dependent on some contingent relationships. Thus, the

257). But it is not clear to me that the public standpoint, as Christiano understands it (at 243–46), is part of democracy and not a moral point of view imposed on democracy. Be that as it may, my main aim is not to place specific authors in specific camps but to distinguish different approaches to the justification of democracy.

[40] This problem is greater in some justice-first theories than others. My objection to Forst, for example, is not that he regards democracy as providing some benefit to the individual, but rather that he ignores the special norm that is created by constitutional democracy.

justice-first justification does not fulfil the robustness requirement of a justification of democracy.

The concern I have just raised entails that justice-first non-instrumentalism doesn't do as well, as we initially thought, regarding the other requirements of a justification of democracy. The justification seems to be in a greater quandary. On the one hand, it can insist on its non-instrumental credentials and maintain that it is not based on substantive interests regarding outcomes. In this way, it is compatible with respect for disagreement on outcomes and the requirement of direct justification. However, it is not clear that this explanation is sufficient to explain standard democratic procedures, because also other decision procedures show equal respect for citizens or treat them as equals, for example a lottery or a coin flip.[41] On the other hand, justice-first theorists can claim that only standard democratic procedures satisfy equal treatment *in the right way*. But this reply depends on a specific conception of equality or a specific theory of justice, which will be controversial, and it will have an instrumental dimension. A third option is to say that this theory of equality is one that is designed to fit democratic procedures and, thus, is not a detached conception of equality.[42] I think the latter is the right direction to go, but it requires fundamental amendments to the justice-first structure of justification, and it pushes us towards the third non-instrumental justification of democracy.

V. Kantian Non-Instrumentalism

Thus, we reach the Kantian account of the non-instrumental value of democracy. Kantian non-instrumentalism seeks to include what the other two get right and avoid what they get wrong. It takes the idea of the constitutive value of democracy from the Aristotelian approach but avoids the latter's commitment to a controversial notion of the good life. From justice-first theories, the Kantian approach takes the norm of egalitarian relationships but it does not regard this norm as fully described in or as part of an independently conceived theory of justice. Rather, it is committed to the idea that democracy's justification lies in a norm that can be fully conceived only in conjunction with the idea of democracy itself.

The third justification of democracy has what I take to be a Kantian form of non-instrumentalism:[43]

[41] Estlund (n 2) ch 4.

[42] This is how Christiano responds to Estlund's objection in Thomas Christiano, 'Debate: Estlund on Democratic Authority' (2009), 17 Journal of Political Philosophy 228, 231.

[43] When I talk about 'Kantian democratic non-instrumentalism' this is not because it is a view held by Immanuel Kant himself, but because it is a form of non-instrumentalism inspired by core Kantian ideas.

The justification of X is non-instrumental, if X is justified by a norm N, which itself can be fully conceived only with reference to X.

This is a constitutive justification in the sense that X constitutes the norm N that justifies X. If X is justified by an N given independently of X, the justification is instrumental, because then X must be seen as a means to N.

In Kant's *Rechtslehre*, we find such a form of justification when he argues that a public legal order is justified by the idea of freedom as independence, while the idea of freedom as independence cannot be fully conceived independently of the idea of a public legal order. Kant's idea of freedom as independence can be fully understood and realized only by the public and reciprocal coercion of a constitutional state 'that contains the conditions under which alone everyone is able to *enjoy* his rights'.[44]

Applying a form of Kantian non-instrumentalism to the justification of democracy, democracy is not merely justified because it gives expression to or promotes some pre-existing value; it is justified as *creating and constituting* something new that is in itself morally obligatory. And this 'something', this norm, cannot be fully conceived without the idea of democracy itself. By establishing and maintaining democratic rule, we create and continually recreate this N, which justifies democracy.

The Kantian account shares with our first non-instrumental justification of democracy the idea of the constitutive value of democracy. Thus, in the Aristotelian view, we cannot fully understand the value of living in a political community without reference to the latter; that is, the value of political activity is constituted and created by the activity itself. However, there are two important differences between the Aristotelian and the Kantian view. First, the good that is constituted by democracy in the Aristotelian view is understood in terms of conferring a form of benefit on individuals, a form of well-being or happiness. In the Kantian view, by contrast, what is constituted is a norm for how individuals ought to relate to one another. There is no reference here to any benefit to individuals but only to an idea of how individuals ought to stand in relation to one another. Second, that which constitutes the value in the Aristotelian view is political activity; it is only by participating in politics that citizens exercise their highest capacities and thus attain true happiness. In the Kantian view, by contrast, what constitutes the norm are public, binding, and entrenched civil and political rights that create the right relationship between citizens and government.

[44] Immanuel Kant, 'The Metaphysics of Morals' in Immanuel Kant, *Practical Philosophy* (Mary J Gregor ed and tr, Cambridge University Press 1996) 6:305–306 (references to Kant are given to volume and page of the *Akademieausgabe*). For Kant's non-instrumentalism, see Ripstein (n 4); Christian F Rostbøll, 'Kant, Freedom as Independence, and Democracy' (2016), 78 The Journal of Politics 792; Ariel Zylberman, 'The Public Form of Law: Kant on the Second-Personal Constitution of Freedom' (2016), 21 Kantian Review 101.

Before we get to the N of the Kantian justification, let me elaborate on the form or structure of the justification. Here the contrast to the first kind of justification is instructive. In the Aristotelian justification, what justifies democracy is an ideal for the *content* of the lives citizens ought to live, namely, the ideal of exercising one's natural capacities to the fullest degree possible. The Kantian justification, by contrast, does not see democracy as constituting some particularly valuable or enjoyable form of life for citizens, but, rather, as constituting a particular and obligatory *relationship* between citizens and government.[45] By establishing democratic government, citizens and government are related to one another in the right way. We might say the same about the justice-first justification, that is, that democratic government is justified because it relate citizens in the right way, for example as equals. However, in the Kantian justification, democratic government does not merely relate citizens to one another in a way that we know is right from an independently conceived theory of justice; rather, it *constitutes* a relationship between citizens and government that we cannot even think without thinking democratic government. The norm that justifies democracy is partly *created* by the democratic organization of the political community.

One recent and important book advancing a form of political-legal non-instrumentalism is Alon Harel's *Why Law Matters*. Harel argues that the constitutional state—with its binding norms and entrenchment of rights—not merely promotes pre-given values, but partly creates values. The constitutive argument that he advances, however, still has an Aristotelian (and Millian) aspect, in so far as he argues that the value that the constitutional state and rights constitute is the value of being able to exercise autonomous choice. For Harel, 'it makes people's life better if, and to the extent that, they exercise [autonomy] in their lives'.[46] The constitution should 'facilitate the realization of autonomy' and sustain 'a liberal autonomy-enhancing society'.[47] Paradoxically, Harel presents his non-instrumentalism as a superior alternative to Joseph Raz's idea that rights exist to promote pre-given values but still holds on to Raz's idea of the grounding value of the exercise of personal autonomy. Kantian non-instrumentalism, as I understand it, is more strictly non-instrumental by rejecting that political-legal institutions should be justified with reference to the promotion of any kind of value for our individual lives, including the value of the free exercise of choice. The idea that we should regard autonomous lives as better lives, moreover, is untenably sectarian.[48]

[45] In this formulation, I concur with Forst, but, as mentioned, I am not convinced that he escapes (or wants to escape) a justice-first approach to the justification of democracy: Forst, 'The Justification of Human Rights and the Basic Right to Justification' (n 31) 59.

[46] Harel (n 4) 40.

[47] ibid 44.

[48] cf Forst, 'The Justification of Human Rights and the Basic Right to Justification' (n 31) 50–52.

On the Kantian justification, democracy is not merely an activity but a constitutional form, a specific, formal organization of the political community. Sometimes 'democracy' is used as a vague reference to a general principle (of collective self-government, participation, or majority rule), rather than to a specific constitutional form. Moreover, Kant himself called (direct) democracy a 'non-form' (*Unform*).[49] Today, however, by 'democracy', we tend to mean representative and constitutional democracy, and this is not a non-form. Democracy, as we commonly use the term, refers to a complex constitutional structure with entrenched constitutional rights, representation, and some division of power. Of course, 'democracy' is used to refer to a range of different institutional set-ups, but normally it is used to refer to a form of government, a constitution. On the Kantian account, it is the constitutional system of democracy that is justified, and which is seen as constituting a specific, legal-political relationship among citizens and government. This is an important point that is often insufficiently emphasized in discussions of the justification of democracy.

The Kantian justification of democracy, then, entails that we view democracy as a way of constituting society. By this, I mean that democracy is a specific way of relating citizens to one another and of relating citizens to their government. I invoke the notion of 'constitution' both to highlight the constitutive aspect of democratic institutions and to emphasize the public, positive, legal, and, thereby, *binding* character of the democratic relation between citizens and government. In the Kantian account, the way citizens and government are related is publicly and legally entrenched in a system of rights. When we see democracy as a constitution of society, and as legally entrenched in a system of rights, this entails that a democratic society is something we—citizens and government—are duty-bound to uphold.[50] The legal-constitutional entrenchment is essential both because it entails common knowledge and acknowledgment of the standing of citizens, and because it involves recognition of this standing as a matter of unconditional importance and good as such (rather than as a contingent and optional means to some good consequences).

I have presented the third justification of democracy more in terms of form than content, and it has been important for me to show how the Kantian justification is unique exactly in terms of structure. However, we cannot justify democracy without also speaking content. This we can see, when we ask why the constitution of society must be democratic. It could be said that other ways of

[49] Immanuel Kant, 'Toward Perpetual Peace' in Immanuel Kant, *Practical Philosophy* (Mary J Gregor ed and tr, Cambridge University Press 1996) 8: 352.

[50] Harel gives a good account of the importance of the bindingness of constitutional norms, but he sees these norms as constraining rather than constituting democracy. For him, 'democracy' most often refers to majority rule and decisions by the legislature, rather than to the democratic constitution of society. See Harel (n 4) 7, 152, 189.

constituting society also constitute rightful relationships between citizens and government. Indeed, Kant himself gave a non-instrumental justification of the *Rechtsstaat*, and his ideal republic does not meet contemporary standards of democracy. Thus, establishing a public legal order, the rule of law, and protecting civil rights might be thought to be sufficient for securing the required standing of citizens and for creating egalitarian relationships among citizens. Why must the constitutional state also be a democratic state? If we want to provide a non-instrumental justification of democracy, we cannot appeal to the idea that democratic states are better at protecting individual rights or at promoting other values. We can answer the question of the non-instrumental importance of democracy only by specifying what is the norm that the democratic constitution of society constitutes and creates. What is it that is realized by a democratic constitution, and which cannot be realized or even fully understood without the idea of democracy? What kind of egalitarian relationships are being created by constitutional democracy?

The very form of the Kantian justification entails that the 'good' realized by political-legal institutions cannot be some independently identified good for the individual person or a benefit one can enjoy on one's own. Nor is it some benefit of communal living in the communitarian sense.[51] Rather, the political constitution is something that relates citizens to one another in the normatively required way. And this normatively required way of relating citizens to one another cannot be explained in terms of—or derived from—some interests individuals have; it has a moral importance in its own right.[52] This means that on the Kantian justification, democracy cannot be grounded in an idea of welfare or even in an interest in being individually self-governing. The latter are independently conceived ideas that would reduce democracy to a means to a given end. This leaves us with some idea of *standing*—a standing that can be fully understood and realized only with the idea and constitution of democracy itself.

What kind of standing, then, does democracy constitute or realize? The predominant answer is the standing of being an equal.[53] It is exactly the idea of egalitarian relationships that we should incorporate from the justice-first approach, even if we must modify its meaning. It is evident that not just any conception of equality will do if we are to meet our second requirement of a justification of democracy, namely, that it should be able to explain democratic procedures, as

[51] cf Michael J Sandel, *Liberalism and the Limits of Justice* (Cambridge University Press 1992) 183: in politics, 'we can know a good in common that we cannot know alone'.

[52] In a similar vein, Forst argues that we can justify the standing secured by human rights independently of the claim that it contributes to the good life: Forst, 'The Justification of Human Rights and the Basic Right to Justification' (n 31) 46.

[53] Hence, the apt title of Christiano's important book on democracy, *The Constitution of Equality*. See also Kolodny, 'Rule Over None II' (n 11) 287, and Eric Beerbohm, *In Our Name: The Ethics of Democracy* (Princeton University Press 2012) 37.

we commonly understand them. Other forms of decision-making, for example, decision by a coin flip, gives every citizen an equal standing. As mentioned at the end of Section IV, this pushes equality theorists to suggest that their conception of equality must be one that fits democratic procedures. Thus, the conception of equal standing that justifies democracy is one that cannot be fully understood without the idea of democratic procedures of decision-making themselves. Elsewhere, I have suggested that we can understand this idea of equality only with the inclusion of a notion of freedom.[54] Thus, the standing constituted by democracy is a form of equal freedom.[55] In Kant, freedom is understood in terms of 'independence from being constrained by another's choice',[56] and it can be realized only in a system that affords everyone equal standing. Only within such a system is no one subordinated to the will of another.

Some theorists have thought that the rule of law or the *Rechtsstaat* is sufficient for equal freedom—indeed, some constitutive legal-political non-instrumentalists, including Kant(ians), have thought so.[57] For them, the rule of law and individual rights secure the impersonality and the distinction between office and person that are essential for equal freedom. However, while the rule of law is crucial for equal freedom, it is insufficient to secure and realize that no one is subject to the will of another. Positive laws must be given by someone and cannot be treated as natural phenomena. Democratizing the constitutional state entails realizing equal freedom more fully than is attained by the rule of law by itself. In a non-democratic constitutional regime, everyone may enjoy equal freedom as subject to law, at least in principle. But, by definition, only some of the members have the standing of rulers and political decision-makers. Thus, the idea that is constituted by democracy and that can be fully understood only with the idea of democracy is the idea of equal standing as co-rulers or participants in common law-making. The idea of democracy entails that laws are some that must be made, and that everyone (or all adult members) must be able equally to participate in doing so. Without democratic equality, some members would be subordinate to the will of others in making law.

The idea of having standing as a co-ruler cannot be grounded in some idea of satisfying an interest in getting what one wants. As many have pointed out,

[54] Rostbøll, 'The Non-instrumental Value of Democracy' (n 27); Rostbøll, 'Kant, Freedom as Independence, and Democracy' (n 44).

[55] A similar notion of standing is central to Forst's justification of human rights and democracy, but, again, for him this standing is understood in terms of a prior idea of a moral right to justification, rather than an independent norm created by constitutional democracy. See Forst, 'The Justification of Human Rights and the Basic Right to Justification' (n 31) 38, 52f, 65.

[56] Kant, 'The Metaphysics of Morals' (n 44) 6:237.

[57] Ripstein, for example, writes: 'The idea that the people are the authors of the laws that bind them is thus a formal rather than material idea . . . positive legislation is only legitimate if it *could* be a law that free persons *could* impose on themselves'. Ripstein (n 4) 213 (emphasis added).

democracy does not secure that the desires or preferences of everyone are satisfied, nor does it make the individual self-governing.[58] The Kantian argument also does not depend on the latter, but only on the idea that democracy constitutes a type of political relationship between citizens and government in which everyone has an equal opportunity to influence law-making. And, crucially, who are elected to office and which laws are passed should be a result of the application of constitutional procedures that treat everyone as equal co-rulers rather than being decided independently of these procedures. When my policy preferences fail to be mirrored in law-making to the extent I would have preferred, I should be able to see this as a result of constitutional procedures that gave me an equal standing as all other citizens rather than the result of some independent factors. When the decision is a result of such procedures and the result does not violate my standing, I must regard the decision as authoritative and legitimate even if I find it substantively unjust. The reason for the latter cannot be explained with reference to some interest in being self-governing or preference satisfaction, but can be grounded in the standing created by a democratic constitution.

While I regard democracy as constituting equal freedom more fully than the rule of law on its own, I don't see the two as justified separately. For the Kantian, what can be justified is *constitutional democracy* and not some unconstitutional form of democracy.[59] The standing afforded citizens by democratic rights of participation augments and completes the standing of the legal person constituted by the *Rechtsstaat*; it does not replace it. Of course, it is vague and indeterminate what this combination of constitutionalism and democracy entails in institutional terms. However, it is exactly the point of our whole enterprise of clarifying the justification of democracy that it can contribute to determine which kind of (constitutional) democracy to establish. How we justify democracy affect what kind of democracy we should favour. The Kantian would look for what kind of political-legal relationships among citizens and government are realized by different institutional configurations or different kinds of democracy. What kind of constitution is required for realizing a system of equal freedom?[60]

On the Kantian account, it becomes clear that democracy is internally related to positive law. On the one hand, it is by positive law with its public and coercive entrenchment of rights that the equal standing and independence of citizens is secured. On the other hand, positive law is the medium through which free

[58] Thomas Christiano, *The Rule of the Many: Fundamental Issues in Democratic Theory* (Westview Press 1996) 15–28.

[59] cf Forst, 'The Rule of Reasons' (n 30) 182.

[60] Again, the idea of a system of equal freedom here cannot be understood independently of the political-legal institutions that constitute it.

and equal citizens rule themselves.[61] In a constitutional democracy, positive law provides assurance and determinacy of our standing not only as subject to law but also as co-rulers.

The idea of co-ruler should not be confused with the notion of autonomy found in Kant's moral philosophy, nor should constitutional democracy be confused with the kingdom of ends. The individual person is morally autonomous by giving and subjecting herself to the moral law. This way of realizing autonomy is not possible in politics that makes use of positive law. As Jürgen Habermas has suggested, 'the positive character of law forces autonomy to split up in a peculiar way' and 'makes it conceptually necessary to distinguish the role of authors who make (and adjudicate) law from that of addressees who are subject to established law'.[62] This split is a consequence of the fact that public law entails setting up a coercive authority, which enforces the law on subjects from the outside. In a social setting with a multitude of mutually affecting persons, the coercive and external character of positive law has the advantage that we are not dependent on the goodwill of other persons for our rights but instead have 'the *dependence* of all upon a single common legislation'.[63]

In contrast to a merely moral relationship of freedom and equality, such as the kingdom of ends, the positive and coercive character of constitutional democracy means that the members are independent of the goodwill of others. As Philip Pettit has argued, freedom is a status 'that we cannot provide for one another on the basis of our own goodwill'; it can be secured only by 'external checks' and, in the final analysis, 'a just and democratic state'.[64] The kingdom of ends cannot provide us status freedom; for this, we need common, positive legislation.

A constitutional democracy, however, does not merely make all dependent on a common positive legislation; it in addition makes everyone equal participants in this common legislation. The common legislation assures us of our equal standing as independent beings and provides us with equal opportunities for participating in legislating in common. Thus, the common legislation of a democracy has an external and coercive dimension that distinguishes it from the moral legislation of the kingdom of ends, but it has also the internal aspect of being given in and by procedures, which provides the opportunity for all members to participate as equals. The justice-first justification of democracy gives us an insufficient account of these relationships of democracy, because it fails to

[61] This is an important theme in Jürgen Habermas, *Between Facts and Norms: Contributions to a Discourse Theory of Law and Democracy* (William Rehg tr, MIT Press 1996) especially chapters 3 and 4.

[62] Jürgen Habermas, 'On the Internal Relation between Law and Democracy' in Jürgen Habermas, *The Inclusion of the Other: Studies in Political Theory* (Ciaran Cronin and Pablo De Greiff eds, Ciaran Cronin and others trs, MIT Press 1998) 257.

[63] Kant, 'Toward Perpetual Peace' (n 49) 8:349f.

[64] Pettit (n 2) 63, 183f.

acknowledge that democracy's egalitarian relationships cannot be fully specified in an independent theory of justice. The relationships of equality described in the last few paragraphs are *created* by constitutional democracy and are not fully intelligible without reference to the latter.

VI. Kantian Non-Instrumentalism and the Requirements of a Justification of Democracy

How does the Kantian justification of democracy fare in relation to the six requirements set out in the Introduction? To begin from the top, is the Kantian justification non-sectarian? It is more accommodating of diversity than the Aristotelian account, because it does not dependent on agreement on a sectarian view of human flourishing. It might be thought that the Kantian account implicitly is dependent on a view of autonomy that some people reasonably reject. However, the account that I am proposing does not rely on that people value a life of autonomous decision-making. Thus, democracy is not defended as maximizing the opportunity for autonomous choice but, rather, as constituting a specific relation between persons.[65] And, this relation between persons is exactly one that respects their different conceptions of the good life and their political disagreements. The Kantian account concurs with disagreement theorists about the latter but is more precise in explaining that and how democracy constitutes the norm that justifies it.

Is the Kantian justification able to explain standard democratic procedures and institutions, such as equal and universal suffrage, the right to run for office and to participate in public deliberation, and so forth? In so far as Kantian non-instrumentalism begins from democratic institutions and is based on the standing realized by these, it clearly fulfils the requirement of fidelity. However, a justification of democracy cannot just take the whole edifice of democracy for granted without losing its point, that is, without becoming viciously circular.[66] In so far as fidelity is a requirement of a *justification* of democracy, it cannot take democracy as already justified. Such an approach would also be plagued by the fact that there are different models of democracy and different institutional specifications of democracy, whereas our justification should help us choosing

[65] Forst explains well how we can combine a Kantian commitment to equal standing, while avoiding a teleological commitment to the superiority of the autonomous life. See Forst, 'The Justification of Human Rights and the Basic Right to Justification' (n 31) 46, 50–52, 65; Rainer Forst, 'A Critical Theory of Multicultural Toleration' in Rainer Forst, *The Right to Justification: Elements of a Constructivist Theory of Justice* (Jeffrey Flynn tr, Columbia University Press 2011) 146.

[66] cf Ariel Zylberman, 'Why Human Rights? Because of *You*' (2016), 24 Journal of Political Philosophy 321, on the charge on vicious circularity in non-instrumental justifications of human rights.

between these models and institutions. Thus, we should not take the second requirement to mean fidelity to an already fully explained and specified model of democracy. Rather, the requirement is that a justification of democracy should be loyal to commonly agreed and fundamental aspects of different models of democracy. The justification of democracy should also, however, be applicable as a critical standard to assess actually existing democracies, as I explain shortly.

I have already opened the question of the third requirement, namely, whether the Kantian justification gives an independent justification of democracy. Non-instrumental accounts are often criticized for being viciously circular and unilluminating, because they are seen as presupposing the validity of that which they aim to justify. Similarly, it might be objected that my Kantian account supplies only an analytical defence of democracy, since the idea of standing as co-ruler seems to be part of the definition of democracy. And, the objection might continue, we have added no substantive weight to the case for democracy if all we have done is to give a justification of democracy that does not go beyond a definition of democracy. However, we should not accept that the only sound justifications of democracy are those that either (1) show that democracy is the best feasible means to some good end, or (2) express or embody some value that can be identified independently of democratic decision-making. This would leave us with only instrumental and justice-first justifications of democracy.[67] My argument is exactly that these are not the only two possibilities. The Kantian justification of democracy is neither analytical, nor is it instrumental, nor does it rely on independently specified values. Rather, it relies on a norm that has some meaning independently of democracy but which can be understood fully only in connection with the idea of (constitutional) democracy, because it is created and constituted by the latter. The Kantian account does more than describe and define democracy, and the ideas of standing as co-ruler, equal freedom, and non-subordination add to the case for democracy. Moreover, when we, for example, clarify that democracy does not promote the good of self-legislation (which the concept might otherwise indicate), but that it constitutes and respects the equal standing of citizens as co-rulers, this also illuminates and contributes to the case for democracy.

The fourth requirement is that a justification of democracy must be robust in face of variable circumstances. My use of the adjective 'Kantian' might suggest to some readers that the justification is regarded as absolutely necessary and *a priori*. However, I don't think we can or should aim for this kind of unconditionality in our justification of democracy. Political theoretical argument depends on

[67] For an example of a critique of merely analytical defences of democracy that makes the only possible justifications of democracy instrumental ones, see Frank Lovett, *A General Theory of Domination and Justice* (Oxford University Press 2010) 210ff.

certain facts about human beings and the natural and social world—and Kant's own legal and political philosophy does, too. Still, it is a desideratum of a justification of democracy that it holds under normal circumstances of human interaction. Now, it might be said that instrumental accounts of democracy are quite robust in this sense, at least in the contemporary world, because it is well established empirically that democracies are more prosperous and just than non-democracies.[68] However, this reply takes for granted agreement on what counts as good and just outcomes. Thus, democratic instrumentalism is only as robust as the agreement on outcome standards. While I accept that the non-instrumental value of democracy is conditional on democratic decision-making not leading to what are broadly agreed to be horrendous outcomes, a justification of democracy should be robust in face of shifting understandings of what counts as good and just outcomes. Moreover, as mentioned earlier, a democratic instrumentalist cannot truly be said to give a justification of democracy, since she has no standards of her own to determine what regimes count as democratic. Thus, a justification of democracy should not merely be robust under a range of variable but normal circumstances; by itself, it should also be able to determine in other than descriptive terms what counts as a democratic regime. I believe the Kantian account is both.

The fifth requirement is that a justification of democracy must show that democracy is not merely good to have but obligatory. Clearly, there is a gap between the evaluation that something is good or valuable and the judgment that we ought to establish it.[69] Does the Kantian justification of democracy show that democracy is not merely good to have but that we ought to establish and maintain it? I have said that in the Kantian account, the standing constituted by constitutional democracy is not merely something that is valuable or good for us but is required as a matter of right. The suggestion is that constitutional democracy is obligatory, because it contains the conditions under which alone it is possible to enjoy the standing of not being subordinate to another person's choice.[70] If we accept that freedom as independence is a fundamental right, we have a moral obligation to establish the form of political system under which alone this freedom can be realized.[71] This formulation does not mean that democracy is reduced to a means to realize freedom as independence, because the meaning of the latter

[68] See eg John Gerring, Strom C Thacker, and Rodrigo Alfaro, 'Democracy and Human Development' (2012), 74 The Journal of Politics 1; Christian Davenport and David A Armstrong, 'Democracy and the Violation of Human Rights: A Statistical Analysis from 1976 to 1996' (2004), 48 American Journal of Political Science 538. Thank you to Rasmus Fonnesbæk Andersen for these references.

[69] Zylberman, 'Why Human Rights? Because of *You*' (n 66) 2–8.

[70] This formulation borrows from Kant, 'The Metaphysics of Morals' (n 44) 6:305f.

[71] For further argument regarding how democracy realizes this standing, see Rostbøll, 'Kant, Freedom as Independence, and Democracy' (n 44).

refers to democracy as a constitutional system. As such, the Kantian argument at least has the right form. There is no gap to be closed between an evaluative judgment about the goodness of democracy and the deontic judgment that we ought to establish it.

However, it might be objected that I have not demonstrated that we ought, as a matter of right, to establish the type of relationship of equal standing and non-subordination that is constituted by democracy. I accept this; to this extent my argument is conditional on accepting (something along the lines of) the Kantian right to freedom as independence. My aim is merely to show that the Kantian justification is a unique type of justification and indicate what would be required of it. Thus, what is distinctive about the Kantian justification of political arrangements is that it does not rely on that they somehow are to the benefit or good of individuals. Rather, the Kantian sees political arrangements as justified by an idea about how citizens ought to be related to one another.

Finally, I have suggested that a justification of democracy must cultivate our understanding of democracy in a way that creates a critical perspective on actually existing democracy. Actually existing democracy consists of both a specific constitutional-legal order and its social-economic context. It is important that we do not reduce the idea of the democratic constitutional state to any actually existing legal order.[72] The Kantian idea is not that any and all actually existing legal orders constitute the right relationships between government and citizens. True, we can understand the obligatory nature of the relations created by constitutional democracy only with reference to constitutional democracy, but the latter is an idea that transcends any actually existing legal and social order, and which can be turned critically against it. The norms of freedom as independence and the status of co-ruler are both part of constitutional democracy *and* can provide a critical perspective on it.[73] With these norms we can gain a better understanding of what democracy is about, the relations it creates, and why we are bound to maintain these relations. Yet the Kantian justification can also be turned critically towards existing institutions and laws as well as their socio-economic context, because the status of enjoying independence and being a co-ruler is demanding and requires specific entrenched rights and institutions, and has strong social and economic preconditions. The norms that are constituted by

[72] Jürgen Habermas, 'Civil Disobedience: Litmus Test for the Democratic Constitutional State' (1985), 30 Berkeley Journal of Sociology 95.

[73] Forst suggests a similar critical perspective that includes normative standards that simultaneously '*transcend* existing procedures [and are] *immanent* to these procedures'. Forst, 'The Rule of Reasons' (n 30) 186.

and justify democracy are never fully realized but provide an ideal for assessing actually existing institutions and practices.[74]

Here you may ask, haven't we, despite of what we claim, justified the standing of a citizen within a constitutional democracy as a type of benefit to or good for the individual? Isn't the freedom of not being subject to the choice of another in private as well as in political life not a good to the individual? To be sure, some might see this as a good or a benefit, but that is not the issue, and the Kantian justification does not rely on it. The reason why Kantians emphasize that political arrangements cannot be justified with reference to some individual or collective good is that this obscures their non-instrumental and constitutive value. Moreover, if political arrangements were seen as justified with reference to some good, we would look for arrangements that maximized that good. But the Kantian justification does not claim and cannot claim that constitutional democracy maximizes some good. Constitutional democracy is justified by the standing that it affords citizens, and *standing is not a good that can be maximized.* Standing is a relational norm and not an individual good; it is something you have in relation to others, not something you can enjoy on your own. You might insist that the Kantian treats constitutional democracy as instrumental to establishing the right kind of relations among citizens and government. Here the point has been that in so far as we can only understand these relations with reference to constitutional democracy, the relationship cannot be seen as instrumental.

In addition, if democracy were justified with reference to its ability to promote certain goods and interests or to supply certain benefits, these goods and benefits should be weighed against other goods and benefits. For example, the good of participation should be balanced against the interests in protection of individual rights. It is exactly this instrumental logic that the Kantian avoids. We do not claim that the standing afforded by constitutional democracy is some supreme benefit that outweighs all other goods. We simply say that it is wrong for some to have a standing that others do not have, and that constitutional democracy is the only form of government that affords all members equal standing as co-rulers.

VII. Conclusion

In sum, I propose that Kantian non-instrumentalism fulfils the six requirements of a sound justification of democracy. First, it respects diversity

[74] Providing an account of what exactly these institutions, rights, and social preconditions are is crucial, but go beyond the aim of the present chapter. Moreover, to answer this question is part of actual democratic politics itself.

because it relies on neither agreement on a substantive theory of outcome-justice nor a sectarian conception of the good life. Second, in so far as it begins from democratic institutions and is based on the standing realized by these, this justification fulfils the requirement of fidelity. Third, Kantian non-instrumentalism relies on a norm that has some meaning independently of democracy but which can be understood fully only in connection with the idea of democracy, and thus it fulfils the requirement of directness and independence. Fourth, the Kantian account is robust, because it applies over a wide range of circumstances of human interaction. Fifth, our third non-instrumental justification can show that democracy is not merely good to have but is authoritative and legitimate. In the Kantian view, the relationship among citizens and government realized by constitutional democracy does not satisfy some interest or good of individuals; it is right in and of itself. Thus, according to the Kantian justification, we should not understand the idea that democracy is good in itself to mean that it realizes some benefit to the citizens but, rather, as a matter of constituting a standing and relationship among citizens and government that is obligatory to establish as a matter of right. Finally, Kantian non-instrumentalism gives us a deep understanding of democracy, which can provide a critical perspective on actual institutions and practices, because it relies on a demanding norm of independence and co-rulership.

References

Anderson ES, 'Democracy: Instrumental vs. Non-Instrumental Value' in Thomas Christiano and John P Christman (eds), *Contemporary Debates in Political Philosophy* (Wiley-Blackwell 2009).

Arendt H, *On Revolution* (Penguin Books 1990).

Arendt H, *The Human Condition* (2nd edn, University of Chicago Press 1998).

Arneson RJ, 'The Supposed Right to a Democratic Say' in Thomas Christiano and John P Christman (eds), *Contemporary Debates in Political Philosophy* (Wiley-Blackwell 2009).

Beerbohm E, *In Our Name: The Ethics of Democracy* (Princeton University Press 2012).

Ceva, E and Ottonelli V, 'Rescuing Democracy from Reductionism', unpublished manuscript.

Christiano T, *The Rule of the Many: Fundamental Issues in Democratic Theory* (Westview Press 1996).

Christiano T, *The Constitution of Equality: Democratic Authority and Its Limits* (Oxford University Press 2008).

Christiano T, 'Debate: Estlund on Democratic Authority' (2009), 17 Journal of Political Philosophy 228.

Christiano T, 'Disagreement and the Justification of Democracy' in Steven Wall (ed), *The Cambridge Companion to Liberalism* (Cambridge University Press 2015).

Cohen J, 'For a Democratic Society' in Joshua Cohen, *The Arc of the Moral Universe and Other Essays* (Harvard University Press 2010).

Davenport C and Armstrong DA, 'Democracy and the Violation of Human Rights: A Statistical Analysis from 1976 to 1996' (2004), 48 American Journal of Political Science 538.

Elster J, 'The Market and the Forum: Three Varieties of Political Theory' in James Bohman and William Rehg (eds), *Deliberative Democracy: Essays on Reason and Politics* (MIT Press 1997).

Estlund DM, *Democratic Authority: A Philosophical Framework* (Princeton University Press 2008).

Forst R, 'A Critical Theory of Multicultural Toleration' in Rainer Forst, *The Right to Justification: Elements of a Constructivist Theory of Justice* (Jeffrey Flynn tr, Columbia University Press 2011).

Forst R, 'The Rule of Reasons: Three Models of Deliberative Democracy' in Rainer Forst, *The Right to Justification: Elements of a Constructivist Theory of Justice* (Jeffrey Flynn tr, Columbia University Press 2011).

Forst R, 'The Justification of Human Rights and the Basic Right to Justification: A Reflexive Approach' in Rainer Forst, *Justification and Critique: Towards a Critical Theory of Politics* (Ciaran Cronin tr, Polity Press 2013).

Forst R, 'Legitimacy, Democracy, and Justice: On the Reflexivity of Normative Orders' in Rainer Forst, *Normativity and Power: Analyzing Social Orders of Justification* (Ciaran Cronin tr, Oxford University Press 2017).

Gerring J, Thacker SC, and Alfaro R, 'Democracy and Human Development' (2012), 74 The Journal of Politics 1.

Griffin C, 'Debate: Democracy as a Non-instrumentally Just Procedure' (2003), 11 The Journal of Political Philosophy 111.

Habermas J, 'Civil Disobedience: Litmus Test for the Democratic Constitutional State' (1985), 30 Berkeley Journal of Sociology 95.

Habermas J, *Between Facts and Norms: Contributions to a Discourse Theory of Law and Democracy* (William Rehg tr, MIT Press 1996).

Habermas J, 'On the Internal Relation between Law and Democracy' in Jürgen Habermas, *The Inclusion of the Other: Studies in Political Theory* (Ciaran Cronin and Pablo De Greiff eds, Ciaran Cronin and others trs, MIT Press 1998).

Harel A, *Why Law Matters* (Oxford University Press 2014).

Kant I, 'The Metaphysics of Morals' in Immanuel Kant, *Practical Philosophy* (Mary J Gregor ed and tr, Cambridge University Press 1996).

Kant I, 'Toward Perpetual Peace' in Immanuel Kant, *Practical Philosophy* (Mary J Gregor ed and tr, Cambridge University Press 1996).

Kolodny N, 'Rule Over None I: What Justifies Democracy?' (2014), 42 Philosophy & Public Affairs 195.

Kolodny N, 'Rule Over None II: Social Equality and the Justification of Democracy' (2014), 42 Philosophy & Public Affairs 287.

Kymlicka W, *Contemporary Political Philosophy: An Introduction* (2nd edn, Oxford University Press 2002).

Lovett F, *A General Theory of Domination and Justice* (Oxford University Press 2010).

Mill JS, 'Considerations on Representative Government' in John Stuart Mill, *On Liberty and Other Essays* (John Gray ed, Oxford University Press 1991).

Mill JS, 'On Liberty' in John Stuart Mill, *On Liberty and Other Essays* (John Gray ed, Oxford University Press 1991).

Ober J, 'Natural Capacities and Democracy as a Good-in-Itself' (2007), 132 Philosophical Studies 59.

Peter F, *Democratic Legitimacy* (Routledge 2009).

Pettit P, *On the People's Terms: A Republican Theory and Model of Democracy* (Cambridge University Press 2012).

Ripstein A, *Force and Freedom: Kant's Legal and Political Philosophy* (Harvard University Press 2009).

Rostbøll CF, 'Statelessness, Domination, and Unfreedom: Arendt and Pettit in Dialogue' in Christian Dahl and Tue A Nexø (eds), *To Be Unfree: Republicanism and Unfreedom in History, Literature, and Philosophy* (Transcript Verlag 2014).

Rostbøll CF, 'The Non-instrumental Value of Democracy: The Freedom Argument' (2015), 22 Constellations 267.

Rostbøll CF, 'Kant, Freedom as Independence, and Democracy' (2016), 78 The Journal of Politics 792.

Rostbøll CF, 'Democratic Respect and Compromise' (2017), 20 Critical Review of International Social and Political Philosophy 619.

Rostbøll CF, 'Kant and the Critique of the Ethics-First Approach to Politics' [2019] 22 Critical Review of International Social and Political Philosophy 55.

Sandel MJ, *Liberalism and the Limits of Justice* (Cambridge University Press 1992).

Valentini L, 'Justice, Disagreement and Democracy' (2013), 43 British Journal of Political Science 177.

Waldron J, *Law and Disagreement* (Oxford University Press 1999).

Wall S, 'Democracy and Equality' (2007), 57 The Philosophical Quarterly 416.

Wall S, 'Perfectionism in Politics: A Defense' in Thomas Christiano and John P Christman (eds), *Contemporary Debates in Political Philosophy* (Wiley-Blackwell 2009).

Zylberman A, 'The Public Form of Law: Kant on the Second-Personal Constitution of Freedom' (2016), 21 Kantian Review 101.

Zylberman A, 'Why Human Rights? Because of *You*' (2016), 24 Journal of Political Philosophy 321.

12
The Concepts of Non-Domination and Justification in EU Security-Related Context

*Ester Herlin-Karnell**

I. Introduction

This chapter explores the implications of a non-domination oriented view for understanding European Union (EU) security regulation. I will ask how the non-domination template fits the constitutional legal model, and what it adds for the understanding of the establishment of an 'Area of Freedom, Security and Justice' (AFSJ) in the specific case of the EU. The concept of non-domination is commonly seen as one of the most central concepts in republican theory.[1] Therefore, I will tentatively look at the relationship between coercion, which is the common term in legal vocabulary for describing force, and the concept of domination in political theory as such. In addition, I will discuss the implications of non-arbitrariness and the right to justification in a new security-related context.[2] Specifically, this chapter links the question of security regulation to the longstanding debate in political theory on the connection between freedom and non-domination and to the constitutional debate on the formation of security regulation in Europe. Examples will be drawn from EU 'Area of Freedom, Security and Justice' law and policy as an expression of how practice matters, and arguably dependent on the use of proportionality, and reflected in the constitutional theory debate on the right to justification.

* Thanks go to Matthias Klatt and Héctor Morales for their insightful suggestions. I would also like to thank the participants in the VU Centre for European Legal Studies, the *NWO* Veni grant and Access Europe workshop 'Exploring structures of proportionality and justification in contemporary constitutional law: methods against injustice in Europe and beyond ' 29 January 2016 Amsterdam, in particular my discussants: Sionaidh Douglas Scott and Mattias Kumm for useful comments. The usual disclaimer applies, of course.

[1] Philip Pettit, *Just Freedom: A Moral Compass for a Complex World* (W.W. Norton & Company 2014).

[2] On the right to justification, Rainer Forst, *The Right to Justification: Elements of a Constructivist Theory of Justice* (Jeffrey Flynn tr, Columbia University Press 2011).

Ester Herlin-Karnell, *The Concepts of Non-Domination and Justification in EU Security-Related Context* In: *Constitutionalism Justified: Rainer Forst in Discourse.* Edited by: Ester Herlin-Karnell and Matthias Klatt, Oxford University Press (2020), © Ester Herlin-Karnell and Matthias Klatt.
DOI: 10.1093/oso/9780190889050.003.0012

But first I should explain what I mean by an AFSJ. When the EU sets out to establish an 'Area of Freedom, Security and Justice' it does so in order to ensure free movement, migration, and asylum policy while developing, maintaining, and adjusting criminal laws and anti-terrorism strategies. The area is chiefly constructed through preventive regulation and the notion of meeting the need for the EU to attain a high level of security through approximating Member States law in various related fields as stated in Article 67 Treaty of the Functioning of the European Union (TFEU). In short, the AFSJ embodies a new and sensitive field in the EU, one which is currently being transformed from largely being an isolated justice and home affairs space, to that of a European security regulation enterprise. This chapter argues that it is through security seen as domination that we will understand the EU's strategy in AFSJ matters and that this pose challenges as to how freedom and justice could be achieved (the EU's promise of securing 'freedom, security and justice'). Specifically, the question to be asked is how the balance should be struck between security needs and the need to ensure adequately high human-rights standards and why this is a question that is best asked through the framework of constitutionalism. Therefore, and as this chapter will seek to demonstrate, the EU security regulation regime will serve as a good test case of non-domination and justice.

On this background, this chapter seeks to elucidate why it is helpful to analyze EU security regulation through the lens of justice as 'non-domination'[3] and how constitutionalism offers a useful framework for this process. This chapter therefore adopts the benchmark of freedom as non-domination for viewing *justice* as 'non-domination' in the AFSJ context, and how it could be achieved through attention to a right to justification in the EU setting.

This chapter is focused on both the broader theoretical and normative understanding of the EU security project as well as its empirical implications. Surely, no civic-minded person would argue against justice as a normative benchmark for a decent society.[4] However, is the concept of justice at risk of losing any concrete meaning, of becoming no more than a metaphor for the political process? In trying to answer this question and the broader implications of 'justice', this chapter will try to cast a clarifying light on the debate and thereby provide a platform, and a theoretical foundation, for understanding the concept of non-domination and justification in political theory, before addressing its forms and shapes in the EU security context. Given the strong emphasis on security and current domination of it, the idea of justice, it seems, is of crucial importance for shaping the future EU security law.

[3] On freedom as non-domination, Philip Pettit, *On the People's Terms: A Republican Theory and Model of Democracy* (Cambridge University Press 2012).

[4] See generally, Avishai Margalit, *The Decent Society* (Harvard University Press 1998).

This chapter is structured as follows. The first section looks at the notion of freedom as non-domination, and also addresses some of the main critiques against this, predominantly, republican benchmark. The second section looks at the relevance of coercion for understanding the concept of domination, and tentatively explores the relationship with the question of power as such. The third section investigates the question of legitimacy and justification as a closely associated question to that of 'non-domination'. Thereafter, this chapter briefly assesses the relationship between judicial review and non-domination before examining the impact of non-domination and legitimacy in the EU constitutional landscape and addressing it in the specific context of security seen as domination and the implications for the Area of Freedom, Security and Justice.

II. The Concept of 'Freedom as Non-Domination' as a Constitutional Set-Up

Certainly, the classic benchmark for testing the level of freedom in a given society is commonly the republican yardstick of 'non-domination'.[5] Thus, in the republican tradition, non-domination is a personal and common good, one which everyone desires.[6] In order to identity the notion of domination, the well-known slave/master example is often used to illustrate the prime example of 'unfreedom'.[7] While the master/slave example is the most obvious instance of domination, it is far from the only one. There are more recent examples in contemporary society, for example, how some states are dominating others, and the difficulty is to translate the 'domination' criteria as a device for measuring freedom, to the meta level.

Because freedom as non-domination is a status that one enjoys in relation to other people, which stems from one person or group (or the state) being able to interfere with another person (or group) arbitrarily, Philip Pettit claims that non-domination is an egalitarian concept.[8] For Rainer Forst, republicanism is 'Kantian' because it respects the autonomy of persons to be both authors and addressees of the law.[9]

[5] See eg Adam Tomkins, *Our Republican Constitution* (Hart Publishing 2005) 46–52.

[6] Pettit, *On the People's Terms* (n 3) and Fabian Schuppert, 'Non-domination, Non-alienation and Social Equality: Towards a Republican Understanding of Equality' (2015), 18 Critical Review of International Social and Political Philosophy 440.

[7] Pettit, *Just Freedom* (n 1) ch 1.

[8] Christian F Rostbøll, 'Non-domination and Democratic Legitimacy' (2015), 18 Critical Review of International Social and Political Philosophy 424, 432.

[9] Rainer Forst, 'A Kantian Republican Conception of Justice as Non-Domination' in Andreas Niederberger and Philipp Schink (eds), *Republican Democracy: Liberty, Law and Politics* (Edinburgh University Press 2013).

Moreover, it is sometimes suggested that a turn to global constitutionalism is in line with the republican vision of freedom as non-domination, as it rests on the idea that individuals do not live 'at the mercy' of national constitutions.[10] In this view there is an intrinsic value in constitutionalism as honouring rights and that the global norm-setting contributes to freedom from static constitutions. With Mattias Kumm, the foundation of constitutionalism, then, is the idea of free and equal persons governing themselves through law as part of an international community of equally sovereign states.[11]

In line with this, for James Bohman, the most robust version of a model of global governance is a theory of republican constitutionalism understood as an obligation to form a political community beyond the nation state.[12] As indicated, the idea of non-domination as the basis for freedom is an essential feature of a republican worldview. In short, as pointed out by Eoin Daly, and, arguably, of importance for the constitutional law project, the notion of 'domination' is a vertically constructed concept and means that some form of inequality, in terms of unfairness or the like, occurs, which is generally considered as 'domination'.[13] The ideal of non-domination is therefore structurally egalitarian in that non-domination can only be achieved if all are equal in some fundamental sense, such as equality before the law. Hence, the idea of non-domination is aimed at ensuring a system of 'free and equal' citizens.

Furthermore, freedom as non-domination is not only a social good, which means that there are legal and social arrangements in place which ensure non-domination but also a common good in so far as it aims at reducing everybody's (and every social group's) vulnerability.[14]

When trying to pin down what exactly is meant by non-domination, it is useful to turn to Isaiah Berlin who famously distinguished between 'two conceptions of liberty', namely, a positive notion and a negative reading of freedom.[15] With the negative conception, of freedom people are free simply to the extent that their choices are not interfered with.[16] The positive conception is trickier: it is freedom

[10] Alon Harel, *Why Law Matters* (Oxford University Press 2014), ch 2; and chapter in this volume.

[11] Mattias Kumm, 'Constituent Power, Cosmopolitan Constitutionalism, and Post-positivist Law' (2016), 14 International Journal of Constitutional Law 697.

[12] James Bohman, 'A Response to My Critics: Democracy Across Borders' (2010), 3 Ethics & Global Politics 71.

[13] Eoin Daly, 'Freedom as Non-Domination in the Jurisprudence of Constitutional Rights' (2015), 28 Canadian Journal of Law & Jurisprudence 289; and chapter in this volume.

[14] Pettit, *Just Freedom* (n 1); and Philip Pettit, *Republicanism: A Theory of Freedom and Government* (Clarendon Press 1997) 122f.

[15] Isaiah Berlin, *Two Concepts of Liberty* (Clarendon Press 1958).

[16] John S Mill, *On Liberty* (John Parker and Son 1859). This is in line with the liberalism expressed by John Stuart Mill, for example, and has been the dominant view of freedom, and has formed much of modern criminal law based upon the harm principle (according to the harm principle, the only purpose for which power can rightfully be exercised over any other member of a civilized community against his or her will is to prevent harm being done to others). For an overview, see Andrew

in the sense that groups or individuals exercise self-control or self-mastery. Berlin associated the positive conception of freedom to the 'enlightened rationalism' of thinkers such as Spinoza and Hegel.[17] Yet, according to the republican understanding of freedom, to be free, it is not sufficient that the person is not coerced or is unlikely to be coerced; to be free, it is also necessary that the potential victim does not live at 'the mercy of' the inclinations of his or her potential violators.[18]

The exact contours of domination are, however, still debatable. Despite its contested nature, the conception of domination is commonly marked by three important features:[19] (1) domination is seen as a problem in specific social relationships; (2) domination is understood as being structure-based, meaning that it is not a particular outcome of domination which matters (eg that I dare not speak my mind), but the structure of the social relationship itself; and (3) domination is identified as the use of arbitrary interference or alien control. Hence, the notion of domination is complex and appears to share something in common with other cognate concepts such as injustice, inequality, and exclusion,[20] and this is why this concept is particularly interesting for constitutional lawyers.[21]

In Pettit's terms, however, domination means something along the lines of, 'living under any agent who possesses the capacity to interfere with choices in an arbitrary manner'.[22] To be free, therefore, requires one consciously to have the personal, natural, and social resources to be able to satisfy one's will. With arbitrary power, Pettit does not seem to mean a decision that is based upon judgment or preference of the agent as such, but rather one based solely upon the agent's subjective *arbitrary* will.[23] This approach has recently been criticized by scholars who suggest that the classic focus on arbitrariness as the central element of domination is mistaken, and what is needed is a Weberian view of domination as being informed by societal strictures.[24] In addition, critics argue that domination in the modern world is often not arbitrary, but very strategic and routinized.[25] According to this view, domination cannot be reduced merely to an

von Hirsch and AP Simester, *Crimes, Harms, Wrongs: On the Principles of Criminalisation* (Hart Publishing 2011) ch 2.

[17] Berlin (n 15) and discussion in Daly (n 13).
[18] ibid.
[19] Schuppert (n 6) 440.
[20] Mira Bachvarova, 'Non-domination's Role in the Theorizing of Global Justice' (2013), 9 Journal of Global Ethics 173.
[21] Daly (n 13).
[22] Pettit, *On the People's Terms* (n 3) 58f; and discussion in Frank Lovett, *A General Theory of Domination and Justice* (Oxford University Press 2010).
[23] Lovett, *A General Theory of Domination and Justice* (n 22).
[24] Michael J Thompson, 'Reconstructing Republican Freedom' (2013), 39 Philosophy & Social Criticism 277.
[25] ibid.

agent, but must be seen as being generated by the logic of social structure. The standard account on non-domination seems to be that, in the words of Frank Lovett, 'Public policies, institutions and so forth ought to be designed with the aim of reducing domination, so far as this is feasible'.[26]

In any case, while many scholars have criticized the republican take on freedom, that is, democracy as grounded in freedom as non-domination rather than equality, more recently, the question of non-domination has reached the limelight anew as a more general stricture for understanding power structures.[27]

According to Forst, and also Arthur Ripstein in his chapter in this volume, on the Kantian model: a discourse-theoretical notion of non-domination, unlike a neo-republican version, does not focus on the robustness of the protection of secured spheres of individual freedom of choice.[28] Instead, it focuses on the normative standing of persons as justificatory equals and normative authorities within a political and social order as an order of justification. [29] From the lens of law, this debate seems related to the discussion on the value of constitutionalism as such.[30] This is confirmed by the approach adopted by Alon Harel and Ripstein on the non-instrumental, or innate value, of constitutionalism and humanity.[31] In the political theory context, as Christian Rostbøll observes, some contemporary political thinkers ground democracy in equality, rather than freedom, and suggest that the value of democracy is instrumental.[32] Thus, on the instrumental view, the value and legitimacy of democracy are derived from the consequences to which it is believed to be the best feasible means.[33] The value and legitimacy of democracy, from a non-instrumental perspective, lies in something that is internal to and expressed by democratic decision-making. Others, like David Estlund, consider the appeal of democracy as associated with the importance of fair procedures.[34] Also Rostbøll himself, as confirmed in his chapter in this edited book, argues for an non-instrumental interpretation of democracy.

In sum the idea of non-domination as the foremost yardstick for testing the level of freedom in a society.[35] Therefore, a common theme in the literature on

[26] Frank Lovett, 'Should Republicans Be Cosmopolitan?' (2016), 9 Global Justice: Theory Practice Rhetoric 28, 35.

[27] Daly (n 13).

[28] Forst, 'A Kantian Republican Conception of Justice as Non-Domination' (n 9); and chapter by Ripstein in this volume.

[29] This seems to bring Forst close to that of the non-instrumental viewpoint: Rainer Forst, 'Noumenal Power' (2015), 23 Journal of Political Philosophy 111.

[30] Harel (n 10) ch 2; and chapter in this volume.

[31] See chapters by Harel and Ripstein in this volume.

[32] Rostbøll (n 8).

[33] ibid.

[34] David M Estlund, *Democratic Authority: A Philosophical Framework* (Princeton University Press 2008); and Rostbøll (n 8).

[35] See, for example, Hirsch and Simester (n 16) 3–7.

domination is the linkage between the basics of democracy and the striving for justice. The notion of non-domination could then be formulated as a constitutional 'right' to freedom, in that nobody is to be subject to arbitrary power.[36]

Let me now briefly address the relationship between coercion and that of domination, which seems relevant in a legal context.

For Rawls, 'political' power is always coercive power.[37] Moreover, any coercive political community must respect the dignity of those over whom it exercises dominion by showing equal concern and respect for them all.[38] For this reason, it has been proposed that the ideal of non-domination can be interpreted as a normative argument for cosmopolitan democracy.[39]

While the idea of non-domination for measuring freedom is a well-known concept in political theory,[40] in a legal context, it seems more common to refer to 'coercion', rather than the notion of domination as such. For example, for Dworkin, any conception of law must explain why law is the legitimate authority for coercion.[41] A state is said to coerce its citizens because it issues commands (laws) backed by the threat of sanctions.[42] Indeed, any textbook on criminal law starts with the question of coercion, and explains how it is an obstacle to freedom as well as a means to it.[43] As Kumm has recently pointed out, individual actors might not always be motivated to do what is required by justice. The institutionalization of a constitutional system seeks to add non-moral incentives—the threat of institutionalized sanctions of some kind— to support and stabilize justice-respecting behaviour and counter domination.[44] But coercion, just like domination, is an essentially contested concept.[45] According to Ripstein any questions about coercion are to be answered by considering the potential costs of giving a certain type of power to the state.[46] Ripstein adopts the Kantian approach in which, without a state, all uses of force are arbitrary. The coercive power of the state, he concedes, may well be needed to deter malefactors and to assure citizens of one another's compliance with the law. The point that he makes

[36] See chapters by Ripstein and Daly in this volume.

[37] John Rawls, *Political Liberalism* (Columbia University Press 1993).

[38] Ronald Dworkin, 'A New Philosophy for International Law' (2013), 41 Philosophy & Public Affairs 2.

[39] James Bohman, 'Nondomination and Transnational Democracy' in Cécile Laborde and John W Maynor (eds), *Republicanism and Theory* (Blackwell Publishing 2008).

[40] But see Andrea Sangiovanni, 'The Irrelevance of Coercion, Imposition, and Framing to Distributive Justice' (2012), 40 Philosophy & Public Affairs 79.

[41] Ronald Dworkin, *Law's Empire* (Hart Publishing 1998) 190.

[42] See eg HLA Hart, *The Concept of Law* (3rd edn, Oxford University Press 2012) ch 3. See also discussion in a global context, eg Laura Valentini, *Justice in a Globalized World: A Normative Framework* (Oxford University Press 2011).

[43] ibid.

[44] Kumm, 'Constituent Power, Cosmopolitan Constitutionalism, and Post-positivist Law' (n 11).

[45] Ian Shapiro, 'On Non-domination' (2012), 62 University of Toronto Law Journal 293.

[46] Arthur Ripstein, 'Authority and Coercion' (2004), 32 Philosophy & Public Affairs 2.

is that the ways in which the state may legitimately exercise its coercive power cannot delimit what justice itself is. As indicated, for Rawls, political power is always coercive power and always backed by the government's use of sanctions.[47] It is also about the legitimacy of the general structure of authority and the idea of public reason is intimately connected. Perhaps, this is in line with Dworkinian course of reasoning: that fundamental values of equal concern and respect are interpreted in the light of their role in a coercive order.[48] After all, it was Dworkin who stated that:

> the various standards governing the state's use of coercion against its citizens be consistent in the sense that they express a single and comprehensive vision of justice.[49]

For him, coercive political organizations undermine the dignity of their members unless each accepts a reciprocal responsibility to the others to respect collective decisions, provided that these decisions meet the appropriate conditions. Moreover, Dworkin famously linked the general justification for the exercise of the coercive power of state with that of the moral obligation of citizens to obey the law.[50] So every conception, in Dworkin's terms, therefore faces the same dilemma, as it asks the question of whether anything can justify coercion in ordinary politics? Rawls's notion of justification is, instead, rather a justification of coercion coupled to the question of the extent to which coercion is a necessary price to pay for people living in a state together.[51]

The question of coercion just like non-domination, then, seems to be tied to the question of legitimacy. As Mira Bachvarova argues, the concept of non-domination in a global context can usefully be turned into a question of legitimacy while retaining the republican idea of freedom.[52] It seems as if the question of legitimacy is also contingent on the right to justification.[53]

[47] Rawls, *Political Liberalism* (n 37) ch 1.

[48] Dworkin, *Law's Empire* (n 41) 190f. See also Ronald Dworkin, *Justice for Hedgehogs* (The Belknap Press of Harvard University Press 2011); AJ Simmons, 'Justification and Legitimacy' (1999), 109 Ethics 739.

[49] Dworkin, *Law's Empire* (n 41) 134.

[50] ibid 190f; Simmons (n 48).

[51] Sangiovanni, 'The Irrelevance of Coercion, Imposition, and Framing to Distributive Justice' (n 40).

[52] Bachvarova (n 20).

[53] And that legitimacy is not only a question of the legitimacy of how states are created but also a question of justification of its 'everyday' business: Simmons (n 48); also discussed in Joel Colón-Ríos, *Weak Constitutionalism: Democratic Legitimacy and the Question of Constituent Power* (Routledge 2012) ch 6. See also Jean L Cohen, *Globalization and Sovereignty: Rethinking Legality, Legitimacy, and Constitutionalism* (Cambridge University Press 2012).

III. Legitimacy and Justification in the Context of Non-Domination

This section will now try to give a brief account of the main linkage between the question of legitimacy and justification and what implications it may have for our understanding of the concept of non-domination. For Forst, every political philosophy raises the question of the justification of legitimate rule, but very few take the principle of justification itself as a principle of discursive practice as their theoretical foundation.[54] Justification applies when what is at stake is exercising rule over others. According to Forst, this applies both in political and moral context. Justification is normative as a basic concept for practical reason and as a practice of moral and political autonomy. But before briefly unfolding the non-domination, legitimacy, and justification turf: it is contended that the freedom component, when viewed against the current domination of security, is a reasonable expectation for ensuring justice. It could be argued, that the notion of justification is deeply associated with the question of how to create a European legal culture in AFSJ matters that genuinely cares for the individual.

In the following I will briefly set out (what I consider) the main points about legitimacy and how it is connected to that of justification. Indeed, Bernard Williams has famously argued that a state 'has to be able to offer a justification of its power to *each subject*'.[55] And, for Hannah Arendt, the question of justification is inherently connected to that of legitimacy, where the former depends on how the purported government has acquired its powers and the quality of the justification given.[56] Legitimacy then speaks to the moral quality of power relations between specific agents.[57] The point, with Dworkin, is to establish the rule of law by setting boundaries to the social power of various actors so that social affairs are governed by principle and not by force (in a democracy, there will always be those who voted against the current regime). For Dworkin, this

[54] Rainer Forst, 'Introduction: On the Idea of a Critique of Relations of Justification' in Rainer Forst, *Justification and Critique: Towards a Critical Theory of Politics* (Ciaran Cronin tr, Polity Press 2013) 5.

[55] See Bernard Williams, 'Realism and Moralism' in Bernard Williams, *In the Beginning Was the Deed: Realism and Moralism in Political Argument* (Geoffrey Hawthorn ed, Princeton University Press 2005) 4; also discussed in David Dyzenhaus, 'Process and Substance as Aspects of the Public Law Form' (2015), 74 The Cambridge Law Journal 284. See also Jan P Beetz and Enzo Rossi, 'The EU's Democratic Deficit in a Realist Key: Multilateral Governance, Popular Sovereignty and Critical Responsiveness' (2017), 8 Transnational Legal Theory 228.

[56] See discussion in Christian Volk, 'Towards a Critical Theory of the Political' (2016), 42 Philosophy & Social Criticism 549. See also Pettit, who argues that there can be no effective system of justice without the state. For him the question of justice is deep down one of legitimacy as non-interference. The distinction non-interference/non-domination appear somewhat vague: Pettit, *On the People's Terms* (n 3).

[57] Simmons (n 48); and Forst (n 2).

is the classic problem of legitimacy, as it rides on the back of another problem, that of political obligation, and is linked to the question of justification of state action.[58]

Likewise, in Rawlsian terms, and according to his 'liberal principle of legitimacy', the use of political power is fully proper only when 'it is exercised in accordance with a constitution the essentials of which all citizens as free and equal may reasonably be expected to endorse in light of the principles and ideals acceptable to their common human reason'.[59] Max Weber, in turn, approached legitimacy as a subcategory of domination, by which he meant the probability that certain specific commands will be obeyed by a given group of persons. Moreover, every genuine form of domination implies a minimum of voluntary compliance, that is, an interest in obedience. Hence, Weber used the word 'legitimate' in order to characterize one type of domination: the type in which obedience is based in part upon the belief that command is binding. In this sense, society has legitimacy when its members are willing to assume the disciplines and burdens which membership entails.[60] Weber saw legitimacy as embedded in an order of domination, in which obedience is based upon the belief that the command in question is binding.[61] Moreover, in Raz's theory of legitimate authority, legitimacy is ultimately derived from the citizens' interest in following the authority's directives, rather than from any facts about the authorities themselves.[62] With Jürgen Habermas, laws are legitimate if they can be conceived as both self-imposed and binding.[63] He is well known for grounding his account of democratic politics with its guiding normative idea of legitimacy in what people would agree to in the absence of coercion.[64] Yet, it has been suggested that Habermas does not specify specific institutions, but instead argues that people would be persuaded to the best arrangement through uncoerced deliberations.[65] Thus, Habermas has been criticized for ignoring the importance of the question of power, in contrast

58 Dworkin, *Law's Empire* (n 41) 191.

59 John Rawls, *Political Liberalism* (expanded edn, Columbia University Press 2005).

60 Discussed in Simmons (n 48), citing Tom R Tyler, *Why People Obey the Law* (Yale University Press 1990).

61 Max Weber's *Economy and Society*, discussed in Alan Cromartie, 'Legitimacy' in Richard Bellamy and Andrew Mason (eds), *Political Concepts* (Manchester University Press 2003).

62 Joseph Raz, *The Morality of Freedom* (Clarendon Press 1986) ch 4. See also Wojciech Sadurski, 'Reason of State and Public Reason' (2014), 27 Ratio Juris 21.

63 Jürgen Habermas, *Between Facts and Norms: Contributions to a Discourse Theory of Law and Democracy* (William Rehg tr, MIT Press 1996); also in Michel Rosenfield, 'Constitutional versus Administrative Ordering in an Era of Globalization and Privatization: Reflections on Sources of Legitimation in the Post-Westphalian Polity' (2011), 32 Cardozo Law Review 2339.

64 Shapiro (n 45).

65 ibid.

to Foucault's view on domination, which is rooted in the recognition of power as the characteristics of politics.[66]

Does that then mean that an unjust society, which is still valued by some of its members, is legitimate? This is where the questions of justice and justification usually enters the debate and in which human rights and the rule of law insists on a quality check of legal measures. For Forst, the concept of legitimacy is partly descriptive, as it owes its overlaying, more salient function of normative criticism or defence to other resources.[67] The question of power, as Forst points out, is the first question of justice.[68] Indeed, a just society demands creativity on how to imagine a just system: and justice is what the power allows in practice. And, as he continues, the concept of justice is integrated in the right to justification, and is at the very heart of a non-domination-oriented conception of law and justice.[69] As Ian Shapiro points out regardless of whether political theorists see freedom as a feature of justice or an alternative to it, they treat it as the coin of the realm in judging the legitimacy of political institutions. Therefore, Shapiro argues that 'democratic competition offers the best hope for mitigating domination. As a result, working to protect and expand it is the best path forward for those who regard non-domination as the bedrock of justice'.[70]

Also, for Allen Buchanan, legitimacy is an ecological notion which makes sense when one thinks of how it fits into the 'system'.[71] With Forst then, instead of imagining justice as a distribution machine which allocates various goods in a just way, justice allows individuals equality and the right to justification for any decisions that concern them and form part of the very idea of human dignity.[72] The question of legitimacy is then interwoven with justification as it requires a good enough justification.

On this background, it is needed to briefly explain why judicial review is an adequate tool in the context of non-domination and the right to justification.

[66] ibid and Michel Foucault, *The Archaeology of Knowledge and the Discourse on Language* (AM Sheridan Smith tr, Pantheon Books 1972).

[67] Rainer Forst, 'Legitimacy, Democracy, and Justice: On the Reflexivity of Normative Orders' in Rainer Forst, *Normativity and Power: Analyzing Social Orders of Justification* (Ciaran Cronin tr, Oxford University Press 2017).

[68] Rainer Forst, 'First Things First: Redistribution, Recognition and Justification' (2007), 6 European Journal of Political Theory 291.

[69] Philip Pettit, 'A Republican Law of Peoples' (2010), 9 European Journal of Political Theory 70; and Shapiro (n 45) 311.

[70] Shapiro (n 45) 335.

[71] Allen E Buchanan, *The Heart of Human Rights* (Oxford University Press 2014) 198.

[72] Rainer Forst, *Justification and Critique: Towards a Critical Theory of Politics* (Ciaran Cronin tr, Polity Press 2013).

IV. Judicial Review and Non-Domination

The idea of judicial review is commonly seen as the hallmark of the constitutionalist way of thinking about law. Central to the idea of freedom as non-domination, according to neo-republican thinkers like Pettit, is a strong form of judicial review as a vital check on arbitrary powers.[73] The reason for this is that what constitutes non-arbitrary intervention is best preformed through a non-political procedure. Perhaps, this appears in contrast to other republican thinkers, such as Richard Bellamy, who view courts as inherently undemocratic.[74] Also scholars like Jeremy Waldron have structurally argued against the institution of judicial review as they see it as fundamentally undemocratic.[75] Others, have suggested that the de-politicization of rights by taking them outside the political domain and to courts could amount to political domination.[76] Yet, Daly's point, in his chapter in this volume, is that even the fiercest opponents of judicial review in the republicanisms camp may, in some instances, agree that judicial review is a good idea. A republican argument in favour of courts taking account of power differentials in certain context while remaining sceptical as to whether judicial power can reduce power differentials in society at large. He argues for a context-based approach as I understand him, in which it is necessary to pay attention to citizens' perceived experience of freedom and unfreedom.[77] As Daly argues in his chapter in this volume, if rights are understood as channelling the kinds of reasons that governments can invoke when they act in certain arenas, and therefore are not trumps *à la* Dworkin, but rather its channels and its pointers, this has a republican flavour.

But in practical terms: What would it take for a court to interfere upon the basis of non-domination in a security context? What sort of argument would hold in a court? The basic right of due process is, of course, also a guarantee against domination in the courtroom. Moreover, in the EU security-related context, this question would seem to turn largely on the elasticity of the proportionality principle as a legal expression of the right to justification. Moreover, clearly, it could be argued that the rights in the EU Charter of Fundamental Rights and the Convention on Human Rights, by themselves, work as a buffer against state domination of the individual.[78] And the problem here is what we create from the proportionality test (as a sword or a shield).

[73] Pettit, *On the People's Terms* (n 3); also discussed in Daly (n 13).

[74] Richard Bellamy, *Political Constitutionalism* (Cambridge University Press 2007) ch 1. See also Jeremy Waldron, *Law and Disagreement* (Oxford University Press 1999) ch 13.

[75] Waldron (n 74).

[76] See chapter by Daly in this volume.

[77] ibid.

[78] Mattias Kumm, 'The Turn to Justification: On the Structure and Domain of Human Rights Practice' in Adam Etinson (ed), *Human Rights: Moral or Political?* (Oxford University Press 2018).

As Aharon Barak has pointed out:

> Real democracy is not just the law of rules and legislative supremacy. Democracy is a multi-dimensional concept. It requires recognition of the power of the majority and limitations on the power of the majority.[79]

For him, proportionality serves as a tool, making sure that law is upheld even in the worst of times.

As Kumm observes, the question of politics is the practice of rights-based justice-seeking among free and equal people under conditions of reasonable disagreement.[80] And yet, in the EU context, this might pre-suppose a shared platform, a culture of values. The question of a common European culture is a very relevant one for this mission of establishing a common solidarity. The idea of solidarity between the Member States is a constitutional obligation in EU law (Article 2 Treaty of the European Union and the EU Charter of Fundamental Rights).[81]

But how can this be done in the EU's emergency-driven security legislation? It seems close to heart for any EU constitutional scholar to think that the principle of proportionality understood critically offers the best available constitutional solution for establishing the idea of solidarity as a workable legal principle through the key of proportionality reasoning.[82] As this section will argue, the merits of proportionality outweigh its downsides, as it could help improve the democratic shortcomings in the AFSJ and secure rights where the legislator has failed to do so. But we still need to explain why it is reflected in a non-domination based view. Borrowing from Daly and Matthias Klatt, proportionality can be interpreted as a mechanism for ensuring that coercive state interference remains non-arbitrary in the republican sense:[83]

> the more technical aspects of the proportionality doctrine—particularly the requirement of a rational connection between the means and end of a

[79] Aharon Barak, 'The Role of a Supreme Court in a Democracy and the Fight Against Terrorism' (2005), 35 Hong Kong Law Journal 287.

[80] Mattias Kumm, 'The Idea of Socratic Contestation and the Right to Justification: The Point of Rights-Based Proportionality Review' (2010), 4 Law & Ethics of Human Rights 141.

[81] On solidarity, see eg Andrea Sangiovanni, 'Solidarity in the European Union' (2013), 33 Oxford Journal of Legal Studies 213.

[82] See, eg Aharon Barak, *Proportionality: Constitutional Rights and Their Limitations* (Doron Kalir tr, Cambridge University Press 2012); Robert Alexy, *A Theory of Constitutional Rights* (Julian Rivers tr, Oxford University Press 2002); Vicki C Jackson, 'Constitutional Law in an Age of Proportionality' (2015), 124 Yale Law Journal 3094; Matthias Klatt and Moritz Meister, *The Constitutional Structure of Proportionality* (Oxford University Press 2012); Kai Möller, *The Global Model of Constitutional Rights* (Oxford University Press 2012); Kumm, 'The Idea of Socratic Contestation and the Right to Justification' (n 80).

[83] See chapters by Daly and Klatt in this volume.

> restriction on rights—helps to show, that constitutional rights are not moral rights, institutionalised, but rather, controls on the predicates of state power.[84]

By understanding the meaning of 'non-domination' as a realization of freedom and justice, this will help us to link the rather abstract right to justification to the more 'graspable' proportionality test, and will confirm the need for both *ex ante* and *ex post* checks of the legislative domain.[85] While the EU's heavy reliance on security as a justificatory tool for the EU's presence both on the internal and the external scene has been criticized by academics in the last decade, it still plays an important role as the main driving force for the furthering of the EU security agenda.[86] From the perspective of 'justice', such an approach has been problematical since the basic due-process fundamentals were not given significant weight in the supranational state of security. However, as the EU is taking on more state-like features, it inevitably has to address some of the core 'old nation state' questions: the need to justify any use of coercive powers and to tackle the issue of what it means to refer to justice within a Union of twenty-eight Member States (alas with one core member state, the U.K., about to leave through its'Brexit' process, which started in 2016). Thus, as the EU pushes forward with deterrent measures to ensure a high level of security, the *status quo* in AFSJ law has become one of a 'too preventive' regime, in which the safeguards of the individual are lost, despite the grand treaty values. Perhaps, it could even be argued that the rights in the EU Charter of Fundamental Rights (Charter) and the European Convention on Human Rights at present appear empty assertions, in so far that not enough is being done at political level to ensure a European culture of due process when the nation state no longer supplies adequate legal safeguards.

But how this is achieved at EU level *in concreto* is trickier. One question that automatically arises when discussing the EU's security mission is how it is related to the identity of the AFSJ, and the extent to which this identity mission is more broadly tied to the EU's symbolic function. This is because, just like 'security', terms such as 'symbolic' run the risk of being used in an overly broad way. Added to this is the tendency for ill-defined legislation, and concealment[87] in the legislative process, arguably constituting domination at the expense of adequate high human-rights protection. A critical notion of justice within the AFSJ is—as this chapter argues—linked to the basic right of justification as a counter-measure to domination.

[84] See chapter by Daly in this volume.

[85] See chapter by Klatt in this volume.

[86] See Sionaidh Douglas-Scott, 'The Problem of Justice in the European Union' in Julie Dickson and Pavlos Eleftheriadis (eds), *Philosophical Foundations of European Union Law* (Oxford University Press 2012).

[87] eg Deirdre Curtin, 'Overseeing Secrets in the EU: A Democratic Perspective' (2014), 52 Journal of Common Market Studies 684.

V. Translating the 'Non-Domination' Question to the Supranational EU Level and Its Relevance for EU Security Regulation

It is worthwhile clarifying in brief why the concept of non-domination is a useful one in the area of EU constitutional law, and why it is linked to the debate on non-domination.[88]

Indeed, the freedom argument coupled to that of non-domination, seems an essential component of the EU legal objectives. While much of the current debate on legitimacy has focused on the notorious democratic deficit within the EU and the need to move away from state templates, EU lawyers have tended to avoid the associated issue of legitimacy as well as the political theory concept of the meanings and critical understanding of freedom as non-domination.

As noted earlier, domination, when debating the supranational structure of the EU, is that of the lack of a monopoly of force, the 'coercion' question. The EU is not a state, even though it increasingly comprises state-like features, and the very lack of coercive power is often highlighted as one of the criteria distinguishing the EU from a nation state.[89] Despite the EU's lack of traditional coercive powers, the entry into force of the Treaty of Lisbon, and therein the increased role of the Union legislator, means that the EU has gained increased sanctioning powers because of being entrusted with some monopoly of force. Yet, perhaps it is worth asking whether the theory of coercion as the benchmark for assessing the legitimacy of the nation state[90] really matters to the EU? From the start, the EU has been built on a decentralized system, in which the Member States act as gatekeepers and enforcers of EU law on the national stage. Not only do the Member States run the risk of infringement procedures being initiated by the EU Commission, but their national courts have been turned into infiltrators by the Court of Justice, and are required to enforce EU law in the domestic setting.[91]

Coercion in the EU context, therefore, involves the use of arbitrary powers and can be traced back, for example, to poorly drafted legislation and deficient legal reasoning in the Court of Justice. As a result, domination was not wiped off the agenda by the creation of the EU and its genesis as a peace project; instead, a

[88] On legitimacy in EU law, see eg Joseph Weiler, 'The Transformation of Europe' (1991), 100 Yale Law Journal 2403; Paul Craig, 'Integration, Democracy, and Legitimacy' in Paul Craig and Gráinne de Búrca (eds), *The Evolution of EU Law* (2nd edn, Oxford University Press 2011); and Anthony Arnull and Daniel Wincott (eds), *Accountability and Legitimacy in the European Union* (Oxford University Press 2002). See also Sangiovanni (n 81).

[89] Jürgen Neyer, *The Justification of Europe: A Political Theory of Supranational Integration* (Oxford University Press 2012).

[90] Andreas Føllesdal and Simon Hix, 'Why There Is a Democratic Deficit in the EU: A Response to Majone and Moravcsik' (2006), 44 Journal of Common Market Studies 533.

[91] On this story, eg Marcus Klamert, *The Principle of Loyalty in EU Law* (Oxford University Press 2014) and Stephen Weatherill, *Law and Values in the European Union* (Oxford University Press 2016).

different form of domination developed: that of the extraordinary powers of the Court of Justice and the Commission, the two strongest EU institutions. The ambitious reading of EU law by the Court is well documented,[92] while the Court has also long been an active player with regard to determining the values to be promoted by the EU.[93] In addition to the more overarching goal of creating an autonomous European legal order that provides adequate safeguards of fundamental rights and grants individuals rights in national courts,[94] the Court of Justice has read values into the idea of loyalty as a holistic mechanism for maintaining and establishing continuing European integration.

In a traditional EU constitutionalist world, the EU has its own constitutional structure in its commitment to human rights, democracy, and the rule of law, and this commitment would be at its heart. The debate about the constitutional character of EU law should therefore be seen as a debate about how to understand the conditions of constitutional legitimacy and European authority.[95] The continuing search for legitimacy, when related to the political theory debate, seems to turn on the EU's need to re-invent its ambitions, and its narrative. When discussing the EU's legitimacy, the starting-point—from an EU legal perspective—is the democratic credentials of the EU, which are also connected to legitimacy, and the latter is a constitutional principle of the EU, as recognized in Article 2 EU, and is listed as one of the principles that inspired the creation of the EU. Central to the rule of law is the idea of bounded government restrained by law from acting outside its powers.[96] For one thing, the question of legitimacy and the aspiration to achieve justice are not necessarily the same thing. After all, law may be 'just' without having been legitimately enacted, and legitimate while failing to be just.[97] The rule of law pre-supposes, therefore, that both of these criteria are fulfilled. So, if we have rule of law, why do we need justification and proportionality are they not already part of the rule of law criteria? The answer, as I see it, is that these concepts are more concrete in legal practice as representing a contextualized approach to justice as a counter mechanism to domination.

[92] See, eg Karen J Alter, *The European Court's Political Power: Selected Essays* (Oxford University Press 2009).

[93] See, eg Case C-159/90 *Society for the Protection of Unborn Children Ireland Ltd. v Grogan* [1991] ECR 4685; Case C-36/02 *Omega Spielhallen- und Automatenaufstellungs-GmbH v Oberbürgermeisterin der Bundesstadt Bonn* [2004] ECR I-9609; Case C-208/09 *Sayn-Wittgenstein v Von Wien* [2011] ECR I-13693.

[94] Case C-6/64 *Costa v ENEL* [1964] ECR 585.

[95] Case C-294/83 *Les Verts* [1986] ECR 1339. Famously, the Court of Justice declared that the Community had a basic constitutional charter based on the rule of law.

[96] See Mattias Kumm, 'The Moral Point of Constitutional Pluralism: Defining the Domain of Legitimate Institutional Civil Disobedience and Conscientious Objection' in Julie Dickson and Pavlos Eleftheriadis (eds), *Philosophical Foundations of European Union Law* (Oxford University Press 2012).

[97] Charles Larmore, 'What Is Political Philosophy?' (2013), 10 Journal of Moral Philosophy 276.

But let us turn once more to the notion of non-domination in the EU security-related context.

VI. Domination and Security, the Specific Case of the AFSJ

In the following, I propose that the core of AFSJ law be properly framed as a question of how the EU justifies its endeavours. As already mentioned, the EU promises to deliver its citizens an area of freedom and security built on (and reconcilable with) the concept of justice, thereby indicating the demand for a balance to be struck between these, sometimes conflicting, values. For this reason, there is a need to identify an adequate legal framework for reference when searching for an appropriate theoretical foundation in this area. Such identification involves pinning down the extent to which we can translate supranational EU principles developed upon the basis of the EU Treaty, and, as such, often in the context of economics to the AFSJ.

Of relevance for this project is how the AFSJ legal framework should be understood in concrete legal terms. The AFSJ as an EU objective is defined in Article 3(2) Treaty of the European Union (TEU). This provision lays down the EU's mission in this area by promising that the EU is to offer its citizens an AFSJ in which the free movement of persons is ensured in conjunction with appropriate measures with respect to external border controls, asylum, immigration, and the prevention and combating of crime. Article 4 TFEU confirms this mission by explicitly acknowledging the EU's competence within the AFSJ, and making it clear that, in achieving such a constitutional space, the EU shares its competences with the Member States. Article 67 TFEU adds to this by setting out the AFSJ objectives in further detail. These objectives are phrased as goals and stipulate that:

> The Union shall endeavour to ensure a high level of security through measures to prevent and combat crime, racism and xenophobia, and through measures for coordination and cooperation between police and judicial authorities and other competent authorities, as well as through the mutual recognition of judgments in criminal matters and, if necessary, through the approximation of criminal laws.[98]

While this remains an important task, what is still lacking, however, is a normative and critical debate on how the EU could construct an AFSJ that integrates its mission of establishing an effective response to the growing global security threat

[98] These EU objectives to be achieved are supplemented by Article 68 TFEU, which stipulates that the European Council 'shall define the strategic guidelines for legislative and operational planning'; part of this planning involves the drawing up agendas of points to be achieved in the future AFSJ. But,

posed by the unstable situation in the world, growing migration moment and political violence and radicalization, with the EU values of human rights and the promotion of justice. In other words, the phenomenon of globalization also affects the EU also and the constitutional skeleton for addressing these problems needs to uphold the rule of law (Article 2 Treaty of the EU).

What are the exact implications of a right to justification with regard to the construction of the AFSJ as a justice space when we are discussing humanitarian questions such as the refugee crisis in 2015–16? Is it even legitimate that the EU sets out to establish an AFSJ within the EU territory? What does it tell us about the EU's obligations towards outsiders?[99] While these questions are indeed big issues, both practically and philosophically, they still need to form the backbone of what we are discussing in the AFSJ. Should we accept a cosmopolitan claim of a duty of justice towards outsiders?[100]

While it would seem politically utopian to claim cosmopolitan-based justice when some 'old' Member States still have problems with the 'new' Member States, the conception of justice could still inform the European Treaty–based interpretation of what it means to refer to solidarity. Increasingly, the EU invokes criminal sanctions as a preventive strategy in dealing with migrants, who are put into detention as part of the securitization of the AFSJ.

Against this background, the EU's new Security Agenda identifies three priorities for the EU: fighting terrorism, organized crime, and the suppression of cyber crime.[101] Indeed, security regulation in the EU is one that is constantly challenged and constantly evolving, the latest Anti-Money Laundering and Counter Terrorism Financing directive and the new directive on the fight against terrorism being recent examples of risk based approaches to security in the EU.[102] To date it has evolved as an enterprise of risk regulation and one which has been largely influenced by administrative practices and market

in order for the EU to draw up a successful future schedule for the EU to develop its justice plan, the EU needs to add positively to the debate, by helping the Member States to structure their national laws and improve due process rights.

---

[99] Ian Ward, 'Identifying the European Other' (2002), 14 International Journal of Refugee Law 219, 221.

[100] On cosmopolitan law, see eg Mattias Kumm, 'The Cosmopolitan Turn in Constitutionalism: An Integrated Conception of Public Law' (2013), 20 Indiana Journal of Global Legal Studies 605; and Alexander Somek, *The Cosmopolitan Constitution* (Oxford University Press 2014).

[101] To address these threats, the Security Agenda 2015-2020, COM (2015) 185 final,) intends to strengthen and make more effective the exchange of information and the operational co-operation between Member States, EU agencies, and the IT sector.

[102] Directive 2018/843, on the prevention of the use of the financial system for the purposes of money laundering or terrorist financing, OJ L 156/43; Directive 2017/541 on combating terrorism and replacing Council Framework Decision 2002/475/JHA and amending Council Decision 2005/671/JHA, OJL 88, 31 March 2017, 6–21.

construction (the mission of creating an internal market) and not as a question of constitutional law. It could be argued that the effect of security regulation in the AFSJ context comes close to domination, in that the EU often adopts security-focused measures upon emergency-based grounds. It could be argued that, at macro level, 'domination' may be identified in the way in which the EU uses security to extend its objectives into new areas. At micro level, conversely, domination may be identified in the way in which the security dogma deprives individuals of some of their basic due process rights which were traditionally guaranteed by the nation state, as the current system is so oriented towards a preventive regime.

And yet, and as outlined earlier, with respect to the broader issue of sanctioning authority in the EU, many commentators on Europe have discussed the EU's lack of coercive power as the main feature that distinguishes it from a nation state.[103]

The significance of achieving security has spilled over to the more general ambition of the market-based approach to the EU's fight against crime and the financing of terrorism, which has led to a preventive approach and a coupling of the market, and to that of achieving security through penal measures.[104] Recent examples here include criminal law measures in the area of financial crimes that combines a threat of the financing of terrorism and endeavours to stabilize the market by getting tough on white-collar crime.[105] These are only brief examples, but, at their core, there is an innate need for the EU to work out a strategy for the AFSJ. It is true that the multi-annual AFSJ programme like the aforementioned EU Security Agenda and the ambitions set out in these ambitious agendas, reflect a wish among the EU institution to be firm on the future application of the rule of law. But there is a striking absence, in the political discussion, of how to shape this area and what, precisely, justice (as part of the AFSJ) can add to the debate.[106]

[103] eg Neyer (n 89).

[104] See eg Directive 2013/40/EU, L 218/8 directive on attacks against information systems and repealing Council Framework Decision 2005/222/JHA.

[105] Ester Herlin-Karnell, 'Constructing Europe's Area of Freedom, Security and Justice through the Framework of "Regulation": A Cascade of Market Based Challenges in the EU's Fight against Financial Crime' (2015), 16 German Law Journal 49. See also discussion in Ester Herlin-Karnell, 'The Domination of Security and the Promise of Justice: On Justification and Proportionality in Europe's "Area of Freedom, Security and Justice"' (2017), 8 Transnational Legal Theory 79.

[106] See Sionaidh Douglas-Scott, 'Human Rights as a Basis for Justice in the European Union' (2017), 8 Transnational Legal Theory 59.

VII. What Kind of Justification and What Kind of Solidarity?

When understanding the legal corpus which forms the AFSJ, we also need to take the political theory dimension as discussed earlier into account and the need for the EU legislator to supply a justification for its action not only to the Member States but also to the citizens. Even if we agree that the EU has adopted an overly preventive stance towards the creation of the AFSJ, what can be done about it and what is the function of justice to remedy this accusation? After all, it seems as if the security focus on emergency is not isolated from, but closely related to, the broader constitutional crisis in Europe, and one that links up with the financial crisis in recent years, in that there is an increased effectiveness focus in the EU system as a whole. The main issue for the EU, in this respect, is its one-sided focus on prevention and enforcement, while it has largely ignored the need to ensure adequate protection of the individual so as to ensure a 'just' AFSJ space. The European Agenda on Migration[107] states that the EU has a duty to contribute its share in helping displaced persons in clear need of international protection, and that smugglers ought already be criminalized before they reached the shores of the EU. Moreover, the EU promises that it must continue engaging beyond its borders and strengthen co-operation with its global partners, address root causes, and promote modalities of legal migration that foster circular growth and development in the countries of origin and destination. Yet, this expansion of legal responsibilities beyond borders poses questions about legitimacy and human rights protection.

The EU is increasingly legislating on migration issues at the borders of Europe, or even outside its territories, extending the reach of EU law. Should there be an obligation for the EU to take into account needs of those outside the EU territory when legislating on new security regulation? And what does non-domination mean in this case? At international level, there seems to be no binding duty among states to assist an overburdened state.[108]

It seems to me that one key underlying issue is the following. What, if any, justification does the EU offer those entering its territory in submitting them to its current forms of regulation? Perhaps this poses the question as to why the EU need to offer a justification in the first place? Could one reasonably claim that this right to justification, amounts merely to 'a right of due process'/'to be treated fairly'? Contemporary constitutional law has for a long time been absorbed with the discussion of the question of 'outsiders' and justification in the context of the

[107] European Agenda on Migration, COM(2015) 240 final.

[108] Matthew J Gibney, 'Refugees and Justice between States' (2015), 14 European Journal of Political Theory 448.

Kantian idea of a 'cosmopolitan right' that requires those who arrive in the territory of a foreign state to be received without hostility or discrimination. Thus, for example, Buchanan stands for a certain cosmopolitan tradition in claiming that the basic idea behind the international legal regime of human rights is to regulate the behaviour of states towards all individuals within their jurisdiction.[109] This, however, is a problem at the regional and global stage if one wants to achieve a universal rights system beyond the state, such as in the case of the EU. This may go even beyond, such as a requirement that EU express and apply its obligation to accord safety and protection through operation that extends beyond its territory by, for example, the European coast guard (Frontex) outside the shores of Europe. Such externalization and extension of EU law would require a compelling discursive construction of the relationship between the EU and, for example, the migrant/refugee/smuggled/ trafficked person whereby the relationship enters into force before the migrant/refugee/trafficked person enters the EU space. Arguably in EU migration governance and the question as to how to tackle the refugee crisis as well as the EU strategies for fighting terrorism, the idea of solidarity has largely replaced the vocabulary of subsidiarity. Such a trajectory would help clarify what solidarity really means and thereby promote an understanding of it which equally respects 'freedom, security and justice'.

VIII. Is Non-Domination Utilized in Law through a Proportionality Test?

The question of a common European solidarity (or culture) is a very relevant one for the mission of establishing a common security area. But how can this be done in the EU's emergency-driven security legislation, driven by political considerations rather than legal concerns? As Kumm points out, the question of politics is the practice of rights-based justice seeking through a constitutional framework (among free and equal people) under conditions of reasonable disagreement.[110] It seems to me that the impact of rights-based proportionality in the EU security-regulated context and the notion of solidarity in the EU could play a significant function in the formation of the AFSJ. For Barak, for example, proportionality links up with the question of justice because: 'There is always law (domestic or international) according to which the state must act. There are no black-holes'.[111] The EU is not a state. But, while, in the EU, there seems currently to be a lot of

[109] See generally, Buchanan (n 71).
[110] Kumm, 'The Turn to Justification' (n 78).
[111] Barak, 'The Role of a Supreme Court in a Democracy and the Fight Against Terrorism' (n 79) 293f.

vacuum in the debate, the principle of proportionality allows for some stability, a rescuer until 'the real work' of legislation and deliberation begins, and this seems particularly important in criminal law and security regulation in order to avoid a 'ticking bomb' of state violence against the individual. Hence, the merits of proportionality outweigh its downsides, as it could help improve the democratic shortcomings in the AFSJ and secure rights where the legislator has failed to do so, assuming that we agree that this is what a democratic system should do.[112] It seems close to heart for any EU constitutional scholar to think that the principle of proportionality understood critically offers the best available constitutional solution for establishing the idea of solidarity as a workable legal principle through the key of proportionality reasoning.

At present, and as charted above, much of the thinking in the AFSJ is currently dominated by security, and the non-domination and justification through the principle of proportionality serves the purpose of ensuring constitutional rights protection at both the abstract and the concrete level. This chapter means to ask the greater question of assessing reasons in the AFSJ by asking how the principle of proportionality as a legal tool is reflected in the political theory debate on the right to justification. And with this concreteness, there is a need to pay more attention to the balancing question in practice through the EU Court of Justice's assessment of public reason in the courtroom.

As Malcolm Thorburn points out, constitutional rights and proportionality justification as a filtering mechanism through which we can determine what sorts of treatment of persons by the state are consistent with their status as free and equal bearers.[113] The legal-doctrinal idea of proportionate 'interference' in rights roughly maps on to the theoretical understanding of *interference without domination*.[114] For republicans, non-dominating interference must pursue a legitimate aim connected to a common public good, and this concern is captured, at least in part, in the existing methodologies of constitutional and human-rights courts.[115] It is true that in some variants, at least, the proportionality test will effectively require judges to make substantive, even intuitive appraisals as to the relative merits of competing claims of public and private right, and that this implicates judges in a more far-reaching normative endeavour, going beyond an assessment as to arbitrariness in its republican sense. In turn, this makes rights-based constitutional adjudication quite consistent with a 'political' concept of rights, and accommodating of the fact of 'disagreement' about rights.[116]

112 Kumm, 'The Idea of Socratic Contestation and the Right to Justification' (n 80).

113 Malcolm Thorburn, 'Proportionality' in David Dyzenhaus and Malcolm Thorburn (eds), *Philosophical Foundations of Constitutional Law* (Oxford University Press 2016). See also chapter by Klatt in this volume; and eg Barak, *Proportionality* (n 81); Alexy (n 81); Möller (n 81).

114 See chapter by Daly in this volume.

115 ibid.

116 Daly (n 13).

What values will be utilized in the proportionality test in EU security law? The right to justification and non-domination in the legislative process could be guaranteed by the more hands-on 'proportionality' test. One of the most sensitive testing fields for the enterprise of ensuring a constitutional rights is that of data protection in contemporary EU security law with the need for the increasing threat posed by cyber-related criminality and the apparent need to safeguard security having to be balanced against the need to protect fundamental rights. The EU has become an active player in fighting criminality in digital space, following the increased cyber-security threat and recent bugging scandals. The recent directive designed to deal with attacks against information systems seems closely linked to the EU's fight against organized crime.[117] This directive is based upon Article 83(1) TFEU, which covers computer crime in a broad sense.[118] For the past ten years, the EU has been making significant efforts to develop a framework capable of dealing with cyber-security in the EU area. At the core of the debate, however, is the sensitive relationship between the protection of human rights and the effective fighting of crime. Finally, in the *Digital Rights* case[119] the Court of Justice annulled the 2006 Data Retention Directive, which was aimed at fighting crime and terrorism, and which allowed data to be stored for up to two years. It concluded that the measure breached proportionality on the grounds that the directive had a too sweeping generality and therefore violated, *inter alia*, the basic right of data protection as set out in Article 8 of the Charter of Fundamental Rights. The directive authorized the gathering of data and far-reaching surveillance mechanisms in order to ensure the effective fight against crime. The approach was confirmed in the recent *Schrems* and *Tele2 Sverige*[120] cases, in which the Court held that:

> a legislation not providing for any possibility for an individual to pursue legal remedies in order to have access to personal data or to obtain the rectification or erasure of such data, does not respect the essence of the fundamental right to effective judicial protection, as enshrined in Article 47 of the Charter.

These judgments add to the construction of the AFSJ field but need to be explored further in theory. They raise a number of questions with regard to the function of the Charter of Fundamental Rights in the future, as well as the need for a clarification of the AFSJ narrative. If the Court is to develop criteria for the increasing

[117] Directive 2013/40/EU.
[118] Directive on attacks against information systems and repealing Council Framework Decision 2005/222/JHA.
[119] Joines Cases C-293/12 and C-594/12 *Digital Rights Ireland and Seitlinger and Others* [2014].
[120] Case C-362/14 *Schrems* [2015]. See also Joined Cases C-203/15 and C-698/15 *Telia 2 Sverige* [2016]. See also Opinion 1/15, delivered on 26 July 2017.

use of proportionality as a balancing principle in connection with the Charter, this will arguably confirm a tentative version of a contextual justice approach.

IX. Conclusion

This chapter has tried to conceptualize the concept of non-domination in political theory discourse and how it is translated into EU constitutional law and its relevance for EU security studies with specific focus on the EU policy area of the AFSJ. It has highlighted the longstanding debate in political theory on freedom as non-domination-oriented theories and equality-oriented ones, and explained why this debate has now been re-routed to that of a connection between the neo-republican concept of non-domination and methods against arbitrariness to that of a constitutional right of justification for arbitrary decisions. Especially, this chapter has sought to elucidate the function and benefits of using non-domination as a threshold for ensuing freedom and guaranteeing justice for all (free and equal).

This chapter has also attempted to show why the concept of non-domination is highly relevant for the understanding of the security architecture of the constitutional structure for the EU-AFSJ nexus, where the quest for justice and freedom is currently being challenged by the security focused make-up of the AFSJ. Finally, this chapter has argued that a contextualized approach to proportionality is important where the legislator has failed in its promise to deliver high quality law which upholds the rule of law and due process rights even in times of emergency.

References

Alexy R, *A Theory of Constitutional Rights* (Julian Rivers tr, Oxford University Press 2002).

Alter KJ, *The European Court's Political Power: Selected Essays* (Oxford University Press 2009).

Arnull A and Wincott D (eds), *Accountability and Legitimacy in the European Union* (Oxford University Press 2002).

Bachvarova M, 'Non-domination's Role in the Theorizing of Global Justice' (2013), 9 Journal of Global Ethics 173.

Barak A, 'The Role of a Supreme Court in a Democracy and the Fight Against Terrorism' (2005), 35 Hong Kong Law Journal 287.

Barak A, *Proportionality: Constitutional Rights and Their Limitations* (Doron Kalir tr, Cambridge University Press 2012).

Beetz JP and Rossi E, 'The EU's Democratic Deficit in a Realist Key: Multilateral Governance, Popular Sovereignty and Critical Responsiveness' (2017), 8 Transnational Legal Theory 22.

Bellamy R, *Political Constitutionalism* (Cambridge University Press 2007).
Berlin I, *Two Concepts of Liberty* (Clarendon Press 1958).
Bohman J, 'Nondomination and Transnational Democracy' in Cécile Laborde and John W Maynor (eds), *Republicanism and Theory* (Blackwell Publishing 2008).
Bohman J, 'A Response to My Critics: Democracy Across Borders' (2010), 3 Ethics & Global Politics 71.
Buchanan AE, *The Heart of Human Rights* (Oxford University Press 2014).
Cohen JL, *Globalization and Sovereignty: Rethinking Legality, Legitimacy, and Constitutionalism* (Cambridge University Press 2012).
Colón-Ríos J, *Weak Constitutionalism: Democratic Legitimacy and the Question of Constituent Power* (Routledge 2012).
Craig P, 'Integration, Democracy, and Legitimacy' in Paul Craig and Gráinne de Búrca (eds), *The Evolution of EU Law* (2nd edn, Oxford University Press 2011).
Cromartie A, 'Legitimacy' in Richard Bellamy and Andrew Mason (eds), *Political Concepts* (Manchester University Press 2003).
Curtin D, 'Overseeing Secrets in the EU: A Democratic Perspective' (2014), 52 Journal of Common Market Studies 684.
Daly E, 'Freedom as Non-Domination in the Jurisprudence of Constitutional Rights' (2015), 28 Canadian Journal of Law & Jurisprudence 289.
Douglas-Scott S, 'The Problem of Justice in the European Union' in Julie Dickson and Pavlos Eleftheriadis (eds), *Philosophical Foundations of European Union Law* (Oxford University Press 2012).
Douglas-Scott S, 'Human Rights as a Basis for Justice in the European Union' (2017), 8 Transnational Legal Theory 59.
Dworkin R, *Law's Empire* (Hart Publishing 1998).
Dworkin R, *Justice for Hedgehogs* (The Belknap Press of Harvard University Press 2011).
Dworkin R, 'A New Philosophy for International Law' (2013), 41 Philosophy & Public Affairs 2.
Dyzenhaus D, 'Process and Substance as Aspects of the Public Law Form' (2015), 74 The Cambridge Law Journal 284.
Estlund DM, *Democratic Authority: A Philosophical Framework* (Princeton University Press 2008).
Føllesdal A and Hix S, 'Why There Is a Democratic Deficit in the EU: A Response to Majone and Moravcsik' (2006), 44 Journal of Common Market Studies 533.
Forst R, 'First Things First: Redistribution, Recognition and Justification' (2007), 6 European Journal of Political Theory 291.
Forst R, *The Right to Justification: Elements of a Constructivist Theory of Justice* (Jeffrey Flynn tr, Columbia University Press 2011).
Forst R, 'A Kantian Republican Conception of Justice as Non-Domination' in Andreas Niederberger and Philipp Schink (eds), *Republican Democracy: Liberty, Law and Politics* (Edinburgh University Press 2013).
Forst R, 'Introduction: On the Idea of a Critique of Relations of Justification' in Rainer Forst, *Justification and Critique: Towards a Critical Theory of Politics* (Ciaran Cronin tr, Polity Press 2013).
Forst R, *Justification and Critique: Towards a Critical Theory of Politics* (Ciaran Cronin tr, Polity Press 2013).
Forst R, 'Noumenal Power' (2015), 23 Journal of Political Philosophy 111.

Forst R, 'Legitimacy, Democracy, and Justice: On the Reflexivity of Normative Orders' in Rainer Forst, *Normativity and Power: Analyzing Social Orders of Justification* (Ciaran Cronin tr, Oxford University Press 2017).
Foucault M, *The Archaeology of Knowledge and the Discourse on Language* (AM Sheridan Smith tr, Pantheon Books 1972).
Gibney MJ, 'Refugees and Justice between States' (2015), 14 European Journal of Political Theory 448.
Habermas J, *Between Facts and Norms: Contributions to a Discourse Theory of Law and Democracy* (William Rehg tr, MIT Press 1996).
Harel A, *Why Law Matters* (Oxford University Press 2014).
Hart HLA, *The Concept of Law* (3rd edn, Oxford University Press 2012).
Herlin-Karnell E, 'Constructing Europe's Area of Freedom, Security and Justice through the Framework of "Regulation": A Cascade of Market Based Challenges in the EU's Fight against Financial Crime' (2015), 16 German Law Journal 49.
Herlin-Karnell E, 'The Domination of Security and the Promise of Justice: On Justification and Proportionality in Europe's "Area of Freedom, Security and Justice"' (2017), 8 Transnational Legal Theory 79.
Hirsch A von and Simester AP, *Crimes, Harms, Wrongs: On the Principles of Criminalisation* (Hart Publishing 2011).
Jackson VC, 'Constitutional Law in an Age of Proportionality' (2015), 124 Yale Law Journal 3094.
Klamert M, *The Principle of Loyalty in EU Law* (Oxford University Press 2014).
Klatt M and Meister M, *The Constitutional Structure of Proportionality* (Oxford University Press 2012).
Kumm M, 'The Idea of Socratic Contestation and the Right to Justification: The Point of Rights-Based Proportionality Review' (2010), 4 Law & Ethics of Human Rights 141.
Kumm M, 'The Moral Point of Constitutional Pluralism: Defining the Domain of Legitimate Institutional Civil Disobedience and Conscientious Objection' in Julie Dickson and Pavlos Eleftheriadis (eds), *Philosophical Foundations of European Union Law* (Oxford University Press 2012).
Kumm M, 'The Cosmopolitan Turn in Constitutionalism: An Integrated Conception of Public Law' (2013), 20 Indiana Journal of Global Legal Studies 605.
Kumm M, 'Constituent Power, Cosmopolitan Constitutionalism, and Post-positivist Law' (2016), 14 International Journal of Constitutional Law 697.
Kumm M, 'The Turn to Justification: On the Structure and Domain of Human Rights Practice' in Adam Etinson (ed), *Human Rights: Moral or Political?* (Oxford University Press 2018).
Larmore C, 'What Is Political Philosophy?' (2013), 10 Journal of Moral Philosophy 276.
Lovett F, *A General Theory of Domination and Justice* (Oxford University Press 2010).
Lovett F, 'Should Republicans Be Cosmopolitan?' (2016), 9 Global Justice: Theory Practice Rhetoric 28.
Margalit A, *The Decent Society* (Harvard University Press 1998).
Mill JS, *On Liberty* (John Parker and Son 1859).
Möller K, *The Global Model of Constitutional Rights* (Oxford University Press 2012).
Neyer J, *The Justification of Europe: A Political Theory of Supranational Integration* (Oxford University Press 2012).
Pettit P, *Republicanism: A Theory of Freedom and Government* (Clarendon Press 1997).
Pettit P, 'A Republican Law of Peoples' (2010), 9 European Journal of Political Theory 70.

Pettit P, *On the People's Terms: A Republican Theory and Model of Democracy* (Cambridge University Press 2012).
Pettit P, *Just Freedom: A Moral Compass for a Complex World* (W.W. Norton & Company 2014).
Rawls J, *Political Liberalism* (Columbia University Press 1993).
Rawls J, *Political Liberalism* (expanded edn, Columbia University Press 2005).
Raz J, *The Morality of Freedom* (Clarendon Press 1986).
Ripstein A, 'Authority and Coercion' (2004), 32 Philosophy & Public Affairs 2.
Rosenfield M, 'Constitutional versus Administrative Ordering in an Era of Globalization and Privatization: Reflections on Sources of Legitimation in the Post-Westphalian Polity' (2011), 32 Cardozo Law Review 2339.
Rostbøll CF, 'Non-domination and Democratic Legitimacy' (2015), 18 Critical Review of International Social and Political Philosophy 424.
Sadurski W, 'Reason of State and Public Reason' (2014), 27 Ratio Juris 21.
Sangiovanni A, 'The Irrelevance of Coercion, Imposition, and Framing to Distributive Justice' (2012), 40 Philosophy & Public Affairs 79.
Sangiovanni A, 'Solidarity in the European Union' (2013), 33 Oxford Journal of Legal Studies 213.
Schuppert F, 'Non-domination, Non-alienation and Social Equality: Towards a Republican Understanding of Equality' (2015), 18 Critical Review of International Social and Political Philosophy 440.
Shapiro I, 'On Non-domination' (2012), 62 University of Toronto Law Journal 293.
Simmons AJ, 'Justification and Legitimacy' (1999), 109 Ethics 739.
Somek A, *The Cosmopolitan Constitution* (Oxford University Press 2014).
Thompson MJ, 'Reconstructing Republican Freedom' (2013), 39 Philosophy & Social Criticism 277.
Thorburn M, 'Proportionality' in David Dyzenhaus and Malcolm Thorburn (eds), *Philosophical Foundations of Constitutional Law* (Oxford University Press 2016).
Tomkins A, *Our Republican Constitution* (Hart Publishing 2005).
Tyler TR, *Why People Obey the Law* (Yale University Press 1990).
Valentini L, *Justice in a Globalized World: A Normative Framework* (Oxford University Press 2011).
Volk C, 'Towards a Critical Theory of the Political' (2016), 42 Philosophy & Social Criticism 549.
Waldron J, *Law and Disagreement* (Oxford University Press 1999).
Ward I, 'Identifying the European Other' (2002), 14 International Journal of Refugee Law 219.
Weatherill S, *Law and Values in the European Union* (Oxford University Press 2016).
Weiler J, 'The Transformation of Europe' (1991), 100 Yale Law Journal 2403.
Williams B, 'Realism and Moralism' in Bernard Williams, *In the Beginning Was the Deed: Realism and Moralism in Political Argument* (Geoffrey Hawthorn ed, Princeton University Press 2005).

PART III
RESPONSES

13
The Constitution of Justification
Replies and Comments

Rainer Forst

It gives me great pleasure to contribute to this very impressive volume that Ester Herlin-Karnell and Matthias Klatt have brought together. It contains chapters by authors whose work I greatly admire and from whom I have learned, and will continue to learn, a lot. That they took the time and trouble to focus on my work in conceptualizing what an order of constitutional democratic justification should look like and what its foundations are, does me great honour while at the same time confronting me with a challenge. The honour is too obvious to require further comment. The challenge is that I find myself compelled to clarify my ideas concerning these marvelous chapters. So I would like to express my sincere gratitude for the opportunity to respond to these great critics and at the same time to apologize in advance for any shortcomings of my responses.

The topics that need to be addressed cover a very wide terrain, ranging from foundational questions about moral universality and the reflexivity of practical reason to questions of legal, political, and social justice, critical theory, the value of democracy, the justificatory practice of judicial review or the European polity. I am not an expert in all of these areas, but I will try to address them from within the theory of justification that I have been developing over the years since writing my first book, *Contexts of Justice* (published in German in 1994). I am still committed to central aspects of that approach, as much as it has been reworked during those years. And if during that time there has been some progress, it was in large part due to critics who alerted me to things I should—or better, should not—have said. I am greatly indebted to them.

There are many common themes running through the various chapters so that it is tempting to discuss them in clusters. In order to do justice to the individual authors, however, I will proceed step by step following the order of the contributions, although still in the hope of constructing a coherent narrative connecting the chapters. I will divide my contributions broadly into replies to the chapters that directly address my work (those in Part One of this book) and comments on the chapters in Part Two, which develop an argument in dialogue with my work without focusing directly on it.

Rainer Forst, *The Constitution of Justification: Replies and Comments* In: *Constitutionalism Justified: Rainer Forst in Discourse.* Edited by: Ester Herlin-Karnell and Matthias Klatt, Oxford University Press (2020),

DOI: 10.1093/oso/9780190889050.003.0013

I. Replies

1. Kantian Republicanism: A Third Way (Reply to Arthur Ripstein)

Thanks to great thinkers like John Rawls and Jürgen Habermas, a lot of recent political philosophy has taken a Kantian turn that seemed unlikely given the predominance of consequentialism in the Anglo-American world and of historicist thinking (in Hegelian or Nietzschean versions) in Europe. This leads to important debates, as the debate between consequentialist luck egalitarians and relational egalitarians (which will play a role later in my response to Christian Hiebaum) attests. In the post-Rawlsian, deontological discourse on justice, however, it was Kant's moral philosophy that played a major role in thinking about a normative order as an order of justification based on a categorical imperative of equal respect. And it is thanks to powerful philosophers such as Arthur Ripstein that in recent years Kant's legal philosophy has been taken much more seriously, shedding new light on what it means to think about a political and legal structure of non-domination, thus elaborating a particular version of Kantian republicanism.[1] Ripstein's interpretation of Kant, whether in *Force and Freedom* or in his new *Kant and the Law of War*,[2] which makes Kant speak to the most pressing questions of current legal and political philosophy, demonstrates in a unique and exemplary way how one can be true to a historical thinker while nevertheless making him into our contemporary.

In his chapter, Ripstein asks me to clarify whether the right to justification should be interpreted in accordance with a wide view of the issues and reasons involved in a structure of justification that he calls the 'co-deliberation' view or in accordance with a narrower version modeled on his reading of the Kantian idea of a person being *sui iuris*, based on 'some antecedent idea of a right to stand in a certain type of normative relation, not exhausted by claims to justification' (R 4).[3] This represents a major challenge, because, as Ripstein suspects, I am indeed somewhat torn between different interpretations of the formal and material implications of the right to justification—but in my view for good reasons, for

[1] I discuss the differences between my view of non-domination and that of Pettit in 'A Kantian Republican Conception of Justice as Nondomination' in Andreas Niederberger and Philipp Schink (eds), *Republican Democracy: Liberty, Law and Politics* (Edinburgh University Press 2013), and in 'Die neorepublikanische Maschine. Zur Unabdingbarkeit des Kantischen Republikanismus' in Violetta L Waibel, Margit Ruffing, and David Wagner (eds), *Natur und Freiheit* (De Gruyter 2019).

[2] Arthur Ripstein, *Force and Freedom: Kant's Legal and Political Philosophy* (Harvard University Press 2009); Ripstein, *Kant and the Law of War*, forthcoming.

[3] Arthur Ripstein, 'The Innate Right of Humanity and the Right to Justification' in this volume, cited in the text as R.

I see myself as constructing a *third way* that avoids the respective shortcomings of the two views that Ripstein lays out.

Briefly, I find the wide co-deliberation view too wide, because in Ripstein's formulation it contains 'no antecedent constraint on acceptable reasons' (R 3), whereas my view does contain such constraints. Substantial limits are placed on the realm of valid or acceptable reasons *both* by the formal justificatory criteria of reciprocity and generality *and* by the material standing of persons as equal normative authorities, both as moral subjects and—in legal and political contexts—as legally, politically, and socially non-dominated equals endowed with basic rights.[4] So this brings me closer to Ripstein's narrow view, which, however, I find too narrow, because it seems to imply a number of rights that are deduced from the 'innate right' of freedom as independence rather than being arrived at through a particular mode of (constrained) justification. I do not see how justification can be reduced to a 'demonstration of consistency' (R 7) based on the notion of innate right. But that depends on how we interpret that right, which Kant defines as follows:

> *Freedom* (independence from being constrained by another's choice), insofar as it can coexist with the freedom of every other in accordance with a universal law, is the only original [*ursprüngliche*] right belonging to every man by virtue of his humanity.[5]

Ripstein (rightly) stresses the part of this definition concerning freedom as independence, where you are your own master and must never be arbitrarily subjected to the will of another. By contrast, I stress the part of the Kantian formulation which states that the freedom of each must coexist under a general (or, depending on how one translates *allgemeine*, a universal) law; and such a law, I would add, must be *self-given*, for otherwise it would not be binding for morally and politically autonomous beings who are, as both Ripstein and I agree, ends in themselves. This moral status provides the deontological foundation for the innate right. This is why for Kant there is a superior 'internal' moral duty of right to honour the '*right* of humanity in your own person',[6] which means that one must never make oneself a means to others nor allow them to turn one into a mere means to their ends. In my own work, I call the lack of consciousness of being such an end a form of 'second-order alienation', where a person disregards his or

[4] I lay out my view of basic rights in 'The Justification of Basic Rights: A Discourse-Theoretical Approach' (2016) 45(3) Netherlands Journal of Legal Philosophy 7.

[5] Immanuel Kant, Ac. 6:237, 'The Metaphysics of Morals', in Immanuel Kant, *Practical Philosophy* (Mary J Gregor ed and tr, Cambridge University Press 1996) 393.

[6] ibid 236; see also Ripstein, *Force and Freedom* (n 2) 37.

her own dignity as an equal normative authority to others.[7] So Ripstein and I do not disagree about the deontological framework within which we think right and politics have to be grounded; but we might have somewhat different views on what this entails. Nevertheless, it does not follow that I embrace the wide view he criticizes.

Let me try to situate myself a bit more clearly with respect to the two views Ripstein distinguishes. The co-deliberation view focuses on non-arbitrary justifications for general norms, and it is wide open for the kinds of reasons and considerations that flow into the process of justification. This means that the reasons in question can also be based on certain interests presumed to be general (R 6), as in Rawls's account, or on other material considerations. Thus, as Ripstein writes, 'the generality of moral and legal rules is the *product* of the reciprocal exercise of the right to justification by citizens' (R 7). I agree with the latter formulation, since it reflects a characteristic feature of the constructivism of my approach. I also think that it is correct to open up the space of justification for critical claims that some norms would be 'burdensome' (R 7) on certain persons, assuming that in the process of justification it can be ascertained what kind of burden is involved and whether the corresponding claim is justifiable or not. This is important for the question of the restrictive or exclusionary character of a justification-based view, which is a source of concern for Lois McNay, for example. But that openness with respect to content and claims does not mean that the justification procedure leads to an unstructured realm of norms, as Ripstein fears, because certain basic rights are justified in a particular way in so far as they secure the standing of persons as *sui iuris* and because the criteria of reciprocity and generality serve to 'filter' justifiable from unjustifiable claims.

According to my account, to put it in a seemingly paradoxical way, certain basic rights are beyond 'normal' justification because they are fundamentally justified on the grounds that they secure the standing of persons as legally, politically, and socially non-dominated equals, and thus are a prerequisite for further political justification. Based on their fundamental right to be respected as normative equals, this kind of respect is transferred into the legal and political realm through the (higher-order) justification of certain non-rejectable basic rights that secure the powers not to be subject to certain forms of domination. As I explain in an essay devoted to that topic, the right to justification thus serves a mediating function between the moral and the legal-political realm similar to Kant's innate or original right, because it also structures and determines the basic legal standing of persons within a legal condition.[8] Some of these rights are as

[7] Rainer Forst, 'Noumenal Alienation: Rousseau, Kant and Marx on the Dialectics of Self-Determination' (2017) 22 Kantian Review 523.

[8] Forst, 'The Justification of Basic Rights: A Discourse-Theoretical Approach' (n 4) 12.

'inalienable' as the dignity of persons as normative equals, and they are justified either by way of a status-based argument concerning what is required to secure the very standing of being a non-dominated equal (such as basic rights to life and liberty and to political self-determination or social standing) or by way of a reciprocity-based argument which demonstrates that certain rights, such as rights to religious liberty or to work, are not mutually rejectable.[9]

Thus reflection on our status as normative equals and independent persons as well as the criteria of reciprocity and generality do a considerable amount of deontological work in structuring political justification, having priority over particular claims about interests, the general good or other impersonal considerations, as Ripstein fears could dominate in the case of the open view. My approach does call for a special realm of narrower justifications for basic rights that secure independence; however, that realm is not deduced from the innate right but is also arrived at through justification (in the way specified earlier). Thus my view is narrower than the wide and open view of co-deliberation, but not quite as narrow as Ripstein's favoured alternative.

When it comes to justifying basic rights, I distinguish between two levels of constructivist justification. On a first, moral-political level, a conception of generally defined basic rights must be determined such as we find in human rights declarations or in constitutional rights bills, leaving the concrete determination to be specified by democratic law. On a second, political level, the particular content of basic rights must be specified discursively. For example, while a right to democratic participation is justified on the first level, the second-level discursive process determines what that means in a given normative order. The latter then constrains and structures arguments on a third level that needs to be added, namely, that of 'normal' democratic justification.

This account has the advantage of taking a more dynamic view of basic rights, which still have a special place as *congealed or solidified justifications* that protect persons from domination; yet it avoids the danger—which Ripstein, I believe, would also regard as a danger—that 'a set of already differentiated entitlements to formal independence' (R 7) will be reified as a set of a priori rights that cannot be critically examined when it comes to, say, claims to property. In every society, such claims must be put to the test of justifiability. So basic rights are essential and must be secured within a legal order; but what they mean when it comes to defining the right to property, to freedom of religion, and so on, must always stand the test of reciprocal and general justifiability in order to avoid dressing up material reifications as formal requirements of independence. Hence the different

[9] ibid 22.

levels mentioned earlier are not sealed off from another, since new insights need to be taken into account on all levels.

To Ripstein, this may sound like wanting to have one's cake and eat it too. In a certain sense this is true, but that is because I see the 'innate' right to justification both as a *ground* of and as a *constraint* on public justification, and I consider this to be a virtue and not a vice. Persons are equal normative authorities who are sheltered and protected by the right to justification that wards off unjustified forms of power; thus they have the normative powers of basic rights—yet these rights are essentially justified reciprocally and generally. That is why my view is *relational* all the way down (something Ripstein also claims for his view); but precisely because no rights are beyond fundamental moral-political justification, they all express relations of respect and have to be justified in relational terms. As such powers, rights secure independence and also the legal right not to have to justify yourself all the time, for example, in court where you can refuse to say anything that can be used against you or in areas of (justified) privacy. So we need to get the levels of justification right. In order to protect persons from unjustifiable justifications in the legal and political realm, their standing is defined by a set of rights justified in fundamental, moral-political terms. Thus my view is more relational than Ripstein's, because I try to achieve through relational justification what he tries to achieve without constructivist justification.

I agree with Ripstein when he says that standing is 'primitive, rather than something that is conferred on us in the service of some other set of moral ideas' (R 11), because such standing is based on the right to justification that protects one against dominating claims of social interests or ethical notions of the good (R 11). My view does not open up the realm of admissible justifications too much, as he fears Rawls, Scanlon, and Habermas do (which I won't comment on here). I also agree that the formal aspects of justification are essential in excluding impermissible justifications; but I regard this as a truth concerning justification that must be shown by way of recursive consideration of the right to justification. This lifts persons out of the danger of being subjected to false justifications, but only based on respect for their status as agents of justification, not as masters over themselves in some non-justification view ('prior to any specific demand for justification'; R 18), as if they already had a set of natural rights before justification begins. That would be a non-relational view of innate right that I consider incompatible with Ripstein's relationalism. I agree with him, however, that the right to justification leads to a higher-order moral-political justification for basic rights that protects them from 'specific' demands for justification that fall below the threshold of justification established by basic rights. Such rights are fundamentally morally and politically justified and establish a level of justification that legal-political norms must not violate.

Ripstein and I also agree that the justification for democracy stems from the innate right or the right to justification seen as its equivalent (R 19f.). But here I think my view has an advantage over his, since the right to justification is not primarily a right to have a justified space of freedom of your own protected from arbitrary interference from others, but rather a right to be the co-author of the norms that bind you. This is a direct implication of our status as equal normative authorities. It is this idea of authority that I think is essential to Kant's view, and the notion of independence can only fully be developed if we interpret the 'general law' that secures it as a democratic law. That is in line with Kant's assertion that 'my external and rightful freedom should be defined as a warrant to obey no external laws except those to which I have been able to give my own consent'.[10] I take this to be part of the definition of innate right, which is why I agree with Ripstein when he emphasizes that public law must be 'self-imposed' (R 20) and democratic. But that is also why I am sceptical of his earlier claim that the 'Universal Principle of Right is not a principle of self-legislation'.[11] I accept the difference he stresses between political and moral self-legislation; but I think that the notion of autonomy as self-legislation and self-government does connect the categorical imperative with the principle of right. But I will leave this for now, because I agree with how Ripstein formulates the deontological notion of 'co-authorship' (R 20) in this volume.

If I tried to express the (small) difference between us in a nutshell, I would say that while Ripstein thinks that 'all of the questions of political philosophy come out of the fact that no person is in charge of another' (R 21), I would say that they stem from the principle of equal normative authority and (co-)authorship in the realm of norms that are binding on all. So my relationalism is a constructivist one, involving differentiated constructions of basic rights and of other norms (which would allow for majority decisions), while his is a relational account of non-subordination that treats this standing as prior to justification. But in my view, such standing means that certain reasons that cast doubt on the status of some persons as equals are unjustifiable, and I see no reason why Ripstein should disagree with this. He is primarily concerned with excluding improper reasons on that basic level, and I share this concern. I think thus that our disagreement becomes very small indeed when he says that, in his view, there is a 'background of a form of interaction in which justificatory resources are available, antecedent to any particular ends or interests either of us might have' (R 22). I completely agree with this. But note that here he is speaking of justificatory resources that can and ought to be used in a fundamental discourse about what rights we have.

[10] Immanuel Kant, Ac. 8:350 (fn), 'Perpetual Peace: A Philosophical Sketch' in Immanuel Kant, *Political Writings* (Hans Reiss ed, HB Nisbet tr, Cambridge University Press 1996) 99.

[11] Ripstein, *Force and Freedom* (n 2) 359.

Such discourse is, as I said earlier, unavoidable; for even if we take the claim 'that I am not in charge of you' (R 22) as fundamental, we need to justify what that means in legal, political, and social relations. Some would draw libertarian conclusions from this, others republican, and others socialist ones. That must be made part of a larger discourse about rights, justice, and responsibilities. Such discourse belongs to the idea of a rightful condition, for that idea cannot be sufficiently developed by arguments of 'direct implication' (R 23) of the innate right. Although this right has fundamental implications, they are a part of justificatory discourse, not something that stands apart from it. Such discourse rules out a lot of arguments about 'private purposes' (R 24) or higher interests by emphasizing reciprocity and generality; but it still has to be conducted within a basic structure of justification. That, I think, is also the lesson of the idea of a 'sequenced justification' that Ripstein endorses and that calls for proper justifications of certain rights based on 'a compelling public purpose' (R 25). And in order to avoid opening the door too wide, one should add: a reciprocally and generally justifiable purpose that can withstand the veto right of persons' basic rights justified in the way I suggested earlier. This preserves the deontological core of the basic standing of persons as normative equals and protects against impermissible exercises of balancing or aggregation of which Ripstein is rightly critical.

In conclusion, I am grateful to Ripstein for challenging me to take sides between the two views he distinguishes, because this helped me realize that I should embrace a third view.

2. Kantian Republicanism in a Discourse-Theoretical Key (Reply to Claudio Corradetti)

Like Arthur Ripstein, Claudio Corradetti asks essential questions about the structure of my Kantian approach to law and politics, but with a different focus. He expresses doubts about the connection between Kant's categorical imperative and the innate right, and also about the relation between a duty of and a right to justification. That forces me to explain in greater detail in what way my view is a neo-Kantian one. Furthermore, Corradetti, in line with his own view as elaborated in his book *Relativism and Human Rights*,[12] raises important issues about moral pluralism and, finally, about the status of being a justificatory subject and about possible exclusionary implications of my view. I am grateful to him for these important challenges.

[12] Claudio Corradetti, *Relativism and Human Rights: A Theory of Pluralistic Universalism* (Springer 2009).

To make a long story short, I take the principle of justification, which states that the validity of norms has to be redeemed or justified in accordance with the criteria that are implicit in their claim to normative validity, to be a principle of reason, and thus I interpret the principle of the reciprocal and general justifiability of reciprocally and generally binding norms of action as a principle of practical reason. It is equally and morally binding on responsible, reason-giving persons as normative authorities, and they have to be able to differentiate moral from legal-political contexts of justification. In the legal-political domain, the norms to be justified are not purely moral norms; however, as fundamental norms of justice, they have a moral core. And in any case the imperative to respect others as justificatory equals holds in every normative context, in moral contexts of the community of all moral persons and in legal-political contexts of the community of all who are subjected to a normative order.

In the moral context, to respect others (and oneself) as ends in themselves is to regard them as normative equals in the sense that you owe them morally justifiable reasons that refer to reciprocal and general norms for your actions. So you have a *moral duty* of justification towards them, as a categorical imperative. According to my neo-Kantian view, this entails that those who are such autonomous ends in themselves have a *moral right* to justification. With the exception of the innate right, Kant did not use the language of moral rights; but I do not see any reason why a categorical moral duty should not imply a general moral right to be treated in accordance with that duty by all other persons. In fact, I think that this follows given the structure of perfect duties.

So why does Corradetti consider it inappropriate to use the language of a right to justification in moral contexts? I think it is because he does not make a distinction between a moral right in the above-mentioned sense and a positive right in the realm of 'volition' and 'protected interest' (C 37f),[13] with the result that he sees every rights claim as an empirical claim of will that demands something specific from another person, thus drawing that person into heteronomy. If you fulfil the claim of another as a claim of will, you are no longer acting autonomously. It seems that, for Corradetti, rights are always 'coercive rights' (C 38) regulating 'external freedom' and something that 'someone else imposes on me' (C 40). That may or may not be true for positive rights (though I think that it is not true for the justification of rights in a general sense); but I fail to see why we cannot conceive of a moral right of autonomous persons to hold others, who are equally autonomous, responsible for respecting that right as part of their duty of justification.

To connect this with the earlier discussion of Ripstein's view, I also do not see why there should be 'no correlation between the categorical duty of morality and

[13] Claudio Corradetti, 'Engaging with Forst's *Right to Justification*: Kantian Analogies and the Problem of Subjectivity' in this volume, cited in the text as C.

the innate right to freedom' (C 38). Kant justifies both with respect to our nature as ends in themselves and thus grounds his Doctrine of Right on the categorical imperative. That does not mean that the sphere of right is no longer the sphere of norms that bind externally but not internally; however, the normative structure of what counts as 'right' follows imperatives of practical reason for persons who respect each other's innate (moral) right to mutual respect as ends in themselves and as subjects and authorities of the law. They are norm-givers, not just norm-takers, in the moral as well as in the political world, with all the differences this involves.

But Corradetti's criticism goes much further. In his view, one should not ground a conception of justice on Kant's deontological conception of morality because that would not do justice to the 'irreducible radical pluralism of moral perspectives that characterizes modern societies' (C 42). He then narrows the critique a bit by pointing to the plurality of 'reasonably comprehensive views' (C 42) in Rawls's sense, indicating that my moral conception would count as a reasonable doctrine but still as comprehensive. I deny this, as I have tried to show elsewhere, especially in my work on toleration.[14] Already the use of 'reasonable' to qualify certain comprehensive doctrines, as well as the search for a reasonably justifiable conception of justice beyond such doctrines, indicate that we must presuppose such a possibility if that search is to be meaningful; and, in my view, a recursive and discursive conception of practical reason as the faculty of justification counts as a strong candidate for grounding such a conception of justice because it is based on the idea of justification and justifiability *itself*. There is no dubious metaphysics at work here, I believe, only a reflexive transcendental argument. And, as I explained earlier, my way of reading Kant's principle of right, which Corradetti suggests as a way out (C 43), is in line with such a recursive view. Already in *Contexts of Justice*, I tried to explain how I view the connection between contexts of moral norms and those of legal norms as coercive norms—and as norms that owe their validity to having undergone a process of justification that is not moral in nature but nevertheless leaves room for moral reasons. We need to be aware of normative contextual differences but we should not reify them.

Corradetti is absolutely right to raise the issue of who counts as a proper subject of justification in legal-political contexts. For we need an account of how the moral status of membership in the human community of responsibility relates to the more concrete status of being a member of a legal community or,

[14] Rainer Forst, *Contexts of Justice: Political Philosophy beyond Liberalism and Communitarianism* (John MM Farrell tr, University of California Press 2002); *The Right to Justification: Elements of a Constructivist Theory of Justice* (Jeff Flynn tr, Columbia University Press 2011) ch 4; *Toleration in Conflict: Past and Present* (Ciaran Cronin tr, Cambridge University Press 2013) pt 2.

in other words, of a normative order of rule or domination. The latter is more specific, and thus, as Corradetti rightly assumes (as does Ripstein near the end of his chapter), its preconditions must also be more specific. And with specificity comes the danger of exclusion, if we do not want to use an undifferentiated notion of 'all affected' in defining the relevant justification community.

Corradetti is concerned that my account of human rights, in which I argue for the right to be a norm-giver and not just a norm-taker, necessarily implies that only those individuals have human rights who are already full members of a political community. But that is an invalid inference, because the normative argument that those subject to a normative order must become its authorities does not imply a restrictive criterion for membership in such an order.[15] I think that subjection to a normative order is a relevant criterion for justice claims; but not only full citizens or recognized legal subjects are subjected to a normative order but also those who have fled into a country or those who are subjected to a country's political actions (such as military interventions) or by structures of rule or domination (for example, economic structures) that the country in question upholds. So the relevant notion of a normative order to which one is subject is a broad one, and I fail to see why my theory supposedly commits me to a narrow view of *Rechtssubjektfähigkeit*, that is, of the capacity to be a legal subject.

The problem of legally 'rightless' persons that Corradetti brings up following Arendt and Agamben raises a further issue that he is right to address and that I need to say something about (as I did, albeit all too briefly, in my previous work).[16] All too often the loss of state citizenship (for whatever reason) lands individuals in a legal void, so that human rights seem absent especially where they are most needed.[17] A conception of human rights must respond to this with a legally valid claim to legal protection and standing, and current regulations of asylum and migration fail to measure up to these standards.[18] Stateless persons or those who are forced to flee their countries should never be devoid of rights; hence the international legal community, which is an existing normative order, should have legally binding rules about the status of such persons and how they can become agents of justification in a legal and political sense, based on their moral status as justificatory agents and on the fact that they are subjected to a normative order of international law, of borders and lots of other regulations.

[15] Compare Rainer Forst, *Normativity and Power: Analyzing Social Orders of Justification* (Ciaran Cronin tr, Oxford University Press 2017) ch 10.

[16] See, for example, my *Contexts of Justice* (n 14) ch 4 as well as 'The Justification of Human Rights and the Basic Right to Justification: A Reflexive Approach' (2010) 120 Ethics 711 [reprinted in *Justification and Critique: Towards a Critical Theory of Politics* (Ciaran Cronin tr, Polity Press 2013) ch 2].

[17] Seyla Benhabib, *The Rights of Others: Aliens, Residents, and Citizens* (Cambridge University Press 2004).

[18] Ayelet Shachar, *The Shifting Border* (Manchester University Press forthcoming).

The duty to secure their status is therefore a duty of justice, not merely a humanitarian issue (as is often claimed).

So I accept that we need principles for an international and transnational normative order of law to ensure that stateless persons are guaranteed standing as subjects of justification in a legal and not just a moral sense. But I fail to see why the theory of moral rights to justification cannot ground such rights, as Corradetti fears. For in my work I try to stress that being a member of a context of justice in which you are subject to a normative order is a ground for certain rights and standing, based on the fact that you have a right to justification. The idea of stressing the moral core is that this provides reasons for legal and political claims; thus it is not correct to say that it is fixed and constrained by the legal status quo—quite the reverse. However, if you think that there is no way that leads from a moral duty to grounding a right, first a moral right, then a legal one, then you risk being held captive by the existing legal frameworks and their limits.

3. Justifying Human Rights and the Limits of Contextualism (Reply to Andrea Sangiovanni)

I greatly welcome the opportunity to continue the (hopefully unending) dialogue with Andrea Sangiovanni about our approaches, close as they in many ways are, such as when we think about contextual and practical justifications for norms and rights, and far apart as they may be in other respects, given his Humean scepticism about Kantian groundings.[19] In the chapter for this volume, he follows up on a recent discussion we had about justifying human rights.[20]

I agree with Sangiovanni that we need to leave behind outworn debates between 'orthodox' moral and 'political' or purely 'legal' approaches to understanding human rights. All of these aspects are important when it comes to human rights, but they must be combined in the right way.[21] We need to think about a moral grounding for legal human rights that does not downplay their political character, especially the reflexive character of securing the status as a norm-giver who has the power and authority to co-determine the particular

[19] See Andrea Sangiovanni, 'Scottish Constructivism and the Right to Justification' in Rainer Forst, *Justice, Democracy and the Right to Justification: Rainer Forst in Dialogue* (Bloomsbury 2014), and my response 'Justifying Justification: Reply to My Critics' in the same volume. See also Andrea Sangiovanni, *Humanity without Dignity: Moral Equality, Respect, and Human Rights* (Harvard University Press 2017) ch 1.

[20] See Andrea Sangiovanni, 'Beyond the Political-Orthodox Divide: The Broad View' in Adam Etinson (ed), *Human Rights: Moral or Political?* (Oxford University Press 2018), and my reply 'Human Rights in Context: A Comment on Sangiovanni' in the same volume.

[21] See my argument in 'The Justification of Human Rights and the Basic Right to Justification' (n 16).

set of rights and laws within the normative order to which one is subject. Like Sangiovanni, I believe that grounding rights in certain moral 'interests' (S 58)[22] is not the correct approach. However, I conclude that they require a deontological grounding in the basic right to justification, while he favours a teleological approach that again focuses on 'fundamental interests/claims that are most threatened by political, legal, social, economic and cultural orders of all types' (S 70). Thus I think it is his rather than my approach that is in danger of reverting to the orthodox one.

I agree with Sangiovanni's interpretation that my approach implies that human rights have to be placed in practical contexts and cannot be logically deduced from the right to justification (S 60). However, in contrast to Sangiovanni, I think that there are good reasons for an abstract conception of basic rights that will be interpreted and laid out in practical contexts by those subject to a normative order. Thus I see two major differences between my view and his as he develops it: first, there *is* a moral-political core conception of human rights in an abstract sense, and second, every binding political-legal form assumed by the interpretation of these core rights must be achieved through reciprocal and general democratic discourses that are part of a normative order equipped with *public authority*.[23] Thus Sangiovanni is correct that human rights apply to sub-state and supranational organizations as well as to private organizations like companies; but that does not turn such organizations into the normative orders in which such rights are justified and institutionalized. When it comes to human rights, we need to make a different distinction between contexts of justification and contexts of application from the one suggested by Sangiovanni (S 61).

Therefore, I think that I have an answer to the role that institutions play in 'fixing the human rights we have' (S 62), but it differs from Sangiovanni's; for only democratic public normative orders are contexts of the concrete *justification* of human rights, whereas many other forms of organization and institution are contexts in which human rights *apply*. Accordingly, I suggest a different three-stage procedure of justifying human rights from Sangiovanni's (S 64). Specifically, I distinguish three contexts of the justification of human rights:[24] first, the moral-political context of basic human rights that are relevant for protecting against forms of legal, political, and social domination. This does

[22] Andrea Sangiovanni, 'Human Rights, Interests, and Variation' in this volume, cited in the text as S.

[23] For a theory concerning that term in the international realm, see Armin von Bogdandy, Matthias Goldmann, and Ingo Venzke, 'From Public International to International Public Law: Translating World Public Opinion into International Public Authority' (2017) 28 European Journal of International Law 115.

[24] See more explicitly Rainer Forst, 'The Point and Ground of Human Rights: A Kantian Constructivist View' in David Held and Pietro Maffettone (eds), *Global Political Theory* (Polity Press 2016), as well as my reply to Sangiovanni 'Human Rights in Context' (n 20).

not involve a deduction or an argument based on human interests, as orthodox views have it, but a reflection on the rights required to secure a status of non-domination in all of the respects that we know from historical and actual experience to be relevant. The result is a general and rather abstract conception and a corresponding list of human rights. And, as I said earlier, Sangiovanni cannot avoid such a basic conception that is required in order to have a sense of human rights at all, nor does this commit one to an orthodox view, since these rights are specific to a certain purpose (as Sangiovanni rightly requires) and are not based on general human ideas of the good (as he also rightly emphasizes). But without such a general conception, our thinking about human rights is too vague.

A second context is that of a particular political-legal normative order with public authority in which such rights are not simply to be 'realized' by such an authority, but where those subject to an order have the right to co-determine that order by interpreting—that is, collectively and concretely justifying—their basic human rights. They determine in a reciprocal and general way which human rights they ought to accord each other and in which form. Thus, for example, they know that they cannot reasonably (reciprocally and generally) reject a right to democratic participation (because they themselves use it abstractly, based on the right to justification); but they have to determine what shape that right should take and what its institutional form will be. The same holds for the other rights. The justification procedure therefore presupposes certain rights in the abstract but lends them concrete shape through processes of justification that are themselves in need of legal institutionalization. This is not a vicious circle, but a virtuous one, because it means justifiably constructing (and constantly reconstructing) a basic structure of justification (or what I call fundamental justice).

The third context that must be taken into account is the one briefly alluded to earlier in my reply to Corradetti, namely, the international and supranational level. Here normative orders of human rights beyond the state must be established that have sufficient public authority to protect human beings from becoming deprived of rights, either in the stateless realm or within their states, for example, by being oppressed by their state or by private companies. Only sufficiently justified institutions with public authority will have any sanctioning force with respect to human rights violations, ie institutions which deserve the name of the rule of law. The conception of human rights to be constructed on this third level beyond the state is thinner than the second level of basic rights within a state order; but it is more concrete than the first abstract level, because it can lead to sanctioning mechanisms. Thus we need to know here what the core of a right is about (level one), how it was or was not institutionalized within a particular normative order (level two), and how we evaluate from a supranational or international perspective when and how it was violated and whether certain sanctions should follow, as justified in a legitimate procedure (level three).

Sangiovanni proposes a very different three-stage procedure for justifying human rights (S 64). After grounding the right to justification, he suggests that it should be employed in various institutional contexts, from the state to private associations, and that it is in these contexts that human rights must be justified, while the normal normative life of such institutions unfolds on the third level. On the second level, the rights of participants must be defined with an eye to the nature of the institution in question, such as whether it is coercive or what goods it provides. Hence, we must tailor a particular conception of human rights to corporations, for example, including possible duties to maintain a health-care or an educational system (assuming that these are justified). As a result, we end up with as many conceptions of human rights as there are institutions that not only could violate them but also may have responsibilities to fulfil them in the form of positive duties. Hence 'the shape, nature, and justification of human rights will differ greatly when considering different kinds of institutions' (S 66). The result would be something like a 'corporation human rights conception', as I would call it, and there would be other conceptions, such as for families, associations of different kinds, and so on (S 68).

I accept Sangiovanni's important point that neither corporations nor other institutions of social life should be exempt from human rights duties, and also the idea that, in making assessments of human rights, we have to be aware of their specific nature. But Sangiovanni's proposal turns an important context of the application of human rights into one of justification, and that entails three major problems. First, it is not clear *who* does the constructive interpretation here: the employees together with the owners of companies, or anyone else involved and concerned or affected? Or is it just the philosopher who understands the point of the practice? Second, it is not clear whether the construction is a democratic and discursive one and how we can avoid power asymmetries that yield particular outcomes of such constructions. And third, it is unclear what is the relevant normative order endowed with sufficient public authority that legitimizes these rights constructions and establishes them as legally binding, including mechanisms for conflict resolution. Thus, I fear that Sangiovanni neglects the democratic, public, political, and legal character of human rights regimes and as a result potentially privatizes the justification as well as the establishment of regimes of human rights. It is almost as if the company itself becomes a normative order. I think that one reason for this is an ambiguity in the notion of what it means to 'fulfil' human rights: companies have to *honour* them, but they should not have the authority to *define* and *institutionalize* them.

Sangiovanni recognizes this danger and reminds us that corporations are 'subject to the legislative authority of a state that determines their legal rights'

(S 65). But then it is the whole political community of a state that has to justify and establish the human rights that are relevant for companies; and if that is the case, I fail to see why the human right to a limited workday, for example, or the human right to adequate health care should lead to a separate conception of human rights specific to companies. Human rights are human rights, and they protect against *specific* forms of domination in a *general* form; but that does not mean that we need specific conceptions or regimes for each social institution. That is a task for the legislative and judicial levels of normative orders, not one that reaches down to the basic conceptual level. This does not lead us back to orthodox views, because my suggestion preserves the practice-relevant character of human rights constructions with an eye, for example, to specific dangers of violations within companies. But when companies violate human rights, they do not violate 'company human rights'—they simply violate human rights, and that is a concern for all. The specific dangers of domination within families, in companies, or in public administrations should not lead to specific conceptions of human rights geared to each of these institutions, but to a robust conception of human rights that can be applied to such contexts. Otherwise, we end up with a pluralism of human rights conceptions and regimes, which would indeed be in danger of arbitrariness, as Sangiovanni himself remarks (S 68f.). I am not convinced by the answer that any specific conception 'is determined by interpretation of what the institution actually does and how it does it' (S 69), because I need to know which public community and authority reciprocally and generally determines what it does and how.

I am still concerned, to link up with my earlier exchange with Sangiovanni to which he refers (S 68), that we should not have different conceptions of human rights for Amnesty International and for international courts such as the European Court of Human Rights. The problem is that this would give the ECtHR leeway, which it in fact exercises, to interpret the 'margin of appreciation' in certain cases in such a way that restrictions of religious liberty, for example, in using Christian symbols in public offices or by banning Muslim dresses from public spaces, are seen as justified.[25] That opens the door to relativism and power politics, whereas the politics of human rights should speak a different language—namely, the critique of power.

To avoid such conclusions, Sangiovanni is ultimately at pains to define the 'single aim' of human rights as that of 'protecting fundamental interests/claims, including general claims' (S 71).[26] But I fear that the reference to basic human interests not only brings him closer to the orthodox view, as remarked earlier, but

[25] *Lautsi and Others v Italy* App no 30814/06 (ECtHR, 18 March 2011); *S.A.S. v France* App no 43835/11 (ECtHR, 1 July 2014).

[26] See also Sangiovanni, *Humanity Without Dignity* (n 19) ch 4.

also raises a question concerning the definition of that single aim that his pluralistic view can't answer.

4. The Authority of Justice (Reply to Christian Hiebaum)

I am grateful to Christian Hiebaum and Bernhard Schlink for requiring me to clarify my view of political and social justice as based on the right to justification. I will begin with Hiebaum, whose discussion of two versions of egalitarianism—namely, in his terminology, distributive and social egalitarianism—is illuminating and leads to his assessment of my view and his own as possible candidates for a more synthetic view combining elements of both approaches.[27] Like him (H 78f.),[28] I find the terminology that usually opposes 'distributive' and 'relational' conceptions of justice unfortunate, because it seems to imply that the former are not interested in relations and the latter are not interested in distributions, which is false. I have suggested that the real difference resides in two ways of thinking about justice, and I have also argued that one of them captures better than the other the task of justice as being to set up a basic political and social framework avoiding arbitrary rule.[29] So I fear that I am somewhat less ecumenical in this respect than Hiebaum.

Hiebaum is right that I believe that there is one single normative source of justice, namely, the categorical right to have standing as a non-dominated legal, political, and social equal in the normative order to which one is subject, so that one co-determines that order. I take this view because I regard arbitrary rule, whether in legal, political, or social contexts, as the source of injustice, although the concrete injustices can assume many forms. The goddess of justice aims to overcome and ban such arbitrariness. And just as an aside, Hiebaum is not quite correct when he says that I first developed the right to justification as the core of the virtue of tolerance and now assume that it grounds justice (H 80f.); rather, it was the other way round, because I think that justice as justification, which I first developed in *Contexts of Justice*, grounds the correct conception of toleration.[30]

[27] Similarly Simon Caney, 'Justice and the Basic Right to Justification' in Rainer Forst, *Justice, Democracy and the Right to Justification* (n 19) 147; Kasper Lippert-Rasmussen, *Relational Egalitarianism: Living as Equals* (Cambridge University Press 2018).

[28] Christian Hiebaum, 'Distributions, Relations, and Justifications: Mixing Flavours of Egalitarianism' in this volume, cited in the text as H.

[29] See my 'Two Pictures of Justice' in Rainer Forst, *Justice, Democracy and the Right to Justification* (n 19) ch 1 [also in Forst, *Justification and Critique* (n 16) ch 1]; 'The Point of Justice: On the Paradigmatic Incompatibility of Rawlsian "Justice as Fairness" and Luck Egalitarianism' in Jon Mandle and Sarah Roberts-Cady (eds), *John Rawls: Debating the Major Questions* (Oxford University Press forthcoming).

[30] Forst, *Toleration in Conflict* (n 14). See also my *Toleration, Power and the Right to Justification* (Manchester University Press forthcoming), with replies to critics.

Hiebaum rightly addresses the question of how the right to justification ought to be situated in social contexts of arbitrary rule (ie domination) where no adequate structure of justification exists (H 83). I actually regard this as a standard case of injustice, for I believe that in most existing societies (including democracies) there are structures of domination that prevent those subject to the law from becoming its authors, and, as Hiebaum remarks, this is even more the case in the international and transnational realm. In that realm, persons, groups, and whole countries are subject to political and/or economic forces of domination and powerlessness that 'trigger' the right to justification to a high degree. As I argue in several places in my work,[31] the main task of political and social justice is to establish structures of justification to curb and overcome domination, following the principle that democratic justice is a recuperating virtue that tracks relations of domination where they exist. Thus, 'demoi of subjection'[32] have to constitute themselves as the constituent powers in order to establish structures of justification that will be strong enough to generate what I call the *force towards the better argument*, that is, at least to expose arbitrary power and to try to overcome it. So I agree with Hiebaum that this presents huge political tasks, involving, as he says, collective action problems; but I fail to see why this is a worry for the normative approach, at least as long as we want to avoid short-circuiting a normative argument by claiming that justice only applies in already established positive normative contexts, a view I criticize as 'justice positivism'.[33] But that is not Hiebaum's position. In that context, I fear that he misunderstands me (H 84) in the passages he quotes, since (in my reply to Eva Erman) I claim that the right to justification *is* a right of those who are subjected to participate in practices of 'establishing proper procedures and institutions of justification'[34] where they do not exist.

Hiebaum is correct when he says that I believe that identifying injustice presupposes the attribution of responsibility, even in complex social systems, but he is wrong to think that I hold a narrow view of such responsibilities. I differentiate between groups that are more or less directly responsible and groups that benefit from injustice in various ways and groups that are implicated very little or not at all but have the power to do something by way of a 'natural duty' (to use

[31] Rainer Forst, 'Towards a Critical Theory of Transnational Justice' (2001) 32 Metaphilosophy 160 [reprinted in *The Right to Justification* (n 14) ch 12]; 'Transnational Justice and Non-Domination: A Discourse-Theoretical Approach' in Barbara Buckinx, Jonathan Trejo-Mathys, and Timothy Waligore (eds), *Domination and Global Political Justice: Conceptual, Historical and Institutional Perspectives* (Routledge 2015) [reprinted in *Normativity and Power* (n 15) ch 10]; 'A Critical Theory of Transnational (In-)Justice: Realistic in the Right Way' in Thom Brooks (ed), *The Oxford Handbook of Global Justice* (Oxford University Press forthcoming).

[32] Forst, *Normativity and Power* (n 15) 167ff.

[33] Forst, 'A Critical Theory of Transnational (In-)Justice' (n 31).

[34] Forst, 'Justifying Justification' (n 19) 205.

Rawls's term) of justice.[35] In any case, I take seriously the point that it will be difficult to locate responsibilities in complex social structures and thus to identify an addressee of the right to justification; but I am less sceptical than Hiebaum who seems to see this as a somewhat Kafkaesque enterprise (H 85f.). In a normative order of rule and domination, there may be lots of 'anonymous' structures of power; but emancipation could never get off the ground if one could not identify any powerful groups as addressees of one's critique or any fellow-community of those who are in solidarity with your critique.

This is important for the point he raises about justice and legitimacy. Like Caney and others,[36] Hiebaum has a tendency to separate political (democratic) legitimacy from substantive justice. But I reject this separation. I believe that the legitimate authority of justice rests with those who, as justificatory equals, accept the criteria of reciprocity and generality and each other's claim to equal authorship and standing as non-dominated subjects and decide collectively how to define the justice of their social institutions. This formulation involves a lot of conditionals, and this is what fundamental justice means; but if they were fulfilled (a huge counterfactual), justice would be constructed democratically. And since, according to the criteria of reciprocity and generality, the worst off have a veto right in such discourses, they would not be relegated to some minimalist welfarism. Thus the form and the substance of justice cohere and are internally connected to democracy.

I am sceptical of philosophical theories that authorize some 'distributor'[37] to 'realize' an independently justified conception of justice. Such authorization is not only a problem of legitimacy; it is also a problem of justice *tout court*. For without the self-determination by way of a process of justification among justificatory equals, there simply *is no* valid or right conception of justice for a collective. So the problem is not just one of democratic illegitimacy; it is also one of the lack of understanding of the *political* point of the *authority* to justify a conception of justice for a normative order. Since Plato, philosophers have made that mistake, and we should not continue to do so.

[35] ibid 207; also Forst, *The Right to Justification* (n 14) 248–50; *Normativity and Power* (n 15) 154 (fn 2); 'A Critical Theory of Transnational (In-)Justice' (n 31). In footnote 43 of his text, Hiebaum misunderstands my example (in *The Right to Justification* (n 14) ch 11) of the poor worker being called to a Court of Global Justice. The counterfactual is meant not just to exhibit the structure of claims about injustice but also the injustice of establishing justice in a non-democratic way. See my summary in *The Right to Justification* (n 14) 250.

[36] Caney, 'Justice and the Basic Right to Justification' (n 27) 151ff.; Philip Pettit, *On the People's Terms: A Theory of Freedom and Government* (Cambridge University Press 2012); Zofia Stemplowska and Adam Swift, 'Dethroning Democratic Legitimacy' in David Sobel, Peter Vallentyne, and Steven Wall (eds) *Oxford Studies in Political Philosophy* (vol 4, Oxford University Press 2018).

[37] In a telling phrase of Gerald A Cohen, *On the Currency of Egalitarian Justice and Other Essays in Political Philosophy* (Princeton University Press 2011) 61.

So I agree with Hiebaum that many struggles for economic or ecological justice today 'take place outside of democratic procedures' (H 88), because there are very few such procedures and the prospects of realizing them are slim. But that does not change the normative point. And to confuse what democracy as fundamental justice means with populism (H 88) is a conceptual mistake that overlooks the conditionals for a meaningful form of democracy mentioned earlier.

Hiebaum's own proposal for combining distributive and social-relational concerns I find illuminating and challenging, since it stresses the rights-based character of social distributive justice. He emphasizes the importance of rights to certain goods and argues that they should be seen as a good to be distributed, contrary to Iris Young or Habermas, who do not think of rights as such goods (H 90). But I am not sure whether Hiebaum understands the difference in the right way, because I am uncertain whether he wants to say that the distribution of rights is nothing but a distribution of goods. On the one hand, this seems to be the case when, for example, he repeatedly says that 'we' (H 90, passim) or a 'legislator' (H 93) distribute such rights goods, as if there were a stock of such rights one could use or as if a power-holder could simply create such rights. That sounds like a non-democratic conception of rights. But on the other hand, he stresses that assigning rights is a horizontal matter of redefining the political community (H 90f.) or an act by 'the members of society recognizing each other as equally or unequally holding such rights' (H 93). If this is done by way of reciprocal and general justification, then rights are not distributed from the top down but instead are created and justified at the horizontal level, and this is what Young and Habermas have in mind (and what Hiebaum seems to affirm; H 93–95). So rather than combining distributional and relational aspects in his theory, the difference reappears as a tension in Hiebaum's account.

This tension may well be one between a deontological and a teleological conception of rights. The former regards rights as a manifestation of mutual respect among normative equals, the latter as a valid claim to some kind of good based on the value of that good (for the individual or for society). Thus within a deontological framework, rights can always be traced back to the essential relation between those who as normative equals recognize these rights, and it is useful to describe their 'original' mutual recognition as a matter of recognizing their authority as having equal moral rights to claim and have rights, including the right to a status of social non-domination.[38] However, a teleological view denies, as does Hiebaum (H 96), that a system of rights can be normatively traced back to a central right of mutual respect of persons as ends in themselves but argues

[38] Although I cannot go into this in detail, this sounds more Fichtean than I would think of it, because Fichte, in contrast to Kant, did not capture the basic kind of moral recognition in the right way.

instead that it depends on other evaluative assessments. This is why, as I understand, he argues that the 'grounding and distribution of such rights and the determination of their content and relative weight may well involve considerations of public interests, the common good, and collective history or identity' (H 97). This raises all the concerns that deontologists like Ripstein and I have about such balancing justifications. And this is ultimately what separates the two pictures of justice (and rights) that cannot be combined at a fundamental level.

5. The Substance of Procedural Justice (Reply to Bernhard Schlink)

It is especially gratifying to have my work challenged by Bernhard Schlink, from whose classical studies on public law[39] and legal philosophy I have benefitted as much as from the conferences on proportionality we organized together and the many conversations we had about questions of justice and law. In his chapter, originally delivered as a lecture in Frankfurt, he takes up Adorno's view that there can be no 'right life in the false society' and argues instead that justice is still a virtue and, more than that, a duty in the false society—but in practical, piecemeal form, as an attempt to do or establish some justice in the unjust world. And for that, he argues, the distributive paradigm is the right one and justice as justifiability, by contrast, a somewhat otherworldly and unrealistic ideal.

But more than that, Schlink poses a fundamental challenge to my view when he reminds us in hermeneutic fashion that no conception of justice can get off the ground without a substantive pre-judgment, as Gadamer would say, about justice. If justice as justifiability denies this, it is empty or contradictory; yet if it allows for this, it is merely another substantive conception on a par with others, and a pretty meager one at that. The procedural discursive justification of justice is always secondary, at best, to a substantive justification of justice. That is a daunting challenge, one which is at the heart of many criticisms against procedural views, especially my own (a point also relevant for Hiebaum's critique earlier), and I am grateful to Schlink for expressing it here in such a succinct way. I will try to defend justice as justification by arguing that it does indeed imply substantive aspects and pre-judgments, but that this does not speak against the procedural theory—for my argument involves a *substantive form of proceduralism*. This seemingly paradoxical formulation may confirm some of the worst suspicions that some people may entertain about Frankfurt dialectics; but I will try to show that these suspicions are unfounded.

39 Bodo Pieroth and Bernhard Schlink, *Grundrechte. Staatsrecht II* (C.F. Müller 2011).

Schlink reconstructs the distributive paradigm within a discursive framework in an extremely illuminating way. According to him, it is not so much about the distribution of goods according to pre-ordained standards and criteria but rather about the distribution of burdens of argumentation (Sch 106).[40] But note that he gives the paradigm an egalitarian twist, such that arguments for unequal treatment have the heavier burden, while equal treatment is the default.[41] That is not implicit in the paradigm itself, but instead reflects a particular version of it. And Schlink agrees, since he holds that such a view 'references the rationality standards of the time and place in which the unequal treatment occurs' (Sch 106). Here already the critical theorist whom Schlink argues against would raise some concerns, because these standards might not deserve to be called 'rational' if they violate reciprocity and generality. This, I think, not only holds for contemporary standards; for if we say, as Schlink does, that it is 'foolish to lambast discrimination against women in the nineteenth century as if it were occurring today' (Sch 106), then we cannot explain what made such a critique seem rational to those who did actually engage in radical criticism of the standards of their day. Was their critique irrational then and rational only today? And is it rational today because these standards are contingent historical products, so that we are committed to some kind of moral Darwinism if we think we should adhere to the standards that won out historically?[42] And even if we did (though we should not), did they really win out, if we come to the conclusion (we both agree on) that '[o]ur world is not just, our society is not just' (Sch 103)? I leave these issues aside for now.

At this point I should mention another concern of critical theory. Schlink rightly emphasizes that public discourse about distributional issues will be more successful the more it functions within established institutions, and he calls that a 'discourse of justification' (Sch 108). But as McNay and others in this volume remind us, such discourses tend to reproduce standard views about who deserves what and these views may discriminate unjustly against certain groups and identities. Thus if we have no recourse to a second, critical layer of criteria of justification and a corresponding discourse among justificatory equals, social justification might merely end up reproducing the unjustifiable. As Bernard Williams reminds us with his 'critical theory principle' following Habermas: 'the acceptance of a justification does not count if the acceptance itself is produced by the coercive power which is supposedly being justified'.[43]

[40] Bernhard Schlink, 'Practical Justice' in this volume, cited in the text as Sch.

[41] See Ernst Tugendhat, *Vorlesungen über Ethik* (Suhrkamp 1993) lec 18, 364; Wilfried Hinsch, *Gerechtfertigte Ungleichheiten: Grundsätze sozialer Gerechtigkeit* (De Gruyter 2002); Stefan Gosepath, *Gleiche Gerechtigkeit: Grundlagen eines liberalen Egalitarismus* (Suhrkamp 2004).

[42] Rainer Forst, 'The Justification of Progress and the Progress of Justification' in Amy Allen and Eduardo Mendieta (eds), *Justice and Emancipation: The Critical Theory of Rainer Forst* (Penn State University Press forthcoming).

[43] Bernard Williams, *In the Beginning Was the Deed* (Princeton University Press 2005) 6.

Thus in all of these considerations about practical justice there is an essential question that must be asked, namely, the one I called in my responses to Sangiovanni and Hiebaum earlier the question of authority: Who is or has the authority to conduct the discourses about proportionality, appropriateness, the *suum cuique*, and all that, once we are in a political situation where we have no benevolent 'mother' (Sch 104) to distribute a cake? Isn't that the *prior and essential* question when it comes to the justice of distributions—namely, the question of political, distributive power?

This brings me to the central point of our debate, the meaningfulness of the critical conception of justice as justifiability. For Schlink's answer when asked whether political, distributive power should be regarded as the primary and essential issue is simply 'no', despite his emphasis on the need for justification. In his view, the question of justificatory power as posed within the framework of justice as justifiability is not prior. As I indicated earlier, he uses an epistemic, hermeneutic argument at this point. He reconstructs my view in such a way that justice as justifiability claims that no knowledge concerning what is just is presupposed by the constructivist procedure; hence justice is collectively produced, almost *ex nihilo*. But such constructivism, he argues, is 'illusionary' (Sch 109), since justification is always a justification of something based on a certain understanding of that something about which those who seek to arrive at a common view have some shared certainty. Thus the acceptance of a procedure of constructing justice does not rest on any different substantive pre-judgment (or judgment, if considered) than other substantive views of justice—and if there were no sufficiently shared substantive view of justice, no procedure would be regarded as just and as bringing about justice. Thus the essential justification of justice 'always exists already prior to' (Sch 110) justice as justifiability. Engaging in such discourses is neither necessary nor sufficient for justice.

I disagree with the conclusion but not with all of Schlink's premises. For I have no doubt that some certainty about justice must already exist in order to get a practical project of justice off the ground, although I have the above-mentioned concerns that the practical certainty in question might rest on ideological views. But I reject the premise that justice as justification (and justifiability, to differentiate the modal forms) does not presuppose any substantive knowledge about justice. On the contrary, it presupposes the *concept* of justice as overcoming or banning arbitrary social and political rule, and it also presupposes substantive views of justificatory equality, equal normative authorship and their social, political, and legal implications when it comes to the conception of justice as justification.[44] Hence, these normative substantive notions are not constructed; rather,

[44] See Forst, 'Two Pictures of Justice' (n 29).

they are *reconstructed* through recursive reflection on the meaning of justice and its practical and normative authority, which is the authority of all as autonomous authors of the norms to which they are subject in accordance with the criteria of reciprocity and generality.[45] Thus there is no construction *ex nihilo* but a substantively justified view of why (proper) procedural justification is necessary and sufficient for constructions of justice—if (and only if) it is conducted in conditions of fundamental justice that secure the status of non-dominated equals. Otherwise, such discourses might only reproduce false (unjustified) certainties. In social situations in which such structures of justification do not exist (Hiebaum's question), establishing them is a duty of justice—of practical justice, I may add. Therefore, I deny that 'the paradigm of justifiability overreaches itself', as Schlink claims, for in my view it does not lack a 'guiding notion of justice' (Sch 111). But this guiding notion of justice is that of justification among justificatory equals, and thus it is substantive and procedural at the same time.

From the perspective of that conception of justice, Schlink is correct when he argues that every concrete interpretation of legal, political, or social equality must be defended with reasons (Sch 112); however, I doubt that a notion of 'self-evidence' about some of these standards helps when it comes to the question of justifiability. For one might doubt that such standards really are self-evident to all, and one might also doubt whether some views regarded as self-evident deserve that epistemic standing. Judgments of justice must aim for standards in terms of which such evidence can be questioned, since it may contain one-sided justifications. Thus I agree with Schlink when he concludes by affirming that '[j]ustice is directed against unexamined traditions and unquestioned assumptions' (Sch 114), and that is why I insist on the both practical and counterfactual imperative of justice as justification.

When Schlink reminds us about the limits of justice and that it needs to be combined with compassion and solidarity and other practical virtues (Sch 115), I am inclined to disagree with respect to some claims, such as the claim that justice does not provide us with sufficient guidance in the context of refugee and migration issues. But behind that, I think there is a larger issue, which brings us back to the initial reference to Adorno. Because the worry might be that from the perspective of 'practical justice' as an innerworldly virtue within our unjust reality, justice as justification and justifiability could turn into a utopian framework that is too far removed from our concerns and realistic aims, even if we strive for justice—a kind of justice for *schöne Seelen* only, in Hegel's terms, who turn ugly once they force reality to conform to their radical views. This is a serious

[45] On constructivism of that kind, see Forst, 'The Justification of Basic Rights' (n 4); *Normativity and Power* (n 15) ch 1; *The Right to Justification* (n 14) chapters 1 and 3.

concern, but I would respond that the imperative to overcome social and political relations in which the right to justification is denied is an essential practical demand of justice, and it is and can be raised in all practical contexts of struggles for concrete justice. These struggles make sense and are justified even when they fail or achieve only little progress—there is no concrete utopia that all of them serve. They serve the end of establishing human beings as ends in themselves, as authors within the normative orders to which they are subject. That this struggle is a never-ending one does not mean that it makes no sense to start or continue it. Democracy is a difficult achievement, both to reach and to defend, but it is worth struggling for, as the political form of justice.

6. Power and Reasons (Reply to Samir Bajaj and Enzo Rossi)

In my replies to Hiebaum and Schlink in particular, I defended the view that the first question of justice is that of power, more precisely, that of gaining the justificatory power required to exercise the right to justification in the political and legal realm. This establishes a connection between justice and power, and I am grateful to Samir Bajaj and Enzo Rossi (and Lois McNay) for inquiring into the theory of power that informs this view, a theory of, as I call it, *noumenal* power.[46]

But as much as my account of power fits my normative conception of justice (or so I hope), it is *not* a normative account, which has been a source of confusion for many critics.[47] Rather, it is in essence a conceptual and descriptive theory that mediates between the empirical and the normative levels, leaving room for a neutral notion of power that can be developed into positive notions of, for example, democratic power, and negative ones such as domination, oppression, or exploitation. Although Bajaj and Rossi rightly stress this point (as well as that my view is not a positivist one), I am afraid that they nevertheless offer too strong a normative reading of my theory. In my view, the *exercise* of power (by which I mean something different from a non-intended effect of power) rests on those subject to power recognizing a justification 'given' to them by those who exercise power, and such recognition can be the recognition of a good reason but also of a threat, it can be a matter of accepting a lie as truth or of accepting an ideological justification and thereby succumbing to delusion. All of these are taken as *effective* justifications and thus as *motivating reasons* for B 'produced' by A; hence the operative conception of 'giving' reasons is a very broad one, and justification

[46] Forst, 'Noumenal Power' in *Normativity and Power* (n 15) ch 2 [originally in (2015) 23 *The Journal of Political Philosophy* 111].

[47] See especially my 'Noumenal Power Revisited: Reply to Critics' (2018) 11 Journal of Political Power 294.

is understood in a non-normative way (hence differently from how it has been used thus far in this text). In this context, I do not necessarily regard a justification as a *good* justification, but I fear that Bajaj and Rossi read me in this way. This is why they reject the fourth step in their reconstruction of my argument, the one that links recognition of a reason with recognition of a justification (BR 121f.).[48] Let me explain my view in response to the careful arguments they develop.

The main reason for my view that to be a subject of power is to be moved by reasons the power-yielder 'gives' a person or group is, as Bajaj and Rossi rightly argue, that I believe (in line with such different thinkers as Foucault or Lukes) that power is exercised over free agents, that is, over agents who are not mere objects of control like machines or a stone I kick away. They are free to the extent that, as subjects of power, their action is still *their* action, being based on their convictions concerning what ought to be done. This is even true of a person who is threatened by someone with a gun as long as that person is still capable of acting in one way or another (in contrast to someone who is fettered or locked up). The mugger 'gives' the person he threatens a very strong reason to hand over her purse; but she could still refuse, even at a very high risk of being shot. Subjects of power are still free agents, even though they are often not equally free as those having power. This is what I call social power, which on my conception is different from physical force. When physical force is exercised against humans, it is not a form of social power; one exercises physical force over those one cannot move by other, social reasons. Thus it is true, as Bajaj and Rossi assert, that I make a categorical distinction between the use of physical force or violence and social power as exercised over free agents. However, it is not accurate to say that according to my view a state that puts someone into jail is not exercising power over that person. Such an act must be viewed within the wider context of the state's claim to recognition of its punitive power, even by the person jailed; thus the act of jailing has a range of noumenal implications and aims, including attempting to convince the jailed person not to break the law in the future. So the sheer act of physical violence has a number of power aims and effects; but viewed in isolation from this context, an act of physical violence demonstrates that one is reducing the target of the violence to a mere object who can no longer be moved by reasons. If we want to understand how coercion (BR 119) works, we need to understand this interplay between physical force and social power; and then it will become apparent that the threat of the use of force is a means of exercising noumenal power.

The point where I fear that Bajaj and Rossi read my view of justification as a normative view, contrary to my intentions in that context, is in their characterization

[48] Sameer Bajaj and Enzo Rossi, 'Noumenal Power, Reasons, and Justification: A Critique of Forst' in this volume, cited in the text as BR.

of what they call my 'justificatory recognition view' (BR 122). According to that view, to recognize a reason is to recognize it on the basis of a normative standard of justification, such that 'only justification can provide recognizable reasons' (BR 122). But that is not what I think—or better, this is what I think about *justified* exercises of power, but in my descriptive theory of power I want to explain *all* exercises of power, not just well-justified ones, as being based on justifications. So, as my example of a threat should make clear, I do of course accept that 'one can recognize that an agent is providing them with a reason (to act, say) even though that agent fails to provide—and perhaps couldn't provide—a justification for why that course of action is required, or is a good idea' (BR 122f.). If I hand over my purse to the mugger with the gun because I believe that the threat he is making is credible, of course I do not require a good justification for what he does; I see his gun as a *justifying and motivating reason* for me to act as he wants me to act. That is how I use and connect the recognition of reasons and justification in my descriptive account of power, and there is no independent normative standard implied here or any attempt to 'ground the right to justification' (BR 122). That right or its grounds are not relevant in this context; here I simply want to understand how power works. In such a situation, the gun provides a reason and a justification for what I do, just as in other contexts, as Bajaj and Rossi argue, to 'fear the power-holder's secret police' (BR 124) is a sufficient reason and justification for complying with a regime. That is how such forms of power work; they are based on the conviction that it is better to comply, which is based in turn on justifying reasons for an agent to hold that conviction and act accordingly. In sum, when Bajaj and Rossi criticize step 4 in my argument, they read a notion of 'good' justification into my argument that is not there.

When it comes to the question of grounding the right to justification (which, again, does not play any role in the discussion of power), Bajaj and Rossi correctly reconstruct my view as a '*practical* transcendental argument' (BR 124), since I analyze the principle of reciprocal and general justification as a principle of practical reason and ground the duty of and the right to justification by appeal to a normative reflection about what it means to understand and use that principle. That is the Kantianism in my approach: if you reason properly with regard to moral practice, you will understand that the principle of justification is not only a principle of reason but also a principle of morality and of respecting yourself and others as equal agents of justification. That is the point of my idea of a higher-order practical insight not just into the *how*, but also into that *that* of justification.[49]

[49] Forst, *The Right to Justification* (n 14) ch 1.

I suspect that Bajaj and Rossi favour a different idea of justification in their criticism. For it is correct to say that people in modern liberal democracies will disagree about the status of the right to justification and its implications; but neither a Rawlsian view[50] nor any other view that defends a principle of *reasonable* justification and *reasonable* disagreement will conclude from the mere fact of disagreement that it is a reasonable disagreement, and thus that favouring a view based on the right to justification is just as arbitrary as those that favour other views, as Bajaj and Rossi argue (BR 126f.). That would amount to a form of social relativism in which the term 'reasonable' does not have any bite or provide any criteria of better and worse views and in which all we can hope for is a modus vivendi of views and groups. I consider such relativism counter-intuitive and contradictory, because it cannot account for how one's own normative stance in any moral or political debate could be justified and justifiable. In addition, it deflates the term 'reasonable' into a contingent set of norms with which powerful groups in a society can live, and is thus positivistic (*contre cœur* of Bajaj and Rossi) in reducing reason to a descriptive term and overlooking the validity claim we necessarily make when we call something 'reasonable'.

In particular, the reflexive and transcendental view I hold does indeed assert, as Bajaj and Rossi anticipate (BR 127f.), that a critique of 'arbitrarily privileging' (BR 126) a certain view over others by its very meaning presupposes that we have certain criteria for arbitrariness. My criteria for arbitrary norms are that they are at odds with the right to justification, mutual respect as normative equals and the criteria of reciprocity and generality. Thus insisting on such respect and on these criteria is precisely not an arbitrary act; rather, it is to insist on non-arbitrary normative justification. However, if we were to claim that holding any view as true and reasonable, including such a formal notion of reasonable justification, is arbitrary and unfounded, then using a term such as 'arbitrariness' would become meaningless—all that would be left is a Nietzschean struggle over which view wins out.

Moreover, insisting on the validity of such principles and forms of respect does not amount to a form of 'ideal theory', as Bajaj and Rossi surmise (BR 127), since the very point of these principles is that individuals as members of political communities should have the justificatory power to create their own justified social structures, and there is no teleological ideal that is given prior to the exercise of that kind of autonomy. No normative theory can do without certain principles and counterfactuals, and that is especially true of a critical theory that has to transcend given power structures and ideologies (a point to which I will return).

50 Rainer Forst, 'Political Liberalism: A Kantian View' (2017) 128 Ethics 123.

This has nothing to do with ideal theory. If realism means not transcending reality, then it falls back into positivism and extreme conservatism.

So I admit to being guilty of regarding the right to justification as the 'correct standard for evaluating political power' (BR 127). But precisely not because I think its claim to truth rests on some ethical or religious comprehensive doctrine but because it rests on a reflexive justification of the very principles that are essential for producing any valid general moral or political norm. We start from within the practice of making such claims and reconstruct the abstract principles and criteria of reason implied; and thus 'practical transcendentalism' in my view means conceptualizing the conditions of possibility of normative validity. There is nothing metaphysical about this nor does it imply any spurious ontology, only a reflection on what it means to make normative sense.

Based on that (neo-Kantian) conception of practical reason, a utilitarian standard for evaluating political power, such as Shivani holds in the example cited by Bajaj and Rossi, fails to meet the standards of reciprocity and generality, because it requires some persons to sacrifice their justifiable claims to the greater good of the greater number of people in accordance with some dubious welfare metric. But that would violate the veto right that the right to justification accords an individual objecting to such a form of disrespect. The truth of deontology resides in the respect it grants the justified claims of justificatory agents who insist on nothing but the very principle of justification. No other justification can trump that respect.

Bajaj and Rossi are willing to concede (provisionally) the transcendental argument but then they reject the substantive moral claim according to which understanding that very argument and knowing *how* to engage in rational moral discourse implies understanding—and having the corresponding moral insight—*that* one has a duty of justification according to the criteria just explained. This is where I differ from Habermas, as they rightly state (BR 128), which raises another major issue, namely, how we ought to understand practical reason. Briefly put, with Kant I believe that reason is only practical if knowing how to make sense and co-produce validity is also to know that in moral practical contexts such justification is not a mere game I can opt into or out of as I wish, but a game that places me under a moral duty. I draw not only on Kant but also on Wittgenstein[51] to argue that a philosophical reconstruction of practical reason must situate the latter in contexts of human practice, and in such contexts, someone who understood what morality demands but did not understand that it is demanded *of him or her* does not really know what that practice means. Thus I deny that 'one can fully engage in rational moral discourse without having the

[51] Forst, *The Right to Justification* (n 14) 41.

moral insight that Forst believes is essential to establishing the normativity of the right to justification' (BR 129). That view is not sufficiently practical, because it does not do justice to the first-person perspective of participants in moral discourses and moral contexts. Morality and moral argument and justification is a practice, as realists would like to say, and participating in that practice requires that you understand and live up to its normative point. In such contexts, morality is a categorical demand—at least in the way I reconstruct the rules of that game.

7. Transcending Reality (Reply to Lois McNay)

I am very grateful to Lois McNay for further pressing me on the issues of reflexivity and the status of transcendental principles already raised by Bajaj and Rossi, and for placing them in the context of a debate about the grounds and aims of critical theory. This is not only important as part of a reflection on my relation to the tradition of the Frankfurt School; it is essential for anyone who thinks that we should aim at critical theories that develop a sociologically informed, conceptually clear critique of domination, and combine it with an emancipatory perspective that is normatively well-grounded (and not arbitrary) and has practical import, at least in directing our criticism of social and political life. It is on the basis of a deep agreement about the value of such an enterprise[52] that our different views matter, I think, and they essentially revolve around what it means to ground critical theory in a non-arbitrary way. McNay believes that my reliance on the principle and right to justification reduces the possibilities of reflexive self-scrutiny and of developing a sense for the 'non-identical elements of social life' (M 132),[53] as she says with reference to Adorno. By contrast, I take the opposite view: without a principle of justification there can be no self-reflexivity, no grounded critique and no critical theory, only an arbitrary affirmation of 'that which doesn't fit in' (M 132) that loses track of a justifiable view of emancipation as a matter of overcoming *unjustified* rule as domination.

There are so many issues here that it is difficult to restrict myself to some essential points, although I will nevertheless try to do so. I will begin by responding briefly to McNay's view that it is one of the 'defining premises of Frankfurt School critical theory' that 'emancipatory political critique necessarily has immanent foundations' (M 131), that it must be guided by 'values and norms that are already embodied, in an incomplete form, in the core institutions, practices, and

[52] See Lois McNay, *Against Recognition* (Polity Press 2008); *The Misguided Search for the Political* (Polity Press 2014).

[53] Lois McNay, 'The Limits of Justification: Critique, Disclosure, and Reflexivity' in this volume, cited in the text as M.

beliefs that structure social life' (M 132). I both agree and disagree with these assertions. I agree in so far as we, as finite creatures, do not have access to a view that is not part of social contexts of meaning. So any claim to a reasonable view or argument is of course situated, but it could never be a *critical* claim if it could not generate a transcending power with respect to its social context. So, although reason is situated, it has the power to reflect on its situatedness; as critical theory in its different versions has shown, reason has a distancing power. Thus my reconstruction of the transcendental principles immanent in the situated social practice of justification is an approach that is *both* immanent and transcendental, one which defies the undialectical opposition between immanent and transcendental thought that McNay uses. Critical theory, as I understand the approach, represents an attempt to reconstruct the counterfactual principles of rationality amidst the factual irrationality of society and to provide adequate concepts for both dimensions (or worlds, as I will explain later).

I fail to see how any theory that pursued the purely immanentist path McNay seems to propose could be called 'emancipatory'. For obviously, libertarians engage in immanent criticism of liberal societies for being insufficiently liberal, fascists criticize authoritarian regimes for being too weak, and so on. The fact that a critique is immanent is not an indication of its emancipatory character; rather, it has no normative value. An emancipatory critique needs certain sufficiently robust criteria of justification, and in my view the theory that (recursively) appeals to the very criteria of critique and justification for that purpose does not suffer from a 'lack of reflexivity' (M 132) but is a truly self-reflexive one. On the contrary, a theory that relies excessively on immanent criteria of emancipation seems to me to suffer from a lack of critical reflexivity. It is doomed to adopt a positivistic view that reaffirms the status quo and takes it as its definitive normative horizon.

I cannot offer a detailed discussion of critical theory here, so I will limit myself to a few brief remarks. As far as I can see, in none of its versions has Frankfurt-style critical theory ever exhibited the historicist relativism that McNay defends. In its first period, Horkheimer and even more so others like Marcuse were unambiguous about a critical 'theory guided at every turn by a concern for reasonable conditions of life',[54] and they asked themselves why the capitalist (and Soviet socialist) societies of their time developed in such irrational ways. Within the Hegelian-Marxist framework in which they operated, the point of immanent critique was to remind bourgeois society of its unfulfilled promises of a rational and free way of life; but it was of course based on the strong assumption that these were the promises of *true* human freedom and rationality and

[54] Max Horkheimer, 'Traditional and Critical Theory' in Max Horkheimer, *Critical Theory: Selected Essays* (Matthew J O'Connell and others trs, Continuum 2002) 199.

not a mere reflection of immanence and historical contingency, simply using what happened to be there. Critique had to be contextual and situated, but its point was *true* emancipation, the overcoming of what Marx had called *das Unrecht schlechthin*.[55] To say that historicist immanentism was their method is to overlook the character of their philosophical ideas about emancipation and to interpret that tradition in Rortyan terms.[56] In fact, the idea that thinkers in a Hegelian-Marxist tradition worthy of the name were historicists is to misunderstand that tradition. They believed that a logic of reason (and unreason) unfolds in history; thus when they spoke about the *Zeitgebundenheit* or *Zeitkern* of normative truths they did so from an overarching perspective of reason in history (in which we have lost faith).

When Horkheimer and Adorno developed their radical critique of rationality in the second phase of critical theory in *The Eclipse of Reason* and the *Dialectic of Enlightenment*, they criticized the perversions of reason as 'instrumental rationality' or 'subjective' reason that follow a derailed logic of *Selbsterhaltung* as domination of outer and inner nature. But they still upheld the idea that this was the victory of unreason or irrationality, which betrays the true meaning of reason: 'What appears as the triumph of subjective rationality, the subjection of all existing things to logical formalism, is bought with the obedient subordination of reason to what is immediately at hand . . . Enlightenment thereby regresses to mythology';[57] or, to cite a later work (1958) by Adorno: 'the excess of rationality, about which the educated class complains and which it registers in concepts like mechanization, atomization, indeed even de-individualization, is a lack of rationality, namely the increase of all the apparatuses and means of quantifiable domination at the cost of the goal, the rational organization of mankind, which is left abandoned to the unreason of mere constellations of power'.[58] We would perpetuate such a mythological dialectical inversion of reason into unreason if we abandoned the critical conception of reason as transcending the status quo and bought into arbitrary, conventionalist immanentism or, even worse, trusted our 'instincts' more than our faculty of critique. It is true that Adorno was sceptical

[55] Karl Marx, 'Zur Kritik der Hegelschen Rechtsphilosophie' in Karl Marx and Friedrich Engels, *Marx Engels Werke* (vol 1, Dietz 1976) 378, 390. In the *Collected Works, das Unrecht schlechthin* is translated with 'the wrong generally', which is misleading; what is meant is 'absolute injustice'; see 'Contribution to the Critique of Hegel's Philosophy of Law' in Karl Marx and Frederick Engels, *Collected Works* (vol 3, Jack Cohen and others trs, *International Publishers* 2005) 186.

[56] As does Amy Allen; see my response in 'The Justification of Progress and the Progress of Justification' (n 42).

[57] Max Horkheimer and Theodor W Adorno, *Dialectic of Enlightenment: Philosophical Fragments* (Edmund Jephcott tr, Stanford University Press 2009) 20 (translation altered).

[58] Theodor W Adorno, 'Reason and Revelation' in Theodor W Adorno, *Critical Models: Interventions and Catchwords* (Henry W Pickford tr, Columbia University Press 2005) 138. Martin Jay develops this very clearly in his *Reason after Its Eclipse: On Late Critical Theory* (The University of Wisconsin Press 2016).

of rationalist constructions of morality that lose touch with moral impulses[59] and experiences; but the idea that, as McNay says, '[w]e instinctively recognize oppression when we see it' (M 147), places an epistemic trust in 'instincts' that Adorno cannot be accused of, since he taught us how little rationality there is in, say, anti-Semitic or other racist instincts. He was far from celebrating arational emotivism.

Nor did he celebrate any form of arational immanentism, since especially after the *Dialectic of Enlightenment* he was convinced that critical theory needs to develop conceptual means to distance itself from the totality of a social form: 'The limit of immanent critique is that the law of the immanent context is ultimately one with the delusion that has to be overcome'.[60] He also warned us against abstract conceptions of reason that turn into reified principles of domination. But he saw reason as a dialectical concept with an inherent power to de-reify itself when combined with the right social theory and moral experience. In this sense, Habermas's reconstruction of the dominating powers of reason versus its communicative forms develops such a dialectical notion of reason and rationality that goes back to Kant's distinction between instrumental rationality and moral practical reason.

In addition to a non-dialectical view that opposes reason and 'instinct' or immanence and transcendence, we should also avoid an empty opposition between historicism and transcendentalism. As I argued earlier, transcendental reflection merely tries to reconstruct the necessary principles of making sense, in our context the principles of valid norms. A critical conception of reason, being situated and historically informed, is aware that such principles often lead to reifications and exclusions of those who don't 'fit in' (M 132), as McNay says. We agree on that point. But I fail to see how such exclusions and reifications could be criticized except in terms of a better understanding of reciprocally and generally justifiable norms that overcomes past reductions of the community and terms of justification. How else would a 'reflection on the non-identical elements of social life' (M 132) be possible, how else would a 'guard against theoretical bias and conceptual reification' (M 137) come about, how else can we analyze the 'complex, often indirect ways in which inequality and oppression are perpetuated' (M 138) if we lack a conception of discursive justification and the radical egalitarian right to question any norm and concrete form of justification? It is true that what we consider 'to be the universal practice of justification may turn out to be a contingent socio-cultural practice that is less inclusive' (M 144) than we assume; but what other capacity to reflect on that do we have except critical reason?

[59] Theodor W Adorno, *Negative Dialectics* (E B Ashton tr, Routledge 2010) 285.
[60] ibid 182.

And furthermore, how much sense does it make to consider the very *principles* of reason and justification that are used to criticize the *social forms* of rationality as themselves completely contingent, as 'a contingent historical achievement' (M 152)? As I explain elsewhere in greater detail and alluded to above in my response to Schlink,[61] that would imply that the criteria for valid justifications are regarded as an 'achievement' only because they are a product of history, a product of dominant historical processes that brought forth these standards. Such an immanentist view thus buys into what I call moral Darwinism, because it holds that we simply adopt and inherit the standards of rationality and normative justification that the winners in history bequeath to us. And if that is the view (again, reminiscent of Rorty), I fail to see why any critical theorist who knows that the history of the winners is usually a moral disaster should hold such a view. It does not make any sense for someone pursuing a critical intention to regard her rational standards as ones that are true because they have been 'achieved' in history if the evaluative standards for what counts as an achievement are products of that same history—see the critical theory principle proposed by Williams cited earlier. We need better criteria for what counts as an achievement. Of course, these cannot be ahistorical or superhistorical; but they must have sufficient normative power to look at history critically, as demanded, for example, by Benjamin. Merely being happy to reproduce the results of history is not a critical stance. And it cannot serve the very critique McNay and I think is important. Historicism that aims to be critical is self-undermining. So too is a conception of transcendental principles that overlooks the finite character of human powers. Thus a claim to reasonable justification must always be aware of its possible exclusions and blind spots; yet it cannot have recourse to any other power than reason itself in such self-criticism.

Historicist immanentism pays a huge price in the form of its blindness to radical critique that transcends the normative horizon of its time. But critical theory has to allow for and even call for such radical critique. Those who rejected slavery when it was very much part of the normative order of its time, those who argued for gender equality when that was 'unheard' of, and those who argued for social equality in feudal times had no 'historical achievements' on their side. Thus a historicist view would have to regard these voices as meaningless or at least as unfounded. But how critical can a theory be that thinks that? Again, if we have no account of the transcending power of the reasonable rejection of a dominant order of justification, we have no critical theory.

The critical theory I aim at always inhabits three worlds simultaneously: the world of given orders of justification, a counterfactual world of the principles

[61] Forst, 'The Justification of Progress and the Progress of Justification' (n 42).

of justification and the world of critique, which is situated in between these two worlds.[62] McNay has a pronounced tendency to read my second world of principles as the real world of existing justifications and as a result thinks that I have no means for critique. Where I speak of abstract principles and criteria of justification, she thinks that I am speaking about concrete and reified forms of justification and reminds me that '[l]atent dynamics of power and authority may subvert formally equal relations, making it far more difficult for certain individuals and groups to be taken seriously as justificatory agents than others' (M 144). I could not agree more, but note that the very ground of that critique is the right to justification, which, as a principle, transcends every actual and historical form. So McNay's criticism that my notion of justification is blind with respect to its own exclusions rests on a category error, because it mistakes the counterfactual for the real. I agree that justice demands the 'development of communicative and interpretative virtues quite different to the standardized norms' (M 149) of given justificatory processes; but to imply that my notion of justification entails such reified norms is unfounded. More than that, any such critique of standardized norms must use my principles of justification if it wants to avoid arguing for arbitrary forms of social life beyond reciprocity and generality.

Finally, McNay also takes issue with my conception of 'noumenal power', which I have already discussed earlier in dialogue with Bajaj and Rossi. She fears that such an approach cannot take note of various 'material' forms of power, such as Foucauldian body power or Bourdieuian 'habitus', which operate 'beneath the radar of reason' (M 140). As I explain in greater detail elsewhere,[63] I think that this critique is based on too narrow and rationalized a reading of my notion of 'noumenal'. Bio-power works through disciplining and forming subjects who 'feel' and 'think' in a certain way, who evaluate themselves and the world in a particular way; but one would not need all of the educational and other disciplinary mechanisms and all of the narratives about what a 'good' girl or boy does if all of this took place at a level that has 'little to do with justification', as McNay asserts (M 140). It has little to do with rational justification if 'rational' means 'reflexively tested and accepted'; but it has a lot to do with the narratives of justification that we grow up with and that 'produce' us as evaluating, thinking, and feeling subjects. The same holds true for habitus formations, where you learn to 'be' a certain kind of social being—and why that is a good thing. So I neither think that the noumenal realm as a realm of power is rational and reflexive, nor do I think that subjects are always free to reject or accept justifications. Most justifications 'creep' into us in various ways; but, as Foucault argued, power only operates on subjects who are at least free to the extent that they are agents who

[62] See Forst, *Normativity and Power* (n 15) ch 1.
[63] Forst, 'Noumenal Power Revisited' (n 47).

are motivated by noumenal considerations, however non-reflexive they may be. The point about noumenal power is not only one about how beliefs became part of our cognitive and emotional makeup; the question is also what work they do there. And that work is cognitive in nature; power motivates us to think and/or do certain things we otherwise would not do. Thus power only works by having noumenal effects on our understanding of ourselves. If it were otherwise, genealogical critique would be pointless, because it cognitively attacks those very noumenal *dispositifs* that make us function in accordance with the rules of disciplinary power.

Another misreading of my view leads to the criticism that I downplay the 'systemic mechanisms that maintain structural inequalities' (M 141), as if I thought that such structures are only reproduced by those subject to them normatively accepting them, even for ideological reasons. But, as McNay (M 142) says, some people 'accept' low-paid and demeaning jobs because they have no other options. Of course, I do not want to deny that; what I am trying to understand is what 'accept' means here. And whatever it means and rests on, such as a conviction of having no alternative, it is a noumenal power effect, since 'acceptance' is a cognitive term. Unpacking such terms is important for anyone who wants to understand how complex forms of power work, and the view operating here is neither a 'hyper-rationalist' (M 143) view nor one that is 'diffuse' in using too broad a notion of the noumenal. I think that at least some broadening is necessary in order to analyze what motivates people to act in given social structures. The view that 'structures' determine how people think and act in a one-dimensional way is too simplistic; rather, certain dominant views about oneself and others must have developed to make people 'function' in social systems. Power has many forms and rests on a plethora of noumenal effects and motives.

II. Comments

1. The Justification of Proportionality (Comments on Matthias Klatt)

In his chapter, Matthias Klatt not only argues for proportionality argumentation as a particular form of the justification of legal rights adjudication;[64] in addition, he argues that the moral basis of the very idea of legal proportionality considerations resides in the moral right to justification. In this respect, his view is

[64] See Matthias Klatt, *Making the Law Explicit: The Normativity of Legal Argumentation* (Jörg Rampacher and Neil Mussett trs, Hart Publishing 2008).

close to that of Mattias Kumm;[65] but Klatt goes further in discussing a number of essential aspects of such a grounding view. I admire the clarity of this way of interpreting the right to justification in the legal context and will try to add some useful remarks.

To begin with, I should comment on Klatt's interpretation of my account of the right to justification as having 'an anthropologic-existentialist basis' (K 165).[66] I shall not quarrel with the immanent-reconstructive view Klatt holds with respect to that right, but I do not agree that from a first-person perspective the ultimate moral normativity of the right to justification rests on 'existentialist decisions' (K 166) about who an agent wants to be. For that would turn what I regard as moral normativity—ie one that is categorically binding—into an ethical one—ie one that is binding for me only in the light of my particular identity. I do not deny that regarding oneself as a moral agent has existential implications; but recognizing oneself as such an agent is a response to an imperative that is regarded as already binding, so that, from the right moral perspective, there is no 'unbound' decision either to be or not be a moral agent. One can decide against morality, but one cannot create morality by deciding in favour of it. It is valid apart from such decisions, because it is grounded in us as 'being' normative equals with all others with respect to the moral space of reasons we inhabit as members of the kingdom of ends, as makers and takers of moral norms. That deontological view is also why I disagree with Klatt's further claim that the validity of the practice of justification is relative in so far as it depends on the decision to respect others as equals. That is factually true, but not with respect to normative validity; for any such decision *responds* to the *prior* claim to moral validity, which, to cut a long story short, is a claim of the other as well as of reason.[67]

Klatt and Kumm are masterly when it comes to translating the right to justification into a theory of legal proportionality, following the discourse-theoretical account of proportionality developed by Robert Alexy.[68] Here we are talking about a particular practice of justification that is constrained by procedural as well as substantive legal norms; thus the discussion is not about the justification of human rights but about how to interpret them and how to justify decisions that might involve, for example, conflicts between human rights. That is why Klatt argues that the claim to legal 'correctness' is 'more fundamental than the right to justification' (K 171). But I think that this is only true if the latter right

[65] Mattias Kumm, 'The Idea of Socratic Contestation and the Right to Justification: The Point of Rights-Based Proportionality Review' (2010) 4 Law & Ethics of Human Rights 142; 'The Turn to Justification: On the Structure and Domain of Human Rights Practice' in Adam Etinson (ed), *Human Rights: Moral or Political?* (Oxford University Press 2018).

[66] Matthias Klatt, 'Proportionality and Justification' in this volume, cited in the text as K.

[67] Forst, *The Right to Justification* (n 14) chapters 1 and 2.

[68] Matthias Klatt (ed), *Institutionalized Reason: The Jurisprudence of Robert Alexy* (Oxford University Press 2012).

is interpreted socially as what 'will be accepted by others', which is a factual interpretation of what that right means, one which neglects the counterfactual question of what 'could' be accepted by others. This question always frames discourses, including legal discourses, if we look at them from a general normative perspective, which might play a role in the general meaning of 'correctness', as Klatt goes on to explain.

When it comes to the substantive and procedural aspects of correct justifications, Klatt is right to argue that my view entails both procedural and substantive aspects (see my remarks earlier in response to Schlink). But here we must distinguish between different levels of justification. On a moral level, the right to justification entails the right to be a subject of reciprocal and general justification, and such justification grounds human rights and the fundamentals of justice in political contexts. Thus the distinction between procedural and substantive is not one of priority or hierarchy, only one of the order of explanation. On a legal level, things might look different, because here procedural notions and substantive aspects (human rights, as Klatt argues) serve different justificatory functions. But in my view Klatt's inference that the right to justification 'is not a sufficient basis to justify the existence of all human rights' (K 175) is mistaken, because it assumes that the right to justification can only justify those rights that are implied in institutionalizing a democratic process. But that is not the case, as I argue in my account of human rights.[69] Human rights are justified as means of establishing the status of persons as legally, politically, and socially non-dominated normative equals, and this includes all human rights, from classical liberal to democratic and social ones. Thus I deny that human rights are analytically and normatively prior to the right to justification, as Klatt argues. Where should these rights come from normatively speaking? Here I fear that Klatt introduces a normative plurality and heterogeneity that might be incompatible with a deontological view, which may point to a deeper source of conflict with proportionality theories.

Such differences become apparent, for example, when Klatt cites 'public interest' as a reason that could justify rights infringements. Although it is true that rights are not absolute, as Klatt and I argue (K 177), in order to counter a rights claim one must show that a particular right or its interpretation violates the rights of others, assuming that proportionality tries to sort out arguments of equal strengths on each level of justification.

In any case, I agree for the most part with Klatt's account of the dialectic of internal and external justification when it comes to basic rights adjudication, although that is a hotly debated issue in legal theory, as Klatt notes (K 180). I think

[69] See my 'The Justification of Human Rights and the Basic Right to Justification' (n 16); 'The Point and Ground of Human Rights' (n 24).

he is right when he says that legal systems must find ways to allow for general moral (deontological) considerations to be brought in at some relevant point, though I also think that such points must be constrained by a certain discipline of justification. In political processes, such discipline might be less stringent, but the application of law must adhere to a strict system of accountability.

I am somewhat puzzled by Klatt's claim that internal justification secures the universality of proportionality while external justification allows for cultural plurality, because I thought the external perspective is that of deontological morality (thus true universality), while the internal perspective is that of the particular rules and norms of a specific legal system. So there may be two notions of the 'external' at work here, and it might be useful to distinguish them. All of this, again, raises the question as to the moral grammar of a proportionality view: Is it a deontological view or one that allows for a plurality of moral aims, concerns, and interests that could possibly trump deontological norms (a worry that Ripstein has, *mutatis mutandis*, with respect to a particular version of justification)?

As far as the complex topic of constitutional review is concerned, I am on shaky ground, since I am far from an expert in this area. I agree that a constitution is a special form of justificatory arrangement and that it must entail reflexive procedures to revisit the question of justification once there is a justified concern that it has been wrongly answered. Institutions of legal and constitutional review play that role. But does this mean, as Klatt argues, that the control competence must be entrusted to a court rather than to a legislative authority (K 187)? I see the rationale for doing so, stressing reason rather than interest and will; but I am not sure whether legislative institutions could not be designed in such a way that minorities, for example, would have a certain veto right with respect to legislation that disadvantages them, and as a result could exercise the force towards the better argument. There are problems with this proposal, if one thinks of the discussion of such veto rights as suggested, for example, by Iris Young;[70] but I think the worries about 'juristocracy' must also be taken seriously. In any case, and this already foreshadows my discussion of Daly and Harel, it is important to distinguish a principle such as the veto right against violations of reciprocity and generality with respect to fundamental standing from particular legal and political forms justified in the light of that principle. No such form can ever exhaust the principle. Once the basic principles are clear, we also know in which light to look at possible forms, and historical experience plays a role when it comes to evaluating them. I think that this holds true for institutions of constitutional review as well as particular accounts of proportionality, and this is true of every 'bridge'—in Klatt's (K 191) apt description—between the moral and the legal world.

70 Iris M Young, *Justice and the Politics of Difference* (Princeton University Press 2011).

2. Republican Rights (Comments on Eoin Daly)

Eoin Daly presents a pointed and convincing republican reading of constitutional rights in general and of proportionality adjudication in particular. According to Daly, basic rights do not carve out asocial spaces of autonomy and cannot serve as absolute 'trumps' against the political will of the majority of citizens; rather, they raise the threshold of justification that needs to be crossed in order to make legitimate, justified law. I basically agree with this view of basic rights as threshold raisers. But since I believe that such rights require a deontological grounding, I would add some remarks with a somewhat different orientation from Daly's, because I think that we need to remind ourselves of the need to ensure the protection of minorities within a (in my view, Kantian) republican framework—for republican, democratic reasons.

I won't spend too much time on the question of whether rights are 'antecedent to politics' (D 198),[71] because I think that in some senses they are and in others they are not. They are in so far as the right to justification, as the *ground* of rights that secure the status of legal, political, and social non-domination, is a right that is not 'given' or 'founded' (as Daly says; D 200) by a political community. Rather, it is a right that one has as member of the *moral* community of all human beings; but the place for its particular construction and institutionalization as a legal-political right is a concrete political community, whether it be a single state or a transnational political unity. These rights only get politically constructed, defined, and interpreted within a political community, and thus their particular form and content is not 'pre-given'. Still, the core of basic rights is not at the disposal of majorities; that is what the higher threshold formulation means in my view. The reason for this is a *democratic* one: since democracy is a normative order of rule where those subject to it are the co-authors of its norms as political equals, securing that latter status is an imperative of democracy itself, not of some other values or principles (such as liberty or the rule of law). Democracy, simply put, is an institution of non-domination; thus it must not be turned into a tool of domination, for example, by the rich, by a religious majority or by men over women.

I will also not go into detail concerning the proper republican view of basic rights. There are many versions of republicanism around. Some Rousseauian versions are sceptical of rights and constitutional review, the Kantian ones less so; and neo-republican ones like Pettit's (*pace* Daly's interpretation) distinguish themselves sharply from Rousseau[72] and emphasize the need to

[71] Eoin Daly, 'Republicanizing Rights? Proportionality, Justification, and Non-Domination' in this volume, cited in the text as D.

[72] Philip Pettit, 'Two Republican Traditions' in Andreas Niederberger and Philipp Schink (eds), *Republican Democracy: Liberty, Law and Politics* (Edinburgh University Press 2013).

'depoliticize' democracy and to establish constitutional courts.[73] Thus even though republicans of all kinds agree, as Daly states, that 'freedom has no sense or meaning outside of, or prior to the political association itself' (D 200), this does not determine what kinds of freedom that association has to secure or in what ways. Ontological statements cannot be translated directly into legal or institutional ones. To argue for individual rights is not to argue for an asocial ontology of monads or anything of the like.[74] As those who have studied the history of toleration know, for example, rights to religious liberty protect the rights of individual believers as much as they protect religious communities and forms of life. Thus I agree with Daly that freedom is 'constituted' (D 206) through politics and that democracy is an exercise of collective autonomy; but that includes the idea that a fundamental disagreement over the rights that secure the basic status of citizens as equals cannot be a reasonable disagreement, and here I differ somewhat from his and Bellamy's view.

Be that as it may, I think Daly's republican notion of rights as 'bulwarks' (D 208) against the arbitrary exercise of political (and we should add, social and economic) power is exactly right, and I also think that a politics of rights should place particular emphasis on the procedures of justification that lead to legitimate law and on procedural safeguards that raise justificatory bars when it comes to essential questions of justice. Having a constitutional court helps when other ways of improving on procedures of justification have failed; but it may be preferable to think about legislative safeguards that avoid the rule of arbitrariness. Here some institutional imagination is required—for example, thinking about a reflexive chamber in parliament.

It is useful to interpret constitutional rights as what I call 'congealed justifications' that equip persons or groups with the normative power to intervene in the justificatory mechanisms of a polity and to ask for better reasons, and thus to exercise the force towards the better argument. This is how the right to justification acquires substantive content and functions within a normative order, demanding reciprocally and generally justifiable reasons for norms. Still, the process of concretization that leads to certain basic rights not only implies that rights are part and parcel of a democratic republic but also that they are rights of individuals. Since the right to justification grants persons or groups a veto right against grave forms of unjustifiable subjection, even if (wrongly) authorized by a majority, the notion of 'subjective' rights still makes sense, and here I cannot go along with Daly's attempt to redefine rights. If a large majority thinks that wearing a *burqa* violates the republican *ordre publique* (as reflected in recent French legislation), they overstep the boundaries of justification, and a veto

[73] Philip Pettit, 'Depoliticizing Democracy' (2004) 17 Ratio Juris 52, 63.
[74] Forst, *Contexts of Justice* (n 14) ch 2.

against such forms of symbolic and social domination is justified. Democracy, to repeat, rests on a principle of non-domination and must not be used for purposes of domination. Respecting others as equals also means tolerating differences when no other rights or principles of justice are violated by these differences.[75]

When it comes to proportionality adjudication as a particular art of legal justification, I agree with Kumm and Daly (D 215) that every interpretation of a rights claim needs to be unpacked with regard to the reasons either side has to claim that its norms or actions are justified. But as every good deontologist must agree (see my response to Ripstein earlier), one should think twice about the exact meaning of a 'balance or calculus of social interests' (D 215). Rights serve the function of placing constraints and thresholds on such balances and especially on aggregated views of what is socially 'good'. In this respect, they do not serve as asocial liberty trumps but as democratic trumps that remind fellow-citizens of standards of equal respect that must not be violated.

3. The Right to Have Rights Secured (Comments on Alon Harel)

Expanding on his powerful arguments in *Why Law Matters*,[76] Alon Harel, contrary to Daly, argues for the intrinsic value of constitutionalism in general and of judicial review in particular. Against consequentialist instrumentalism, he holds that constitutions do not serve further ends or desirable outcomes, but rather that they *express* what justice means. He combines a deontological notion of human dignity and a republican notion of freedom (Ha 226)[77] to argue for the conclusion that such dignity and freedom call for securing the right to have rights (in an expression used by Hannah Arendt in a different context)[78] in a constitution that is not at the disposal of legislatures, for otherwise the threat of being dominated by majorities is too great: 'The citizens in constitutional polities do not live "at the mercy" of their legislature' (Ha 226).

I agree with this emphasis on dignity and non-domination, but would give the argument a somewhat different twist. The reasons for constitutionalism given by Harel imply that the constitution in question *truly* expresses the basic rights of persons, and thus that the constitution itself must include democratic ways of questioning and improving it. This does not make it into an instrumental tool for the realization of rights; but it does make it into a dynamic form of the realization

[75] Forst, *Toleration in Conflict* (n 14) ch 12.
[76] Alon Harel, *Why Law Matters* (Oxford University Press 2014).
[77] Alon Harel, 'Constitutionalism and Justice' in this volume, cited in the text as H.
[78] Hannah Arendt, 'The Perplexities of the Rights of Men' in Hannah Arendt, *The Origins of Totalitarianism* (Penguin Books 2017) ch 9.2.

of rights that are constituted by a proper procedure of justification. Thus a constitution is a self-corrective, learning structure of justification that secures justified rights and norms and that leads to further justifications of rights and norms. I call such a form of constitutionalism a reflexive one, and I believe it rests on the correct interpretation of the right to justification and non-domination as the basis for a constitutional regime (as Harel agrees; Ha 220).

On such a dynamic understanding of constitutionalism, constitutions express the right to justification and the rights justified on that basis; however, that founding right transcends all concrete forms of constitutions and where necessary calls for their revision. Thus no such concrete form can claim to have intrinsic value in the sense that it ought not to be changed; but any such change has to be done through structures and procedures of justification that are in conformity with the requirements of generality and reciprocity. If that is the case, such structures and procedures and the constitutions that secure and enable them are justified directly and non-instrumentally by the only 'absolute' moral value there is in a deontological framework, namely, human beings as ends in themselves. No notion of the 'intrinsic value' of particular norms or institutions can rival that value; in fact, all claims to be valuable must be justified in such a way that they are expressions and realizations of that highest value. If a constitution secures the right to justification procedurally and substantively, it can claim to be justified as an expression of the principle of respect for humans as equal normative agents and is thus justified in a non-instrumental way as an extension and realization of that principle. But if it is such a realization, it also contains reflexive procedures for overcoming its own possible shortcomings. In that sense, I am inclined to take issue with the strong claim that particular constitutions have intrinsic value.

That leaves it open to Harel to argue that he defends the *idea* of a constitution that enshrines basic rights, but not their particular forms. I agree with this in principle, but I think that this argument would hold for any reliable sociopolitical regime in which the basic standing of persons as having a right to justification and enjoying the liberties and equalities grounded on that basis was secure. And I agree with Harel that in our social life, based on our historical experiences, a system of law and of constitutional rights may be the best way of institutionalizing this status and respect that we can conceive. But this does not mean that we could not use our moral and social imagination to think of alternative normative orders of equal respect in which the law plays a less prominent role, allowing for other ways of regulating possible conflicts. Again, the right to justification transcends the particular forms in which it is realized, although it provides strong justifications for such forms if they are sufficiently reflexive.

Harel interprets the right to justification in a specific way as grounding a right to constitutional judicial review as 'the right to a hearing' (Ha 229f.) which is triggered if a person's right has been 'infringed unjustifiably' (Ha 230) even within a democratic procedure. That is why, in his view, having a deliberative democracy is not sufficient to establish justice as justification; rather, judicial review is required.

I shall not take issue with the core of this argument, but would like to add a few thoughts regarding its normative grounding and institutional implications. First, as I argued earlier in dialogue with Daly, the right to justification gives a veto right to those who are subjected to norms that cannot be reciprocally and generally justified to them. From this it follows that this right to a fair hearing, or even a revision of democratic decisions, is not an extra-democratic right but is part of democracy itself, since democracy is the political form of justice among normative equals, and the veto right only affirms that status as an equal. Hence we should avoid thinking of democracy and basic rights as separate values.

Second, I agree with Harel that the institution which secures the veto right, or the 'adjudicative process' (Ha 232) in his words, need not be a court but could also be a particular institution of the legislature. And I agree that this should be seen as an exercise of justification, stressing the criteria of justification. But does this mean that that process 'is in fact the end itself' (Ha 232)? Here my deontological view suggests that the process should be regarded as being required by the right to justification in a non-instrumental sense, as its expression and extension; but I don't think that this makes it an end in itself. What would we sacrifice for it? As I said before, I only consider human beings to be ends in themselves, and thus am more reluctant to use such strong language. There is a third way between instrumental justifications of democracy (and other institutional forms) and ascribing them intrinsic value as ends in themselves—which brings me to Rostbøll's contribution.

4. The Value of Democracy (Comments on Christian Rostbøll)

Christian Rostbøll is a kindred Kantian spirit whose work in democratic theory I hold in very high regard.[79] In his excellent chapter, arguing along similar (but not the same) lines to Harel, he defends a Kantian non-instrumental justification of democracy and argues against instrumental justifications as well as two kinds of non-instrumental justifications, namely, an Aristotelian one and one that puts justice first. He criticizes my view as falling into the latter category. According to Rostbøll, my claim that democracy is the political form of justice as justification does not allow for a 'special or additional value that is constituted and created

[79] Christian F Rostbøll, *Deliberative Freedom: Deliberative Democracy as Critical Theory* (State University of New York Press 2008).

by democracy itself' (Ro 246)[80] because it is based entirely on a prior norm, the right to justification. By contrast, the Kantian argument for democracy he is seeking 'regards relationships of equal freedom as the norm which justifies democracy' (Ro 236)—which sounds like the view he criticizes—but also holds that 'the meaning of this norm' is 'constituted—created and made conceivable—by democracy itself' (Ro 236) and thus does not rest on a prior, independent norm. I find this view somewhat puzzling, but before I comment on it and try to find ways to accommodate what I think is right about it, I shall explain why my view is not a 'justice-first' view in the way Rostbøll thinks.

It seems to me to be a logical truth that any justification of democracy that does not tautologically assert that democracy justifies itself must refer to a *prior* grounding norm or principle. Thus, instrumental justifications point to independent values that democracy contingently realizes to a greater or lesser extent (depending on whether we are dealing with stronger or weaker instrumental justifications), whereas intrinsic arguments point to principles or norms that democracy expresses or realizes as a necessary political form or at least one which is justified in a direct, immanent way (again allowing for stronger and weaker versions of the immanent arguments).

In my own view, a deontological Kantian justification (or at least my neo-Kantian justification) provides a moral argument for the political form of justice as justification that we call democracy. That is how I view a 'robust' (Ro 237) non-instrumental justification of democracy, and I think I am in agreement with Rostbøll here, since he also argues for a moral duty (he uses the term moral obligation, Ro 258) to honour and realize democracy. But while Rostbøll does not want to adopt the Kantian idea of moral and, *mutatis mutandis*, political autonomy as basic (Ro 255) and prefers a weaker notion of legal independence and equal political participation (Ro 253ff.), I think that the notion of *equal normative co-authority and co-authorship* of moral and—again, in a different context—political norms is basic. The difference between these contexts matters, because political norms are not moral norms and bind only through legal authorization. However, the ground of the arguments for moral or political autonomy is the same: the right to justification as the right of members of the moral kingdom of ends who have the right to be equal co-authors of the laws within their normative order(s), given their moral-political status (or dignity) as norm-givers and norm-takers. Justice as justification expresses this status and realizes it in the political realm, but as an expression of mutual respect among free and equal normative authorities, not as 'producing' some other value, as in a consequentialist picture.

[80] Christian F Rostbøll, 'Democracy as a Good in Itself: Three Kinds of Non-Instrumental Justification' in this volume, cited in the text as Ro.

In this justificatory account, a lot of terms form a complex unity and explain each other: the right to justification, practical reason as the faculty of justification, normative authority, dignity, respect, justificatory freedom and equality, moral and political autonomy, legal, political, and social non-domination, public reason, constructivism, justice as justification, democracy, basic rights, etc. Taken together they form what I hope is a coherent grounding story. But as remarked earlier, for Kantians the only 'absolute' and independent value is that of human beings as ends in themselves.[81] It would be a mistake, from a deontological view, to regard democracy as a 'good in itself' that could ever trump the value of human beings. This is why we must be wary of independent 'intrinsic' justifications of democracy and not only of 'instrumental' justifications, which is why I prefer to speak of a deontological grounding.

Democracy thus *expresses* the right form of respect for equal normative authorities in the political realm and is the *political* form of justice. It *realizes* political and social justice. But given the plethora of terms of the grounding story and the deontological core argument about persons as ends in themselves, it seems inappropriate, as Rostbøll does, to pick out the term justice and to claim that my view is a 'justice-first' view. One could also call it a justification-first, a respect-first, a dignity-first, or whatever view. In any case, such 'first' views do not do justice to the complexity of the grounding story, although if one had to accord anything priority, it would be persons as ends in themselves.

But the more interesting question is where Rostbøll and I really differ in our Kantian grounding accounts. One major difference I have already mentioned is that, while I uphold a notion of normative co-authorship, he relies on freedom as independence within the public order of a constitutional democracy. The citizens are 'co-rulers' but are not 'self-governing' (Ro 253f.). I will leave the difference between these approaches unexplored, but since Rostbøll and I agree that political equal relationships are morally grounded, I wonder which moral grounding he can give for that. Is it Kant's 'innate right' or some other moral notion of equal standing and respect? And how does it differ from my account?

The core of Rostbøll's argument is the complex idea that, as I cited earlier, democracy is based on a certain norm (of equal standing) but at the same time regards that norm as being 'constituted'—or 'created and made conceivable' (Ro 236, passim)—by democracy. That is a bit puzzling, for here democracy is both justified by a prior norm and constitutes that very norm, thus is prior to that norm. What could this mean? How can we accept a justification for something if only the existence of that something produces the justification? I think that

[81] See Kant, Ac. 4:428, *Groundwork of the Metaphysics of Morals* (Mary J Gregor and Jens Timmermann eds and trs, Cambridge University Press 2012) 40.

Rostbøll is trying to capture something important, namely, the 'unique nature' (Ro 236) or 'additional value' (Ro 246) of democratic relationships; but his description of the justificatory relation is not felicitous. It is unclear what could be meant by a 'special norm that is created by constitutional democracy' (Ro 247 n. 40), whereas the weaker formulation of 'a norm that can be fully conceived only in conjunction with the idea of democracy itself' (Ro 248) might help. To be sure, the additional value that democracy provides cannot be anything like the Arendtian 'fun' in acting together, because she saw this as part of the good life and also not as something 'morally obligatory' (Ro 249). Thus the additional value Rostbøll has in mind must supervene on the moral norm of equal standing.

Thus I suggest that we interpret Rostbøll's argument, *pace* his words, as not saying that democracy 'creates' (Ro 256) a particular norm of equal standing, but that it *realizes* this moral norm in a *unique* and enriching way. To return to my own normative language and not put too many words into Rostbøll's mouth, it realizes a form of *collective political co-authorship* that cannot be realized in the moral realm and also in no other political form. We can then say that being recognized as such a political co-author who has equal standing and exercises collective self-rule both realizes the right to justification in the form of democratic justice and lends it a *new meaning* in the political context—although not a totally new meaning, morally speaking. We can describe this new meaning in colourful ways with reference to the many facets of being a democratic agent, but we can also tone this down a bit and merely say that it realizes a political-moral right.

As far as I see, this comes close to saying that Rostbøll is looking for a justification for democracy that explains its particular value, but that also explains its moral point and falls neither into the trap of tautology nor of contradiction. He alludes to such a view in some formulations, I think, such as when he says that '[t]he norm that justifies democracy is *partly* created' (Ro 250, my emphasis) by democracy or that his Kantian justification of democracy 'relies on a norm that has some meaning independently of democracy but which can be understood fully only in connection with the idea of (constitutional) democracy' (though the problem arises again when he continues 'because it is created and constituted by the latter'; Ro 257). In any case, while I think we need to stress the moral foundations of democracy as the exercise of normative co-authorship, he is right to argue that the realization of this in a democratic framework adds new meaning to that prior norm. We have to take the difference between moral and political contexts and the respective forms of autonomy into account.[82]

[82] See the various forms of autonomy discussed in Forst, *Contexts of Justice* (n 14) ch 5.2.

5. Justificatory Non-Domination in the European Union (Comments on Ester Herlin-Karnell)

I very much welcome Ester Herlin-Karnell's reflections, as an expert on EU constitutional law, on the importance of a justification-based theory of non-domination in the EU context. Various attempts have been made by scholars to apply the right to justification to the EU political structure (as it is), most notably Jürgen Neyer's *The Justification of Europe*.[83] But in my view such attempts tend to downplay the critical and democratic implications of the theory of justice as justification.[84]

Herlin-Karnell defends a different view. She critically reflects on the relation between non-domination and how the term 'security' is understood and used in the context of EU policy to establish an 'Area of Freedom, Security and Justice' (AFSJ). Her main concern is with securing individual liberties, and thus, like Klatt and Daly, she considers proportionality adjudication to be a bulwark against false justifications that allow for political domination (HK 276f.)[85]—such as policies justified by appeal to security (and thus also to 'secured freedom') which in reality restrict liberties or have the potential to do so, as non-domination theories rightly criticize.

Herlin-Karnell also importantly points out that a supranational polity like the EU is a very powerful entity and a potential source of domination, even though it does not have the coercive forces that a state does. But EU legal mechanisms have power over states, especially through the Court of Justice and the Commission (HK 279f.). This shows that focusing on state power often runs the risk of overlooking other forms of power and potential domination.

In the specific case of the AFSJ, Herlin-Karnell analyzes the dangers of EU security regulations below the level of constitutional law, which lead to a 'preventive regime' that restricts basic rights, especially when they are justified on the basis of cases of emergency (HK 283).[86] She not only criticizes the lack of justificatory justice with respect to such legal mechanisms; in addition, she argues that there is a lack of a political realm of justifications for these kinds of policies (HK 283). In my view, there is an important lesson to be learned here: justice as justification comes in many forms and aspects, such as within legal proceedings; but

[83] Jürgen Neyer, *The Justification of Europe: A Political Theory of Supranational Integration* (Oxford University Press 2012).

[84] See my reply to Neyer in 'Justice, Democracy and the Right to Justification: Reflections on Jürgen Neyer's Normative Theory of the European Union' in Dimitry Kochenov, Gráinne de Búrca, and Andrew Williams (eds), *Europe's Justice Deficit?* (Hart Publishing 2015).

[85] Ester Herlin-Karnell, 'The Concepts of Non-Domination and Justification in EU Security-Related Context' in this volume, cited in the text as HK.

[86] See also Jonathan White, 'Emergency Europe' (2015) 63 Political Studies 300.

the idea of democracy is the idea of a general structure of justification that can open up spaces of justification with regard to certain institutions and policies.

Finally, as Herlin-Karnell reminds us, such a democratic structure of justification cannot draw a tight circle around the justification community in such a way that it denies justificatory standing to persons outside its territories who are subjected to its policies of securitization. Hence, states have duties to establish 'a universal rights system beyond the state' (HK 285). I fully agree with this, and would add that such a system must also be a democratic system and cannot be merely an inter-state contractual system. For the most vulnerable individuals within states as well as weaker states must have secure standing in a system of international law-making.

In short, the logic of justice as justifiability does not stop at the borders of national normative orders. Both within such an order and beyond it in trans-, supra-, and international political and legal contexts, the right to justification has a meaning of non-domination, preventing subjection to an order that cannot and could not be justified to those subject to it. We are subject to multiple of such orders, and thus we need analyses like Herlin-Karnell's if we are to understand the nature of our subjection and possible remedies against the dangers of domination connected with it.

III. Afterword

The foregoing replies and comments are the product of a long journey through vast continents of topics and arguments, and they involved more challenges than I have been able to address within the confines of this text. Moreover, my way of addressing them may be deficient in certain respects, owing to the limitations of my approach. In particular, my clinging to the principle of justification in justifying my view and in laying out a structure of justification may occasionally express more of a transcendental hope than transcendental security.

But if I have made any progress in clarifying and developing my position, as was my aim, it is due to the respective contributions of the thirteen colleagues who took the trouble to refer to my work in such careful ways. I remain extremely humbled by this honour and deeply grateful. The challenge of such an abundance of critical thinking to respond to is more than I could wish for as an author.[87]

[87] I am also greatly indebted to Ciaran Cronin, Felix Kämper, and Paul Kindermann for their help in preparing this text.

References

Adorno TW, 'Reason and Revelation' in Theodor W Adorno (ed), *Critical Models: Interventions and Catchwords* (Henry W Pickford tr, Columbia University Press 2005).

Adorno TW, *Negative Dialectics* (EB Ashton tr, Routledge 2010).

Arendt H, *The Origins of Totalitarianism* (Penguin Books 2017).

Benhabib S, *The Rights of Others: Aliens, Residents, and Citizens* (Cambridge University Press 2004).

Bogdandy A von, Goldmann M, and Venzke I, 'From Public International to International Public Law: Translating World Public Opinion into International Public Authority' (2017) 28 European Journal of International Law 115.

Caney S, 'Justice and the Basic Right to Justification' in Rainer Forst, *Justice, Democracy and the Right to Justification: Rainer Forst in Dialogue* (Bloomsbury 2014).

Cohen GA, *On the Currency of Egalitarian Justice and Other Essays in Political Philosophy* (Princeton University Press 2011).

Corradetti C, *Relativism and Human Rights: A Theory of Pluralistic Universalism* (Springer 2009).

Forst R, 'Towards a Critical Theory of Transnational Justice' (2001) 32 Metaphilosophy 160 [reprinted in *The Right to Justification: Elements of a Constructivist Theory of Justice* (Jeff Flynn tr, Columbia University Press 2011)].

Forst R, *Contexts of Justice: Political Philosophy beyond Liberalism and Communitarianism* (John MM Farrell tr, University of California Press 2002).

Forst R, 'The Justification of Human Rights and the Basic Right to Justification: A Reflexive Approach' (2010) 120 Ethics 711 [reprinted in *Justification and Critique: Towards a Critical Theory of Politics* (Ciaran Cronin tr, Polity Press 2013)].

Forst R, *The Right to Justification: Elements of a Constructivist Theory of Justice* (Jeff Flynn tr, Columbia University Press 2011).

Forst R, *Toleration in Conflict: Past and Present* (Ciaran Cronin tr, Cambridge University Press 2013).

Forst R, *Justification and Critique: Towards a Critical Theory of Politics* (Ciaran Cronin tr, Polity Press 2013).

Forst R, 'A Kantian Republican Conception of Justice as Nondomination' in Andreas Niederberger and Philipp Schink (eds), *Republican Democracy: Liberty, Law and Politics* (Edinburgh University Press 2013).

Forst R, 'Two Pictures of Justice' in Rainer Forst, *Justice, Democracy and the Right to Justification: Rainer Forst in Dialogue* (Bloomsbury 2014) [also in *Justification and Critique: Towards a Critical Theory of Politics* (Ciaran Cronin tr, Polity Press 2013)].

Forst R, 'Justifying Justification: Reply to My Critics' in Rainer Forst, *Justice, Democracy and the Right to Justification: Rainer Forst in Dialogue* (Bloomsbury 2014).

Forst R, 'Justice, Democracy and the Right to Justification: Reflections on Jürgen Neyer's Normative Theory of the European Union' in Dimitry Kochenov, Gráinne de Búrca, and Andrew Williams (eds), *Europe's Justice Deficit?* (Hart Publishing 2015).

Forst R, 'Transnational Justice and Non-Domination: A Discourse-Theoretical Approach' in Barbara Buckinx, Jonathan Trejo-Mathys, and Timothy Waligore (eds), *Domination and Global Political Justice: Conceptual, Historical and Institutional Perspectives* (Routledge 2015) [reprinted in *Normativity and Power: Analyzing Social Orders of Justification* (Ciaran Cronin tr, Oxford University Press 2017)].

Forst R, 'Noumenal Power' (2015) 23 *The Journal of Political Philosophy* 111 [reprinted in *Normativity and Power: Analyzing Social Orders of Justification* (Ciaran Cronin tr, Oxford University Press 2017)].

Forst R, 'The Justification of Basic Rights: A Discourse-Theoretical Approach' (2016) 45(3) Netherlands Journal of Legal Philosophy 7.

Forst R, 'The Point and Ground of Human Rights: A Kantian Constructivist View' in David Held and Pietro Maffettone (eds), *Global Political Theory* (Polity Press 2016).

Forst R, 'Noumenal Alienation: Rousseau, Kant and Marx on the Dialectics of Self-Determination' (2017) 22 Kantian Review 523.

Forst R, 'Political Liberalism: A Kantian View' (2017) 128 Ethics 123.

Forst R, *Normativity and Power: Analyzing Social Orders of Justification* (Ciaran Cronin tr, Oxford University Press 2017).

Forst R, 'Human Rights in Context: A Comment on Sangiovanni' in Adam Etinson (ed), *Human Rights: Moral or Political?* (Oxford University Press 2018).

Forst R, 'Noumenal Power Revisited: Reply to Critics' (2018) 11 Journal of Political Power 294.

Forst R, 'Die neorepublikanische Maschine. Zur Unabdingbarkeit des Kantischen Republikanismus' in Violetta L Waibel, Margit Ruffing, and David Wagner (eds), *Natur und Freiheit* (De Gruyter 2018).

Forst R, 'The Justification of Progress and the Progress of Justification' in Amy Allen and Eduardo Mendieta (eds), *Justice and Emancipation: The Critical Theory of Rainer Forst* (Penn State University Press forthcoming)

Forst R, 'The Point of Justice: On the Paradigmatic Incompatibility of Rawlsian "Justice as Fairness" and Luck Egalitarianism' in Jon Mandle and Sarah Roberts-Cady (eds), *John Rawls: Debating the Major Questions* (Oxford University Press forthcoming)

Forst R, *Toleration, Power and the Right to Justification* (Manchester University Press forthcoming).

Forst R, 'A Critical Theory of Transnational (In-)Justice: Realistic in the Right Way' in Thom Brooks (ed), *The Oxford Handbook of Global Justice* (Oxford University Press forthcoming).

Gosepath S, *Gleiche Gerechtigkeit: Grundlagen eines liberalen Egalitarismus* (Suhrkamp 2004).

Harel A, *Why Law Matters* (Oxford University Press 2014).

Hinsch W, *Gerechtfertigte Ungleichheiten: Grundsätze sozialer Gerechtigkeit* (De Gruyter 2002).

Horkheimer M, 'Traditional and Critical Theory' in Max Horkheimer (ed), *Critical Theory: Selected Essays* (Matthew J O'Connell and others trs, Continuum 2002).

Horkheimer M and Adorno TW, *Dialectic of Enlightenment: Philosophical Fragments* (Edmund Jephcott tr, Stanford University Press 2009).

Jay M, *Reason after Its Eclipse: On Late Critical Theory* (The University of Wisconsin Press 2016).

Kant I, 'The Metaphysics of Morals', in Immanuel Kant (ed), *Practical Philosophy* (Mary J Gregor ed and tr, Cambridge University Press 1996).

Kant I, 'Perpetual Peace: A Philosophical Sketch' in Immanuel Kant, *Political Writings* (Hans Reiss ed, HB Nisbet tr, Cambridge University Press 1996).

Kant I, *Groundwork of the Metaphysics of Morals* (Mary J Gregor and Jens Timmermann eds and trs, Cambridge University Press 2012).

Klatt M, *Making the Law Explicit: The Normativity of Legal Argumentation* (Jörg Rampacher and Neil Mussett trs, Hart Publishing 2008).
Klatt M (ed), *Institutionalized Reason: The Jurisprudence of Robert Alexy* (Oxford University Press 2012).
Kumm M, 'The Idea of Socratic Contestation and the Right to Justification: The Point of Rights-Based Proportionality Review' (2010) 4 Law & Ethics of Human Rights 142.
Kumm M, 'The Turn to Justification: On the Structure and Domain of Human Rights Practice' in Adam Etinson (ed), *Human Rights: Moral or Political?* (Oxford University Press 2018).
Lippert-Rasmussen K, *Relational Egalitarianism: Living as Equals* (Cambridge University Press 2018).
Marx K, 'Zur Kritik der Hegelschen Rechtsphilosophie' in Karl Marx and Friedrich Engels (eds), *Marx Engels Werke* (vol 1, Dietz 1976).
Marx K, 'Contribution to the Critique of Hegel's Philosophy of Law' in Karl Marx and Frederick Engels (eds), *Collected Works* (vol 3, Jack Cohen and others trs, *International Publishers* 2005).
McNay L, *Against Recognition* (Polity Press 2008).
McNay L, *The Misguided Search for the Political* (Polity Press 2014).
Neyer J, *The Justification of Europe: A Political Theory of Supranational Integration* (Oxford University Press 2012).
Pettit P, 'Depoliticizing Democracy' (2004) 17 Ratio Juris 52.
Pettit P, *On the People's Terms: A Theory of Freedom and Government* (Cambridge University Press 2012).
Pettit P, 'Two Republican Traditions' in Andreas Niederberger and Philipp Schink (eds), *Republican Democracy: Liberty, Law and Politics* (Edinburgh University Press 2013).
Pieroth B and Schlink B, *Grundrechte. Staatsrecht II* (C.F. Müller 2011).
Ripstein A, *Force and Freedom: Kant's Legal and Political Philosophy* (Harvard University Press 2009).
Ripstein A, *Kant and the Law of War*, forthcoming.
Rostbøll CF, *Deliberative Freedom: Deliberative Democracy as Critical Theory* (State University of New York Press 2008).
Sangiovanni A, 'Scottish Constructivism and the Right to Justification' in Rainer Forst, *Justice, Democracy and the Right to Justification: Rainer Forst in Dialogue* (Bloomsbury 2014).
Sangiovanni A, *Humanity without Dignity: Moral Equality, Respect, and Human Rights* (Harvard University Press 2017).
Sangiovanni A, 'Beyond the Political-Orthodox Divide: The Broad View' in Adam Etinson (ed), *Human Rights: Moral or Political?* (Oxford University Press 2018).
Shachar A, *The Shifting Border: Legal Cartographies of Migration and Mobility* (Manchester University Press forthcoming).
Stemplowska Z and Swift A, 'Dethroning Democratic Legitimacy' in David Sobel, Peter Vallentyne, and Steven Wall (eds), *Oxford Studies in Political Philosophy* (vol 4, Oxford University Press 2018).
Tugendhat E, *Vorlesungen über Ethik* (Suhrkamp 1993).
White J, 'Emergency Europe' (2015) 63 Political Studies 300.
Williams B, *In the Beginning Was the Deed* (Princeton University Press 2005).
Young IM, *Justice and the Politics of Difference* (Princeton University Press 2011).

Index

For the benefit of digital users, indexed terms that span two pages (e.g., 52–53) may, on occasion, appear on only one of those pages.